White-Collar Crime Online

Petter Gottschalk · Christopher Hamerton

White-Collar Crime Online

Deviance, Organizational Behaviour and Risk

palgrave
macmillan

Petter Gottschalk
Department of Leadership
and Organizational Behaviour
BI Norwegian Business School
Oslo, Norway

Christopher Hamerton
Sociology, Social Policy and Criminology
University of Southampton
Southampton, UK

ISBN 978-3-030-82131-9 ISBN 978-3-030-82132-6 (eBook)
https://doi.org/10.1007/978-3-030-82132-6

Cover credit: Ronnie Li/Getty

This Palgrave Macmillan imprint is published by the registered company Springer Nature Switzerland AG
The registered company address is: Gewerbestrasse 11, 6330 Cham, Switzerland

Contents

List of Figures

1
Introduction

White-collar offenders are privileged individuals who abuse their legitimate access to resources to commit and conceal their financial crime (Benson, 2020; Dodge, 2009; Friedrichs et al., 2018; Piquero and Schoepfer, 2010; Pontell et al., 2014; Stadler et al., 2013; Sutherland, 1939, 1983). Traditionally, white-collar offenders have worked offline when committing and concealing corruption, fraud, theft, manipulation, and other forms of financial crime. As documented in this book, working online is not only a matter of opportunity; it is also a matter of motive and willingness. For example, the distance created by working online, and the possibility of anonymity and fake identity might influence the willingness for deviant behavior. White-collar offenders online commit cybercrime through legitimate professions in privileged positions.

This book addresses cybercrime committed through legitimate professions. The book applies the offender-based perspective on white-collar crime. The offender-based perspective emphasizes characteristics of actors such as social and professional status, respectability, and power (Dodge, 2009; Friedrichs et al., 2018; Piquero & Schoepfer, 2010; Pontell et al., 2014, 2021; Stadler et al., 2013; Sutherland, 1939, 1983). The offender-based definition emphasizes some combination of the

P. Gottschalk and C. Hamerton, *White-Collar Crime Online*,
https://doi.org/10.1007/978-3-030-82132-6_1

actors' high social status, power, and respectability as the key features of white-collar crime (Benson, 2020). As evidenced by Payne and Hadzhidimova's (2020) review of cybercrime research, the offender-based perspective has been completely absent from the research agenda.

The integrated and deductive theory of convenience applies offender-based rather than offense-based perspectives on acts of white-collar crime by implicating individual and organizational motive for illegitimate financial gain, opportunities for crime in organizational settings, and personal willingness to engage in deviant behavior (Braaten & Vaughn, 2019; Chan & Gibbs, 2020; Hansen, 2020; Kireenko et al., 2019; Vasiu & Podgor, 2019). The convenience triangle thus consists of financial motive, organizational opportunity, and personal willingness (Gottschalk, 2020).

This book addresses a gap in the literature in the area of white-collar computer crime termed white-collar offenders online in the perspective of convenience theory. The book explores technology-aided white-collar crime caused by professional deviance. White-collar crime committed using technology has its special convenience characteristics. The book advanced the novel theoretical approach of convenience theory that was introduced only a few years ago (Gottschalk, 2020; Vasiu & Podgor, 2019). The book explores the intersections of white-collar crime and cybercrime. The book combines insights from organizational behavior, information technology, management, business administration, psychology, sociology, and criminology. The book explores white-collar crime from the perspective of online crime and discusses the various motives, opportunities, and behaviors. Convenient white-collar crime online is a unique concept that advances insights into the convenience of cybercrime for members of the elite in society. The digitally embedded workplace has its unique characteristics that influence the extent of crime convenience (Teubner & Stockhinger, 2020: 1):

> Although driven by technology, digitalization is not a mere technological phenomenon but has fundamental economic and societal consequences that can be seen in many aspects of our professional and private lives.

This book brings together two significant domains of criminological inquiry and research, namely those dealing with white-collar crime and with cybercrime. The two combined domains are studied in the perspective of convenience theory.

This book applies the term cybercrime as computer-oriented crime, which is crime that involves a computer and a network (Kshetri, 2005). The computer may be used as an instrument in the commission of crime, and it may be the target of crime. Cybercrime is not limited to the cyberspace, which is describing a widespread, interconnected digital technology. Rather, insider attacks on technologies of database management and information storage are just as much cybercrime as are attacks on the internet and the World Wide Web, as well as Facebook and other online services. In response, a new discipline named cyber criminology emerged with Jaishankar (2007) defining cyber criminology as the study of causation of crime that occurs in the digital space and its impact on the physical space.

Like so many other terms in research, there is still no precise and clear definition of cybercrime in academic contexts. Some call it electronic crime, computer crime, computer-related crime, hi-tech crime, technology-enabled crime, e-crime, or cyberspace crime (Sarre et al., 2018). With our focus on white-collar offenders online, it is not an issue to attempt to distinguish the various terms from each other. White-collar offenders commit both cyber-dependent crime and cyber-enabled crime. A cyber-dependent crime, sometimes labeled true cybercrime, is an offense that cannot occur without computer and network technology (Akdemir & Lawless, 2020). The case study of movie piracy in this book is an example of cyber-dependent crime (Borgarting, 2019; Høyesterett, 2019; Stone, 2015) similar to music piracy (Hinduja, 2012; Popham & Volpe, 2018).

When studying cyber fraud, Drew and Farrell (2018) distinguished between cybercrime that is directed at computers and related technology and cybercrime where technology is an enabler and integral part of the offense. Cyber fraud offenses under the first category include illegal access, illegal interception, data interference, system interference, misuse of devices, and hacking offenses. Cyber fraud offenses under the second category include advance fee fraud, investment scams, fraudulent financial transactions, and identity theft.

White-collar offenders online commit both occupational crime and corporate crime. The professional dimension of white-collar crime becomes particularly evident when financial crime is committed to benefit the organization rather than the individual. This is called corporate crime as opposed to occupational crime for personal benefit (Bittle & Hébert, 2020). Hansen (2009) argues that the problem with occupational crime is that it is committed within the confines of positions of trust and in organizations, which prohibit surveillance and accountability. Heath (2008) found that individuals who are further up the chain of command in the firm tend to commit bigger and more severe occupational crime. Corporate crime sometimes labeled organizational offending, on the other hand, is resulting from offenses by collectivities or aggregates of discrete individuals. If a corporate official violates the law in acting for the corporation, we still define it as corporate crime. However, if he or she gains personal benefit in the commission of a crime against the corporation, we regard it as occupational crime. A corporation cannot be subject to imprisonment, and therefore, the majority of penalties to control individual violators are not available for corporations and corporate crime. Detected corporate crime can harm executives involved, since "corporate outcomes such as misconduct serve as signals of the underlying quality of the individuals employed by the firm" (Naumovska et al., 2020: 883).

An example of corporate crime is online consumer fraud. White-collar offenders as legitimate online marketplace participants facilitate fraudulent transactions using various tactics (Harrison et al., 2020: 61):

> These include deception tactics where deceivers create inaccurate representations, negotiation tactics that are used to coerce victims into purchasing nonexistent or overpriced gods, and shill bidding by a fraud perpetrator or his conferates to inflate the selling price of goods.

By limiting attention to computer crime as financial crime by white-collar offenders, we focus on the profit-orientation of such crime. This definition excludes incidents of computer crime to cause damage without a gain, and it excludes incidents of computer-assisted financial crime by people who do not have legitimate access to premises, resources, and systems in professional settings. For example, Nigeria-related financial crime is extensive and 122 out of 138 countries at an Interpol meeting complained about Nigerian involvement in financial fraud in their countries. The most notorious type of non-white-collar crime attempted daily on office workers all over the world is probably the so-called advance fee fraud (Dion, 2010; Webster & Drew, 2017). The sender will seek to involve the recipient in a scheme to earn millions of dollars if the recipient pays an advance fee (Ampratwum, 2009). Even if malware infection, hacking, and other incidents are frequently reported in the popular press (Hagen et al., 2008), these kinds of computer crime are only of interest here if they have a profit motive. Computer crime is here profit-driven crime to gain access to and control over assets that belong to someone else.

While cybercrime is a criminological domain of computer-oriented and -enabled offences, white-collar crime is a criminological domain of occupationally and organizationally based offences. These two areas are the subject of concerted consideration in tandem in this book and studied in the perspective of convenience theory.

White-collar offenders online are trusted cybercriminals, who abuse trust to commit and conceal financial crime. Trust is a general characteristic of all white-collar offenders (Hamerton, 2020; Hansen, 2009; Jordanoska & Schoultz, 2020; Kempa, 2010; Podgor, 2007). Trust is an important contribution to the convenience of white-collar crime. Dearden (2016) argues that violation of trust is at the core of white-collar crime opportunity. Trust implies that vulnerability is accepted based upon positive expectations of the motives and actions of another. Controlling a trusted person is often considered both unnecessary and a signal of mistrust. In many cultures, the opposite of showing trust is to monitor and question what a person is doing. For example, a board can tell management what to do, but they do not tell them how to do it. The board shows trust that management will do it in an acceptable manner. If the board would move from only controlling what management has done to how management did it, then it might be perceived as mistrust. Yip et al. (2013) argue that trust is a mechanism for people to cope with risk and uncertainty in interactions with others. Kim et al. (2009: 401) define trust as "a psychological state comprising the intention to accept vulnerability based on positive expectations of the intentions or behavior of another". The positive expectations can relate to what another does, how it is done, and when it is done. The positive expectations can relate to the reaction of another, where it is expected that the reaction will be understandable, acceptable, and favorable. Vulnerability means that trust can easily be violated without detection or correction of deviant behavior. Trust is associated with dependence and risk (Chan et al., 2020: 3):

> The trustor depends on something or someone (the trustee or object of trust), and there is a possibility that expectations or hopes will not be satisfied, and that things will go wrong. Trust is not absolute, but conditional and contextual.

Just like the concept of trust is relational, such that trust inherently requires a target, so too is the concept of felt trust relational. It is the felt trust that can influence an individual's tendency to crime, while it is the actual trust that is part of the opportunity structure for crime. The gap between the two represents how accurately people understand others' perceptions of them (Campagna et al., 2020: 994):

> The concept of felt trust reflects what the more general interpersonal perception literature refers to as a dyadic meta-perception – one person's belief about the thought, attitude, or perception held by another person.

Uygur (2020) studied fraud in the charity sector in England and Wales. He analyzed 42 fraud and 42 no-fraud charities. His findings suggest that excessive trust towards the charities creates the opportunity for fraud to take place. Similarly, Gottschalk (2017: 121) studied detection and neutralization of economic crime in religious organizations and phrased the following question:

> Are there too much trust, too much freedom, too much individual authority, too little skepticism, too much loyalty, and too little control of the financial side in religious organizations?

Gottschalk and Gunnesdal (2018) have estimated a detection rate for white-collar crime of less than one out of twelve offenders in Norway, which seems supported by an empirical study of bribery detection in Norway by Andresen and Button (2019). The detection rate in the United States seems even lower based on estimates of the magnitude of white-collar crime by the National White-Collar Crime Center (Huff et al., 2010) and the Association of Certified Fraud Examiners (ACFE, 2008, 2014, 2016), which estimates the total annual loss from white-collar crime to be between $300 and $660 billion (Wall-Parker, 2020). Offenders tend to move under the radar (Williams et al., 2019). This book documents that the detection rate for white-collar offenders online certainly must be even lower than the detection rate for white-collar offenders who operate offline.

As argued by Walburg (2020: 343), too little insight exists about the extent, structures, and development of white-collar crime and its multifaceted varieties, especially when it comes to corporate crime:

> (…) this is largely explicable by the well-known and persistent difficulties of measuring undetected acts of corporate wrongdoing (…)

Even when an observer believes to have noticed a crime signal, the observer can be reluctant to report the observation (Bjørkelo et al., 2011; Bookman, 2008; Bowman & Gilligan, 2008; Bussmann et al., 2018; Mpho, 2017). In most countries, there are no benefits from reporting misconduct and crime in the organization (Brown et al., 2016; Keil et al., 2010). Rather, retaliation and reprisals can be the result for the observer (Mesmer-Magnus & Viswesvaran, 2005; Park et al., 2020; Rehg et al., 2009; Shawver & Clements, 2019). This book documents that the whistleblowing rate for online incidents certainly must be even lower than the whistleblowing rate for offline incidents.

Therefore, white-collar crime can remain conveniently concealed even when others have noticed and observed it (Bussmann et al., 2018). Lack of trust in the legitimacy, capacity, and competence of the police and the criminal justice system in general causes a further reduction in the willingness to blow the whistle on observed wrongdoing (Tankebe, 2019).

This book has the following structure. Chapter 2 introduces the theory of convenience that is applied throughout the book. The theory suggests that crime convenience can be found in three dimensions: the financial motive where the offender conveniently can benefit from possibilities and avoid threats, the professional convenient opportunity to commit and conceal crime, and the personal willingness for convenient deviant behavior.

Chapter 3 focuses on characteristics of online convenience for white-collar offenders. A distinction is made between outsider business cyber-crime and insider business cybercrime. Some cases from the Cambridge cybercrime database are presented.

Chapter 4 presents a number of case studies of outsider business cyber-crime. The cases cover movie piracy, foreign aid fraud, crypto currency crime, industrial espionage, Covid-19 fraud, and CEO fraud.

Chapter 5 presents a number of case studies of insider business cyber-crime. The cases cover embezzlement, money laundering, internal bank fraud, and accounting manipulation. In addition, gendered white-collar crime is discussed.

Chapter 6 raises a number of technology issues related to white-collar offenders online. The first issue is the digitally enabled identity gap, where an offender randomly or intentionally has a different identity online compared to the real-world identity. The second issue is special characteristics of the internet that set online offenses apart from offline offenses. The third issue is online crime terminology, where not only offender language can help disguise wrongdoing, but also underground terminology can prevent people from understanding what is going on. The fourth technology issue is special services in terms of infrastructure and software that is available on underground markets to help commit and conceal white-collar online crime. White-collar offenders can engage in crime online without high-level technical skills.

Chapter 7 discusses policing cybercrime including law enforcement approaches, digital forensics, and intelligence strategy, as well as detectives as knowledge workers. Chapter 8 continues on the path of knowledge workers by introducing theoretical knowledge requirements as well as empirical knowledge requirements to detect, investigate, and prosecute cybercriminals.

Chapter 9 introduces a completely different, yet well-researched group of cybercriminals for comparison. The chapter is concerned with online child grooming where pedophiles attract children for sexual abuse. While some of the aspects of child grooming are very different from white-collar crime, there are interesting issues related to stages in the criminal process as well as the existence of social communities of offenders online where analogy is relevant for discussion.

Chapter 10 introduces three offline case studies for comparison. The case studies are from Austria, Congo, and Denmark describing recent internal investigations into suspicions of white-collar crime.

References

ACFE. (2008). *2008 Report to the nations on occupational fraud and abuse*. Association of Certified Fraud Examiners.

ACFE. (2014). *2014 Report to the nations on occupational fraud and abuse, 2014 Global Fraud Study*. Association of Certified Fraud Examiners.

ACFE. (2016). *CFE code of professional standard*. Association of Certified Fraud Examiners. www.acfe.com/standards/

Akdemir, N., & Lawless, C. J. (2020). Exploring the human factor in cyber-enabled and cyber-dependent crime victimization: A lifestyle routine activities approach. *Internet Research, 30*(6), 1665–1687.

Ampratwum, E. F. (2009). Advance fee fraud "419" and investor confidence in the economies of sub-Saharan African (SSA). *Journal of Financial Crime, 16*(1), 67–79.

Andresen, M. S., & Button, M. (2019). The profile and detection of bribery in Norway and England & Wales: A comparative study. *European Journal of Criminology, 16*(1), 18–40.

Benson, M. L. (2020). Theoretical and empirical advances in the study and control of white-collar offenders. *Justice Evaluation Journal*, published online. https://doi.org/10.1080/24751979.2020.1808855

Bittle, S., & Hébert, J. (2020). Controlling corporate crimes in times of de-regulation and re-regulation. In M. L. Rorie (Ed.), *The handbook of white-collar crime* (Chapter 30, pp. 484–501). Wiley.

Bjørkelo, B., Einarsen, S., Nielsen, M. B., & Matthiesen, S. B. (2011). Silence is golden? Characteristics and experiences of self-reported whistleblowers. *European Journal of Work and Organizational Psychology, 20*(2), 206–238.
Bookman, Z. (2008). Convergences and omissions in reporting corporate and white collar crime. *DePaul Business & Commercial Law Journal, 6*, 347–392.
Borgarting. (2019, February 1). *Court case 17–170796AST-BORG/01.* Borgarting lagmannsrett (Borgarting court of appeals), judges Mats Wilhelm Ruland, Marit Bjøränesset Frogner and Bjørn E. Engstrøm. Prosecutor Esben Kyhring, defense attorney Christian Fredrik Bonnevie Hjort, Oslo, Norway.
Bowman, D., & Gilligan, G. (2008). Public awareness of corruption in Australia. *Journal of Financial Crime, 14*(4), 438–452.
Braaten, C. N., & Vaughn, M.S. (2019). Convenience theory of cryptocurrency crime: A content analysis of U.S. federal court decisions. *Deviant Behavior*, published online. https://doi.org/10.1080/01639625.2019.1706706
Brown, J. O., Hays, J., & Stuebs, M. T. (2016). Modeling accountant whistleblowing intentions: Applying the theory of planned behavior and the fraud triangle. *Accounting and the Public Interest, 16*(1), 28–56.
Bussmann, K. D., Niemeczek, A., & Vockrodt, M. (2018). Company culture and prevention of corruption in Germany, China and Russia. *European Journal of Criminology, 15*(3), 255–277.
Campagna, R. L., Dirks, K. T., Knight, A. P., Crossley, C., & Robinson, S. L. (2020). On the relation between felt trust and actual trust: Examining pathways to and implications of leader trust meta-accuracy. *Journal of Applied Psychology, 105*(9), 994–1012.
Chan, F., & Gibbs, C. (2020). Integrated theories of white-collar and corporate crime. In M. L. Rorie (Ed.), *The handbook of white-collar crime* (Chapter 13, pp. 191–208). Wiley.
Chan, J., Logan, S., & Moses, L. B. (2020). Rules in information sharing for security. *Criminology & Criminal Justice*, 1–19, published online. https://doi.org/10.1177/1748895820960199
Dearden, T. E. (2016). Trust: The unwritten cost of white-collar crime. *Journal of Financial Crime, 23*(1), 87–101.
Dion, M. (2010). Advance fee fraud letters as Machiavellian/narcissistic narratives. *International Journal of Cyber Criminology, 4*(1–2), 630–642.
Dodge, M. (2009). *Women and white-collar crime*. Prentice Hall.

Drew, J. M., & Farrell, L. (2018). Online victimization risk and self-protective strategies: Developing police-led cyber fraud prevention programs. *Police Practice & Research, 19*(6), 537–549.

Friedrichs, D. O., Schoultz, I., & Jordanoska, A. (2018). *Edwin H. Sutherland, Routledge key thinkers in criminology*. Routledge.

Gottschalk, P. (2017). White-collar crime: Detection and neutralization in religious organizations. *International Journal of Police Science & Management, 19*(2), 120–126.

Gottschalk, P. (2020). *Convenience dynamics and white-collar crime*. Routledge Publishing.

Gottschalk, P., & Gunnesdal, L. (2018). *White-collar crime in the shadow economy: Lack of detection, investigation, and conviction compared to social security fraud*. Springer.

Hagen, J. M., Sivertsen, T. K., & Rong, C. (2008). Protection against unauthorized access and computer crime in Norwegian enterprises. *Journal of Computer Security, 16*, 341–366.

Hamerton, C. (2020). White-collar cybercrime: Evaluating the redefinition of a criminological artifact. *Journal of Law and Criminal Justice, 8*(2), 67–79.

Hansen, L. L. (2009). Corporate financial crime: Social diagnosis and treatment. *Journal of Financial Crime, 16*(1), 28–40.

Hansen, L. L. (2020). Review of the book "convenience triangle in white-collar crime: Case studies of fraud examinations". *ChoiceConnect, 57*(5). Association of College and Research Libraries.

Harrison, A. J., Dilla, W. N., & Mennecke, B. E. (2020). Relationships within the fraud diamond: The decision processes that influence fraudulent intentions in online consumer fraud. *Journal of Information Systems, 34*(1), 61–80.

Heath, J. (2008). Business ethics and moral motivation: A criminological perspective. *Journal of Business Ethics, 83*, 595–614.

Hinduja, S. (2012). General strain, self-control, and music piracy. *International Journal of Cyber Criminology, 6*(1), 951–967.

Høyesterett. (2019). Dom avsagt 13. mai 2019 i anke over Borgarting lagmannsretts dom 23. oktober 2018 [Verdict announced May 13, 2019 regarding appeal for Borgarting court's verdict October 23, 2018]. Høyesterett (Norwegian Supreme Court).

Huff, R., Desilets, K., & Kane, J. (2010). *The national public survey on white collar crime*. National White Collar Crime Center, Fairmont. www.nw3c.org

Jaishankar, K. (2007). Cyber criminology: Evolving a novel discipline with a new journal. *International Journal of Cyber Criminology, 1*(1), 1–6.

Jordanoska, A., & Schoultz, I. (2020). The discovery of white-collar crime: The legacy of Edwin Sutherland. In M. Rorie (Ed.), *The handbook of white-collar crime* (Chapter 1, pp. 3–15). Wiley.

Keil, M., Tiwana, A., Sainsbury, R., & Sneha, S. (2010). Toward a theory of whistleblowing intentions: A benefit-cost differential perspective. *Decision Sciences, 41*(4), 787–812.

Kempa, M. (2010). Combating white-collar crime in Canada: Serving victim needs and market integrity. *Journal of Financial Crime, 17*(2), 251–264.

Kim, P. H., Dirks, K. T., & Cooper, C. D. (2009). The repair of trust: A dynamic bilateral perspective and multilevel conceptualization. *Academy of Management Review, 34*(3), 401–422.

Kireenko, A. P., Nevzorova, E. N., & Fedotov, D. Y. (2019). Sector-specific characteristics of tax crime in Russia. *Journal of Tax Reform, 5*(3), 249–264.

Kshetri, N. (2005). Pattern of global cyber war and crime: A conceptual framework. *Journal of International Management, 11*(4), 541–562.

Mesmer-Magnus, J. R., & Viswesvaran, C. (2005). Whistleblowing in an organization: An examination of correlates of whistleblowing intentions, actions, and retaliation. *Journal of Business Ethics, 62*(3), 266–297.

Mpho, B. (2017). Whistleblowing: What do contemporary ethical theories say? *Studies in Business and Economics, 12*(1), 19–28.

Naumovska, I., Wernicke, G., & Zajac, E. J. (2020). Last to come and last to go? The complex role of gender and ethnicity in the reputational penalties for directors linked to corporate fraud. *Academy of Management Journal, 63*(3), 881–902.

Park, H., Bjørkelo, B., & Blenkinsopp, J. (2020). External whistleblowers' experiences of workplace bullying by superiors and colleagues. *Journal of Business Ethics, 161*, 591–601.

Payne, B. K., & Hadzhidimova, L. (2020). Disciplinary and interdisciplinary trends in cybercrime research: An examination. *International Journal of Cyber Criminology, 14*(1), 1–25.

Piquero N. L., & Schoepfer A. (2010). Theories of white-collar crime and public policy. In H. D. Barlow & S. H. Decker (Eds.), *Criminology and public policy: Putting theory to work*. Temple University Press.

Podgor, E. S. (2007). The challenge of white collar sentencing. *Journal of Criminal Law and Criminology, 97*(3), 1–10.

Pontell, H. N., Black, W. K., & Geis, G. (2014). Too big to fail, too powerful to jail? On the absence of criminal prosecutions after the 2008 financial meltdown. *Crime, Law and Social Change, 61*(1), 1–13.

Pontell, H. N., Tillman, R., & Ghazi-Tehrani, A. K. (2021). In-your-face Watergate: Neutralizing government lawbreaking and the war against white-collar crime. *Crime, Law and Social Change*, 19, published online. https://doi.org/10.1007/s10611-021-09954-1

Popham, J. F., & Volpe, C. (2018). Predicting moral disengagement from the harms associated with digital music piracy: An exploratory, integrative test of digital drift and the criminal interaction order. *International Journal of Cyber Criminology, 12*(1), 133–150.

Rehg, M. T., Miceli, M. P., Near, J. P., & Scotter, J. R. V. (2009). Antecedents and outcomes of retaliation against whistleblowers: Gender differences and power relationships. *Organization Science, 19*(2), 221–240.

Sarre, R., Lau, L. Y. C., & Chang, L. Y. C. (2018). Responding to cybercrime: Current trends. *Police Practice & Research, 19*(6), 515–518.

Shawver, T., & Clements, L. H. (2019). The impact of value preferences on whistleblowing intentions of accounting professionals. *Journal of Forensic and Investigative Accounting, 11*(2), 232–247.

Stadler, W. A., Benson, M. L., & Cullen, F. T. (2013). Revisiting the special sensitivity hypothesis: The prison experience of white-collar inmates. *Justice Quarterly, 30*(6), 1090–1114.

Stone, B. (2015, March 2–March 8). Too good to be legal. *Bloomberg Businessweek*, pp. 31–33.

Sutherland, E. H. (1939). White-collar criminality. *American Sociological Review, 5*, 1–12.

Sutherland, E. H. (1983). *White collar crime—The uncut version.* Yale University Press.

Tankebe, J. (2019). Cooperation with the police against corruption: Exploring the roles of legitimacy, deterrence and collective action theories. *British Journal of Criminology, 59*, 1390–1410.

Teubner, R. A., & Stockhinger, J. (2020). Literature review: Understanding information systems strategy in the digital age. *Journal of Strategic Information Systems*, published online. https://doi.org/10.1016/j.jsis.2020.101642

Uygur, S. A. (2020). *Fraud in the charity sector in England and Wales: Accountability and stakeholder oversight*. A thesis submitted in fulfillment of the requirement for the degree of Doctor of Philosophy of Royal Holloway, University of London, United Kingdom.

Vasiu, V. I., & Podgor, E. S. (2019, July). Organizational opportunity and deviant behavior: Convenience in white-collar crime. In *Criminal Law and Criminal Justice Books*. Rutgers, The State University of New Jersey. www.clcjbooks.rutgers.edu

Walburg, C. (2020). White-collar and corporate crime: European perspectives. In M. L. Rorie (Ed.), *The handbook of white-collar crime* (Chapter 21, pp. 337–346). Wiley.
Wall-Parker, A. (2020). Measuring white collar crime. In M. L. Rorie (Ed.), *The handbook of white-collar crime* (Chapter 3, pp. 32–44). Wiley.
Webster, J., & Drew, J. M. (2017). Policing advance fee fraud (AFF): Experiences of fraud detectives using a victim-focused approach. *International Journal of Police Science & Management, 19*(1), 39–53.
Williams, M. L., Levi, M., Burnap, P., & Gundur, R. V. (2019). Under the corporate radar: Examining insider business cybercrime victimization through an application of routine activities theory. *Deviant Behavior, 40*(9), 1119–1131.
Yip, M., Webber, C., & Shadbolt, N. (2013). Trust among cybercriminals? Carding forums, uncertainty and implications for policing. *Policing & Society, 23*(4), 516–539.

2

Convenience Dimensions

Researchers have studied the explanatory power of various perspectives that might explain the likelihood and occurrence of cybercrime among white-collar offenders. Payne and Hadzhidimova (2020) reviewed such disciplinary and interdisciplinary cybercrime research and found that important general perspectives include low or lack of self-control, reaction to stress and strain, learning from others, application of neutralization techniques, and abuse of routine activities. These perspectives are important elements in the theory of convenience, where reaction to stress and strain (Hinduja, 2012; Langton & Piquero, 2007; Thaxton & Agnew, 2018) belongs in the motive dimension, routine activities (Cohen & Felson, 1979; Huisman & Erp, 2013) belong in the opportunity dimension, while self-control (Craig & Piquero, 2016; Hinduja, 2012; Holtfreter et al., 2010), learning (Leasure & Zhang, 2018; Sutherland, 1983), and neutralization (Kaptein & Helvoort, 2019; Sykes & Matza, 1957) belong in the willingness dimension of convenience theory.

The theory of convenience is an integrated and deductive perspective on white-collar offenders where individual and organizational themes interact with each other (Chan & Gibbs, 2020; Gottschalk, 2020;

P. Gottschalk and C. Hamerton, *White-Collar Crime Online*,
https://doi.org/10.1007/978-3-030-82132-6_2

Vasiu & Podgor, 2019). To integrate is to form, coordinate, or blend into a functioning or unified whole. Integration is to add perspectives and propositions that improve the validity, generalizability, and utility of a theory to explain a phenomenon and to predict potential outcomes (Fried & Slowik, 2004; Hambrick & Lovelace, 2018).

The theory of convenience integrates various perspectives on convenience into a single theory with greater comprehensiveness and explanatory value than any one of its component perspectives. As such, convenience theory attempts to explain white-collar crime by bringing together several different theories and invoking multiple levels of analysis at the individual, organizational, as well as societal levels as suggested by Friedrichs (2010: 479):

> The number of different theories or levels, and the formality, with which the relationship between the theories or variables on different levels of analysis is posited, varies.

Convenience theory explains white-collar offenders' financial motives, organizational opportunities, and personal willingness for deviant behaviors.

Convenience in Financial Motive

It is convenient to use illegitimate financial gain to explore possibilities and avoid threats. Climb the hierarchy of needs for status and success (Maslow, 1943), realize the American dream of prosperity (Schoepfer & Piquero, 2006), satisfy the need for acclaim as a narcissist (Chatterjee & Pollock, 2017), and restore the perception of equity and equality (Leigh et al., 2010) are some of the perspectives integrated in the motive dimension of convenience theory. In addition, goal setting is a common practice in the field of organizational behavior, where high performance goals tend to encourage unethical behavior (Welsh et al., 2019). The extra profit from financial crime enables the offender to handle desired possibilities and potential threats. It is mainly the convenience of extra profit, rather than the convenience of illegal profit, that is important in the motive dimension of convenience theory.

However, under certain circumstances, there might be some extra benefits from illegal extra profit rather than extra profit in general, since illegal funds avoid the attention of external and internal control mechanisms, including compliance functions (Kawasaki, 2020). Illegitimate financial gain can thus find its ways into exploring possibilities and avoiding threats that recorded funds cannot. It has been argued that convenience does not provide a motive and thus does not make someone want to climb the hierarchy of needs. However, illegitimate gain is a strong motive to do what you otherwise would not have done, where convenience can be found in the use of illegal gain.

White-collar offenders online can explore the special benefits from illegal gain as the money might be transferred on digital networks according to financial motives that are unattainable for legal gain. If the motive is to have money placed in tax havens, commit corruption, receive bribes, finance terrorism, or has other purposes for which many nations have control mechanisms, then it is more convenient in the motive dimension to have money from fraud and other forms of financial crime than from regular and legal business practices. A financial motive thus becomes relevant for offenders online.

Some white-collar offenders have the financial motive of reaching business objectives that justify means (Jonnergård et al., 2010), satisfying the desire to help others as social concern (Agnew, 2014), satisfying greed where nothing is ever enough (Goldstraw-White, 2012), avoiding corporate collapse and bankruptcy (Kang & Thosuwanchot, 2017), or enjoying mutual benefits in exchange relationships (Huang & Knight, 2017). Some offenders have the motive of avoiding loss of self-esteem after organizational failure (Crosina & Pratt, 2019), removing strain, pain, and uncertainty (Hinduja, 2012; Langton & Piquero, 2007), avoiding falling from position in the privileged elite (Piquero, 2012), adapting to profitable criminal market forces (Schoultz & Flyghed, 2020a, 2020b, 2021), or joining profitable criminal networks (Goncharov & Peter, 2019).

Greed is the most acknowledged motive for financial crime by white-collar offenders. Goldstraw-White (2012) defines greed as socially constructed needs and desires that can never be completely covered or contended. Greed can be a very strong quest to get more and more of something, and there is a strong preference to maximize wealth. To outsiders it may seem strange that rich people have such a strong desire to become even richer that they are willing to break the law. However, as the definition indicates, greedy individuals are never happy with what they have, as they desperately want more all the time. Prosperity is not a means, but a goal for greedy individuals. Greed can grow when the organization does not have an adequate reaction (Haynes et al., 2015). Greed is a typical motive for occupational crime where individuals enrich themselves. Greed implies that some people never become satisfied with what they earn or what they own. There is a lack of satisfaction with whatever one has. Greed can be a strong quest to maximize wealth as wealth is also a symbol of success. Greed leads to a need for an increasingly larger home, several chalets, and summerhouses, bigger boat, luxurious vacations, and ownership in various enterprises. Greed is a desire among all sorts of people. When there are simple possibilities for financial gain to enjoy prosperity, then economic crime can be a convenient action. Both Bucy et al. (2008) and Hamilton and Micklethwait (2006) emphasize greed as the most common cause of criminal acts by white-collar offenders.

In many organizations, ends justify means (Campbell & Göritz, 2014). If ends in terms of ambitions and goals are difficult to realize and achieve in legal ways, illegal means represent an alternative in many organizations (Jonnergård et al., 2010). Among most executives, it is an obvious necessity to achieve goals and objectives, while it is an obvious catastrophe failing to achieve goals and objectives. Welsh and Ordonez (2014) found that high performance goals cause unethical behavior.

Convenience in Professional Opportunity

There is convenient access to resources to commit and conceal financial crime. Legitimate access to premises and systems (Benson & Simpson, 2018), specialized access in routine activity (Cohen & Felson, 1979), blame game by misleading attribution to others (Eberly et al., 2011), and institutional deterioration (Rodriguez et al., 2005) are some of the perspectives integrated in the opportunity dimension of convenience theory. A typical white-collar offender does not go into hiding as many street criminals do. Rather, the offender conceals financial crime among legal transactions to make illegal transactions seem legitimate, or the offender conceals financial crime by removing certain activities from the books. A typical white-collar offender who has convenient legitimate access to commit crime might spend most of the energy on concealing crime in the professional context.

White-collar offenders offline can use executive language that people do not understand (Ferraro et al., 2005), while white-collar offenders online can use digital techniques that people do not understand. Misleading attribution to others is possible in the digital space, where email addresses and webpage labels can attribute deviant behavior and thus blame to others (Resodihardjo et al., 2015). Offender humor can distract from deviant behavior by application of various digital symbols online (Yam et al., 2018). There is power inequality between the elite and others (Patel & Cooper, 2014), where offenders online can pretend to have the necessary authority.

Since offenders have legitimate access to their own premises and systems (Benson & Simpson, 2018), they have the opportunity to exploit their legitimate access to move electronically into other digital spaces. Opportunity creation by entrepreneurship is indeed possible (Ramoglou & Tsang, 2016), where the entrepreneurial effort online is concentrated on both committing and concealing crime. Offenders may have convenient specialized access in routine activity (Cohen & Felson, 1979) and legitimate access to strategic resources in terms of digital tools and techniques (Adler & Kwon, 2002). Scheaf and Wood (2021: 2) found that entrepreneurial fraud has stimulated a wide array of research related to white-collar crime, where they provided the following definition of entrepreneurial fraud:

> Enterprising individuals (alone or in groups) deceiving stakeholders by sharing statements about their identity, individual capabilities, elements of new market offerings, and/or new venture activities that they know to be false in order to obtain something of value.

While the common understanding of entrepreneurship is focused on the positive and productive aspects, entrepreneurial fraud focuses on the dark aspects. It is all about deception used to obtain valuable resources from stakeholders (Scheaf & Wood, 2021).

An important element of the opportunity structure is deterioration in computer systems lacking technical guardianship and lacking supervising competence from absence of technology expertise. A consequence is institutional deterioration (Rodriguez et al., 2005), where nobody feels responsible for whatever goes on in computer systems. There is an inability to control because of social disorganization (Hoffmann, 2002), where online activities are neither coordinated nor reviewed.

The lack of information technology competence in the organization makes it difficult—if not impossible—to distinguish between digital noise and digital crime signals (Karim & Siegel, 1998; Szalma & Hancock, 2013). While executives are spending their working days in meeting rooms talking, technology employees try to fix digital issues when often failing to communicate with others. There is thus a failure of coordination in the principal–agent relationship between executives and experts (Bosse & Phillips, 2016). It is often extremely difficult for outsiders to make sense of what is going on in computer systems (Holt & Cornelissen, 2014; Weick et al., 2005). Computer systems tend to be considered as black box, where people only understand what goes into systems and what comes out of systems, while being unable to understand what happens inside the systems. People thus fail in sense making, where sense making is the process of creating meaning through interpretation of cues (Hällgren et al., 2020). Surprisingly often, people trust computer systems although they are unable to make sense of what is going on inside them.

Even when someone notices deviance and potential wrongdoing, most people are reluctant to blow the whistle and notify relevant entities. It is well-known that whistleblowers often experience retaliation and reprisals without any benefits from whistleblowing for themselves (Bjørkelo et al., 2011; Keil et al., 2010). In addition, there can be an ethical climate conflict (Victor & Cullen, 1998), which strengthens the opportunity structure for offenders.

Convenience in Behavioral Willingness

White-collar offenders online can conveniently justify crime and neutralize potential guilt feelings. By neutralizing guilt feelings, offenders do not feel accountable, ashamed, or responsible (Chen & Moosmayer, 2020). Application of neutralization techniques (Sykes & Matza, 1957), sliding on the slippery slope (Welsh et al., 2014), lack of self-control (Gottfredson & Hirschi, 1990; Hinduja, 2012), narcissistic identification with the organization (Galvin et al., 2015), learning from others by differential association (Sutherland, 1983), and professional deviant identity (Obodaru, 2017) are some of the perspectives integrated in the willingness dimension of convenience theory. When a white-collar offender justifies crime, then it is obvious to him or her that wrongdoing occurred. However, the offender can claim that the act of wrongdoing is morally justifiable (Schnatterly et al., 2018), and that a negative life event has occurred and is to blame (Engdahl, 2013). When a white-collar offender denies a guilty mind, then the offender applies neutralization techniques (Kaptein & Helvoort, 2019; Whyte, 2016). When a white-collar offender makes crime as a choice, it is convenient based on identity (Galvin et al., 2015), rationality (Pratt & Cullen, 2005), and learning from others (Sutherland, 1983). Convenience in behavior refers to convenience of the rationalizations, excuses, and neutralizations.

White-collar offenders online can have a professional deviant identity (Obodaru, 2017). The identity perspective suggests that individuals develop professional identities where they commit to a chosen identity. It is a process of generating possible selves, selecting one, and discarding others. Professional identity is how an individual sees himself or herself in relation to work. The self-concept is a complex cognitive structure containing all of a person's and possibly an organization's self-representations (Cloutier & Ravasi, 2020; Graham et al., 2020). An online offender can have a self-concept of a technology expert, where victims are considered losers incapable of protecting themselves. According to the identity perspective, roles and identities are interdependent concepts. Identity enactment refers to acting out an identity or claiming the identity by engaging in behaviors that conform to role expectations and that allow the identity to become manifest. Deviant behavior finds an anchor in a person's professional identity (Crank, 2018), where the deviant leader must claim and assume a leader identity by their followers.

Labeling can influence the deviant personality offender mind (Mingus & Burchfield, 2012). The labeling perspective suggests that individuals adapt to the reputation created by others (Crank, 2018). A white-collar offender online might act according to the label of a technology expert, where the limits are not whether or not an act is illegal, but rather whether or not an act is technologically feasible to commit and conceal. The labeling perspective argues that the deviant reputation stigmatizes a person into a stereotype. Formal societal reaction to the individual can be a stepping-stone in the development of a criminal career. The deviant label is over time embedded in the individual. The labeled person is increasingly likely to become involved in social groups that consist of social deviants and unconventional others without feeling any doubt or regret since the behavior is in accordance with the label glued to the person by others (Bernburg et al., 2006).

The choice of crime might derive from sensation seeking. Craig and Piquero (2017) suggest that the willingness to commit financial crime by some white-collar offenders has to do with their inclination for adventure and excitement. Offenders are not only seeking new, intense, and complicated experiences and sensations, as well as exciting adventures, they are also accepting the legal, physical, financial, and social risks associated with these adventures. They attempt to avoid boredom by replacing repetitive activities such as regular meetings with thrill and adventures. They search risky and exciting activities and have distaste for monotonous situations. A white-collar offender online can experience new, intense, and complicated adventure, sensation, and excitement when attacking internal and external digital networks and systems for illegitimate financial gain.

White-collar offenders can take on professional deviant identities depending on the space where activities take place. As suggested by Al-Suwaidi et al. (2018), people behave differently when they move from one space to another. For example, in email communication, people tend to have an overemphasis on the sender role rather than the receiver role as compared to face-to-face interaction. In the digital space it can therefore be more convenient to offend compared to the physical space. Moral disengagement from harms associated with online offenses may seem more convenient than moral disengagement from harms associated with offline offenses (Popham & Volpe, 2018).

Structural Convenience Model

Figure 2.1 illustrates the structural convenience model with convenience themes associated with convenience dimensions. In the convenience dimension of financial motive, there are both possibilities and threats

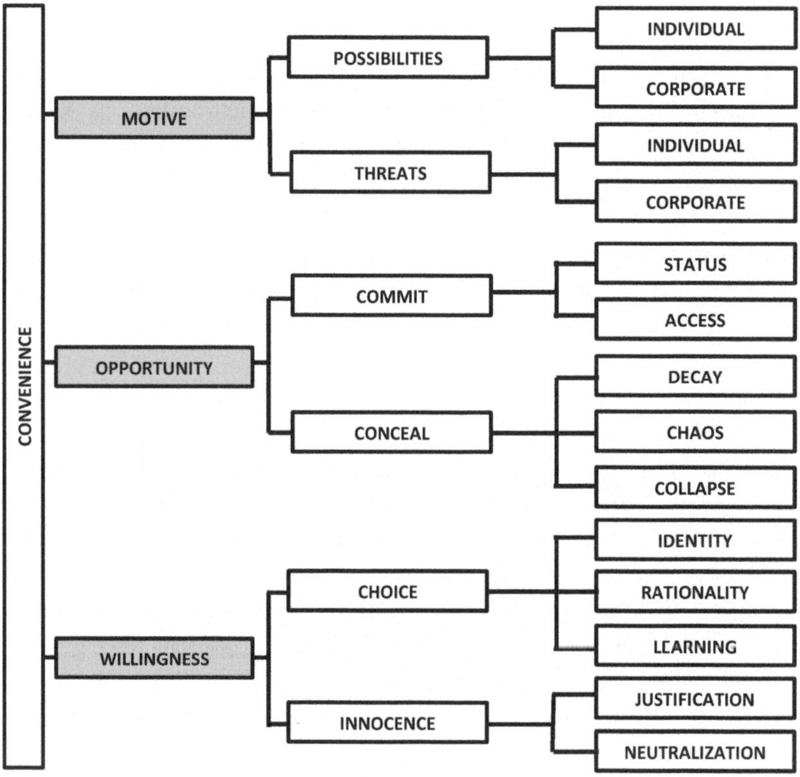

Fig. 2.1 Structural model of convenience theory

that can motive white-collar crime to benefit individuals and organizations. In the convenience dimension of professional opportunity, there are avenues both to commit and conceal crime. Status of offender and access to resources to offend are enablers of crime. Decay, chaos, and collapse are enablers of concealment of crime. In the convenience dimension of willingness, deviant behavior can be the result of choice and a perception of innocence. Offender identity, rational consideration, and learning from others can explain choice of crime. Justification of action and neutralization of guilt feelings can explain the perception of innocence.

Low or lack of self-control is one of the convenience themes in the willingness dimension that can cause the offender to have a perception of innocence. As argued by Gottfredson and Hirschi (1990), human behavior finds innocence in the self-centered quest for satisfaction and avoidance of suffering. Self-control is the blockade that stands between the individual and criminal activity. Lack of self-control is lack of such a blockade, making the short-term pleasure seeking dominate the mind. Lack of self-control implies that the offender lacks the ability and tendency to consider potential implications of a deviant action (Kroneberg & Schultz, 2018), as they are impulsive and unstable (Craig & Piquero, 2016; Jones et al., 2015). Those lacking self-control will typically have a short-term focus and be adventuresome, risk-willing, and indifferent.

Kroneberg and Schultz (2018: 59) link lack of self-control (Gottfredson & Hirschi, 1990) to the situational action perspective, when they find that "personal moral rules play a crucial role in the process of perception of action alternatives, whereas self-control matters only in the subsequent process of choice should actors start to deliberate on whether or not to break the law". While the perception of action alternatives belongs to the organizational opportunity dimension of white-collar offending, the subsequent lack of self-control belongs to the personal willingness dimension of white-collar offending. Gottfredson and Hirschi (1990) suggest that involvement in criminal behavior can be a by-product of low self-control, or crime-propensity. Self-control shapes an individual's response to criminal opportunities with either deviance or refrain from criminal behavior. The presence of a developed sense of self-control prevents involvement in deviance in a similar manner as an underdeveloped sense of self-control, or low or lack of self-control, allows an individual to view criminal behavior as pleasurable (Nodeland & Morris, 2020).

Crime Convenience Triangle

The convenience triangle consists of financial motive, professional opportunity, and deviant behavior as illustrated in Fig. 2.2. There are six hypothetical links between the three dimensions in convenience theory. The links might be causal in nature. For example, the offender can have a stronger desire for profits that can cause an expansion in organizational opportunity over time.

The convenience triangle for white-collar crime has similarities with the well-known fraud triangle (Cressey, 1972), which suggests three conditions for fraud: (1) incentives and pressures, (2) opportunities, and (3) attitudes and rationalization (Steinmeier, 2016). However, there are

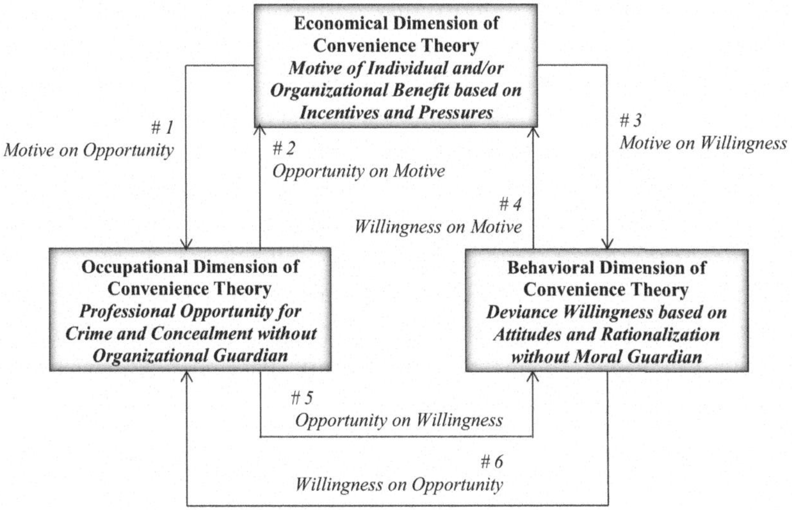

Fig. 2.2 Hypothetical links between constructs in the triangle of convenience

three distinct differences. First, convenience is a relative concept, indicating that offenders have the option of alternative actions to reach their goals that do not represent illegitimate behavior. While the fraud triangle suggests that opportunities will stimulate crime, the convenience triangle suggests that relative opportunities will stimulate crime. There is no reason to commit crime, even if there are many opportunities, as long as alternative convenient decisions may lead to the same result. It is the extent of relative convenience, and not the extent of opportunity, that determines whether an offense is attractive. A very conveniently oriented decision-maker may resort to illegal activities when legal activities are slightly more stressful. A less conveniently oriented decision-maker may try intensely to solve problems and explore opportunities without violating the law.

Second, it is in the occupational and professional setting where offenders have access to resources so that opportunity arises to commit and conceal crime. While the fraud triangle emphasizes opportunity in general, the convenience triangle concentrates on the privileged position that offenders can abuse to commit and conceal crime. There is trust and lack of control, obedience, and fear, which create convenient opportunities. The convenient opportunity derives from legitimate access to resources in a trusted position without guardians, where resources are enablers to carry out activities that are not available to others. Opportunity convenience emerges because of an occupational structure and a professional culture where members of the elite may feel above the law.

Third, a white-collar offender can influence the professional opportunity over time. Therefore, opportunity in convenience theory is a dynamic rather than a static condition. By collecting decision rights, by controlling information flows, and by authoritarian leadership styles a potential offender develops an opportunity space that grows over time. Whether intentional or not, the opportunity space changes over time as a reaction to the potential offender's behavior.

Financial Crime Categories

In this book, computer crime is classified as financial crime (Fletcher, 2007). Financial crime can be defined as crime against property, involving the unlawful conversion of property belonging to another to one's own personal use and benefit. Financial crime is sometimes labeled economic crime (Larsson, 2006). Financial crime is profit-driven crime to gain access to and control over property that belonged to someone else. Pickett and Pickett (2002) define financial crime as the use of deception for illegal gain, normally involving breach of trust, and some concealment of the true nature of the activities. They use the terms financial crime, white-collar crime, and fraud interchangeably.

The term financial crime expresses different concepts depending on the jurisdiction and the context. Nevertheless, Henning (2009) argues that financial crime generally describes a variety of crimes against property, involving the unlawful conversion of property belonging to another to one's own personal use and benefit, more often than not involving fraud but also bribery, corruption, money laundering, embezzlement, insider trading, tax violations, cyber-attacks, and the like. Criminal gain for personal benefit seems to be one of the core characteristics of financial crime.

Financial crime often involves fraud. Financial crime is carried out via check and credit card fraud, mortgage fraud, medical fraud, corporate fraud, bank account fraud, payment (point of sale) fraud, currency fraud, and health care fraud, and they involve acts such as insider trading, tax violations, kickbacks, embezzlement, identity theft, cyber-attacks, money laundering, and social engineering. Embezzlement and theft of labor union property and falsification of union records used to facilitate or conceal such larcenies remain the most frequently prosecuted Labor-Management Reporting and Disclosure Act offences in the US (Toner, 2009).

Financial crime sometimes, but not always, involves criminal acts such as elder abuse, armed robbery, burglary, and even murder. Victims range from individuals to institutions, corporations, governments, and entire economies. Interpol (2009) argues that financial and high-tech crimes—currency counterfeiting, money laundering, intellectual property crime, payment card fraud, computer virus attacks, and cyber-terrorism, for example—can affect all levels of society.

We find a great variety of criminal activities that can be classified as financial crime. The four main categories can be labeled fraud, theft, manipulation, and corruption, respectively. Within each main category there are a number of subcategories.

Fraud can be defined as intentional perversion of truth for the purpose of inducing another in reliance upon it to part with some valuable thing belonging to him or to surrender a legal right. Fraud is unlawful and intentional making of a misrepresentation, which causes actual prejudice, or which is potentially prejudicial to another. Fraud refers to the intentional misrepresentation of the truth in order to manipulate or deceive a company or individual. Fraud is to create a misjudgment or maintain an existing misjudgment to induce somebody to do something that the person or organization otherwise would not do (Elisha et al., 2020). Bank fraud is a typical example. Bank fraud is a criminal offence of knowingly executing a scheme to defraud a financial institution.

Theft can be defined as the illegal taking of another person's, group's, or organization's property without the victim's consent. For example, identity theft combined with identity fraud is the unlawful use of another's personal identifying information. It involves financial or other personal information stolen with the intent of establishing another person's identity as the thief's own. It occurs when someone uses personally identifying information, like name, social security number, date of birth, government passport number, or credit card number without the owners' permission, to commit financial crime.

Manipulation can be defined as a means of gaining illegal control or influence over others' activities, means, and results. For example, bankruptcy crime is criminal acts committed in connection with bankruptcy or liquidation proceedings. A person filing for bankruptcy or a business that has gone into liquidation can hide assets after proceedings have been initiated, and thereby preventing creditors from collecting their claims. However, most of the criminal acts are typically committed before bankruptcy/liquidation proceedings are initiated, e.g., the debtor has failed to keep accounts or has unlawfully withdrawn money from the business.

Corruption can be defined as the giving, requesting, receiving, or accepting of an improper advantage related to a position, office, or assignment (Ashforth et al., 2008). The improper advantage does not have to be connected to a specific action or to not doing this action. It will be sufficient if the advantage can be linked to a person's position, office, or assignment (Artello & Albanese, 2021). An individual or group is guilty of corruption if they accept money or money's worth for doing something that he is under a duty to do anyway, that he is under a duty not to do, or to exercise a legitimate discretion for improper reason. Corruption is to destroy or pervert the integrity or fidelity of a person in his discharge of duty, it is to induce to act dishonestly or unfaithfully, it is to make venal, and it is to bribe. Corruption involves behavior on the part of officials in the public or private sectors, in which they improperly and unlawfully enrich themselves and/or those close to them, or induce others to do so, by misusing the position in which they are placed. Corruption covers a wide range of illegal activity such as kickbacks, embezzlement, and extortion. Corruption entails "mistreatment of suppliers, customers, or competitors" (Kolthoff, 2020: 434).

The various main categories and subcategories of financial crime imply varying sanctions and penalties around the globe. An example is corruption, where there is demand for a bribe and supply of a bribe. In the United States, the most serious offense is to offer and supply a bribe. In China, the most serious offense is to request and receive a bribe (Wang, 2020). In Norway, the law does not distinguish the extent of seriousness between bribe-giver and bribe-taker, but the courts punish bribe-takers more harshly.

By defining computer crime as financial crime and sometimes even as white-collar crime, like in this book, we focus on the profit-orientation of such crime. This definition excludes incidents of computer crime to cause damage without a gain. Even if malware infection, hacking, and other incidents are frequently reported in the popular press (Hagen et al., 2008), these kinds of computer crime are only of interest here if they have a profit motive. Computer crime is here profit-driven crime to gain access to and control over property that belonged to someone else.

References

Adler, P. S., & Kwon, S. W. (2002). Social capital: Prospects for a new concept. *Academy of Management Review, 27*(1), 17–40.

Agnew, R. (2014). Social concern and crime: Moving beyond the assumption of simple self-interest. *Criminology, 52*(1), 1–32.

Al-Suwaidi, N., Nobanee, H., & Jabeen, F. (2018). Estimating causes of cyber crime: Evidence from panel data FGLS estimator. *International Journal of Cyber Criminology, 12*(2), 392–407.

Artello, K., & Albanese, J. S. (2021). Culture of corruption: Prosecutions, persistence, and desistence. *Public Integrity*, 1–21, published online. https://doi.org/10.1080/10999922.2021.1881300.

Ashforth, B. E., Gioia, D. A., Robinson, S. L., & Trevino, L. K. (2008). Re-reviewing organizational corruption. *Academy of Management Review, 33*(3), 670–684.

Benson, M. L., & Simpson, S. S. (2018). *Understanding white-collar crime—An opportunity perspective* (2nd ed.). Routledge.

Bernburg, J. G., Krohn, M. D., & Rivera, C. (2006). Official labeling, criminal embeddedness, and subsequent delinquency. *Journal of Research in Crime and Delinquency, 43*(1), 67–88.

Bjørkelo, B., Einarsen, S., Nielsen, M. B., & Matthiesen, S. B. (2011). Silence is golden? Characteristics and experiences of self-reported whistleblowers. *European Journal of Work and Organizational Psychology, 20*(2), 206–238.

Bosse, D. A., & Phillips, R. A. (2016). Agency theory and bounded self-interest. *Academy of Management Review, 41*(2), 276–297.

Bucy, P. H., Formby, E. P., Raspanti, M. S., & Rooney, K. E. (2008). Why do they do it? The motives, mores, and character of white collar criminals. *St. John's Law Review, 82,* 401–571.

Campbell, J. L., & Göritz, A. S. (2014). Culture corrupts! A qualitative study of organizational culture in corrupt organizations. *Journal of Business Ethics, 120*(3): 291–311.

Chan, F., & Gibbs, C. (2020). Integrated theories of white-collar and corporate crime. In M. L. Rorie (Ed.), *The handbook of white-collar crime* (Chapter 13, pp. 191–208). Wiley.

Chatterjee, A., & Pollock, T. G. (2017). Master of puppets: How narcissistic CEOs construct their professional worlds. *Academy of Management Review, 42*(4), 703–725.

Chen, Y., & Moosmayer, D. C. (2020). When guilt is not enough: Interdependent self-construal as moderator of the relationship between guilt and ethical consumption in a Confucian context. *Journal of Business Ethics, 161,* 551–572.

Cloutier, C., & Ravasi, D. (2020). Identity trajectories: Explaining long-term patterns of continuity and change in organizational identities. *Academy of Management Journal, 63*(4), 1196–1235.

Cohen, L. E., & Felson, M. (1979). Social change and crime rate trends: A routine activity approach. *American Sociological Review, 44,* 588–608.

Craig, J. M., & Piquero, N. L. (2016). The effects of low self-control and desire-for-control on white-collar offending: A replication. *Deviant Behavior, 37*(11), 1308–1324.

Craig, J. M., & Piquero, N. L. (2017). Sensational offending: An application of sensation seeking to white-collar and conventional crimes. *Crime & Delinquency, 63*(11), 1363–1382.

Crank, B. R. (2018). Accepting deviant identities: The impact of self-labeling on intentions to desist from crime. *Journal of Crime and Justice, 41*(2), 155–172.

Cressey, D. (1972). *Criminal organization: Its elementary forms.* Harper and Row.

Crosina, E., & Pratt, M. G. (2019). Toward a model of organizational mourning: The case of former Lehman Brothers bankers. *Academy of Management Journal, 62*(1), 66–98.

Eberly, M. B., Holley, E. C., Johnson, M. D., & Mitchell, T. R. (2011). Beyond internal and external: A dyadic theory of relational attributions. *Academy of Management Review, 36*(4), 731–753.

Elisha, O. S., Johnson, U. J., Olugbemi, K. O., Olugbemi, M. D., & Emefiele, C. C. (2020). Forensic accounting and fraud detection in Nigerian universities. *Journal of Accounting and Financial Management, 6*(4), 1–12.

Engdahl, O. (2013). Ensuring regulatory compliance in banking and finance through effective controls: The principle of duality in the segregation of duties. *Regulation & Governance, 8*(3), 332–349.

Ferraro, F., Pfeffer, J., & Sutton, R. I. (2005). Economics language and assumptions: How theories can become self-fulfilling. *Academy of Management Review, 30*(1), 8–24.

Fletcher, N. (2007). Challenges for regulating financial fraud in cyberspace. *Journal of Financial Crime, 14*(2), 190–207.

Fried, Y., & Slowik, L. H. (2004). Enriching goal-setting theory with time: An integrated approach. *Academy of Management Review, 29*(3), 404–422.

Friedrichs, D. O. (2010). Integrated theories of white-collar crime. In F. T. Cullen & P. Wilcox (Eds.), *Encyclopedia of criminological theory* (Vol. 1, pp. 479–486). Sage.

Galvin, B. M., Lange, D., & Ashforth, B. E. (2015). Narcissistic organizational identification: Seeing oneself as central to the organization's identity. *Academy of Management Review, 40*(2), 163–181.

Goldstraw-White, J. (2012). *White-collar crime: Accounts of offending behavior*. Palgrave Macmillan.

Goncharov, I., & Peter, C. D. (2019). Does reporting transparency affect industry coordination? Evidence from the duration of international cartels, *The Accounting Review, 94*(3), 149–175.

Gottfredson, M. R., & Hirschi, T. (1990). *A general theory of crime*. Stanford University Press.

Gottschalk, P. (2020). *Convenience dynamics and white-collar crime*. Routledge Publishing.

Graham, K. A., Resick, C. J., Margolis, J. A., Shao, P., Hargis, M. B., & Kiker, J. (2020). Egoistic norms, organizational identification, and the perceived ethicality of unethical pro-organizational behavior: A moral maturation perspective. *Human Relations, 73*(9), 1249–1277.

Hagen, J. M., Sivertsen, T. K., & Rong, C. (2008). Protection against unauthorized access and computer crime in Norwegian enterprises. *Journal of Computer Security, 16*, 341–366.

Hällgren, M., Lindberg, O., & Rantatalo, O. (2020). Sensemaking in detective work: The social nature of crime investigation. *International Journal of Police Science and Management*, published online. https://doi.org/10.1177/1461355720980759.

Hambrick, D. C., & Lovelace, J. B. (2018). The role of executive symbolism in advancing new strategic themes in organization: A social influence perspective. *Academy of Management Review, 43*(1), 110–131.

Hamilton, S., & Micklethwait, A. (2006). *Greed and corporate failure: The lessons from recent disasters*. Palgrave Macmillan.

Haynes, K. T., Josefy, M., & Hitt, M. A. (2015). Tipping point: Managers' self-interest, greed, and altruism. *Journal of Leadership & Organizational Studies, 22*, 265–279.

Henning, J. (2009). Perspectives on financial crimes in Roman-Dutch law: Bribery, fraud and the general crime of falsity. *Journal of Financial Crime, 16*(4), 295–304.

Hinduja, S. (2012). General strain, self-control, and music piracy. *International Journal of Cyber Criminology, 6*(1), 951–967.

Hoffmann, J. P. (2002). A contextual analysis of differential association, social control, and strain theories of delinquency. *Social Forces, 81*(3), 753–785.

Holt, R., & Cornelissen, J. (2014). Sensemaking revisited. *Management Learning, 45*(5), 525–539.

Holtfreter, K., Beaver, K. M., Reisig, M. D., & Pratt, T. C. (2010). Low self-control and fraud offending. *Journal of Financial Crime, 17*(3), 295–307.

Huang, L., & Knight, A. P. (2017). Resources and relationships in entrepreneurship: An exchange theory of the development and effects of the entrepreneur-investor relationship. *Academy of Management Review, 42*(1), 80–102.

Huisman, W., & Erp, J. (2013). Opportunities for environmental crime. *British Journal of Criminology, 53,* 1178–1200.

Interpol. (2009). *Financial and high-tech crimes*. International Criminal Police Organizaton (Interpol). http://www.interpol.int/Public/FinancialCrime/.

Jones, S., Lyman, D. R., & Piquero, A. R. (2015). Substance use, personality, and inhibitors: Testing Hirschi's predictions about the reconceptualization of self-control. *Crime & Delinquency, 61*(4), 538–558.

Jonnergård, K., Stafsudd, A., & Elg, U. (2010). Performance evaluations as gender barriers in professional organizations: A study of auditing firms. *Gender, Work and Organization, 17*(6), 721–747.

Kang, E., & Thosuwanchot, N. (2017). An application of Durkheim's four categories of suicide to organizational crimes. *Deviant Behavior, 38*(5), 493–513.

Kaptein, M., & Helvoort, M. (2019). A model of neutralization techniques. *Deviant Behavior, 40*(10), 1260–1285.

Karim, K. E., & Siegel, P. H. (1998). A signal detection theory approach to analyzing the efficiency and effectiveness of auditing to detect management fraud. *Managerial Auditing Journal, 13*(6), 367–375.

Kawasaki, T. (2020). Review of comparative studies on white-collar and corporate crime. In M. L. Rorie (Ed.), *The handbook of white-collar crime* (Chapter 27, pp. 437–447). Wiley.

Keil, M., Tiwana, A., Sainsbury, R., & Sneha, S. (2010). Toward a theory of whistleblowing intentions: A benefit-cost differential perspective. *Decision Sciences, 41*(4), 787–812.

Kolthoff, E. (2020). Criminological responses to corruption. In A. Graycar (Ed.), *Handbook on corruption, ethics and integrity in public administration* (Chapter 30, pp. 434–448). Edward Elgar.

Kroneberg, C., & Schulz, S. (2018). Revisiting the role of self-control in situational action theory. *European Journal of Criminology, 15*(1), 56–76.

Langton, L., & Piquero, N. L. (2007). Can general strain theory explain white-collar crime? A preliminary investigation of the relationship between strain and select white-collar offenses. *Journal of Criminal Justice, 35,* 1–15.

Larsson, P. (2006). Developments in the regulation of economic crime in Norway. *Journal of Financial Crime, 13*(1), 65–76.

Leasure, P., & Zhang, G. (2018). "That's how they taught us to do it": Learned deviance and inadequate deterrents in retail banking. *Deviant Behavior, 39*(5), 603–616.

Leigh, A. C., Foote, D. A., Clark, W. R., & Lewis, J. L. (2010). Equity sensitivity: A triadic measure and outcome/input perspectives. *Journal of Managerial Issues, 22*(3), 286–305.

Maslow, A. H. (1943). A theory of human motivation. *Psychological Review, 50*(4), 370–396.

Mingus, W., & Burchfield, K. B. (2012). From prison to integration: Applying modified labeling theory to sex offenders. *Criminal Justice Studies, 25*(1), 97–109.

Nodeland, B., & Morris, R. (2020). The impact of low self-control on past and future cyber offending. *International Journal of Cyber Criminology, 14*(1), 106–120.

Obodaru, O. (2017). Forgone, but not forgotten: Toward a theory of forgone professional identities. *Academy of Management Journal, 60*(2), 523–553.

Patel, P. C., & Cooper, D. (2014). Structural power equality between family and nonfamily TMT members and the performance of family firms. *Academy of Management Journal, 57*(6), 1624–1649.

Payne, B. K., & Hadzhidimova, L. (2020). Disciplinary and interdisciplinary trends in cybercrime research: An examination. *International Journal of Cyber Criminology, 14*(1), 1–25.

Pickett, K. H. S., & Pickett, J. M. (2002). *Financial crime investigation and control*. Wiley.

Piquero, N. L. (2012). The only thing we have to fear is fear itself: Investigating the relationship between fear of falling and white-collar crime. *Crime and Delinquency, 58*(3), 362–379.

Popham, J. F., & Volpe, C. (2018). Predicting moral disengagement from the harms associated with digital music piracy: An exploratory, integrative test of digital drift and the criminal interaction order. *International Journal of Cyber Criminology, 12*(1), 133–150.

Pratt, T. C., & Cullen, F. T. (2005). Assessing macro-level predictors and theories of crime: A meta-analysis. *Crime and Justice, 32,* 373–450.

Ramoglou, S., & Tsang, E. W. K. (2016). A realist perspective of entrepreneurship: Opportunities as propensities. *Academy of Management Review, 41,* 410–434.

Resodihardjo, S. L., Carroll, B. J., Eijk, C. J. A., & Maris, S. (2015). Why traditional responses to blame games fail: The importance of context, rituals, and sub-blame games in the face of raves gone wrong. *Public Administration, 94*(2), 350–363.

Rodriguez, P., Uhlenbruck, K., & Eden, L. (2005). Government corruption and the entry strategies of multinationals. *Academy of Management Review, 30*(2), 383–396.

Scheaf, D. J., & Wood, M. S. (2021). Entrepreneurial fraud: A multidisciplinary review and synthesized framework. *Theory and Practice*, published online. https://doi.org/10.1177/0422587211001818,pages1-36.

Schnatterly, K., Gangloff, K. A., & Tuschke, A. (2018). CEO wrongdoing: A review of pressure, opportunity, and rationalization. *Journal of Management, 44*(6), 2405–2432.

Schoepfer, A., & Piquero, N. L. (2006). Exploring white-collar crime and the American dream: A partial test of institutional anomie theory. *Journal of Criminal Justice, 34*(3), 227–235.

Schoultz, I., & Flyghed, J. (2020a). From "we didn't do it" to "we've learned our lesson": Development of a typology of neutralizations of corporate crime. *Critical Criminology, 28,* 739–757.

Schoultz, I., & Flyghed, J. (2020b). Denials and confessions: An analysis of the temporalization of neutralizations of corporate crime. *International Journal of Law, Crime and Justice*, published online. https://doi.org/10.1016/j.ijlcj.2020.100389.

Schoultz, I., & Flyghed, J. (2021). "We have been thrown under the bus": Corporate versus individual defense mechanisms against transnational corporate bribery charges. *Journal of White Collar and Corporate Crime, 2*(1), 24–35.

Steinmeier, M. (2016). Fraud in sustainability departments? An exploratory study. *Journal of Business Ethics, 138*, 477–492.

Sutherland, E. H. (1983). *White collar crime—The uncut version.* Yale University Press.

Sykes, G., & Matza, D. (1957). Techniques of neutralization: A theory of delinquency. *American Sociological Review, 22*(6), 664–670.

Szalma, J. L., & Hancock, P. A. (2013). A signal improvement to signal detection analysis: Fuzzy SDT on the ROCs. *Journal of Experimental Psychology: Human Perception and Performance, 39*(6), 1741–1762.

Thaxton, S., & Agnew, R. (2018). When criminal coping is likely: An examination of conditioning effects in general strain theory. *Journal of Quantitative Criminology, 34*, 887–920.

Toner, G. A. (2009). New ways of thinking about old crimes: Prosecuting corruption and organized criminal groups engaged in labor-management racketeering. *Journal of Financial Crime, 16*(1), 41–59.

Vasiu, V. I., & Podgor, E. S. (2019, July). Organizational opportunity and deviant behavior: Convenience in white-collar crime. In *Criminal Law and Criminal Justice Books*. Rutgers, The State University of New Jersey. www.clcjbooks.rutgers.edu.

Victor, B., & Cullen, J. B. (1988). The organizational bases of ethical work climates. *Administrative Science Quarterly, 33,* 101–125.

Wang, P. (2020). How to engage in illegal transactions: Resolving risk and uncertainty in corrupt dealings. *British Journal of Criminology, 60,* 1282–1301.

Weick, K. E., Sutcliffe, K. M., & Obstfeld, D. (2005). Organizing and the process of sensemaking. *Organization Science, 16*(4), 409–421.

Welsh, D. T., & Ordonez, L. D. (2014). The dark side of consecutive high performance goals: Linking goal setting, depletion, and unethical behavior. *Organizational Behavior and Human Decision Processes, 123,* 79–89.

Welsh, D. T., Bush, J., Thiel, C., & Bonner, J. (2019). Reconceptualizing goal setting's dark side: The ethical consequences of learning versus outcome goals. *Organizational Behavior and Human Decision Processes, 150,* 14–27.

Welsh, D. T., Ordonez, L. D., Snyder, D. G., & Christian, M. S. (2014). The slippery slope: How small ethical transgressions pave the way for larger future transgressions. *Journal of Applied Psychology, 100*(1), 114–127.

Whyte, D. (2016). It's common sense, stupid! Corporate crime and techniques of neutralization in the automobile industry. *Crime, Law and Social Change, 66*(2), 165–181.

Yam, K. C., Christian, M. S., Wei, W., Liao, Z., & Nai, J. (2018). The mixed blessing of leader sense of humor: Examining costs and benefits. *Academy of Management Journal, 61*(1), 348–369.

3
Online Convenience

Convenience is a term frequently used in the marketing literature (Farquhar & Rowley, 2009; Locke & Blomquist, 2016; Sundström & Radon, 2015). People moving from offline to online have changed life dramatically and conveniently for most of us. An example is online shopping, where we replace visits to shopping malls and other shopping areas to order goods and services online instead. Online shopping is influenced by online reviews. Schoenmueller et al. (2020) argue that consumer online reviews have become an integral part of the consumers' decision-making process. Online reviews can influence purchase decisions for 93% of consumers, and 91% of consumers trust online reviews as much as personal recommendations.

Online opportunities are a double-edge sword providing many opportunities for individuals and organizations to develop and prosper, but at the same time has brought with it new opportunities to commit crime (Salifu, 2008). Most studies seem to apply the victim perspective of computer crime. This perspective implies that an individual, a group, an organization, or a society is the victim of crime. In this book, we apply the offender perspective. The offender perspective implies that an

P. Gottschalk and C. Hamerton, *White-Collar Crime Online*,
https://doi.org/10.1007/978-3-030-82132-6_3

individual, a group, an organization, or a society is the criminal responsible for computer crime. In the victim perspective, a survey revealed that next to malware infection and theft of IT equipment, hacking was the most commonly reported computer crime incident. The findings of Hagen et al. (2008) document that computer crime causes extra work for the victim and loss of earnings as well. Several of the reported crime incidents in their study could be countered by improved access control and data protection measures in addition to awareness raising activities. Their survey revealed that there are large differences in security practices between large and small enterprises, even when it comes to measures one might have thought that all enterprises independent of size would have implemented.

Offenders from Offline to Online

We know from other crime areas that moving from offline to online has changed offending in dramatic ways. An example is sexual offending pathways and chat conversations in online environments. For example, people from all over the world pay for live streaming video images of minors, also called webcam child sex tourism (Tejeiro et al., 2020). Kleijn and Bogaerts (2020) studied the approaches used by offenders who commit webcam child sex tourism. Evidence was found for an avoidant pathway. Direct, manipulative, and discussing sexual topics sub-pathways, and a mixed pathway were also found. These pathways distinguish online from offline offending of vulnerable children. Similarly, Webster et al. (2015) found that online groomers behave differently from offline groomers by means of their hidden or fake identities when grooming children for online or offline abuse. Online child grooming is the solicitation of children for sexual purposes (Klimek, 2020).

Online fraud in the form of fake invoicing differs from offline fake invoicing. In the offline setting, someone internally has to approve the invoice before payment can occur. In the online setting, a computer system checks all elements in the invoice in comparison to the order placed. If there is complete match between the order and the invoice, then the computer system can trigger payment. This happened at a university in Norway where a completely correct invoice for medical research equipment was approved online, causing transfer of more than one million US dollars to an unknown offender (Lie, 2020).

When white-collar offenders move from offline to online, many of the convenience themes presented in the previous chapter can change in importance. An example is the level of self-control. Nodeland and Morris (2020) studied the impact of low self-control on past and future cyber offending. They found that the expansion of the internet and personal technology devices can be coupled with the development and increase in cyber offending behaviors. Furthermore, they found that the level of self-control is of greater importance in cyber offending compared to the past. Self-control shapes an individual's response to criminal opportunities with either deviance or refrain from criminal behavior. Lower self-control online compared to offline might result from weaker ability at resisting online temptation, less refusal of things that may seem bad, easier to break good habits, more convenient to be lazy, more convenient to do inappropriate things, absence of self-discipline online, stronger desire for pleasure and fun, lower concentration when working online, and acting more quickly online without thinking through all the alternatives. This is in line with the situational action perspective (Kroneberg & Schulz, 2018; Wikstrom et al., 2018), where the perception of action alternative, the process of choice, and well as the action itself all differ online compared to offline.

The traditional bank robbery is not particularly profitable anymore for offline offenders. A small team of white-collar offenders can more conveniently transfer millions without causing any physical damage. An example is a rich widow in Norway who was defrauded by a team of white-collar offenders. One team member pretended to be the widow, another team member was at the receiving end in Dubai, a third team member employed in the bank leaked information to team members, while a few more people were involved. The team had set up a legitimate business enterprise involved in housing construction in Dubai, where the widow's money was transferred as payment for a number of housing facilities without the widow's consent (NTB, 2011).

Previously in the offline setting, an unfaithful employee who left the company to join a competitor had to steal documents by copying material from the former employer that would be useful for the future employer. In the online setting, useful material can be transferred digitally out of one company into the other company. For example, a trusted computer programmer leaving to join a competing software firm transferred the whole system digitally so that it immediately was operational at the new employer (Borgarting, 2010).

White-collar offenders online operate in organizational structures that are different from white-collar offenders offline. The typical offline structure is a hierarchy or a pyramid, where executives are found on the top, while other employees are further down in the structure. Decision-making occurs at the top, while others in the organization implement decisions from above. Some are leaders and some are followers. The typical online structure is a network, where some people are more central to activities than others, but there are no roles for leaders or followers. In cybercriminal networks there is division of labor among network participants (Broadhurst et al., 2014). For example, some network members can be money mules who register bank accounts or businesses under their names, which are actually exploited by the criminal network (Leukfeldt & Jansen, 2015).

An online convenience element in white-collar crime is that many businesses may not realize their vulnerability, or the fact that they have become victims (Sarre et al., 2018) . While unnoticed financial crime also occurs in the offline setting, such as tax evasion where the tax collection agency is unable to notice that they are missing some income, unnoticed financial crime is more common in the online setting since digital paths can leave fewer traces. Even when financial crime online is detected by victims, they may be reluctant to report it to the police because they feel ashamed and stressed by the challenge of documenting what has happened online (Cross, 2018; van de Weijer et al., 2020). Graham et al. (2020) found that reporting intentions are lower for online offenses compared to offline offenses. Therefore, cybercrime is often seen as both much safer to commit and much more lucrative than its real-world counterpart (Loveday, 2017).

An important part of the online convenience for white-collar offenders is law enforcement reluctance and lack of capability in policing cybercrime. Loveday (2017) describes inappropriate capability in the United

Kingdom, while Harkin et al. (2018) report lack of specialists in Australia, and Popham et al. (2020) found that police-reported cybercrime varies significantly across jurisdictions in Canada. Generally, Paek et al. (2020: 878) found that there is "a dearth of police personnel who can conduct cybercrime investigation". Burruss et al. (2020: 114) found that most police officers hold "negative views toward their confidence in police response to cybercrimes generally". Later in this book we return to the issue of policing cybercrime.

Computer Crime Research

Computer crime is defined as any violations of criminal law that involve knowledge of computer technology for their perpetration, investigation, or prosecution (Laudon & Laudon, 2010). Kshetri (2005) defines computer crime as any crime that employs a computer network at any phase of the crime. The initial role of information and communication technology was to improve the efficiency and effectiveness of organizations. However, the quest of efficiency and effectiveness serves more obscure goals as fraudsters exploit the electronic dimension for personal profits. Computer crime is a challenge for law enforcement as it has brought an array of new crime types (Picard, 2009). Examples of computer-related crime types include sabotage, software piracy, and stealing personal data (Pickett & Pickett, 2002).

In computer crime terminology, the term cracker is typically used to denote a hacker with a criminal intent. No one knows the magnitude of the computer crime problem—how many systems are invaded, how many people engage in the practice, or the total economic damage. According to Laudon and Laudon (2010), the most economically damaging kinds of computer crime are denial-of-service attacks, where customer orders might be rerouted to another supplier.

Eleven white-collar offenders in five countries carried out one of the worst data thefts for credit card fraud ever (Laudon & Laudon, 2010: 326):

In early August 2008, U.S. federal prosecutors charged 11 men in five countries, including the United States, Ukraine, and China, with stealing more than 41 million credit and debit card numbers. This is now the biggest known theft of credit card numbers in history. The thieves focused on major retail chains such as OfficeMax, Barnes & Noble, BJ's Wholesale Club, the Sports Authority, and T.J. Marxx.
The thieves drove around and scanned the wireless networks of these retailers to identify network vulnerabilities and then installed sniffer programs obtained from overseas collaborators. The sniffer programs tapped into the retailers' networks for processing credit cards, intercepting customers' debit and credit card numbers and PINs (personal identification numbers). The thieves then sent that information to computers in the Ukraine, Latvia, and the United States. They sold the credit card numbers online and imprinted other stolen numbers on the magnetic stripes of blank cards so they could withdraw thousands of dollars from ATM machines. Albert Gonzales of Miami was identified as a principal organizer of the ring.
The conspirators began their largest theft in July 2005, when they identified a vulnerable network at a Marshall's department store in Miami and used it to install a sniffer program on the computers of the chain's parent company, TJX. They were able to access the central TJX database, which stored customer transactions for T.J. Marxx, Marshalls, HomeGoods, and A.J. Wright stores in the United States and Puerto Rico, and for Winners and HomeSense stores in Canada. Fifteen months later, TJX reported that the intruders had stolen records with up to 45 million credit and debit card numbers.
TJX was still using the old Wired Equivalent Privacy (WEP) encryption system, which is relatively easy for hackers to crack. Other companies had switched to the more secure Wi-Fi Protected Access (WPA) standard with more complex encryption, but TJX did not make the change. An auditor later found that TJX had also neglected to install firewalls and data encryption on many of the computers using the wireless network and did not properly install another layer of security software it had purchased. TJX acknowledged in a Securities and Exchange Commission filing that it transmitted credit card data to banks without encryption, violating credit card company guidelines.

Cybercrime is a term used for attacks on the cybersecurity infrastructure of business organizations that can have several goals. One goal pursued by criminals is to gain unauthorized access to the target's sensitive information. Most businesses are vitally dependent on their proprietary information, including new product information, employment records, price lists, and sales figures. According to Gallaher et al. (2008), an attacker may derive direct economic benefits from gaining access to and/or selling such information or may inflict damage on an organization by impacting upon it. Once access has been attained, attackers can not only extract and use or sell confidential information, but they can also modify or delete sensitive information, resulting in significant consequences for their targets.

Payne and Hadzhidimova (2020) reviewed cybercrime research. They found that types of cybercrime examined by criminologists include bullying, sex crime, fraud, identity theft, and hacking. Regarding the consequences of cybercrime, researchers have explored individual consequences for victims, legal consequences, and the criminal justice system's response to cybercrime. These studies indicate a wide range of consequences arising from cyber offending and cyber victimization.

However, as mentioned in the introduction, the review of cybercrime research shows that studies of offenders are completely absent. Rather than surveying or interviewing offenders, criminologists have surveyed victims and experts, and interviewed other researchers (Payne & Hadzhidimova, 2020: 83):

> One researcher studied hacker motivations by surveying computer security experts and asking them about their hacking behaviors and motivations.

The lack of offender studies is compensated in this book by a number of case studies of white-collar offenders online in movie piracy, foreign aid fraud, crypto currency crime, CEO fraud, embezzlement, money laundering, and bank fraud.

Traditional computer crime research as reviewed by Payne and Hadzhidimova (2020) has applied surveys, experiments, secondary sources, and ethnographies. The latter approach is a kind of studies where social scientists immerse themselves into the world of the research subject, either through in-depth interactions and interviews with the research subject or full immersion into their world. Cyber ethnography can learn about cyber subculture from interactions online with potential offenders.

Hutchings and Holt (2018) discuss interviewing cybercrime offenders. Due to the inherent difficulties researchers experience in accessing cybercrime offender groups, there is a need to understand the ways that the obstacles can be overcome in practice. Participants in interviews seemed incentivized by non-monetary rewards, such as having a medium in which to safely have their voice heard and having access to the published work.

When summing up the state of cybercrime research, Payne and Hadzhidimova (2020) found three trends. First, criminologist use traditional forms of research. Second, the interdisciplinary nature of cybercrime provides the opportunity for interdisciplinary research efforts. Third, the international nature of the behavior warrants the need for internationally focused studies on cybercrime. Multiple case studies in this book illustrate both the interdisciplinary and the international nature of white-collar crime online research.

Holt (2015, 2017a, 2017b) and Jaishankar (2007, 2010, 2018) seem to be the most relevant scholars for our perspective on computer crime by white-collar offenders online. For example, Holt and Graves (2007) conducted a qualitative analysis of advance fee fraud email schemes, while Holt et al. (2012) examined the social networks of malware writers and hackers. Jaishankar (2018) suggest that as an academic discipline, cyber criminology encompasses a multidisciplinary field of inquiry—criminology, sociology, psychology, victimology, information technology, and computer science. Cyber criminology involves the examination of criminal behavior and victimization online.

As argued by Hutchings (2016), various forms of cybercrime are not necessarily unique in that they reflect crime that also takes place in physical space. However, it is the technical environment in which offenders operate that makes these types of offences distinctive. It is the transformation of the offender as well as the offense that make online crime unique.

Hutchings and Holt (2016: 610) applied crime script analysis in their computer crime research:

> This study provides an overview of the script actions typically found when interacting in online black markets. Using a qualitative content analysis of 3 English- and 10 Russian-speaking forums, we identified a number of actors and processes of the market through crime script analysis. These included sellers, buyers, suppliers, moderators (who maintained order on the forums and applied the rules), administrators (who organized the platforms and the hosting of the actual forums) and teachers (who wrote tutorials and provided advice). These roles were not mutually exclusive, as one individual may take no multiple roles, such as seller and buyer or administrator and moderator. Script actions included preparation, namely setting up the necessary client software and creating accounts and learning about and taking steps towards anonymity and security.

Hutchings and Holt (2016) found that the online stolen data market enables black markets trading in drugs, firearms, skimming devices, and pill presses, in addition to digital commodities such as credit card details, other personal information, malware, and infrastructure services. Marketplaces also provide guidelines on how to commit offences and how to recruit co-offenders. Furthermore, marketplaces can be used to advertise code writing, websites development, botnets renting, denial of service attacks, and money laundering. A denial-of-service attack is when an offender makes an online service unavailable by overwhelming it with traffic, often from multiple sources, causing it to collapse (Sarre et al., 2018).

The traditional theoretical lenses on cybercrime is routine activity theory (RAT) that defines the opportunity structure (Horgan et al., 2021: 2):

> Cybercrime research has taken a particular interest in RAT (Cohen & Felson, 1979), which it has used to explain the presence or absence of crime online, drawing attention in particular to the convergence of motivated offender and suitable victim or target, and to how the anonymizing and concealed nature of the internet may generate frequent absences of 'capable guardianship'. This transformation of crime's relationship

> with space with the advent of the internet has driven a large body of research which has applied this perspective, often from a micro sociological perspective focusing on the interactions in time and space that do or do not present an 'opportunity' for an offender to commit crime; as such, these analyses bear theoretical similarities with the perspectives associated with rational choice theory, situational crime prevention and crime science.

As suggested in this quote, several researchers have expanded routine activity theory beyond direct-contact offenses to online situations (e.g., Buil-Gil et al., 2021; Ghazi-Tehrani & Pontell, 2021; Reyns, 2013, 2018; Williams et al., 2019). In our perspective of convenience theory, routine activities as defined by Cohen and Felson (1979) belong in the opportunity dimension, while rational choice belongs in the willingness dimension. A shortcoming in published computer crime research, in addition to the lack of the offender perspective rather than the offense perspective, is the one-dimensional focus on opportunity structures for white-collar offenders online. As argued by the theory of convenience, offenders online do not only face different convenience levels in the opportunity structure online compared to offline. Offenders also experience different levels of convenience in financial motives, and they experience different convenience levels in personal willingness. In the financial motive dimension, possibilities and threats at the individual as well as the corporate level are addressed. Enjoying mutual benefits in exchange relationships (Huang & Knight, 2017), adapting to profitable criminal market forces (Holt et al., 2016; Leonard & Weber, 1970; Schoultz & Flyghed, 2020a, 2020b, 2021; Vu et al., 2020), and joining profitable criminal networks (Goncharov & Peter, 2019; Holt et al., 2012; Leukfeldt & Jansen, 2015) might be stronger motives in the online setting compared to the offline world. In the personal willingness dimension, lack of self-control (Gottfredson & Hirschi, 1990) might trigger a faster kind of action online than offline, and the distance to unknown victims might enable more convenient application of neutralization techniques (Sykes & Matza, 1957).

Outsider Business Cybercrime

Outsider business cybercrime is online attacks by white-collar outsiders, whether committing identity theft illegally to transfer funds to themselves (PwC, 2020), state-sponsored hackers committing economic espionage (Williams et al., 2019), movie piracy (Høyesterett, 2019), music piracy (Hinduja, 2012; Popham & Volpe, 2018), crypto currency crime (Braaten and Vaughn), or CEO fraud (Keyworth & Wall, 2016).

During the Covid-19 pandemic (Horgan et al., 2021; Niesche, 2020; Vu et al., 2020), digital government represented an attractive and convenient arena for fraud against public compensation programs. Digital government, e-government, and e-governance have become synonymous with the use of information and communication technology (ICT) in government organizations (Rawat, 2020). Businesses that suffered from government sanctions, such as closing of restaurants to prevent virus spreading, were entitled to compensation of fixed costs from the government. E-government solutions enabled the handling of compensation requests without the involvement of humans. White-collar offenders online who knew how to formulate a request that would satisfy criteria set in the computer system could automatically receive illegitimate financial gain.

Outsider business crime can take on many types. Miro-Llinares et al. (2020: 140) found that email-based social engineering attacks are one of the most commonly reported types of cybercrime:

> Fraudulent emails, including spam and phishing emails, typically seek to gain personal or financial information from the victim in order to directly financially exploit the victim or are used as steps in identity theft and subsequent, fraud. Infection by malware, delivered through fraudulent emails or websites, is conducted to infect the users' computers to gain access to personal and financial information. It can involve the installation of software that allows the offender to monitor all actions undertaken by the victim on the infected system, such as is the case with key logging software, allowing the offender to harvest online passwords to, for example, bank accounts.

An interesting example of outsider business cybercrime is enterprises involved in identities trading. Legal businesses are trading stolen identities on dark web marketplaces. Like any other marketplace, identity pricing is dependent on supply and demand. Steel (2019) found that basic identity information becoming a commodity has a pricing of $1 for 250 identities. Large volumes of identities for resale can easily be obtained from single sources when attacking servers at companies with several thousand employees. The online market for stolen identities has evolved over the course of three generations, where white-collar offenders entered in the third generation. White-collar offenders were not interested in small and random acquisitions of identities in the first generation or only experimental identity fraud schemes in the second generation (Steel, 2019: 70):

> The third and current generation is showing further market maturity, with the differentiation of wholesale and retail markets. The dark web and crypto currencies have led to direct-to-consumer sales of identities, which has had a significant impact on the marketing and pricing of stolen identities.

The dark web is a portion of the internet not indexed by normal search engine parameters. It is intentionally messy, chaotic, and confusing to navigate on the dark web. Prior to entering the dark web, offenders often install a virtual private network (VPN) to disguise the originating internet protocol (IP) address. In order to access the dark web, an offender has to download and use Onion Router or Tor browser to behave anonymously (Guccione, 2019) .

Many dark web fora are dedicated to the illegal exchange of various goods and services (Bruggen & Blokland, 2021: 2):

> Members communicate by submitting posts and by reacting to postings of other forum members. Over time, this user-generated content develops into discussions, or "threads", centered on certain topics.

In the third generation of identity theft and fraud (Drew & Farrell, 2018), white-collar offenders online have the opportunity for value-added services including step-by-step guides to cashing in on stolen identities. Criminal marketplaces for stolen identities allow trading partners to connect in a largely anonymous fashion to sites that are hosted at anonymous locations. Trading partners are not only loners and peers, but also teams and formal organizations (Holt, 2013) . The third generation overcame the barrier of payment transactions with the rise of Bitcoin and similar blockchain-based currencies that allows for the digital equivalent of the anonymity offered through cash transactions offline (Steel, 2019).

Yip et al. (2013) as well as Vu et al. (2020: 1) found that trust and reputation play a core role in underground cyber markets, where offenders are anonymous, and there is little or no legal recourse for dispute arbitration:

> These underground markets exist in tension between two opposing forces: the drive to hide incriminating information, and the trust and stability benefits that greater openness yields.

In the third generation, there are underground cyber markets for specialist services that drive the professionalization of cybercrime. White-collar offenders operating online no longer need to build their own botnet or send their own spam because they can pay others to do the job. Specialist suppliers develop new strains of malware and operate infrastructure for other cybercriminals (Collier et al., 2020). There is a division of labor where some organized criminals develop technical capabilities, while others pay for the capabilities to commit white-collar crime. This is similar to the market for identities, where some steal and establish databases of identity information, while others pay for the structured information to commit identity fraud. There is thus a separation between identity theft and identity fraud similar to the separation of malware development and malware application, where pricing mechanisms exist to regulate supply and demand for identities and supply and demand for malware and other specialist services. White-collar offenders can engage in crime online without the need for high-level technical skills (Sarre et al., 2018) .

Similarly, on the market for illicit online prescription drugs, there are technical experts who develop and operate the infrastructure of white-collar offenders. Unlicensed pharmacies are businesses by white-collar offenders online who sell both legitimate drugs and drugs that include an active ingredient with incorrect and potentially dangerous dosages. Unlicensed online pharmacies provide access to unapproved drugs. Information about the drugs is usually inappropriate, insufficient, or nonexistent, making the use of such products unsafe and harmful to user health (Leontiadis & Hutchings, 2015). This is outsider business cybercrime that harms not only users but also licensed pharmacies.

Button et al. (2015) compared offline fraud to online fraud. One of the first differences is the potential for mass targeting across borders relatively cheaply. Another difference is the lower degree of interaction with online perpetrators. Offline perpetrators tend to interact with victims in cooperative ways before the fraudulent incident (Lokanan & Liu, 2021). A third difference is the lack of police reporting of online fraud compared to offline fraud.

Insider Business Cybercrime

Insider business crime is online attacks by white-collar insiders, whether committing embezzlement based on privileged access to internal computer systems (Kammeradvokaten, 2019; PwC, 2019), helping organized criminals conduct money laundering in the bank (Bruun Hjejle, 2018), committing fraud by privileged access to debt collection system (Kleppe, 2011), or providing remote access to internal information resources (Williams et al., 2019).

Employees of the organization commit most computer crime, and the crime occurs inside company walls (Hagen et al., 2008: Nykodym et al., 2005). In our perspective of financial crime by white-collar offenders, we define computer crime as a profit-oriented crime rather than a damage-oriented crime, thereby excluding the traditional focus of dissatisfied and frustrated employees wanting to harm their own employers.

Hutchings and Jorna (2015) found that internal unauthorized computer use is a major contributor to data breaches, as employees use legitimate access to computer systems in inappropriate and unauthorized ways. Williams et al. (2019) studied corporate insider threats and victimization. They distinguished between malicious insider threat and unintentional insider threat. Malicious insider threat is a current or former employee, contractor, or other businessperson who has authorized access to an organization's network, system, or data. The person has intentionally exceeded or intentionally used that access in a manner that negatively affected the confidentiality, integrity, or availability of the organization's information or information systems. Integrity is the quality of acting in accordance with the moral values, norms, and rules that are considered valid and relevant within the context in which the actor operates (Loyens et al., 2021). Unintentional insider threat is a current or former employee, contractor, or other business partner who has authorized access to an organization's network, system, or data. The person has no malicious intent associated with an action or an inaction that caused harm or substantially increased the probability of future serious harm to the confidentiality, integrity, or availability of the organization's information or information systems (Collins et al., 2016).

In our perspective of white-collar offenders, only the malicious insider threat is of relevance. Furthermore, in our perspective, the offender has intentionally exceeded or intentionally used his or her authorized access to extract illegitimate financial gain that negatively affected the organization's economic situation.

In their survey of UK companies, Williams et al. (2019) found that fewer than 1 in 10 companies were victimized from corporate insiders. Storing confidential data increased the likelihood of victimization. Bringing own devices and remote working increased the likelihood of victimization. Organizational guardianship practices, including presence of security managers, worry of insider threats, and awareness of risks reduced the likelihood of victimization. Larger size companies were more likely to experience victimization compared to smaller size companies.

When studying criminal profiling and insider cybercrime, Nykodym et al. (2005) found that most of the crime types occurring within organizational walls were innocent and petty. Examples include reading newspapers online, following sporting events while at work, or gambling online. Most of the perpetrators were between 30 and 35 years old.

Some of the crime types were serious, for example, theft. Persons over 35 years did the most damage. For more serious crime types, Kshetri (2005) found that almost 25% of cyber criminals were professionally involved with the organization they attacked.

Profiling of criminals is based on the idea that an individual committing crime in digital space using a computer can fit a certain outline or profile. A profile consists of offender characteristics that represent assumptions of the offender's personality and behavioral appearance. Characteristics can include physical build, offender sex, work ethic, and mode of transportation, as well as criminal history, skill level, race, marital status, passiveness/aggressiveness, medical history, and offender residence in relation to the crime (Nykodym et al., 2005).

Nykodym et al. (2005: 413) made distinctions between four main categories of cybercrime: espionage, theft, sabotage, and personal abuse of the organizational network:

> Unlike saboteurs and spies, the thief is guided only by mercantile motives for his own gain. The only goal in front of the cyber thief is to steal valuable information from an organization and use it or sell it afterwards for money.

"Very skill intensive" is how Kshetri (2005: 552) describes the difference between conventional criminals and computer criminals. He continues with a claim that minimal skill is needed for opportunistic attacks where targeted attacks require more knowledge and competence to succeed. In terms of motive for committing computer crime, he mentions ideology where ideology is an important component of cognitive institutions that energize the behavior of many computer hackers.

In terms of criminal profiling, Nykodym et al. (2005) found that there is a strong pattern in the age of the cyber robbers. If the crime is for less than one hundred thousand dollars, then most likely the attacker is young and 20–25 years old, male or female, and still in the low hierarchy of the organization. If the crime involves more money, then the offender is probably an older male from a management level in the organization. His crime is not driven by hate or revenge but by greed and hunger for money.

Cambridge Cybercrime Database

Before we move into the following two chapters with case studies of external white-collar offenders and internal white-collar offenders, respectively, it is interesting to review some of the cases in the Cambridge computer crime database. It is a database of computer crime events where the offender or alleged offender has been arrested, charged and/or prosecuted in the United Kingdom, dating from January 1, 2010. Most of the cases in the database www.cl.cam.ac.uk fall outside our definition of white-collar offenders online. Here are some of the events that qualify for our criteria of financial motive, professional opportunity, and personal willingness. There are four cases of external white-collar offenders online and four cases of internal white-collar offenders online:

- He was one of five members in a criminal white-collar organization. He pleaded guilty to conspiracy to conceal, disguise, convert, transfer, and remove criminal property. The criminal organization deployed malware and associated fraudulent methods targeting the bank accounts of businesses and organizations across the UK. The fifty-six-year-old man received a two-year sentence. He was an external white-collar offender online.
- He pleaded guilty to five offenses related to phishing. He created websites designed to look just like the websites of legitimate companies. These were used to help others defraud victims out of an estimated £41.6 million after sending phishing emails. The thirty-seven-year-old man received a nine-year sentence. He was an external white-collar offender online.
- He pleaded guilty to conspiring to conceal, disguise, convert, transfer, and remove criminal property. It was money laundering following business email compromise. There were twenty-four companies identified as victims around the world. They would receive a fraudulent email claiming to be from their client, who had previously invoiced them, informing them about a change of their bank account details. Sixteen companies, believing they were paying their genuine clients, transferred more than £2.4 million in total to the offender's bank account. They would not know that they had been defrauded until

their real clients started chasing the payments. The thirty-two-year-old man received a five years and nine months sentence. He was an external white-collar offender online.

- He pleaded guilty to fraud by false representation. Using a business email compromise attack, he posed as a supplier to Imperial Tobacco Group and requested payment of several invoices totaling £459,000. The funds were subsequently frozen and returned to the victim. The thirty-four-year-old man received a three years and two months sentence. He was an external white-collar offender online.
- As a software and analytical engineering expert, he leaked highly sensitive military information to hostile foreign states. He pleaded guilty to recording digital information and making damaging disclosure. He disclosed top secret details of a UK missile system. He had worked at BAE Systems and QinetiQ, which provide contracted services to the Ministry of Defense. The fifty-year-old man received a four years and six months sentence. He was an internal white-collar offender online.
- She stole more than £100,000 while employed by Croydon Council. As part of her duties, she had access rights that allowed her to make amendments to an electronic system, which made payments to those providing services within foster care for the most vulnerable children in the borough. She created false records of fictitious foster service providers, who would, if they truly existed, have been entitled to payments from the council for services they performed. She attached legitimate bank account details, in her name, and the names of a number of her associates to these false service provider records allowing payments to be released to personal accounts. The thirty-year-old woman received a four-year sentence. She was an internal white-collar offender online.
- He worked as an apprentice cashier at Barclays. He moved money into mule accounts, but also handed thousands from customer accounts to people who were clearly not the accounts' owners over the counter. He had managed to gain the login credentials of a former colleague. The twenty-two-year-old man received a four years and six months sentence. He was an internal white-collar offender online.
- She was a Universal Credit claims manager for the Department of Work and Pensions. She fraudulently claimed the benefit through

her access to the computer system. She misrepresented her own circumstances on two Universal Credit applications and hijacked five additional identities, submitting fraudulent claims in their names and submitting her own bank account details. She also diverted advance payments from three other Universal Credit claims into her own bank account. The thirty-year-old woman received a sixteen-month sentence. She was an internal white-collar offender online.

The Cambridge computer crime database created by the computer laboratory at the University of Cambridge includes offences that involve the use of computers, which fall under various legislations including the Computer Misuse Act. It includes cases of fraud, conspiracy, misconduct in public office, data protection, and money laundering offenses where there is a link to computer technology.

References

Borgarting. (2010, September 8). *Court case LB-2010–18170*. Borgarting lagmannsrett (Borgarting court of appeals), Oslo, Norway.

Broadhurst, R., Grabosky, P., Alazab, M., & Chon, S. (2014). Organizations and cyber crime: An analysis of the nature of groups engaged in cyber crime. *International Journal of Cyber Criminology, 8*(1), 1–20.

Bruggen, M., & Blokland, A. (2021). Profiling darkweb child sexual exploitation material forum members using longitudinal posting history data. *Social Science Computer Review*, published online. https://doi.org/10.1177/0894439321994894.

Bruun Hjejle. (2018). *Report on the non-resident portfolio at Danske bank's Estonian branch* (Report of investigation, p. 87). Law Firm Bruun Hjejle.

Buil-Gil, D., Miro-Llinares, F., Moneva, A., Kemp, S., & Diaz-Castano, N. (2021). Cybercrime and shifts in opportunities during Covid-19: A preliminary analysis in the UK. *European Societies*, published online. https://doi.org/10.1080/14616696.2020.1804973.

Burruss, G., Howell, C. J., Bossler, A., & Holt, T. J. (2020). Self-perceptions of English and Welsh constables and sergeants preparedness for online crime: A latent analysis. *Policing: An International Journal, 43*(1), 105–119.

Button, M., Nicholls, C. M., Kerr, J., & Owen, R. (2015). Online fraud victims in England and Wales: Victims' views on sentencing and the opportunity for restorative justice. *The Howard Journal of Criminal Justice, 54*(2), 193–211.

Cohen, L. E., & Felson, M. (1979). Social change and crime rate trends: A routine activity approach. *American Sociological Review, 44*, 588–608.

Collier, B., Clayton, R., Hutchings, A., & Thomas, D. R. (2020). *Cybercrime is (often) boring: Maintaining the infrastructure of cybercrime economies.* Workshop on the Economics of Information Security, Brussels. www.weis2020.econinfosec.org.

Collins, M., Theis, M., Trzeciak, R., Strozer, J., Clark, J., Costa, D., Cassidy, T., Albrethsen, M., & Moore, A. (2016). *Common sense guide to mitigating insider threats* (5th ed.). Software Engineering Institute, PA.

Cross, C. (2018). Victims' motivations for reporting to the 'fraud justice network.' *Police Practice & Research, 19*(6), 550–564.

Drew, J. M., & Farrell, L. (2018). Online victimization risk and self-protective strategies: Developing police-led cyber fraud prevention programs. *Police Practice & Research, 19*(6), 537–549.

Farquhar, J. D., & Rowley, J. (2009). Convenience: A services perspective. *Marketing Theory, 9*(4), 425–438.

Gallaher, M. P., Link, A. N., & Rowe, B. R. (2008). *Cyber security—Economic strategies and public policy alternatives.* Edward Elgar.

Ghazi-Tehrani, A. K., & Pontell, H. N. (2021). Phishing evolves: Analyzing the enduring cybercrime. *Victims & Offenders, 16*(3), 316–342.

Goncharov, I., & Peter, C. D. (2019). Does reporting transparency affect industry coordination? Evidence from the duration of international cartels, *The Accounting Review, 94*(3), 149–175.

Gottfredson, M. R., & Hirschi, T. (1990). *A general theory of crime.* Stanford University Press.

Graham, K. A., Resick, C. J., Margolis, J. A., Shao, P., Hargis, M. B., & Kiker, J. (2020). Egoistic norms, organizational identification, and the perceived ethicality of unethical pro-organizational behavior: A moral maturation perspective. *Human Relations, 73*(9), 1249–1277.

Guccione, D. (2019, November 18). What is the dark web? How to access it and what you'll find, The state of cybersecurity. *CSO Online.* www.csoonline.com.

Hagen, J. M., Sivertsen, T. K., & Rong, C. (2008). Protection against unauthorized access and computer crime in Norwegian enterprises. *Journal of Computer Security, 16*, 341–366.

Harkin, D., Whelan, C., & Chang, L. (2018). The challenges facing specialist police cyber-crime units: An empirical analysis. *Police Practice & Research, 19*(6), 519–536.
Hinduja, S. (2012). General strain, self-control, and music piracy. *International Journal of Cyber Criminology, 6*(1), 951–967.
Holt, T. J. (2013). Exploring the social organization and structure of stolen data markets. *Global Crime, 14*(2–3), 155–174.
Holt, T. J. (2015). Qualitative criminology in online spaces. In H. Copes & J. M. Miller (Eds.), *The Routledge handbook of qualitative criminology* (pp. 189–204). Routledge.
Holt, T. J. (2017a). Situating the problem of cybercrime in a multidisciplinary context. In T. J. Holt (Ed.), *Cybercrime through an interdisciplinary lens* (pp. 1–16). Routledge.
Holt, T. J. (2017b). On the value of honeypots to produce policy recommendations. *Criminology & Public Policy, 16*(3), 739–747.
Holt, T. J., & Graves, D. C. (2007). A qualitative analysis of advance fee fraud e-mail schemes. *International Journal of Cyber Criminology, 1*(1), 137–154.
Holt, T. J., Smirnova, O., & Hutchings, A. (2016). Examining signals of trust in criminal markets online. *Journal of Cybersecurity, 2*(2), 137–145.
Holt, T. J., Strumsky, D., Smirnova, O., & Kilger, M. (2012). Examining the social networks of malware writers and hackers. *International Journal of Cyber Criminology, 6*(1), 891–903.
Horgan, S., Collier, B., Jones, R., & Shepherd, L. (2021). Re-territorialising the policing of cybercrime in the post-Covid-19 era: Towards a new vision of local democratic cyber policing. *Journal of Criminal Psychology*, published online. https://doi.org/10.1108/JCP-08-2020-034.
Høyesterett. (2019). Dom avsagt 13. mai 2019 i anke over Borgarting lagmannsretts dom 23. oktober 2018 [Verdict announced May 13, 2019 regarding appeal for Borgarting court's verdict October 23, 2018]. Høyesterett (Norwegian Supreme Court).
Huang, L., & Knight, A. P. (2017). Resources and relationships in entrepreneurship: An exchange theory of the development and effects of the entrepreneur-investor relationship. *Academy of Management Review, 42*(1), 80–102.
Hutchings, A. (2016). Cybercrime trajectories: An integrated theory of initiation, maintenance, and desistance. In T. J. Holt (Ed.), *Crime online: Correlates, causes, and context* (pp. 117–140). Carolina Academic Press.
Hutchings, A., & Holt, T. J. (2016). A crime script analysis of the online stolen data market. *British Journal of Criminology, 55*, 596–614.

Hutchings, A., & Holt, T. J. (2018). Interviewing cybercrime offenders. *Journal of Qualitative Criminal Justice & Criminology, 7*(1), 75–94.

Hutchings, A., & Jorna, P. (2015). *Misuse of information and communications technology within the public sector*. Trends & Issues in Crime & Criminal Justice Series, No. 470. Australian Institute of Criminology.

Jaishankar, K. (2007). Cyber criminology: Evolving a novel discipline with a new journal. *International Journal of Cyber Criminology, 1*(1), 1–6.

Jaishankar, K. (2010). The future of cyber criminology: Challenges and opportunities. *International Journal of Cyber Criminology, 4*(1 & 2), 26–31.

Jaishankar, K. (2018). Cyber criminology as an academic discipline: History, contribution, and impact. *International Journal of Cyber Criminology, 12*(1), 1–8.

Kammeradvokaten. (2019). *Ansvarsvurdering vedrørende sagen om svindel med tilskudsmidler – Offentlig rapport* [Assessment of liability regarding the case of fraud with benefit funds—Public report], report of investigation (p. 163), law firm Kammeradvokaten Poul Schmith.

Keyworth, M., & Wall, M. (2016, January 8). The 'bogus boss' email scam costing firms millions. *BBC*. www.bbc.com.

Kleijn, M., & Bogaerts, S. (2020). Sexual offending pathways and chat conversations in an online environment. *Sexual Abuse*, 1–20, published online. https://doi.org/10.1177/1079063220981061.

Kleppe, M. K. (2011, December 6). Banktopp dømt til tre års fengsel [Bank top convicted to three years prison]. *Finansavisen*, pp. 30–31.

Klimek, L. (2020). European responses criminalizing online solicitation of children for sexual purposes. *Balkan Social Science Review, 16*, 7–21.

Kroneberg, C., & Schulz, S. (2018). Revisiting the role of self-control in situational action theory. *European Journal of Criminology, 15*(1), 56–76.

Kshetri, N. (2005). Pattern of global cyber war and crime: A conceptual framework. *Journal of International Management, 11*(4), 541–562.

Laudon, K. C., & Laudon, J. P. (2010). *Management information systems: Managing the digital firm* (Eleventh). Pearson Education.

Leonard, W. N., & Weber, M. G. (1970). Automakers and dealers: A study of criminogenic market forces. *Law & Society Review, 4*(3), 407–424.

Leontiadis, N., & Hutchings, A. (2015). Scripting the crime commission process in the illicit online prescription drug trade. *Journal of Cybersecurity, 1*(1), 81–92.

Leukfeldt, R., & Jansen, J. (2015). Cyber criminal networks and money mules: An analysis of low-tech and high-tech fraud attacks in the Netherlands. *International Journal of Cyber Criminology, 9*(2), 173–184.

Lie, T. (2020, December 26). UiT gir opp forsøk på å få tilbake svindel-millioner [UiT gives up attempt to get scam millions back]. *Khrono.*
Locke, S. L., & Blomquist, G. C. (2016). The cost of convenience: Estimating the impact of communication antennas on residential property values. *Land Economics, 92*(1), 131–147.
Lokanan, M., & Liu, S. (2021). Predicting fraud victimization using classical machine learning. *Entropy, 23*, 1–19.
Loveday, B. (2017). Still plodding along? The police response to the changing profile of crime in England and Wales. *International Journal of Police Science & Management, 19*(2), 101–109.
Loyens, K., Claringbould, I., Heres-van Rossem, L., & van Eekeren, F. (2021). The social construction of integrity: A qualitative case study in Dutch football. *Sports in Society*, published online. https://doi.org/10.1080/17430437.2021.1877661.
Miro-Llinares, F., Drew, J., & Townsley, M. (2020). Understanding target suitability in cyberspace: An international comparison of cyber victimization processes. *International Journal of Cyber Criminology, 14*(1), 139–155.
Niesche, C. (2020, October–November). Thei heightened risk of fraud in the Covid era. *Acuitymag*. www.acuitymag.com.
Nodeland, B., & Morris, R. (2020). The impact of low self-control on past and future cyber offending. *International Journal of Cyber Criminology, 14*(1), 106–120.
NTB. (2011, July 1). Fem tiltalt for Nordea-bedrageri [Five charged with Nordea fraud]. *Dagens Næringsliv*. www.dn.no.
Nykodym, N., Taylor, R., & Vilela, J. (2005). Criminal profiling and insider cyber crime. *Computer Law & Security Report, 21*, 408–414.
Paek, S. Y., Nalla, M. K., & Lee, J. (2020). Determinants of police officers' support for the public-private partnerships (PPPs) in policing cyberspace. *Policing: An International Journal, 43*(5), 877–892.
Payne, B. K., & Hadzhidimova, L. (2020). Disciplinary and interdisciplinary trends in cybercrime research: An examination. *International Journal of Cyber Criminology, 14*(1), 1–25.
Picard, M. (2009). Financial services in trouble: The electronic dimension. *Journal of Financial Crime, 16*(2), 180–192.
Pickett, K. H. S., & Pickett, J. M. (2002). *Financial crime investigation and control*. Wiley.
Popham, J., McCluskey, M., & Ouellet, M. (2020). Exploring police-reported cybercrime in Canada: Variation and correlates. *Policing: An International Journal, 43*(1), 35–48.

Popham, J. F., & Volpe, C. (2018). Predicting moral disengagement from the harms associated with digital music piracy: An exploratory, integrative test of digital drift and the criminal interaction order. *International Journal of Cyber Criminology, 12*(1), 133–150.

PwC. (2019). *Ekstern undersøgelse af tilskudsadministrationen 1977–2018: Udarbejdet for Socialstyrelsen* [External investigation of benefits administration 1977–2018: Provided to the social security administration]. Report of investigation, 80 pages, audit firm PricewaterhouseCoopers, Copenhagen, Denmark.

PwC. (2020, June 30). *Independent assessment of the LOLC incident: Report developed for Norfund, report of investigation* (p. 34). PricewaterhouseCoopers.

Rawat, P. (2020). A systematic review of multiple terminologies for ICT in government: A mesh of concentric and overlapping circles. *Bulletin of Science, Technology & Society*, published online. https://doi.org/10.1177/0270467620980996.

Reyns, B. W. (2013). Online routines and identity theft victimization: Further expanding routine activity theory beyond direct-contact offenses. *Journal of Research in Crime and Delinquency, 50*, 216–238.

Reyns, B. W. (2018). Routine activity theory and cybercrime. In K. Steinmetz & M. Nobles (Eds.), *Technocrime and criminological theory*. Routledge.

Salifu, A. (2008). The impact of internet crime on development. *Journal of Financial Crime, 15*(4), 432–443.

Sarre, R., Lau, L. Y. C., & Chang, L. Y. C. (2018). Responding to cybercrime: Current trends. *Police Practice & Research, 19*(6), 515–518.

Schoenmueller, V., Netzer, O., & Stahl, F. (2020). The polarity of online reviews: Prevalence, drivers and implications. *Journal of Marketing Research, 57*(5), 853–877.

Schoultz, I., & Flyghed, J. (2020a). From "we didn't do it" to "we've learned our lesson": Development of a typology of neutralizations of corporate crime. *Critical Criminology, 28*, 739–757.

Schoultz, I., & Flyghed, J. (2020b). Denials and confessions: An analysis of the temporalization of neutralizations of corporate crime. *International Journal of Law, Crime and Justice*, published online. https://doi.org/10.1016/j.ijlcj.2020.100389.

Schoultz, I., & Flyghed, J. (2021). "We have been thrown under the bus": Corporate versus individual defense mechanisms against transnational corporate bribery charges. *Journal of White Collar and Corporate Crime, 2*(1), 24–35.

Steel, C. M. S. (2019). Stolen identity valuation and market evolution on the dark web. *International Journal of Cyber Criminology, 13*(1), 70–83.

Sundström, M., & Radon, A. (2015). Utilizing the concept of convenience as a business opportunity in emerging markets. *Organizations and Markets in Emerging Economies, 6*(2), 7–21.

Sykes, G., & Matza, D. (1957). Techniques of neutralization: A theory of delinquency. *American Sociological Review, 22*(6), 664–670.

Tejeiro, R., Alison, L., Hendricks, E., Giles, S., Long, M., & Shipley, D. (2020). Sexual behaviours in indecent images of children: A content analysis. *International Journal of Cyber Criminology, 14*(1), 121–138.

van de Weijer, S., Leukfeldt, R., & van der Zee, S. (2020). Reporting cybercrime victimization: Determinants, motives, and previous experiences. *Policing: An International Journal, 43*(1), 17–34.

Vu, A. V., Hughes, J., Pete, I., Collier, B., Chua, Y. T., Shumailov, I., & Hutchings, A. (2020, October). Turning up the dial: The evolution of a cybercrime market through set-up, stable, and Covid-19 eras, IMC'20. In *Proceedings of the ACM Internet Measurement Conference* (pp. 551–566). https://doi.org/10.1145/3419394.3423636.

Webster, S., Davidson, J., & Gottschalk, P. (2015). Understanding online grooming—Findings from the EOGP study. In S. Webster, J. Davidson, & A. Bifulco (Eds.), *Online offending behaviour and child victimisation* (pp. 55–90). Palgrave Macmillan.

Wikstrom, P. O. H., Mann, R. P., & Hardie, B. (2018). Young people's differential vulnerability to criminogenic exposure: Bridging the gap between people- and place-oriented approaches in the study of crime causation. *European Journal of Criminology, 15*(1), 10–31.

Williams, M. L., Levi, M., Burnap, P., & Gundur, R. V. (2019). Under the corporate radar: Examining insider business cybercrime victimization through an application of routine activities theory. *Deviant Behavior, 40*(9), 1119–1131.

Yip, M., Webber, C., & Shadbolt, N. (2013). Trust among cybercriminals? Carding forums, uncertainty and implications for policing. *Policing & Society, 23*(4), 516–539.

4
External Offenders

External white-collar offenders are individuals who have legitimate access to premises and systems that they use to commit and conceal financial crime harming other individuals and organizations online. This chapter presents three case studies of external white-collar offenders online. The first case study is concerned with movie piracy, where the perpetrator was able to commit financial crime in terms of advertising revenues from illegal access to the software platform Popcorn Time. The second case study is concerned with fraud against the foreign aid organization, Norfund, where the perpetrator used the method of business email compromise to pretend to be the legitimate recipient of foreign aid funds. The third case study is concerned with cryptocurrency crime. This chapter also presents the general issue of chief executive officer (CEO) fraud, where the external offender pretends to be head of the organization asking for transfer of funds out of the organization.

P. Gottschalk and C. Hamerton, *White-Collar Crime Online*,
https://doi.org/10.1007/978-3-030-82132-6_4

Case Study of Movie Piracy

The theory of convenience suggests that characteristics of white-collar offenders include motive, opportunity, and willingness for deviant behavior. This chapter section discusses the case of offenders developing and supporting the software platform Popcorn Time. The motive seems to be sensation seeking with a deviant identity in addition to illegitimate financial gain. The opportunity seems to be unknown and anonymous identity of offenders based on the lack of oversight and guardianship on the internet. The willingness seems to be lack of self-control as well as disclaim of responsibility for violations of intellectual property rights.

Popcorn Time is a software platform to access and view video streaming without paying for it (Stone, 2015). The legality of the software depends on the jurisdiction. A website created in Norway explained and provided access to Popcorn Time. Both the software and the website are illegal violations of intellectual property laws in Norway (NTB, 2018). A court order revoked the domain name for the website to the Norwegian state, after hearings in the court of appeals (Borgarting, 2019) and the Supreme Court (Høyesterett, 2019).

The Norwegian National Authority for Investigation and Prosecution of Economic and Environmental Crime (Økokrim) prosecuted the case in court. Both courts defined the perpetrator as unknown (Borgarting, 2019; Høyesterett, 2019). Therefore, no individual could appear as defendant in court. The organization behind the website in Norway was making money on advertising in the legal form of an independent association. The chairperson of the association witnessed in court, but he was never prosecuted (NTB, 2018). Similarly, the developers of Popcorn Time remained anonymous and unknown (Stone, 2015).

"Too Good to Be Legal" was the heading of an article in Bloomberg BusinessWeek, where Stone (2015: 31) described Popcorn Time as making piracy easier than ever:

> In the past year, a program called Popcorn Time has become the kinder, gentler face of piracy online, taming BitTorrent to make it far more user-friendly and less obviously sketchy. Free incarnations for PCs, phones, and tablets look pretty much like Netflix, Hulu, or Amazon Instant Video.

Digital piracy is the illegal act of copying digital goods—software, digital documents, digital audio (including music and voice) and digital video—for any reason other than backup without explicit permission from and compensation to the copyright holder. Pirates are responsible for digital piracy (Smallridge & Roberts, 2013).

The daily Norwegian newspaper "Aftenposten" told the story about Popcorn Time under the article heading, "Norwegians violated the law by watching movies through Popcorn Time" (NTB, 2018):

> Hundreds of thousands of Norwegians have broken the law after watching movies and TV shows through the free service Popcorn Time, Follo district court states in a recent verdict.
> Popcorn Time is a free service that offers streaming of movies and TV shows in the same manner as other suppliers on the market, such as Netflix. The difference is that Popcorn Time neither pays the licensees nor has obtained permission to show the contents.
> A recent sentence from Follo district court states that the individual user violates the intellectual property law by watching films and series through the streaming service.
>
> - The verdict is clear and clarifying that even those who watch movies and TV shows through Popcorn Time, violate the intellectual property law, says police lawyer Maria Bache Dahl at Økokrim.
> - A special feature of this technology is that parts of the file are retrieved from an infinitely large number of users. Users who watch movies and TV shows through Popcorn Time will usually contribute to this file sharing by allowing others to retrieve parts of the file from them while watching movies. It is this kind of availability by the users that Follo district court says is undoubtedly in violation of the intellectual property law says Dahl.
>
> Licensees in Norway may have lost as much as NOK 500 million, Willy Johansen said in court. He is the head of the Rights Alliance and secretary general of the Norwegian Videogram Association. It was also referred to an article in Aftenposten in May 2015, where a survey by TNS Gallup showed that 315,000 Norwegians used Popcorn Time weekly.
> Økokrim hopes and believes that the verdict will be preventive against copyright infringements on the internet. However, it is unclear whether Norwegian users of Popcorn Time risk being prosecuted.

- Users of illegal file sharing services cannot subsequently claim that they were unaware of the actions being illegal and will hopefully result in more users abstaining from such offenses. Generally, Økokrim does not comment on the cases that we will investigate, but it is clear that users of Popcorn Time can, in principle, be prosecuted, says Dahl.

She makes a point that the licensees have other tools that they can use and refers to a ruling from Oslo district court in November last year. Telenor and 12 other network providers were required to block customers' access to various domain names related to the streaming service. The plaintiffs were American film companies Disney Entertainment, Paramount Pictures, Columbia Pictures, Twentieth Century Fox Film, Universal City Studios and Warner Bros. Entertainment.
The case in Follo district court was about whether the right to use the domain popcorn-time.no should be revoked, which the district court now has determined that it should be. Økokrim seized the domain in March last year.
While Popcorn Time has provided a quick and easy way to download and view movies and TV shows that are copyrighted material, the Norwegian domain has reinforced the opportunity of illegal use, the court states.
The domain popcorn-time.no is owned by Imcasreg8, an association created by the company Internet Marketing Consult. The company has created this and a number of associations with similar names to register domain names for their customers.

- The verdict is very clear that the participation actions on the Norwegian domain, which were the topic of the court case, constitute intentional and very clandestine complicity. It is stated in the verdict about Popcorn Time, among other things, that the service cannot be considered to have any function or purpose other than providing access to protected films and TV shows, without the licensees' consent, says police lawyer Dahl.

The verdict in Norwegian courts (Borgarting, 2019; Høyesterett, 2019) is in line with the statement that "if you are seen as encouraging people to infringe, then you have a copyright problem" (Stone, 2015: 32).

Defense attorney Ola Tellesbø argued in court for dismissal of the case (Borgarting, 2019: 5):

> Popcorn Time is software that integrates several features including a browser, a BitTorrent client and a player. The software and technology behind it is not in itself illegal, as the prosecution has acknowledged. Nor is the BitTorrent technology, which enables efficient file sharing, illegal. The fact that the software can be used to share copyrighted material cannot lead to criminal liability for those behind the Norwegian domain. Based on the content of popcorn-time.no, it is most natural to compare the website with a technology blog. This cannot be confused with the software Popcorn Time and possible copyright infringements when using it.
> The main purpose of the domain has been to sell advertisements and VPN solutions, not to facilitate or contribute to copyright infringement. This is substantiated by the fact that there was a disclaimer on the website, as well as information that use and downloading might be illegal and is done at the user's own risk.
> The contents of the Norwegian domain also have protection under the Norwegian Constitution (§ 100) and the European Convention on Human Rights (Article 10), which protect the freedom of expression and information.
> The prosecuting authority has not established a causal link between the content of the Norwegian domain and alleged copyright infringements. There is a clear weakness in the investigation that it has not been investigated how many users (if any) have visited the Norwegian domain, possibly clicked further on from the Norwegian site and downloaded the software, and then used the software for copyright infringements. The fraction of legal material in the directories that the software's search features are linked to is also not examined.
> There is no basis for concluding that physical or mental involvement has taken place. The decisive factor in the scope of the responsibility is the relevance of penalty for the actions. The Napster sentence and Filmspeler case from the European Court of Justice do not apply as comparable cases and are irrelevant to determine the extent of participation.

Napster was a piracy site hosting infringing files. Pirate Bay did not host such files, nor link to them. Instead, Pirate Bay hosted trackers, that is, files which tell users of individual BitTorrent apps which other BitTorrent users to link to in order to download large files. Nevertheless, the

European Court of Justice ruled that Pirate Bay was infringing copyright (Hern, 2017).

The reference to Filmspeler at the European Court of Justice was a case where the Dutch citizen Jack Wullens sold a multimedia device online called the Filmspeler. The device acts as a medium between an audiovisual data source and a TV. Wullems' player made it possible for users to watch free programming on their TVs regardless of copyright protection. The court noted that the sole purpose of the device was intentionally to access copyrighted work, where Wullens made money on sale of his device while depriving the rights holders of their economic benefit (Dotinga, 2017).

The unknown perpetrator referred to in the Norwegian court documents (Borgarting, 2019; Høyesterett, 2019) is the team of anonymous developers of Popcorn Time (Stone, 2015: 32):

> Creating a less cumbersome wrapper for BitTorrent was the primary objective of Popcorn Time's anonymous developers, a group of friends in Argentina, ways a Dutch blogger who goes by Ernesto van der Sar and runs TorrentFreak, a news site that covers file sharing. The creators abandoned Popcorn Time just a few weeks after its launch, writing on their website that they needed to 'move on with our lives' (…)
> Popcorn Time survived. Its code is open source, so several other groups of coders quickly released versions after the site shut down. 'We were users of the original and were sad to watch it go', wrote a developer of one of the spinoff versions, who answered an e-mail sent through his group's website and insisted on communicating through anonymous Internet chat software to protect his identity. 'The amount of attention this project has been receiving is HUGE, groundbreaking and way above anything we expected when we first picked it up'.

In the motive dimension of convenience theory, sensation seeking seems to be an important driving force for anonymous and unknown developers of piracy software such as Popcorn Time. Sensation seeking to experience adventure is a common characteristic of some white-collar offenses (Craig & Piquero, 2017). Sensation seeking is a psychological trait where the offender seeks excitement. The offender seeks variation, novelty, complexity, and intensity. The offender may be willing to take physical, social, legal, and financial risks for the sake of such experiences. Even when the sensation seeking is not particularly strong, many white-collar crime acts may involve sensations that some find exciting.

Sensation seeking does not necessarily represent anti-social behavior. For example, bribing a potential customer during contract negotiations can be both social and exciting. When executives from the German bus manufacturer MAN bribed public officials from a Norwegian transportation agency, they went for a walk in a German forest where the Germans handed over envelopes containing euros to the Norwegians (Solem & Kleppe, 2014). For both briber and bribed, the forest tour in itself might have been exciting. The memory of the Black Forest (Schwarzwald) at night will probably remain with the participants. Long and boring meetings, reading volumes of documents, and writing minutes of meetings, on the other hand, might be activities that participants soon forget.

Craig and Piquero (2017: 1367) mention other examples where individuals can be sensation seeking:

> Those qualities could fit a businessman adding false charges to his expense account to make some extra money just to see if he can get away with it. These factors may also describe a retail employee stealing money from the cash drawer, or an individual committing an elaborate Ponzi scheme that requires complex planning and intense pressure.

Sensation seekers such as hackers and pirates attempt to avoid boredom by replacing repetitive activities such as status meetings in software projects, computer operations monitoring, and documentation of applications with thrill and adventures. They search out risky and exciting activities and have distaste for monotonous situations.

Figure 4.1 illustrates the convenience theme of sensation seeking as a possibility for the individual piracy developer.

In their empirical study involving students, Craig and Piquero (2017) included embezzlement and credit card fraud. Stealing money from an employer by embezzlement is risky not only because of legal implications but also because of the probable job loss. Abusing a roommate's credit card cannot only result in legal punishment but also an interpersonal cost if caught. At the same time, the offender can perceive both embezzlement

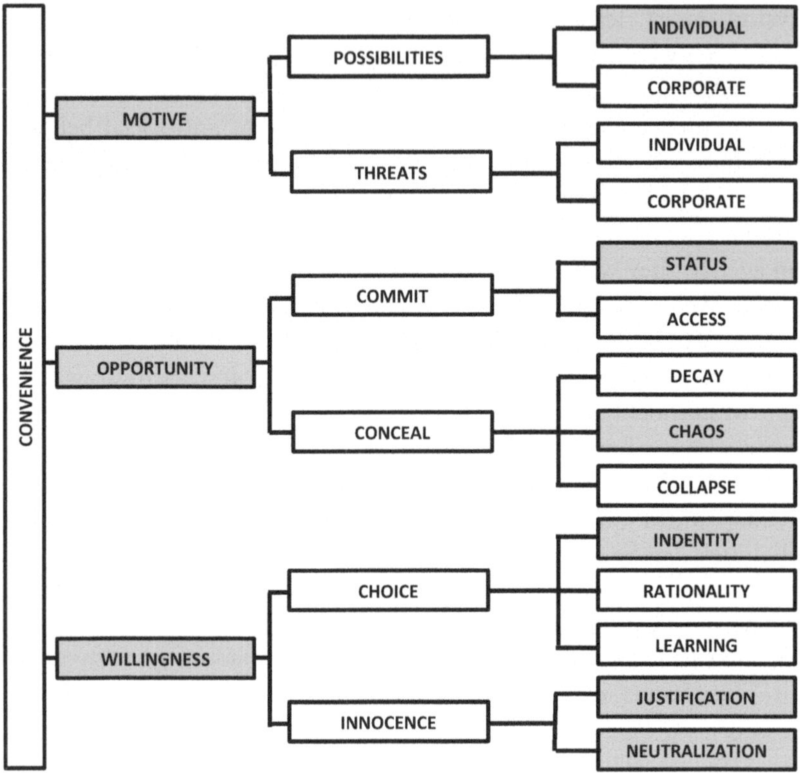

Fig. 4.1 Convenience themes in the case of Popcorn Time

and credit card abuse as thrilling adventures in a situation characterized by boredom. These offenses can also represent acts involving new and intense experiences. To claim to be the roommate is a fraudulent behavior that the offender may perceive as a high-pressure event.

In the empirical study, Craig and Piquero (2017) made a distinction between socialized sensation seeking and un-socialized sensation seeking. While thrill and adventure seeking represents social experience, disinhibition and boredom avoidance represents unsocial experience. The researchers found that unsocial—but not social—sensation seeking was a positive predictor of intentions to engage in shoplifting, embezzlement, and credit card fraud.

In the opportunity dimension of convenience theory, being an anonymous and unknown perpetrator makes it possible to rescue software and avoid detection (Stone, 2015: 32):

> The anonymous Popcorn Time developer says the added pressure is motivating him and his colleagues to finish a version of the software that operates entirely by connecting viewers' computers and doesn't rely at all on central servers. "When we release this, there will be nothing to be taken down again," he says.

Figure 3.1 indicates the high social status among insiders when committing piracy crime as white-collar crime (Slyke & Bales, 2012). Status-related factors such as influential positions in the technological underworld make offenders untouchable (Hausman, 2018).

Figure 3.1 indicates that lack of oversight and guardianship against pirates on the internet is another element of the opportunity structure characterized by chaos when it comes to policing the internet. The climate encourages deviant behavior as normal and acceptable among hackers and pirates (Murphy & Dacin, 2011). Offenders can play the blame game to avoid attention (Eberly et al., 2011; Lee & Robinson, 2000).

In the willingness dimension of convenience theory, lack of self-control (Gottfredson & Hirschi, 1990) seems related to sensation seeking in that willingness for sensation seeking increases with deterioration of self-control. Low self-control individuals give in more easily to their impulsive desires. Nodeland and Morris (2020) found that individuals who engage in digital piracy typically possess characteristics of low self-control.

Lack of self-control is a frequent explanation for executive deviance and crime in general (Gottfredson & Hirschi, 1990). While many might be tempted, only those lacking self-control will actually do it. Self-regulation monitors self-control, where self-regulation represents a process of using self-regulatory resources to control undesirable impulses and override subsequent behavioral responses. As argued by Mawritz et al. (2017), individuals possess varying and limited self-regulatory resources that inhibit responses that may arise from physiological processes, habit, learning, or the strain of the situation. When resources that regulate self-control are depleted, individuals struggle to constrain their urges and engage in behavior almost unwittingly, using quick, thoughtless responses. They move down the slippery slope from the right side of the law to the wrong side of the law (Arjoon, 2008). Self-control processes deplete self-regulatory resources and impair one's ability to control subsequent inappropriate responses.

Kroneberg and Schulz (2018: 59) link lack of self-control (Gottfredson & Hirschi, 1990) to the situational action perspective, when they find that "personal moral rules play a crucial role in the process of perception of action alternatives, whereas self-control matters only in the subsequent process of choice should actors start to deliberate on whether or not to break the law". While the perception of action alternatives belongs to the organizational opportunity dimension of white-collar offending, the subsequent lack of self-control belongs to the personal willingness dimension of white-collar offending. The situational action perspective addresses how environments shape crime opportunities and, subsequently, how modifications in environments can increase criminal opportunities (Huisman & Erp, 2013). When the situational action perspective by Wikstrom et al. (2018) distinguishes between three stages, (1) perception of action alternatives (legal alternatives, illegal alternatives), (2) process of choice (habit, rational deliberation), and (3) action, then Kroneberg and Schulz (2018) conceptualize lack of self-control as well as lack of deterrence on the axis from (2) to (3). The situational action perspective aims to integrate personal and environmental explanatory perspectives within the framework of a situation.

Lack of self-control as described by Gottfredson and Hirschi (1990), combined with sensation seeking as described by Craig and Piquero (2017), can substantially increase the level of willingness among potential white-collar offenders. The researchers also found that unsocial as well as social sensation seeking correlates positively with low self-control.

In addition to lack of self-control, justification of action and neutralization of guilt are typical sources of willingness in deviant behavior. The developers of Popcorn Time thought they did nothing wrong (Stone, 2015: 32):

> The developers don't call themselves pirates. Asked about consequences of making illicit file sharing easier, the anonymous developer claims Popcorn Time doesn't break any laws because it's just an index of other BitTorrent sites and doesn't host any pirated material. 'The torrent world was here with millions of users way before us and will be here BILLIONS of users way after us', he wrote.

The neutralization technique of disclaiming responsibility for crime is relevant here (Sykes & Matza, 1957), where piracy developers claim not being responsible for what happens. They argue that the responsibility for obeying copyright laws should fall to users. Generally, when applying this neutralization technique, the offender claims that one or more of the conditions of responsible agency did not occur. The person committing a deviant act defines himself or herself as lacking responsibility for his or her actions. In this technique, the person rationalizes that the action in question is beyond his or her control. The offender views himself as a billiard ball, helplessly propelled through different situations. He denies responsibility for the event or sequence of events (Jordanoska, 2018; Kaptein & Helvoort, 2019; Schoultz & Flyghed, 2020a, 2020b, 2021; Siponen & Vance, 2010).

Robert Red English, a developer of a separate Popcorn Time spinoff who communicated over Skype Instant Messenger from Ontario with Stone (2015: 32), also argued that the responsibility for obeying copyright laws should fall to users:

> 'I'm not going to justify it', he wrote. 'If it's stealing or not varies by country and each user is given the choice to use the program, and warned we use torrents. It's up to them to choose if they wish to continue'.
> That's common defense among people who collect links to pirated videos, but judicial precedent doesn't back it up. The founders of Pirate Bay, a popular BitTorrent hub, made similar arguments in Swedish court and received prison sentences. Older file-sharing networks such as Napster and Grokster shut down, because U.S. courts ruled that they were emboldening users to break laws.

Smallridge and Roberts (2013) identified two new techniques of neutralization specific to digital piracy. The first technique is the claim of future patronage where offenders diminish their guilt feeling of their actions by rationalizing that they are only sampling the material they are pirating. Digital pirates buy approximately thirty percent more digital products compared to people who do not participate in digital piracy. Based on this, it is possible to imagine that offender may use the idea of sampling content as a justification for digital piracy. The second technique is the claim of digital rights management software defiance where offenders diminish their guilt feeling of their actions by rationalizing that the rights management software is extremely troublesome while a pirated version is more user-friendly. For example, one form of rights management software requires the user to be constantly connected to the internet in order that authentication checks can verify the legitimacy of the product periodically. Such restrictive forms of rights controls negatively affect legitimate customers by making the use of the product cumbersome. If a legitimate user's experience with a digital product is cheapened by rights controls, then the user may begin to see piracy as a viable alternative. The neutralization technique represents the rationalization that digital piracy is permissible when it is used to protect or circumvent troublesome digital rights management software.

Figure 3.1 indicates that deviant identity might also be a cause of willingness among piracy developers. Some white-collar offenders take on a professional deviant identity (Obodaru, 2017). The identity perspective suggests that individuals develop professional identities where they commit to a chosen identity. It is a process of generating possible selves, selecting one, and discarding the others. Professional identity is how an individual sees himself or herself in relation to work. The self-concept is a complex cognitive structure containing all of a person's self-representations. According to the identity perspective, roles and identities are interdependent concepts. Identity enactment refers to acting out an identity or claiming the identity by engaging in behaviors that conform to role expectations and that allow the identity to become manifest. Deviant behavior finds an anchor in a person's professional identity, where the deviant leader must claim and assume a leader identity by their followers.

Labeling can influence the deviant personality offender mind. The labeling perspective suggests that individuals adapt to the reputation created by others. The labeling perspective argues that the deviant reputation stigmatizes a person into a stereotype. Formal societal reaction to the individual can be a stepping-stone in the development of a criminal career. The deviant label is over time embedded in the individual. The labeled person is increasingly likely to become involved in social groups that consist of social deviants and unconventional others without feeling any doubt or regret since the behavior is in accordance with the label glued to the person by others (Bernburg et al., 2006).

In conclusion, this case study has illustrated how the convenience theory applies to hackers and pirates on the internet. The theory of convenience suggests that characteristics of white-collar offenders include motive, opportunity, and willingness for deviant behavior. This chapter section discussed the case of offenders developing and supporting the software platform Popcorn Time. The motive seems to be sensation seeking with a deviant identity for the developers. The opportunity seems to be unknown and anonymous identity of offenders based on the lack of oversight and guardianship on the internet. The willingness seems to be lack of self-control as well as disclaim of responsibility for violations of intellectual property rights, in addition to deviant identity.

Case Study of Foreign Aid Fraud

When white-collar offenders apply business email compromise online, they tend to target companies that frequently work with foreign suppliers or businesses and utilize wire transfers as their regular method of transferring funds. Norfund became victim of such an email scam by transferring funds to offenders.

Norfund is the Norwegian government's investment fund for developing countries. The mission is to create jobs and to improve lives by investing in businesses that drive sustainable development. Norfund is owned and funded by the Norwegian government and is the government's most important vehicle for strengthening the private sector in developing countries and for reducing poverty. Norfund had total commitments of USD 2.5 billion in 2019 in various developing countries.

Norfund reported on May 13, 2020 that the fund had been exposed to s serious case of fraud through a data breach. Two months earlier, on March 16, Norfund transferred USD 9.888.055 to a bank account in Banco Mercantil del Norte, Mexico, which Norfund believed belonged to its client, the Cambodian financial institution LOLC. In fact, the bank account was controlled by a so-called threat actor, who managed to compromise an email account belonging to an employee at Norfund, to register fake domains, and to impersonate Norfund's and LOLC's employees in the conversation (Solgård, 2020; Speed, 2020; Stave, 2020).

In their press release on May 13, 2020, Norfund (2020) claimed to be a victim of "a serious case of fraud through an advanced data breach". The term "advanced" is interesting, as it sometimes indicates and reflects lack of knowledge about the digitalization, applications of information technology, and digital forensics (Wilson-Kovacs, 2020). Norfund hired PwC (2020) to investigate the matter.

The assumption in the following is that the so-called threat actor committing so-called advanced data breach is a criminal organization, which found it convenient to defraud Norfund based on the criminal business's financial motive, organizational opportunity, and willingness for deviant behavior. A business founded on crime will follow the same business phases and logic in its operation and development as any legal or legitimate business venture. The main difference between a legal and illegal business is one of legislation and not one of performance (Dean et al., 2010). Both types of business organizations need entrepreneurialism to survive and succeed, where entrepreneurship is the practice of starting new organizations or revitalizing mature organizations, particularly new businesses generally in response to identified opportunities. Entrepreneurial activity is substantially different from operational activity as it is mainly concerned with creativity and innovation. Just like digitalization by application of information technology created new business models and value configurations for legitimate business ventures, so did the communication and technology revolution create new business opportunities for criminal organizations. Criminal organizations—like non-criminal organizations—develop opportunities by entrepreneurship. Criminal organizations—like non-criminal organizations—can organize their business in hierarchies, networks, or other forms of structures (Gottschalk & Smith, 2011; McElwee & Smith, 2015; Ramoglou & Tsang, 2016; Smith, 2009; Tonoyan et al., 2010; Welter et al., 2017).

Figure 4.2 illustrates convenience themes for the criminal organization Threat Actor when targeting Norfund. First of all, the financial motive for the criminal organization is the possibility of corporate economic gain. Maybe members of the organization want to climb the hierarchy of needs for status and success (Goldstraw-White, 2012; Maslow, 1943), and they suffer from the American dream of prosperity (Cullen, 2010;

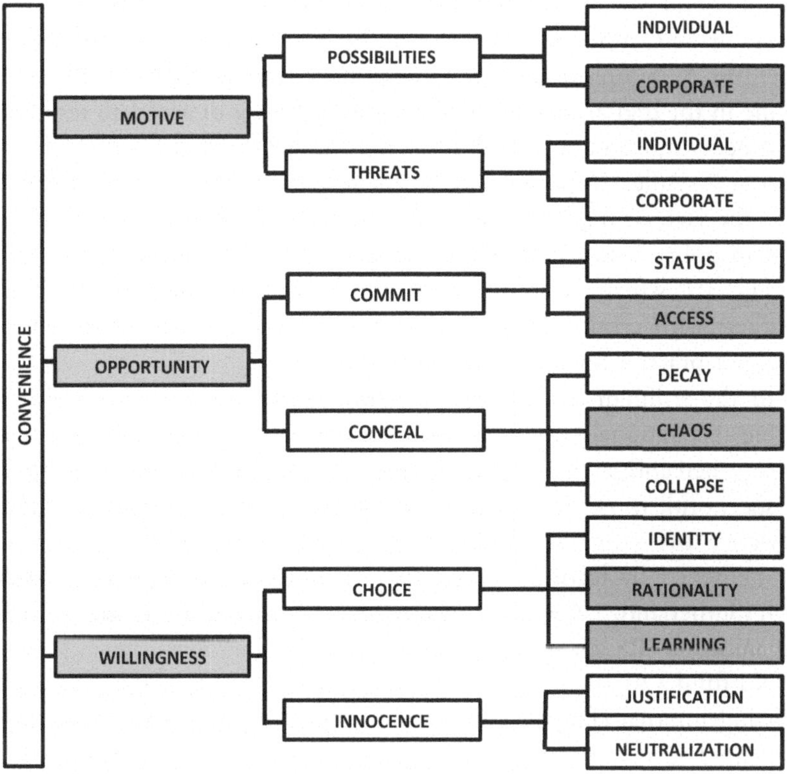

Fig. 4.2 Convenience themes in the case of Norfund

Schoepfer and Piquero, 2006). The choice of crime might also derive from sensation seeking. Craig and Piquero (2017) suggest that the willingness to commit financial crime by some white-collar offenders has to do with their inclination for adventure and excitement. Offenders are not only seeking new, intense, and complicated experiences and sensations, as well as exciting adventures, they are also accepting the legal, physical, financial, and social risks associated with these adventures. They attempt to avoid boredom by replacing repetitive activities such as regular meetings with thrill and adventures. They search risky and exciting activities and have distaste for monotonous situations.

In the opportunity dimension of convenience theory, most criminals have no status in society (Pontell et al., 2014), but they have access to tools and vehicles to compromise email accounts and register fake domains and impersonate employees involved in financial transactions (Benson & Simpson, 2018; Ramoglou & Tsang, 2016). Concealing crime in the digital financial world is also a matter of access to resources to quickly move money away from the Mexican account while deleting all traces (Adler & Kwon, 2002). An important opportunity theme is also the lack of digital knowledge in the victim organization Norfund and in police forces in Norway and globally that is indicated by chaos in Fig. 3.2, where participation in crime networks (Nielsen, 2003) and markets with crime forces (Chang et al., 2005) represents convenient business practice for the criminal organization.

In the willingness dimension of convenience theory, the choice of crime is a rational choice by the criminal organization. The criminals have a perception of benefits exceeding costs (Pratt & Cullen, 2005). If successful, the criminals can experience behavioral reinforcement of deviance over time (Benartzi et al., 2017). The choice of crime is strengthened by learning from other criminals by differential association (Sutherland, 1983) and collectivist value orientations in the criminal organization (Bussmann et al., 2018).

Norfund (2020) hired fraud examiners from PwC (2020) to assess existing internal controls and routines regarding payments. They were not hired to investigate the fraud case, but they nevertheless provide a description of the sequence of events as follows.

Prior to the fraud on March 16, 2020, the criminal organization Threat Actor compromised an email account belonging to an employee at Norfund on September 27, 2019. The Threat Actor then monitored Norfund's communication for seven months. On March 9, 2020, the criminal actor intercepted email correspondence between Norfund and LOLC about the forthcoming transaction. LOLC is located in Sri Lanka, and the money was destined for Cambodia. Threat Actor managed to change bank account details in the disbursement notice and convinced Norfund that a Mexican bank was used to avoid several bank intermediaries in the transaction. Threat Actor used the Corona virus as a factor to convince LOLC that the bank transfer was delayed. At the same time, the criminals sent emails to Norfund confirming that the funds were received by LOLC to prevent immediate suspicion and potential review by Norfund management.

On April 24, 2020, Threat Actor tried to manipulate a transaction with another Norfund client in Cambodia, First Finance, and asked to change the bank account details to Banco Mercantil del Norte. Norfund's investment manager requested First Finance to confirm the change of banking details. In the meantime, Norfund received an email April 30 from LOLC stating that the bank account details in the transfer March 16 were incorrect. Following the discovery of the fraud and fraud attempt, Norfund started reviewing the incident in cooperation with their Norwegian bank DNB, their IT service provider Visolit, as well as reporting the incident to the police.

Police attorney Eivind Kluge at Oslo police district contacted Interpol in France about the case. The Norwegian ministry of foreign affairs contacted Mexican authorities through the Norwegian embassy in Mexico City. However, the police expressed early on that they believed that they would never be able to capture the criminals or retrieve the money stolen (Speed, 2020). Rather than admitting the police force's potential lack of competence and insights into digital fraud locally and globally, the police argued that the criminals were very sophisticated by an "advanced data breach". Key persons at Norfund, such as chairperson Olaug Svarva, chief executive officer Tellef Thorleifsson, and communications executive Per Kristian Sbertoli communicated a similar message that was supported by PwC's (2020) fraud examiners (Solgård, 2020; Stave, 2020).

However, examiners at PwC (2020: 5) identified the approach used by Threat Actor to defraud Norfund as the well-known technique of Business Email Compromise (BEC):

> In this type of scam, a criminal threat actor uses email to impersonate a business executive or other employees to request fraudulent payments. In Norfund's case, the threat actor leveraged relatively simple techniques in terms of circumventing existing IT security controls. PwC found no signs of malicious software being used.

Norfund had no appropriate IT security controls that could have helped detect the breach, and they had no competent technology expert internally. By intercepting Norfund's email system, Threat Actor had acquired knowledge of Norfund's operations generally and money transfers particularly. Threat Actor was successfully able to manipulate communication between Norfund and its client. The combination of Threat Actor's technical capabilities, digital experience, and understanding of Norfund's communication with clients made the fraud convenient for the criminal organization. Convenience was also caused by Norfund's inability to detect fraud and the Norfund employee's ignorance and naivety, which examiners phrase politely (PwC, 2020: 5):

> It's PwC's assessment that the risk management framework could be further developed and improved to ensure Norfund's operational resilience.

The BEC scam that was used against Norfund is quite a common technique (Bakarich & Baranek, 2020: A1):

> Business email compromise (BEC) is a sophisticated email scam targeting companies that frequently work with foreign suppliers or businesses and utilize wire transfers as their regular method of transferring funds. These scams usually involve the compromise of legitimate business email accounts to conduct unauthorized transfers of funds, although other variations include requesting personally identifiable information.

Criminal organizations may use insiders in victim organizations to leak relevant information, bank clerks to open legitimate bank accounts, attorneys to keep secrets because of the attorney–client privilege, police officers to look another way, and various other helpers who the criminals pay off or threaten. When fraud is completed, then money laundering of proceeds from the criminal activity is important.

PwC (2020: 14) identified no singular control failure as the root cause of the incident at Norfund, but rather institutional deterioration that they label "unanticipated interaction of multiple failures in a complex system":

> In hindsight, the reasons why such accidents occur may be obvious. However, they are challenging to predict due to the number of actions and pathways that may lead up to them.

Examiners at PwC (2020) conclude that "a chain of unfortunate events, insufficient controls, and human error, all contributed to the incident".

After stealing the money from Norfund by business email compromise, Threat Actor needed to commit money laundering. Money laundering means the securing of the proceeds of the criminal act. The proceeds must be integrated into the legal economy before the perpetrators can use it. The purpose of laundering is to make it appear as if the proceeds were acquired legally as well as disguising its illegal origins. Money laundering takes place within all types of profit-motivated crime, such as embezzlement, fraud, misappropriation, corruption, robbery, distribution of narcotic drugs, trafficking of human beings, and trafficking of human organs (Stamatel, 2018).

Money laundering has often been characterized as a three-stage process that requires (1) moving the funds from direct association with the crime, (2) disguising the trail to foil pursuit, and (3) making them available to the criminal organization once again with their occupational and geographic origins hidden from view. The first stage is often the riskiest one for the criminals because money from crime is introduced into the financial system. In the Norfund case, the money was already in the financial system. Stage 1 is often called the placement stage. Stage 2 is often called the layering stage, in which money is moved in order to disguise or remove direct links to the offense committed. The money may be channeled through several transactions, which could involve a number of accounts, financial institutions, companies, and funds as well as the use of professionals such as lawyers, brokers, and consultants as intermediaries. Stage 3 is often called the integration stage, in which a legitimate basis for asset origin has been created. The money is made available to the criminal organization and can be used freely for regular expenditures and investments in legal businesses (Menon & Siew, 2012; Naheem, 2020).

PwC (2020) suggests that banks located in China, Hong Kong, UK, Mexico, and China are often involved in fraudulent transfers. Recent money laundering by criminal organizations in Russia involved Danske Bank in Denmark (Bruun Hjejle, 2018) and Swedbank in Sweden (Clifford Chance, 2020).

According to Joyce (2005), criminal money is frequently removed from the country in which the crime occurred to be cycled through the international payment system to obscure any audit trial. The third stage of money laundering is done in different ways. For example, a credit card might be issued by offshore banks, casino "winnings" can be cashed out, capital gains on option or stock trading might occur, and real estate sale might cause profit. When crime generates significant proceeds, the perpetrators need to find a way to control the assets without attracting attention to themselves or the offense committed. Thus, the money laundering process is decisive in order to enjoy the proceeds without arousing suspicion.

The proceeds of crime find their ways into different sectors of the economy. A survey in Canada indicates that deposit institutions are the single largest recipient, having been identified in 114 of the 149 proceeds of crime cases (Schneider, 2006). While the insurance sector was implicated in almost 65% of all cases, in the vast majority, the offender did not explicitly seek out the insurance sector as a laundering device. Instead, because motor vehicles, homes, companies, and marine vessels were purchased with the proceeds of crime, it was often necessary to purchase insurance for the assets.

Transnational criminals such as Threat Actor represent a challenge to societies all over the world. Transnational crime encompasses illegal activities that are carried out across national borders, which includes the planning and execution of illegal activities. Globalization has quickly facilitated the spread of these criminal activities. Transnational criminal organizations are organizations that conduct and carry out criminal operations across international borders. A transnational criminal organization may plan a crime in one country, carry it out in another, escape to a third, and keep the proceeds in a fourth country (Gottschalk & Markovic, 2016). An example might be cybercrime across the Taiwan Strait that became a global issue according to Chang (2013: 540):

> Due to the large number of Internet users and the special political situation across the Taiwan Strait, the Republic of China (Taiwan hereafter) and the People's Republic of China (China hereafter) are two countries where malicious computer activity is rampant. Malicious computer activity across the Taiwan Strait has an impact not only on Taiwan and China but also on many other countries. For example, it has been reported that there have been computer attacks against the USA originating from computers in Taiwan but controlled by command-and-control servers in China.

Transnational crime has three broad objectives: provision of illicit goods, provision of illicit services, and the infiltration of business and government operations (Albanese, 2012). The Norfund fraud is an example of the latter, where Threat Actor infiltrated Norwegian government operations to steal ten million dollars. Transnational criminal organizations include mafia organizations such as La Cosa Nostra based in Italy, Los Zetas based in Mexico, and Hells Angels Motorcycle Club headquartered in the United States. Such organizations vary in their structure, culture, and fields of activity (Paraschiv, 2013). Some organizations recruit members based on ethnicity, while others recruit criminals based on competence and network. To join Threat Actor, computer skills and finance knowledge are probably required.

Traditional crime generally concerns personal or property offences that law enforcement has continued to combat for centuries. Cybercrime is characterized by being technologically different, it can occur almost instantaneously, and it is difficult to observe and detect by traditional investigative methods. Cybercrime is sometimes easy to track, as digital detectives can follow electronic traces. While the crime scene in terms of computers involved may be easy to track, the criminals as actors are more difficult to find and prosecute. The problem of offender identification occurs because of the relative anonymity afforded by the internet as well as the transcendence of geographical and physical limitations in cyberspace. Also, decentralized peer-to-peer networks may prevent material from being tracked to a specific location, and sophisticated encryption lets criminals keep online chats private from those policing the web.

Transnational cybercrime encompasses illegal activities carried out across national borders using information technology. Criminals can take advantage of a virtually limitless pool of potential victims. This is the case, for example, in online grooming where pedophile offenders find child victims across borders. Similarly, transnational music piracy is committed through a multitude of modus operandi. Also, financial crime in terms of, for example, electronic money laundering is frequently transnational between banking sectors with different legislations and secrecy practices (Akinbowale et al., 2020).

Similar to Norfund who used the term "advanced data breach"; PwC (2020: 14) claims that "the fraud was carried out by a resourceful and highly motivated threat actor who had an in-depth knowledge of financial transactions, and access to a global payment infrastructure". Such statements seem to be in contrast to PwC's (2020: 5) claim earlier in their report that the technique used is common and "relatively simple":

> In the past few years, the cyber threat landscape has undergone significant changes. Tools, techniques, and capabilities that were previously exclusively available to highly resourceful threat actors have not only become easily accessible to less-skilled threat actors but have also become easier to use. While substantial in terms of the financial losses incurred by Norfund, the LOLC incident was by no means exceptional.

In addition to the seemingly helpless approach to understanding digital fraud, criminal organizations, and identity of potential offenders, the PwC (2020) report seems like a biased work to satisfy the client. The report creates an impression that the main purpose of the review was to confirm that Norfund does what they can to prevent future fraud, for example (PwC, 2020: 27):

> PwC's assessment is that Norfund has a strong commitment to change and sets an appropriate "tone at the top". It is PwC's opinion that following the Alios incident, Norfund conducted a thorough assessment and identified appropriate measures to improve IT security.

In the summer of 2018, one of Norfund's borrowers, Alios, suffered an incident which appears similar to the LOLC incident (PwC, 2020: 26):

> In this incident, a threat actor infiltrated the communication between Alios and Norfund and manipulated Alios to make a payment to an account under the threat actor's control. Following the incident, Norfund conducted an internal investigation in cooperation with third parties.

PwC (2020) argues that Norfund learned from the episode, while examiners at the same time present excuses for the LOLC incident that happened less than two years later. The client Norfund is probably happy with the PwC report that seems less critical and more client friendly than is expected of work by objective and independent examiners.

In conclusion, this case study documents the convenience for white-collar offenders online as neither victim nor others have the competence to reduce offender convenience.

Case Study of Cryptocurrency Crime

Braaten and Vaughn (2019) studied cryptocurrency crime. They examined cryptocurrency cases decided in United States district and circuit courts to determine the applicability of the theory of convenience to cryptocurrency crime by white-collar offenders online. Analysis of court cases indicated that offenders in cryptocurrency litigation perpetrated a number of cryptocurrency schemes. Some offenders operated unlicensed money transmitting business and/or money laundering. Some offenders engaged in commodities fraud, while others orchestrated securities fraud. Some offenders created bitcoin scams, committed bitcoin exchange fraud, and other criminal activities related to bitcoin. Some offenders were convicted of owning, administering, or selling on the dark web.

Virtual currencies or cryptocurrencies are digital assets used as a medium of exchange. They facilitate decentralized peer-to-peer payment networks that are powered by users with no central authority or middlemen. Cryptocurrencies are stored electronically in digital wallets and transacted online through a direct peer-to-peer system (Malladi & Dheeriya, 2021).

One of the cryptocurrency crime cases studied by Braaten and Vaughn (2019: 3) involved a Tokyo-based bank:

> In Greene v. Mizuho Bank, Ltd. (2016), defendant Mizuho, a Tokyo-based bank, was motivated by the desire to continue earning service fees from processing incoming Mt. Gox wire deposits. Mt. Gox, a bitcoin exchange based in Tokyo, Japan started experiencing internal problems because (1) defendant Karpeles (President, CEO, and majority shareholder) was stealing bitcoins belonging to Mt. Gox users and (2) Mizuho was pressuring Karpeles to close the Mt. Gox bank account at Mizuho due to concerns about a U.S. investigation into money laundering on the Mt. Gox account and potential legal liability or reputational harm to Mizuho. When Karpeles refused to close the account, Mizuho stopped processing international wire withdrawals for Mt. Gox, meaning that Mt. Gox users who wired fiat currency to Mizuho could not withdraw their money. Mizuho, however, did not publicly disclose that it had stopped all international wire transfers out of the Mt. Gox account; instead, defendants continued to accept deposits, which earned revenue from service fees. The plaintiffs were U.S. residents who had wired fiat money to Mizuho for trading in Mt. Gox. After Mt. Gox filed for bankruptcy in Japan on February 28, 2014, plaintiffs could not withdraw the U.S. currency that they wired to Mizuho. Plaintiffs filed a class action lawsuit against Mizuho Bank and Karpeles, asserting claims for tortious interference with contract, unjust enrichment, fraudulent concealment, and accounting. Plaintiffs sought to recover financial losses arising from collapse and bankruptcy of the exchange.

Braathen and Vaughn applied the convenience theory to this kind of cryptocurrency cases. The act of the defendant in the above case was Mizuho Bank stopping the processing of international wire withdrawals for bitcoin exchange Mt. Gox but continued accepting deposits from Mt. Gox users, thereby earning revenue from the associate service fee. The white-collar online offender was Mizuho Bank causing harm to U.S. enterprises and residents. In the economical motive dimension of convenience theory, there were corporate profits from service fees on processing of Mt. Gox wire deposits as illustrated in Fig. 4.3. In the organizational opportunity dimension of convenience theory, Japan-based Mizuho Bank was physically and geographically in a distant jurisdiction

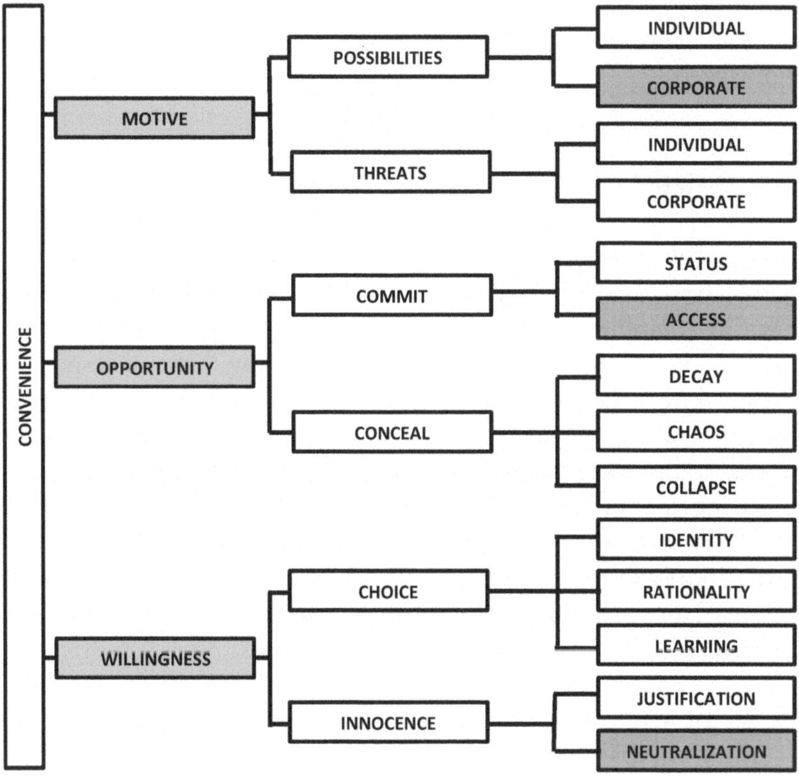

Fig. 4.3 Convenience themes in the case of Mizuho

from its victims in the United States. In the willingness dimension of convenience theory, Mizuho Bank executives argued legal mistake and considered infringement irrelevant because of error of the law.

Claiming legal mistake is a neutralization technique to remove any potential guilt feeling (Benson, 1985; Schoultz & Flyghed, 2020a, 2020b; Sykes & Matza, 1957). The offender argues that this should never pop up as illegal in the first place. The offender argues that the law is wrong, and what the person or enterprise did should indeed not pop up as illegal. One may therefore break the law since the law is unreasonable, unfair, and unjustified. The offender may argue that lawmakers sometimes criminalize behaviors and sometimes decriminalize more or less randomly over time. For example, money involved in bribing people were treated as legal marketing expenses in accounting some decades ago, while corruption today is considered a misconduct and therefore criminalized.

Case Study of Industrial Espionage

Scandinavian Airline System (SAS) committed industrial espionage against the airline Norwegian Air Shuttle. SAS gained illegal access to sensitive business secrets about Norwegian via the booking system Amadeus. It was the management at SAS Norway that was responsible for the white-collar crime online, which took place over several years. Using the Amadeus system, SAS management received updated information on passenger numbers on the routes of Norwegian. SAS was in Borgarting court of appeal sentenced to pay Norwegian the equivalent of USD 20 million in compensation, in addition to legal costs from the district court and the court of appeal that amounted to USD 2 million.

While Norwegian was happy with the verdict, SAS was dissatisfied (Grutle, 2010):

- We are very pleased that the court of appeal has sentenced SAS to pay Norwegian almost NOK 175 million in compensation for the industrial espionage that we were exposed to, says CEO Bjørn Kjos of Norwegian in a press release.

- It is with great disappointment that we receive the verdict from the court of appeal. We have noticed that the court's administrator has advocated a complete acquittal of SAS, so we are interested in finding out what this means, says information manager at SAS Norway, Knut Morten Johansen to TV2 news channel. He assures that SAS plans to appeal the verdict further if the terms for the verdict allows for this. –We do not think that Norwegian has suffered financially, says Johansen.

The case revolved in court about allegations that SAS robbed internal and sensitive information from Norwegian's booking system Amadeus, which several airlines use. It was Braathen's airline, which later became part of SAS that had access to information through the Amadeus system, because Norwegian initially collaborated with Braathen. SAS Norway had access to Norwegian's booking system in Amadeus because former airline Braathen assisted Norwegian on the route Stavanger–Newcastle. SAS Norway continued, according to the ruling, to use the access to the Amadeus system even after the route was closed.

It was corporate crime rather than occupational crime. The professional and organizational dimension of white-collar crime online becomes particularly evident when financial crime is committed to benefit the organization rather than the individual. This is called corporate crime as opposed to occupational crime for personal benefit (Bittle & Hébert, 2020; Hansen, 2009). Corporate crime sometimes labeled organizational offending is resulting from offenses by collectivities or aggregates of discrete individuals (Heath, 2008; Holtfreter, 2015; Kennedy, 2020; Naumovska et al., 2020).

Norwegian Air Shuttle was established as a result of the bankruptcy of airline Busy Bee in 1993. Norwegian started immediately collaboration with Braathen's S.A.F.E., where Norwegian served some short routes locally on the west coast of Norway for Braathen with the plane Fokker 50. The agreement was that Norwegian made planes, crews, and service personnel available to Braathen for their routes. In May 2001, SAS bought the majority of shares at Braathen, and the Norwegian competition authority approved the merger in October the same year. Braathen became a subsidiary of the corporation SAS. Both airlines continued to fly their own routes, but the route offers were nevertheless coordinated. The airline business of SAS was at that time divided into several business areas. Norway was such a business area. The business areas were not independent legal entities but subordinated SAS in Sweden. From the spring 2004, the activities of the Norwegian part of SAS and Braathen were operated under the name SAS Braathens. On March 1, 2005, Braathen was merged with the Norwegian part of SAS Sweden to SAS Braathen's, and Braathen ceased to be a separate company. SAS Braathen's later changed its name to Scandinavian Airlines Norge (Borgarting, 2010).

In January 2002, Norwegian created its own route between Stavanger and Newcastle, a route that Braathen had previously withdrawn from. In the absence of its own organization, Norwegian entered into an agreement with Braathen on February 8, 2002 that the latter would be in charge of selling tickets and handling luggage for Norwegian. Prior to this—probably in connection with the creation of the route—Norwegian was linked to Amadeus, which is a global distribution system for ordering and selling airline tickets through all sales channels. Both Braathen and SAS were already connected to the system (Borgarting, 2010).

Amadeus has open access to information about tickets that all users—including travel agents and competing airlines—have access to, and closed pages with information that basically only the airline that the information concerns can access. In a separate agreement on so-called Extended Ownership Security entered into between Amadeus and Norwegian on January 7, 2001, Norwegian opened up for employees at Braathen to gain access to Norwegian's closed area, so that the airline could serve Norwegian's passengers. Through this special agreement, employees at Braathen thus gained access to so-called PNR data (Passenger Name Record) about Norwegian's passengers. The data included passenger name, travel distance, time of travel, ticket category, ticket price, ordering channel, and time of purchase. For the first eight months of 2002, it was employees at Braathen who entered the information in the system for Norwegian's sales of tickets (Borgarting, 2010).

The complete information about the passengers for a single flight appears on a separate screen in Amadeus. The individual flight is entered into Amadeus up to 365 days before departure, and the airlines have their own computer systems that automatically, and employees who manually, seek to maximize revenues during this period by adjusting the supply of tickets in the various price ranges. This is called revenue management. PNR data are deleted from Amadeus the day after the flight has taken place (Borgarting, 2010).

Braathen terminated the agreement with Norwegian concerning local flights on the west coast on March 21, 2002, with a notice period of 18 months. Braathen later entered into an agreement with Norwegian for a shorter termination period against a financial compensation of 65 million Norwegian kroner. As a result of the termination, Norwegian decided to transform itself into a low-cost carrier using leased Boeing 737 planes. Norwegian started to compete with Braathen and SAS on September 1, 2002. Braathen and SAS closed down its ticket sales and service functions for Norwegian for the route Stavanger–Newcastle on the previous day, August 31, 2002. Norwegian closed the route three months later on December 1 (Borgarting, 2010).

Norwegian started on September 1, 2002 its own routes from Oslo to Bergen, Stavanger, Trondheim, and Tromsø. These routes, and also routes Oslo–Bodø, Oslo–Evenes, Oslo–Alta, and Bergen–Trondheim, have been running continuously since their inceptions. Since September 1, 2002, the need for Braathen employees to access Norwegian's closed pages in Amadeus was no longer present. However, Norwegian did not report to Amadeus that Braathen's access to the airline's PNR data should be closed. Some employees at Braathen continued to exploit the possibility of retrieving information about Norwegian, including information about the number of passengers in various ticket categories. The access was not closed until November 18, 2005. The termination was initiated by SAS Braathen's (Borgarting, 2010).

On July 1, 2005, Norwegian reported SAS Braathen's to the police for illegitimate insights into confidential information in the form of PNR data in Amadeus about Norwegian's passengers. The Norwegian national authority for investigation and prosecution of economic and environmental crime (Økokrim) charged SAS Braathen's on June 13, 2006. The district court in Asker and Bærum passed its verdict in the

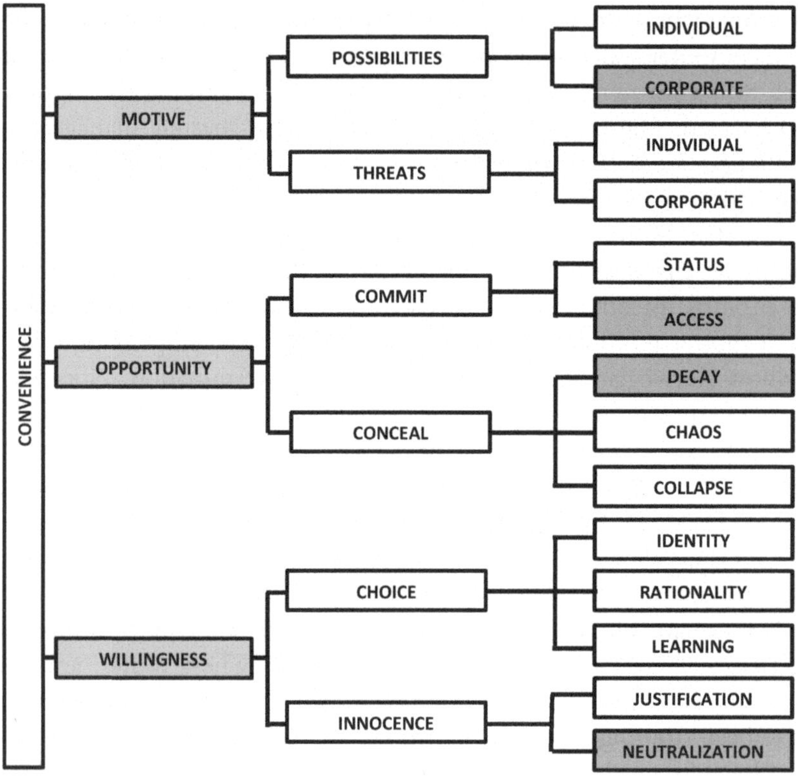

Fig. 4.4 Convenience themes in the case of SAS

case on September 20, while the court of appeal at Borgarting (2010) passed its final verdict on March 16, 2010.

Norwegian was in a very vulnerable start-up phase for the airline exposed to a gross and cynical industrial espionage on the part of SAS, according to the court of appeal. Norwegian is said to have lost several hundred million kroner as a result of SAS illegally robbing itself of internal and sensitive information about Norwegian from the booking system Amadeus. It is this espionage that SAS is convicted of (Grutle, 2010).

On September 28, 2010, the Supreme Court's appeal committee rejected the appeal from SAS regarding Borgarting court of appeal's verdict of March 6 in the same year. The sentence of the court of appeal thus became final. SAS was legally convicted of white-collar crime in the form of computer crime. The same year, SAS was convicted of white-collar crime in the form of cartel activity. SAS, together with ten other airlines, was convicted of illegal price collusion and cartel activities in air freight. The illegal price collusion and cartel activities lasted for six years. SAS was sentenced to pay a fine of 570 million kroner (Valvik & Strømsheim, 2010).

Figure 4.4 illustrates the convenience themes in the industrial espionage conducted by SAS against Norwegian. The possibility motive was corporate crime. SAS management had legitimate access to Amadeus. They neutralized their guilt feeling by Norwegian's negligence to tell Amadeus to terminate SAS's access to Norwegian's PNR data at Amadeus.

Case Study of Covid-19 Fraud

As mentioned in the discussion of outsider business crime, during the Covid-19 pandemic (Horgan et al., 2021; Niesche, 2020; Vu et al., 2020), digital government represented an attractive and convenient arena for fraud against public compensation programs, in addition to new avenues for digital fraud generally during the pandemic (Buil-Gil et al., 2020). Digital government, e-government, and e-governance have become synonymous with the use of information and communication technology (ICT) in government organizations (Rawat, 2020). Businesses that suffered from government sanctions, such as closing of restaurants to prevent virus spreading, were entitled to compensation of fixed costs from the government. E-government solutions enabled the handling of compensation requests without the involvement of humans. White-collar offenders online who knew how to formulate a request that would satisfy criteria set in the computer system could automatically receive illegitimate financial gain.

When the corona virus Covid-19 spread to Norway, the country closed down most sectors on March 12, 2020. The wealthy state provided financial compensation to businesses as well as individuals.

Some explored and exploited the compensation arrangements because they found it convenient. They had a convenient motive, a convenient opportunity, as well as a convenient willingness for deviant behavior. The convenient motive was the fear of bankruptcy despite receipt of some legitimate compensation from the state. The convenient motive was also the greed to climb the hierarchy of needs. The convenient opportunity was the lack of controls and guardianship as the state based its payments on trust to be able to provide financial support quickly to victims of the close-down already in April (Ogre, 2020). The convenient willingness was the attribution of guilt to the state that had closed down the economy and the society. The convenient willingness was also the assumption that a number of other people and businesses did abuse the financial compensation arrangements as well. These convenience themes are illustrated in Fig. 4.5 for the following white-collar offender online who was detected, prosecuted, and convicted to three years and six months in prison (NTB, 2020).

The convicted offender was Lars Hansen who was the chief executive at a company that did not meet the criteria set by the government for financial aid during the pandemic. His company experienced a dramatic decline in revenues during the pandemic. In his digital application online, he redefined his business to fit the criteria, and he created fake employment lists for salaries to individuals who did not exist (NTB, 2020).

He was sentenced to prison, to pay compensation, and confiscation for corona fraud. He received a confession sentence in Oslo district court for fraud of about NOK 6.2 million (USD 700,000) of the corona support scheme administered by the tax administration and the social security service in Norway. The case against Hansen was prosecuted by prosecutor Jens Bachke at the Norwegian national authority for investigation and prosecution of economic and environmental crime (Økokrim). The convicted man received a confession discount, and the court wrote in the judgment that before the deduction it considered that an appropriate punishment would be imprisonment for about four years and eight months (Ogre, 2020).

Prosecutor Jens Bachke commented after the verdict that the case was very serious and concerns fraud of the support scheme which is intended

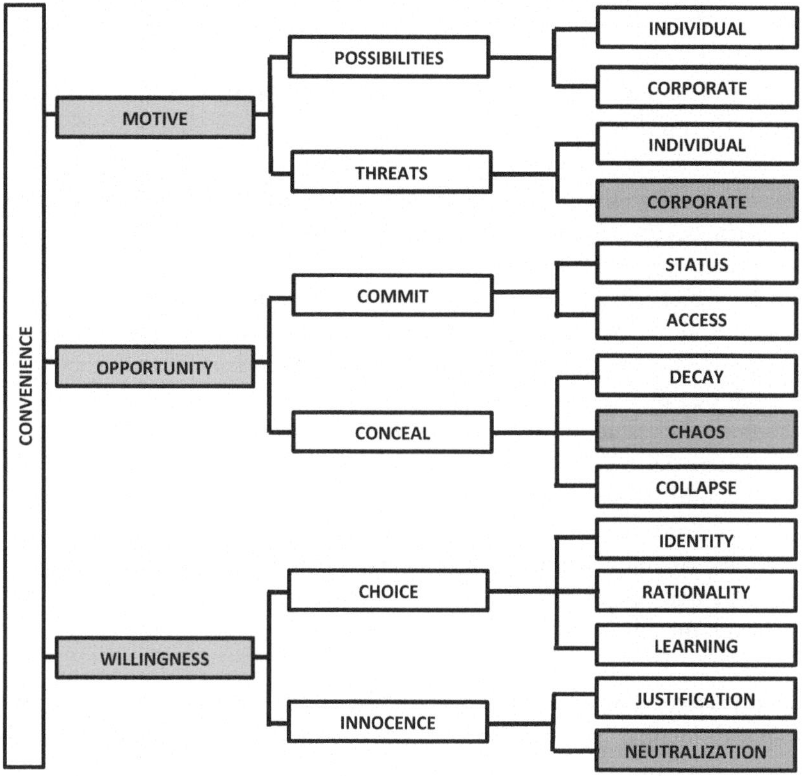

Fig. 4.5 Convenience themes in the case of Covid-19

to benefit the business community in a difficult time. He found that the severe punishment reflects the court's view of how serious it is that such a scheme is abused. The average sentence for white-collar offenders in Norway is two years and two months in prison. The judge Ailu Gaup Stadigs at Oslo district court wrote in the judgment that the defendant's choices and actions in this pandemic situation show in the court's view that the defendant has had a complete lack of respect for the penal rules that are intended to protect the distinctly trust-based support scheme.

The compensation to be paid by Hansen was NOK 5.4 million, and the confiscation amounted to NOK 2.6 million. Asset recovery occurred among others by confiscating luxury items that were bought for the fraudulent money.

Prosecutor Petter Nordeng was head of Økokrim's task force against Covid-19 fraud (Ogre, 2020):

- The money should go out as fast as possible, and we know that such circumstances attract criminals, so we mobilized early, says first prosecutor Nordeng.
- It is aggravating that one attacks national solutions after the biggest crisis since World War II. When the population is doing voluntary work, these people see the opportunity to absorb more than they are entitled to.
- Both the tax administration and the social security agency have barely gotten started. Now auditors have started to look into corporations' accounting figures, these are things you do not discover immediately, says Nordeng.
- These are more complicated cases, which can be very extensive. Several gaps that open up for fraud are currently closed, but I think we will work on this for a long time, says the first prosecutor.

As emphasized by Niesche (2020: 59) Covid-19 fraud is not limited to fraud against government support schemes as illustrated by the Norwegian case:

> Spurious websites set up with information about Covid-19; fraudsters posing as members of the World Health Organization; bogus online shops selling surgical masks; and phony doctors demanding payment for treatments. The Covid-19 pandemic has increased opportunities – and motivation – for fraud, and regulators and accountants are warning auditors they need to be on the alert.

At the time of writing this case study about a convicted white-collar offender who committed online fraud against the government rescue fund in Norway, the pandemic was still going on. When the pandemic is over, research studies will probably be able to identify characteristics of motive, opportunity, and willingness that can distinguish pandemic situations from other online situations for white-collar offenders.

Chief Executive Officer Fraud

BEC fraud is often associated with CEO fraud. Chief executive officers (CEOs) typically enjoy substantial individual freedom in their professions with little or no control. The CEO is the only person at that hierarchical level in the organization. Below the CEO, there are several executives at the same hierarchical level. Above the CEO, there are several board members at the same hierarchical level. But the CEO is alone at his or her level. The CEO is supposed to be controlled by the board, but the board only meets occasionally to discuss business cases. Executives below the CEO are typically appointed by the CEO and tend to be loyal to the CEO. Therefore, power, influence, and freedom are characteristics of CEOs.

CEO power and influence can be illustrated by what is labeled CEO fraud in law enforcement. CEO fraud is not fraud by CEOs. Rather, CEO fraud is fraud committed by someone claiming to be the CEO. If someone claims to be the CEO, most people in the organization will do what they are told. As long as they believe that the message stems from the real CEO, they are completely obedient and do as they are told by the fake CEO. The U.S. Federal Bureau of Investigation (FBI) warned in 2016 about a dramatic increase in CEO fraud, email scams in which the attacker spoofs a message from the boss and tricks someone at the organization into wiring funds to the fraudsters. The FBI estimates these scams cost organizations in the United States more than one billion dollars per year. Organizations that are victimized by CEO fraud can be characterized by a combination of CEO power and obedience culture.

CEO fraud is an external cyberattack in which high-level executives are impersonated, giving employees urgent and confidential orders to make financial transactions in a way that does not follow the company's standard procedure (Keyworth & Wall, 2016). White-collar offenders attempt online to build trust in their victims by using information that is publicly available online in addition to information from identity theft online. CEO fraud is a version of phishing attack that uses the authority of a senior executive to achieve a malicious goal. Phishing is defined as a scalable act of deception whereby impersonation is used to obtain information from a target (Jansen & Leukfeldt, 2016). Phishing is the fraudulent attempt to obtain sensitive information by disguising oneself as a trustworthy entity via electronic communication (Ghazi-Tehrani & Pontell, 2021). By impersonating a CEO, the white-collar attacker directs fake email to an employee, usually in the finance department, demanding the employee to make a deposit to the bank account of the offender. To minimize skepticism, control, and reflection, the offender creates a sense of urgency in the impersonated email message.

Some of the surprises for new CEOs arise from time and knowledge limitations—there is so much to do in complex new areas, with imperfect information and never enough time. Others stem from unexpected and unfamiliar new roles and altered professional relationships. Still others occur because of the frequent paradox that the more power you have, the harder it is to use it. While several of the challenges may appear familiar, Porter et al. (2004) discovered that nothing in a leader's background, even running a large business within his or her company fully prepare them to be CEO. Given the required struggle for CEOs to succeed under such circumstances, their subordinates must cope with initiatives and decisions that may seem random without any clear pattern. After a while with a new CEO, little will surprise those who have to executive CEO decisions. This opens for CEO fraud, where external criminals can take advantage of an institutional climate where every decision by a CEO is expected to be executed, whether the decision makes sense.

CEOs have long been recognized as the principal architects of corporate strategy and major catalysts of organizational change, and the extent to which CEOs can effect change in corporate strategy is thought to be determined largely by the power they possess, and how they decide to apply it (Hambrick & Lovelace, 2018). Thus, CEO fraud is enabled by change initiatives, where CEO behavior itself changes in ways so that there is no suspicion when deviant requests for money transfers occur.

While strategy development as well as organizational change may be at the center of CEO work, many CEOs spend much more time on other—and more minor—matters and issues. Conflicts between individuals in the organization take time to resolve and sudden media attention can steal even more time—and sometimes sleep—from important strategic thinking. Trivial matters tend to occupy much of CEO time. Given an understanding for a stressful situation among employees, CEO fraud is enabled based on the lack of formal rules guiding CEO decision-making and implementation.

Many CEOs discover that they are alone, particularly in difficult times. They have nobody on their side at the same organizational level with whom they can openly discuss how to get out of a crisis. Rather, others in the organization may speculate whether the CEO will survive in the position and act accordingly to rescue their own future in the organization. Therefore, employees who receive strange requests from an alleged CEO will be reluctant to contact the real CEO to check whether they should execute money transfer as requested.

Problem-solving is at the core of CEO work. Mind-sets are conceived as distinct cognitive operations that facilitate problem-solving. The concept dates to the end of the nineteenth century and the experimental psychologist Oswald Külpe, who showed that most of human thinking happens without images (imageless thoughts) and that most of it also occurs outside of our awareness. The resulting term, "Bewusstseinslage", literally a "state of mind", was later translated into the concept of mind-sets, "Einstellung". Subordinates tend to spend time speculating in the mind-set of the CEO and thus feel distant from communicating with the CEO.

Külpe showed that subjects would single out the features related to their tasks, while unimportant or irrelevant features were rejected from their attention. For example, faced with the task of observing the number of letters presented to them, subjects may be totally unable to recall the color and may even deny that color has been experienced at all. This is the original meaning of the term "mind-set": the brain is "set" to perceive the world according to predefined criteria. During his research, it was observed that, while given tasks were conscious initially, after a few repetitions the tasks would gradually disappear from consciousness. Upon increased practice, conscious awareness concerning the task waned, although the task could be completed even if there was no awareness of it. Subjects had no phenomenological awareness of inner speech at the time of study, i.e., there was no longer conscious reflection about the tasks. The original purpose is duly forgotten, and appearance of the stimulus automatically activated the prescribed conduct. In our perspective of speculation with lack of communication, subordinates can be fearful of the possible response by the CEO if they contact the person concerning a requested money transfer. Again, this phenomenon is an enabler of CEO fraud.

The word "set" in "mind-set" describes how the actor is perceptually prepared or "set" to detect and respond to a given situation, a cognitive recognition pattern that is automatically evoked when scanning the environment. The core aspect is that mind-sets are (a) caused by repetitive tasks; (b) automatic behaviors set in play with little or no awareness; and (c) replace personality-based dispositions with mind-set content. Mind-sets can be extremely effective in terms of seizing business opportunities but are in themselves neither lawful nor unlawful since the ethical implications may not be a part of the mind-set. Instead, they may be automated recognition of opportunity with instrumental value as profit maximizing in a competitive setting.

Bigley and Wiersema (2002) argue that CEOs' cognitive orientation should influence how they wield their power to affect corporate strategy. On the other hand, predictions about a CEO's use of power require an understanding of the CEO's cognitive orientation toward his or her firm's strategy, because power is simply the ability to bring about a preferred or intended effect. Hypothesized association between a CEO's cognitive orientation and corporate strategy presupposes that the CEO has sufficient power to bring about the preferred or intended effects.

At the core of a CEO's mind-set, we sometimes find himself or herself. Being alone at the top with rivaling executives as main contacts, the CEO must enter the role of team player without really believing that it will work. There is no top management team, and the CEO is alone. Over time, a CEO may focus more and more on managing the role rather than managing the company.

Not all CEOs work for change. Some are more committed to status quo—particularly to their organization's current strategy and leadership profile—than others. Hambrick and Lovelace (2018) found that many organizations do not adapt effectively to changes in their environments because of CEO commitment to status quo. Organizational inertia can thus be caused by the CEO, making the organization unable to change at the same rate as its environment. McClelland et al. (2010) found that CEO commitment to status quo is influenced by variables at the individual, firm, and industry levels. Increasing CEO age and tenure are associated with greater status quo commitment. CEOs in firms with financial slack view change more favorably. In contrast, CEOs at firms with liquidity problems may be more committed to the status quo out of necessity.

CEOs' mind-sets and strategic beliefs are likely to be instantiated to a significant degree in their firms' current strategies. When a top executive seeking advice confirms and/or restores his or her confidence in the correctness of strategic beliefs, the CEO will be less inclined to alter firm strategy. The mind-sets of CEOs are expected to cause them to be the principal architects of corporate strategy and major catalysts of organizational change. Belonging to their mind-sets is how to use power and secrecy, building alliances with some people and keeping others in the dark about their dispositions, as shown by Bigley and Wiersma (2002). McDonald and Westphal (2003) theorized that relatively poor firm performance can prompt CEOs to seek more advice from executives of other firms who are their friends or like them and less advice from acquaintances or dissimilar others and suggest how and why this pattern of advice seeking could reduce firms' propensity to change corporate strategy in response to poor performance.

Similarly, CEOs can tend to listen more to executives in their top management teams who confirm rather than disconfirm their beliefs. Differential association theory postulates that CEO learning occurs in association with those who find their behavior and thinking favorable and in isolation from those who find it unfavorable. Differential association is the process whereby one is exposed to normative definitions favorable or unfavorable to illegal or law-abiding behavior. Whether CEOs engage in white-collar crime is largely based on their socialization within certain peer groups (Holtfreter, 2015).

McDonald and Westphal (2003) tested their hypothesis that relatively poor firm performance can prompt CEOs to seek self-confirming advice. The results from a large sample confirm their hypothesis and show that executives' social network ties can influence firms' responses to economic adversity, particularly by inhibiting strategic change in response to relatively poor organizational performance. Additional findings indicate that CEOs' advice seeking in response to low performance may ultimately have negative consequences for subsequent performance, suggesting how CEOs' social network ties could play an indirect role in organizational decline and downward spirals in form performance.

References

Adler, P. S., & Kwon, S. W. (2002). Social capital: Prospects for a new concept. *Academy of Management Review, 27*(1), 17–40.

Akinbowale, O. E., Klingelhöfer, H. E., & Zerihun, M. F. (2020). Analysis of cyber-crime effects on the banking sector using the balanced score card: A survey of literature. *Journal of Financial Crime*, 945–958.

Albanese, J. S. (2012). Deciphering the linkages between organized crime and transnational crime. *Journal of International Affairs, 66*(1), 1–16.

Arjoon, S. (2008). Slippery when wet: The real risk in business. *Journal of Markets & Morality, 11*(1), 77–91.

Bakarich, K. M., & Baranek, D. (2020). Something phish-y is going on here: A teaching case on business email compromise. *Current Issues in Auditing, 14*(1), A1–A9.

Benartzi, S., Beshears, J., Milkman, K. L., Sunstein, C. R., Thaler, R. H., Shankar, M., Tucker-Ray, W., Congdon, W. J., & Galing, S. (2017). Should governments invest more in nudging? *Psychological Science, 28*(8), 1041–1055.

Benson, M. L. (1985). Denying the guilty mind: Accounting for involvement in a white-collar crime. *Criminology, 23*(4), 583–607.

Benson, M. L., & Simpson, S. S. (2018). *Understanding white-collar crime—An opportunity perspective* (2nd ed.). Routledge.

Bernburg, J. G., Krohn, M. D., & Rivera, C. (2006). Official labeling, criminal embeddedness, and subsequent delinquency. *Journal of Research in Crime and Delinquency, 43*(1), 67–88.

Bigley, G. A., & Wiersma, M. F. (2002). New CEOs and corporate strategic refocusing: How experience as heir apparent influences the use of power. *Administrative Science Quarterly, 47*, 707–727.

Bittle, S., & Hébert, J. (2020). Controlling corporate crimes in times of de-regulation and re-regulation. In M. L. Rorie (Ed.), *The handbook of white-collar crime* (Chapter 30, pp. 484–501). Wiley.

Borgarting. (2010, March 16). *Court case LB-2008–133972*. Borgarting lagmannsrett (Borgarting court of appleals), Oslo, Norway.

Borgarting. (2019, February 1). *Court case 17–170796AST-BORG/01*. Borgarting lagmannsrett (Borgarting court of appeals), judges Mats Wilhelm Ruland, Marit Bjørånesset Frogner and Bjørn E. Engstrøm. Prosecutor Esben Kyhring, defense attorney Christian Fredrik Bonnevie Hjort, Oslo, Norway.

Braaten, C. N., & Vaughn, M. S. (2019). Convenience theory of cryptocurrency crime: A content analysis of U.S. federal court decisions. *Deviant Behavior*, published online. https://doi.org/10.1080/01639625.2019.1706706

Bruun Hjejle. (2018). *Report on the non-resident portfolio at Danske bank's Estonian branch* (Report of investigation, p. 87). Law Firm Bruun Hjejle.

Buil-Gil, D., Lord, N., & Barrett, E. (2020). The dynamics of business, cybersecurity and cyber-victimization: Foregrounding the internal guardian in prevention. *Victims & Offenders, 16*(3), 286–315.

Bussmann, K. D., Niemeczek, A., & Vockrodt, M. (2018). Company culture and prevention of corruption in Germany China and Russia. *European Journal of Criminology, 15*(3), 255–277.

Chang, L. Y. C. (2013). Formal and informal modalities for policing cybercrime across Taiwan Strait. *Policing & Society, 23*(4), 540–555.

Chang, J. J., Lu, H. C., & Chen, M. (2005). Organized crime or individual crime? Endogeneous size of a criminal organization and the optimal law enforcement. *Economic Inquiry, 43*(3), 661–675.

Clifford Chance. (2020). *Report of investigation on Swedbank* (Report of investigation, 218 pages, law firm Clifford Chance). Washington, DC.

Craig, J. M., & Piquero, N. L. (2017). Sensational offending: An application of sensation seeking to white-collar and conventional crimes. *Crime & Delinquency, 63*(11), 1363–1382.

Cullen, F. T. (2010). Cloward, Richard A., and Lloyd E. Ohlin: Delinquency and opportunity. In F. T. Cullen & P. Wilcox (Eds.), *Encyclopedia of Criminological Theory* (Vol. 1, pp. 170–174). Sage.

Dean, G., Fahsing, I., & Gottschalk, P. (2010). *Organized crime—Policing illegal business entrepreneurialism*. Oxford University Press.

Dotinga, W. (2017, April 26). EU court finds copyright issues with streaming player. *Courthouse News Service*. www.courthousenews.com

Eberly, M. B., Holley, E. C., Johnson, M. D., & Mitchell, T. R. (2011). Beyond internal and external: A dyadic theory of relational attributions. *Academy of Management Review, 36*(4), 731–753.

Ghazi-Tehrani, A. K., & Pontell, H. N. (2021). Phishing evolves: Analyzing the enduring cybercrime. *Victims & Offenders, 16*(3), 316–342.
Goldstraw-White, J. (2012). *White-collar crime: Accounts of offending behavior*. Palgrave Macmillan.
Gottfredson, M. R., & Hirschi, T. (1990). *A general theory of crime*. Stanford University Press.
Gottschalk, P., & Markovic, V. (2016, June–December). Transnational criminal organizations (TCOs): The case of combating criminal biker gangs. *International Journal of Criminal Justice Sciences*, 30–44.
Gottschalk, P., & Smith, R. (2011). Criminal entrepreneurship, white-collar criminality, and neutralization theory. *Journal of Enterprising Communities: People and Places in the Global Economy, 5*(4), 300–308.
Grutle, H. F. (2010, March 16). SAS dømt for industrispionasje mot Norwegian [SAS convicted of industrial espionage against Norwegian]. *TV2*. www.tv2nyhetene.no
Hambrick, D. C., & Lovelace, J. B. (2018). The role of executive symbolism in advancing new strategic themes in organization: A social influence perspective. *Academy of Management Review, 43*(1), 110–131.
Hansen, L. L. (2009). Corporate financial crime: Social diagnosis and treatment. *Journal of Financial Crime, 16*(1), 28–40.
Hausman, W. J. (2018). Howard Hopson's billion dollar fraud: The rise and fall of associated gas & electric company. *Business History, 60*(3), 381–398.
Heath, J. (2008). Business ethics and moral motivation: A criminological perspective. *Journal of Business Ethics, 83*, 595–614.
Hern, A. (2017, June 15). European court of justice rules Pirate Bay is infringing copyright. *The Guardian*. www.theguardian.com
Holtfreter, K. (2015). General theory, gender-specific theory, and white-collar crime. *Journal of Financial Crime, 22*(4), 422–431.
Horgan, S., Collier, B., Jones, R., & Shepherd, L. (2021). Re-territorialising the policing of cybercrime in the post-Covid-19 era: Towards a new vision of local democratic cyber policing. *Journal of Criminal Psychology*. https://doi.org/10.1108/JCP-08-2020-034
Huisman, W., & Erp, J. (2013). Opportunities for environmental crime. *British Journal of Criminology, 53*, 1178–1200.
Høyesterett. (2019). Dom avsagt 13. mai 2019 i anke over Borgarting lagmannsretts dom 23. oktober 2018 [Verdict announced May 13, 2019 regarding appeal for Borgarting court's verdict October 23, 2018]. Høyesterett (Norwegian Supreme Court).

Jansen, J., & Leukfeldt, R. (2016). Phishing and malware attacks on online banking customers in the Netherlands: A qualitative analysis of factors leading to victimization. *International Journal of Cyber Criminology, 10*(1), 79–91.

Jordanoska, A. (2018). The social ecology of white-collar crime: Applying situational action theory to white-collar offending. *Deviant Behavior, 39*(11), 1427–1449.

Joyce, E. (2005). Expanding the international regime on money laundering in response to transnational organized crime, terrorism, and corruption. In P. Reichel (Ed.), *Handbook of Transnational Crime and Justice* (pp. 79–97). Sage.

Kaptein, M., & Helvoort, M. (2019). A model of neutralization techniques. *Deviant Behavior, 40*(10), 1260–1285.

Kennedy, J. P. (2020). Organizational and macro-level corporate crime theories. In M. L. Rorie (Ed.), *The handbook of white-collar crime* (Chapter 12, pp 175–190). Wiley.

Keyworth, M., & Wall, M. (2016, January 8). The 'bogus boss' email scam costing firms millions. *BBC*. www.bbc.com

Kroneberg, C., & Schulz, S. (2018). Revisiting the role of self-control in situational action theory. *European Journal of Criminology, 15*(1), 56–76.

Lee, F., & Robinson, R. J. (2000). An attributional analysis of social accounts: Implications of playing the blame game. *Journal of Applied Social Psychology, 30*(9), 1853–1879.

Malladi, R. K., & Dheeriya, P. L. (2021). Time series analysis of cryptocurrency returns and volatilities. *Journal of Economics and Finance, 45*, 75–94.

Maslow, A. H. (1943). A theory of human motivation. *Psychological Review, 50*(4), 370–396.

Mawritz, M. B., Greenbaum, R. L., Butts, M. M., & Graham, K. A. (2017). I just can't control myself: A self-regulation perspective on the abuse of deviant employees. *Academy of Management Journal, 60*(4), 1482–1503.

McClelland, P. L., Liang, X., & Barker, V. L. (2010). CEO commitment to the status quo: Replication and extension using content analysis. *Journal of Management, 36*(5), 1251–1277.

McDonald, M. L., & Westphal, J. D. (2003). Getting by with the advice of their friends: CEOs' advice networks using content analysis. *Administrative Science Quarterly, 48*(1), 1–32.

McElwee, G., & Smith, R. (2015). Towards a nuanced typology of illegal entrepreneurship: A theoretical and conceptual overview. In G. McElwee & R. Smith (Eds.), *Exploring criminal and illegal enterprise: New perspectives on research, policy & practice: Contemporary issues in entrepreneurship research* (Vol. 5). Emerald.

Menon, S., & Siew, T. G. (2012). Key challenges in tackling economic and cybercrimes—Creating a multilateral platform for international co-operation. *Journal of Money Laundering Control, 15*(3), 243–256.

Murphy, P. R., & Dacin, M. T. (2011). Psychological pathways to fraud: Understanding and preventing fraud in organizations. *Journal of Business Ethics, 101*, 601–618.

Naheem, M. A. (2020). The agency dilemma in anti-money laundering regulation. *Journal of Money Laundering Control*, published online. https://doi.org/10.1108/JMLC-01-2016-0007

Naumovska, I., Wernicke, G., & Zajac, E. J. (2020). Last to come and last to go? The Complex Role of Gender and Ethnicity in the Reputational Penalties for Directors Linked to Corporate Fraud. *Academy of Management Journal, 63*(3), 881–902.

Nielsen, R. P. (2003). Corruption networks and implications for ethical corruption reform. *Journal of Business Ethics, 42*(2), 125–149.

Niesche, C. (2020, October–November). Thei heightened risk of fraud in the Covid era. *Acuitymag*. www.acuitymag.com

Nodeland, B., & Morris, R. (2020). The impact of low self-control on past and future cyber offending. *International Journal of Cyber Criminology, 14*(1), 106–120.

Norfund. (2020, May 15). *Norfund er utsatt for alvorlig svindel* [Norfund is exposed to serious fraud]. *Norfund*. www.norfund.no

NTB. (2018, January 19). Nordmenn brøt loven ved å se filmer gjennom popcorn time [Norwegians violated the law by watching movies through Popcorn Time]. *Aftenposten*. www.aftenposten.no

NTB. (2020, December 17). Mann dømt til fengsel for koronasvindel [Man sentenced to prison for corona fraud]. Norwegian daily business newspaper *Sunnmørsposten*. www.smp.no

Obodaru, O. (2017). Forgone, but not forgotten: Toward a theory of forgone professional identities. *Academy of Management Journal, 60*(2), 523–553.

Ogre, M. (2020, December 17). Mann dømt for massiv koronasvindel – Økokrim tror dette bare er begynnelsen [Man convicted of massive corona fraud – Økokrim thinks this is just the beginning]. *TV2*. www.tv2.no

Paraschiv, G. (2013). Conceptualizing transnational organized crime. *Economics, Management, and Financial Markets, 8*(2), 173–178.

Pontell, H. N., Black, W. K., & Geis, G. (2014). Too big to fail, too powerful to jail? On the absence of criminal prosecutions after the 2008 financial meltdown. *Crime, Law and Social Change, 61*(1), 1–13.

Porter, M. E., Lorsch, J. W., & Nohria, N. (2004, October). Seven surprises for new CEOs. *Harvard Business Review*, 62.

Pratt, T. C., & Cullen, F. T. (2005). Assessing macro-level predictors and theories of crime: A meta-analysis. *Crime and Justice, 32*, 373–450.

PwC. (2020, June 30). *Independent assessment of the LOLC incident: Report developed for Norfund, report of investigation* (p. 34). PricewaterhouseCoopers.

Ramoglou, S., & Tsang, E. W. K. (2016). A realist perspective of entrepreneurship: Opportunities as propensities. *Academy of Management Review, 41*, 410–434.

Rawat, P. (2020). A systematic review of multiple terminologies for ICT in government: A mesh of concentric and overlapping circles. *Bulletin of Science, Technology & Society*, published online. https://doi.org/10.1177/0270467620980996

Schneider, S. (2006). Privatizing economic crime enforcement: Exploring the role of private sector investigative agencies in combating money laundering. *Policing & Society, 16*(3), 285–312.

Schoepfer, A., & Piquero, N. L. (2006). Exploring white-collar crime and the American dream: A partial test of institutional anomie theory. *Journal of Criminal Justice, 34*(3), 227–235.

Schoultz, I., & Flyghed, J. (2020a). From "we didn't do it" to "we've learned our lesson": Development of a typology of neutralizations of corporate crime. *Critical Criminology, 28*, 739–757.

Schoultz, I., & Flyghed, J. (2020b). Denials and confessions: An analysis of the temporalization of neutralizations of corporate crime. *International Journal of Law, Crime and Justice*. https://doi.org/10.1016/j.ijlcj.2020.100389

Schoultz, I., & Flyghed, J. (2021). "We have been thrown under the bus": Corporate versus individual defense mechanisms against transnational corporate bribery charges. *Journal of White Collar and Corporate Crime, 2*(1), 24–35.

Siponen, M., & Vance, A. (2010). Neutralization: New insights into the problem of employee information security policy violations. *MIS Quarterly, 34*(3), 487–502.

Slyke, S. V., & Bales, W. D. (2012). A contemporary study of the decision to incarcerate white-collar and street property offenders. *Punishment & Society, 14*(2), 217–246.

Smallridge, J. L., & Roberts, J. R. (2013). Crime specific neutralizations: An empirical examination of four types of digital piracy. *International Journal of Cyber Criminology, 7*(2), 125–140.
Smith, R. (2009). Understanding entrepreneurial behavior in organized criminals. *Journal of Enterprising Communities: People and Places in the Global Economy, 3*(3), 256–268.
Solem, L. K., & Kleppe, M. K. (2014, December 3). Seks dømt for korrupsjon i Unibuss-saken [Six convicted in the Unibuss case]. Norwegian daily business newspaper *Dagens Næringsliv*. https://www.dn.no/korrupsjon/unibuss/kriminalitet/seks-domt-for-korrupsjon-i-unibuss-saken/1-1-5245586
Solgård, J. (2020, July 9). Norfund ble svindlet for 100 millioner: -Vi har gjort mye, men ikke raskt nok for å styrke våre rutiner og systemer [Norfund was defrauded for 100 million: -We have done a lot, but not fast enough to strengthen our routines and systems]. Norwegian daily business newspaper *Dagens Næringsliv*. www.dn.no
Speed, J. (2020, May 15). *Politiet: Lite trolig at Nordfun får igjen svindelpenger* [The police: It is unlikely that Norfund will get back fraud money]. *BistandsAktuelt*. www.bistandsaktuelt.no
Stamatel, J. P. (2018). The international trafficking of human organs. *Police Practice & Research, 19*(6), 618–620.
Stave, T. K. (2020, July 9). Norfund tar selvkritikk etter gigantsvindel [Norfund takes self-criticism after giant fraud]. Norwegian daily newspaper *Aftenposten*. www.e24.no
Stone, B. (2015, March 2–March 8). Too good to be legal. *Bloomberg Businessweek*, pp. 31–33.
Sutherland, E. H. (1983). *White collar crime—The uncut version*. Yale University Press.
Sykes, G., & Matza, D. (1957). Techniques of neutralization: A theory of delinquency. *American Sociological Review, 22*(6), 664–670.
Tonoyan, V., Strohmeyer, R., Habib, M., & Perlitz, M. (2010). Corruption and entrepreneurship: How formal and informal institutions shape small firm behavior in transition and mature market economies. *Entrepreneurship: Theory & Practice, 34*(5), 803–831.
Valvik, M. E., & Strømsheim, G. (2010, November 10). SAS dømt til å betale 570 millioner i bot [SAS convicted to pay 570 million kroner in fine]. Norwegian daily newspaper *Aftenposten*. www.aftenposten.no
Vu, A. V., Hughes, J., Pete, I., Collier, B., Chua, Y. T., Shumailov, I., & Hutchings, A. (2020, October). Turning up the dial: The evolution of a cybercrime market through set-up, stable, and Covid-19 eras, IMC'20. In *Proceedings*

of the ACM Internet Measurement Conference (pp. 551–566). https://doi.org/10.1145/3419394.3423636

Welter, F., Baker, T., Audretsch, D. B., & Gartner, W.B. (2017). Everyday entrepreneurship: A call for entrepreneurship research to embrace entrepreneurial diversity. *Entrepreneurship: Theory and Practice, 41*(3), 323–347.

Wikstrom, P. O. H., Mann, R. P., & Hardie, B. (2018). Young people's differential vulnerability to criminogenic exposure: Bridging the gap between people- and place-oriented approaches in the study of crime causation. *European Journal of Criminology, 15*(1), 10–31.

Wilson-Kovacs, D. (2020). Effective resource management in digital forensics: An exploratory analysis of triage practices in four English constabularies. *Policing: An International Journal, 43*(1), 77–90.

5
Internal Offenders

Internal white-collar offenders are individuals who have legitimate access to premises and systems that they use to commit and conceal financial crime harming their own organization online. This chapter presents three case studies of internal white-collar offenders online. The first case study is concerned with a trusted employee in the social security agency in Denmark who committed embezzlement online. The second case study is concerned with employees at the Estonian branch of a Danish bank helping organized criminals in Russia conduct money laundering of proceeds from crime online. The third case study is concerned with a trusted employee who committed bank fraud online. Two out of three case studies presented in this chapter are concerned with female white-collar offenders online, which invite the introduction of the issue of gendered crime at the end of this chapter.

P. Gottschalk and C. Hamerton, *White-Collar Crime Online*,
https://doi.org/10.1007/978-3-030-82132-6_5

Case Study of Embezzlement

From 2000 to 2007, she abused the PAS system, while she later abused the TAS system for benefits payments. TAS (tilskuddsadministrationssystem/benefits administration system) did not separate between users of the system who registered information about potential receivers of benefits and users of the system who initiated actual benefit payments. She was a trusted offender in the Danish social security agency (BBC, 2020; Kammeradvokaten, 2019; Newth, 2018; NTB, 2019; Ottermann, 2020; PwC, 2019).

The National Board of Social Services in Denmark hired corporate examiners from global auditing firm PwC (2019) to investigate the matter. The social services board (Socialstyrelsen) is a government agency under the Ministry of Social Affairs and Interior. Socialstyrelsen aims at actively contributing to social initiatives for the benefit of citizens. Socialstyrelsen is responsible for a variety of tasks and projects in the social area, including children, young people and families, disabilities, aids and psycho-social initiatives, and adults with social problems. Socialstyrelsen does not only support vulnerable groups such as unemployed and homeless people, but it also provides social benefits to a large fraction of the Danish population.

The initial account from Socialstyrelsen was denial of any misconduct internally in the organization. Denial is a false response about occurrence of misconduct, wrongdoing, and crime (Gago-Rodriguez et al., 2020). Denial of knowledge, denial of deviance, denial of responsibility as well as scapegoating represent typical initial responses to accusations and allegations (Gottschalk & Benson, 2020; Schoultz & Flyghed, 2020a, 2020b, 2021). A scapegoat is a person burdened with the wrongdoing of others (Eren, 2021).

Allegations of fraud at Socialstyrelsen were not consistent with the self-image of the Danish state that Transparency International and other global organizations have regarded as having the lowest rate of corruption in the world. However, allegations that trusted employee Britta Nielsen had embezzled funds amounting to more than one hundred million Danish kroner (sixteen million USD) over the course of twenty-five years became evident in August 2018 and then taken seriously. The agency terminated her employment, and she fled to South Africa. In November 2018, South African police arrested her and extradited her to Denmark. In February 2020, a Danish court sentenced her to prison (Ottermann, 2020).

"Britta Nielsen is a committed employee, who takes on significant tasks in grant administration and is always willing when extra work is required". This is what Danish Britta Nielsen's (64) employer wrote in a recommendation for the Queen's Merit Medal in 2016. Nielsen received the medal in silver. The occasion was 40 years of service as an employee at Socialstyrelsen. It is from that point in time that Nielsen faces suspicion and then allegation of having embezzled 117 million Danish kroner. In 2018, the police arrested her in South Africa, having been on the run for more than a month (Newth, 2018).

The following year, Britta Nielsen was the defendant in court facing the charge of embezzlement (NTB, 2019):

> The 65-year-old woman faced the accusation of stealing DKK 117 million from Socialstyrelsen. When she appeared in court on Thursday, she admitted the charges, but not the amount for which the prosecution charged her.

BBC (2020) reported the following year:

> A Danish court is due to deliver its verdict in the case of a woman accused of stealing 117 million Danish kroner (£13m; $17m) of government funding. Britta Nielsen worked at Denmark's social services board for 40 years, distributing funding to people in need.

In their report, PwC (2019: 3) label Britta Nielsen as BN and mentions that acronym 141 times in the 80-page report, for example:

> In the period from 1993 to 2018, a total of 66 bank accounts have been identified, which belong to BN, spread to nine Danish financial institutions or credit card institutions.

By exploitation of fundamental insights into the social security processes and because of her central employment in benefits administration, Britta

Nielsen was able to conceal her fraud for a very long period. From 2000 to 2007, she abused the PAS system, while she later abused the TAS system for benefits payments. TAS (tilskuddsadministrationssystem / benefits administration system) did not separate between users of the system who registered information about potential receivers of benefits and users of the system who initiated actual benefit payments. Nobody controlled Nielsen when she created fake receivers with her bank accounts attached, and when she initiated payments to the same fake benefit receivers (Benson & Simpson, 2018; Cohen & Felson, 1979). There was obviously a lack of control in principal–agent relationships (Bosse & Phillips, 2016). She was supposed to distribute funding to people in need. Instead, she took some of the money herself. Maybe she had traces of sensation seeking to experience adventure (Craig & Piquero, 2017).

Britta Nielsen embezzled funds intended for vulnerable and disabled people by creating fake receivers of social benefits. She received a sentence of six and a half years in prison for embezzling 117 million Danish kroner of government funding intended for social security needs (Ottermann, 2020).

Nielsen did not only create fictitious receivers of benefits in the computer system. She also created fictitious projects—one of them she called "help for self-help"—that were eligible of funding. However, most of the money ended up in her personal bank accounts. Her defense lawyer argued in court that barriers against fraud were nonexistent, and that all colleagues knew how easy it was to embezzle money (Ottermann, 2020):

> Nielsen reportedly told the court: "It was a standing joke that you could easily add your own account number and then be off to the Bahamas".

Nielsen's motive was greed (Goldstraw-White, 2012; Schoepfer & Piquero, 2006), as she over the years had acquired luxury properties in Denmark and South Africa. She gave some of the embezzled money to her three adult children who all pleaded guilty of gross robbery for each of them receiving funds. One of the daughters had allegedly spent the money on a competition horse. The Danish treasury had thus hard time retrieving money from Nielsen's swindle (Ottermann, 2020).

"She has betrayed the trust she was given when she became employed by the National Board of Social Services", prosecutor Lisbeth Jorgensen told the court during the trial (Ottermann, 2020), maybe because of a professional deviant identity (Obodaru, 2017) and a rational choice (Pratt & Cullen, 2005). During the trial, Nielsen explained that she had moved involuntarily into a vicious circle where she wanted to improve the lifestyle for her children, thereby indicating social concern for others (Agnew, 2014). Her lawyer, Nima Nabipour, pleaded mitigating circumstances, including Nielsen's age and health. On several occasions, the trial was interrupted when Nielsen felt bad and needed transportation by ambulance for medical checks in hospital.

Figure 5.1 illustrates convenience themes suggested above. Her perceived innocence—lack of a guilty mind—might be explained by a disappointing work context that caused entitlement (Nichol, 2019), sliding on a slippery slope to the wrong side of the law (Arjoon, 2008; Welsh et al., 2014), as well as lack of self-control (Gottfredson & Hirschi, 1990) .

Fraud examiners from PwC (2019: 6) concluded that the main convenience theme in the organizational opportunity dimension was lack of division of functions:

> We can ascertain that the main reason why it has been possible for BN to carry out the presumptive fraud against the grant administration has been the lack of functional separation between persons with access to change recipients' master data, including account numbers, and persons who can make payments to the beneficiaries.

The investigative approach chosen by fraud examiners from PwC (2019) was mainly to review accounts and accounting. They followed financial transactions from TAS payments to Navision Stat, a system for business accounting. They reviewed accounting statements from 1993 to 2018 and identified 37 bank accounts belonging to Nielsen. However, the individual banks were not able to retrieve all relevant transactions that Nielsen conducted.

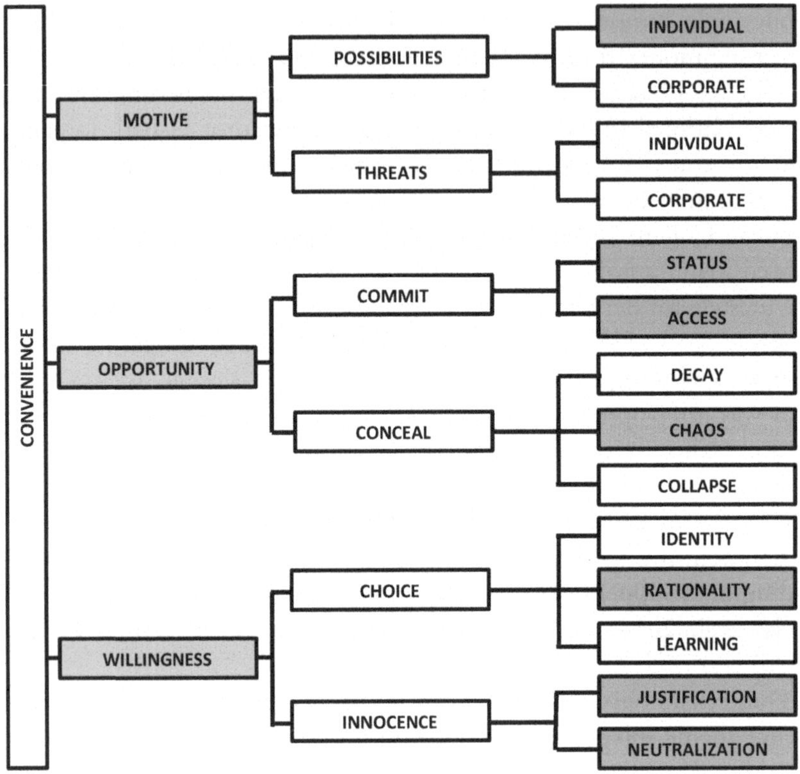

Fig. 5.1 Convenience themes in the case of Socialstyrelsen

The fraud examiners found that the grant administration since 2016 automatically issued notifications to grant recipients' email addresses when allocation of grants occurred. As email addresses are part of the basic data, administrative case handlers had the opportunity to change email addresses without any barriers. By changing email addresses, the entitled receivers of funds had no way of knowing that the grant administration had approved their applications.

The Auditor General in Denmark had conducted performance audits at Socialstyrelsen, but fraud examiners from PwC failed in obtaining their results. Therefore, they ignored other sources of information related to the Auditor General's work. Instead, fraud examiners simply state that if they had looked into the matter in documents from the Auditor General, then investigation conclusions might have been different. However, fraud examiners emphasized that the Auditor General had made recommendations in the past that might have prevented the extent of convenience experienced by Nielsen.

To the extent that fraud examiners were able to retrieve the contents in Nielsen's email accounts they claim to have made some interesting findings. They applied simple search words and search combinations based on their knowledge of the case so far. Unfortunately, these pages in the report are blank in the publicly available version.

The PwC (2019) report describes 13 control weaknesses in the Danish social security agency. The main flaw was the ability for an employee to both create projects and pay grants (Nielsen, 2019). Management was not required to approve transfers or to control who had access to financial systems. The investigation confirmed that a number of control functions had failed that might explain the convenience of Nielsen's embezzlement.

PwC (2019) conducted no interviews, at least do they not write about interviews in their report of investigation. This is surprising, as informants and witnesses typically have observed behaviors that can lead to new disclosures and more evidence related to disclosures that have already occurred. While the embezzled amount confirmed is already significant, there is in similar cases often more money out there that professional examiners might detect. Typically, offenders admit to amounts that are already subject to hard evidence, while being reluctant to tell about further instances of fraud that investigators have not detected. In such situations, other people can lead investigators into new avenues for their inquiries. Very often, colleagues and others are willing to tell what they have observed, as long as interviewers treat interviewees fairly and honestly (Goodman-Delahunty & Martschuk, 2020).

Fraud examiners were unable to find more embezzled money than was already known (PwC, 2019: 31):

> Thus, there is still a risk that there will be disbursements to accounts where we do not know the real owners for all or part of the period 2002 to 2018. To address this, we have attempted to obtain account information from banks, curators, and tax authorities to identify as many of BN's accounts as possible.

The mandate for PwC's (2019) investigation was to reconstruct sequences of events for abuse of social benefit payments and to explain how such financial abuse could take place. Furthermore, the mandate asked investigators to determine the magnitude of the fraud for the period from 1977 to 2018. Finally, the mandate asked investigators to evaluate the control systems and control culture at Socialstyrelsen.

The Danish government hired the law firm Paul Schmith (Kammeradvokaten, 2019) in parallel with PwC (2019) hired by Socialstyrelsen to determine whether executives had failed in the management of controls, which made it convenient for Britta Nielsen to commit fraud over such a long period (BBC, 2020; Newth, 2018; Nielsen, 2019; NTB, 2019; Ottermann, 2020). The mandate asked investigators to examine whether any official responsibility could transfer into blame at individuals. Relevant individuals worked as executives in the social security service in Denmark, in the ministry, or elsewhere.

This is an interesting mandate, as attribution of guilt is a frequent issue in private policing of economic crime. Attribution theory (Keaveney, 2008) and the blame game hypothesis (Lee & Robinson, 2000) suggest that establishing causality for a negative event is concerned with efforts by suspects to assign misleading attribution to others (Eberly et al., 2011). Self-blame is rare and often nonexistent. Nobody will blame oneself for a negative event. Self-blame is attributing a negative event to one's behavior or disposition. Some are too powerful to blame. Pontell et al. (2014) found that the financial crisis obviously had its cause in mismanagement in the financial sector, but all in the financial sector avoided serious blame. Status-related factors such as influential positions often preclude perceptions of blameworthiness (Slyke & Bales, 2012).

Compared to the PwC (2019) examination, Kammeradvokaten (2019) included a responsibility analysis and personal contact reflection with the social security agency. However, Kammeradvokaten builds to a substantial extent on the work by PwC, which in turn builds on information from the whistleblower Søren Madsen. Law firm Kammeradvokaten (2019) reached the conclusion that no former or current executives at Socialstyrelsen deserved blame for such failures. This was in contrast to Nielsen's defense attorney, who argued in court that the safeguards around welfare were too lax, and that both management and her colleagues knew how convenient it was to commit embezzlement at work (Ottermann, 2020).

The investigators found that there were no indications or suspicion of fraud or similar irregularities in the ministry and other authorities responsible for social security services. Based on this finding, they conclude that boards and others had no reason to react to something they did not know was taking place (Kammeradvokaten, 2019: 123):

> Based on the available material, we first assess that the management's handling of the government audit's comments on accounts and reports was immediately deficient, given that the situation was not completely rectified over a period of at least three years. However, this criticism for not following up the national audit office's comments regarding accounts and reports cannot be directly linked to the alleged audit weakness number 6 identified by PwC regarding accounts and reports. The alleged control weakness number 6 concerns Britta Nielsen's ability to override the reminder function for these, and thus not, as pointed out by the auditor general, that the accounting review has been slow. Regardless of the fact that it must be considered obvious that the large casefile of accounts and reports has been instrumental in creating a control environment where it has been easier for Britta Nielsen to hide her fraud, the criticism here must be compared with the fact that there is not necessarily correlation between Britta Nielsen's fraud and the lack of review of accounts and reports.

In this quote, lawyers from Kammeradvokaten (2019) express disagreement with auditors from PwC (2019) and thereby create some confusion. One reason for the gap in their understanding of weaknesses might be the different levels of probability for evidence. If auditors apply the rule of more likely than not, while lawyers apply the rule of beyond any doubt, then they may certainly conclude differently about various pieces of evidence.

However, Kammeradvokaten (2019) continue in their report to downplay the lack of management attention as identified by PwC (2019):

> In addition, it could immediately appear questionable that the management did not seem to adequately respond to the government audit's

> comments regarding control of disbursements and user access. However, we cannot rule out, on the present basis, that there was a follow-up to this in the period.

While attorneys at Kammeradvokaten (2019) according to the mandate should identify potentially responsible individuals and institutions for lack of controls, they do instead contribute to diffusion of responsibility in their report. The examiners conclude that no responsibility or blame belongs in the grant administration or the national board of health and welfare either personally or functionally, and therefore suggest no actions, except what PwC already had emphasized. The only thing examiners suggest is that the national board of health and welfare may, if they desire, improve their own control mechanisms to compensate for weaknesses.

Case Study of Money Laundering

The branch office of the Danish bank had its own separate computer system in Estonia, which was programmed and administered in a language that bank auditors did not understand. Local employees in Estonia could cooperate with organized criminals in Russia to launder money for the criminals by transferring funds via the local Danish bank system in Estonia to other Danish bank systems and potentially over to other banks where the money then got rid of its links to crime. White-collar offenders in the Estonian branch office benefitted from helping organized criminals online.

In September 2018, the money laundering scandal at Danske Bank's Estonian branch became public when the bank presented a report of investigation by fraud examiners. The 87-pages report provides an empirical description of misconduct and potential crime that is suited for research by application of the theory of convenience. Convenience theory suggests that executive deviance occurs when there is a strong financial motive, ample organizational opportunity to commit and conceal offenses, and a personal willingness for deviant behavior. This section presents empirical evidence for the theory in the Estonian case. In particular, financial motive derived from non-residents providing most of bank profits, and organizational opportunity existed because of a different IT platform in Estonia that prevented insights and controls from compliance and auditing functions in the bank.

At the end of their inquiry, fraud examiners write a report of investigation and hand it over to the client organization as their property (Gottschalk & Benson, 2020; Gottschalk & Tcherni-Buzzeo, 2017). This was also the case when there was a suspicion of lacking anti-money laundering control at Danske Bank's Estonian branch (Binham & Milne, 2018). The 87-pages report by Bruun Hjejle (2018) provides an empirical description of misconduct and potential crime that is suited for research by application of the theory of convenience. This section addresses the following research question: What evidence of convenience emerges from the investigation report in terms of motive, opportunity, and willingness for lacking anti-money laundering in the bank?

The research method applied in this empirical study of an investigation report is content analysis. Content analysis is any methodology or procedure that works to identify characteristics within texts attempting to make valid inferences (Krippendorff, 1980; Patrucco et al., 2017). Content analysis assumes that language reflects both how people understand their surroundings and their cognitive processes. Therefore, content analysis makes it possible to identify and determine relevant text in a context (McClelland et al., 2010). Content analysis is to make inferences by objectively and systematically identifying characteristics of messages (Tejeiro et al., 2020).

The report of investigation written by a Danish law firm found that it is clear that anti-money-laundering procedures "at the Estonian branch had been manifestly insufficient and inadequate, including, inter alia, lack of identification of 'controlling interests' of customers, lack of screening of customers, and lack of independence and possible collusion in the Estonian branch" (Bruun & Hjejle, 2018: 78).

Researching the use of financial institutions in money laundering is important. Nguyen (2018) discuss the implication of money laundering preventive measures for financial privacy, with the focus on banking secrecy. Jaara and Kadomi (2017) discuss factors related to the Central Bank instructions on money laundering, while Mugarura (2015) presents the jeopardy of the bank in enforcement of normative anti-money laundering and countering financing of terrorism regimes. This research contributes to the stream of research into the use of financial institutions in money laundering as well as to the stream of research into lacking governance in the banking sector, where important issues include secrecy and problem of international cooperation (Emmenegger, 2015), ensuring regulatory compliance in banking and finance (Engdahl, 2013), and shadow banking (Rixen, 2013).

Money laundering has often been characterized as a three-stage process that requires (1) moving the funds from direct association with the crime, (2) disguising the trail to foil pursuit, and (3) making them available to the criminal organization once again with their occupational and geographic origins hidden from view. The first stage is often the riskiest one for the criminals because money from crime is introduced into the financial system. In the Norfund case, the money was already in the financial system. Stage 1 is often called the placement stage. Stage 2 is often called the layering stage, in which money is moved in order to disguise or remove direct links to the offense committed. The money may be channeled through several transactions, which could involve a number of accounts, financial institutions, companies, and funds as well as the use of professionals such as lawyers, brokers, and consultants as intermediaries. Stage 3 is often called the integration stage, in which a legitimate basis for asset origin has been created. The money is made available to the criminal organization and can be used freely for regular expenditures and investments in legal businesses (Menon & Siew, 2012; Naheem, 2020).

In the period from 2007 to 2015, customers in the non-resident portfolio generated an increasing part of profits in Danske Bank's Estonian branch. While the share in percent of profits was 49% in 2007, the share of profits reached its peak in 2013 with 99% of the profits in the branch from non-residents. Thus, while non-residents provided all profits in 2013, they only represented one-fourth of the ten thousand customers in the Estonian branch. Therefore, it is obvious that non-residents were attractive bank customers so that bank executives in the Estonian branch could report profits to the headquarters in Denmark. Executive deviance by ignoring money-laundering controls must have been convenient to secure profits in the local bank. In addition, several bank executives had personal financial benefits from the ignorance. Therefore, both individual and corporate benefits were motives as illustrated in Fig. 4.2.

Supporting the "Russian Laundromat" was thus profitable for executives at the Estonian branch. Bruun Hjelle (2018: 21) identified 177 bank customers who received payments through Modindconbank and Trasta Komercbanca from 21 "core companies" listed in the media as money laundering organizations. Therefore, the 177 customers were likely involved in the Russian Laundromat. The majority of the 177 customers were limited partnerships or limited liability partnerships incorporated in the U.K. or in countries generally considered tax havens, such as British Virgin Islands.

The Estonian branch had its own IT platform preventing people at the headquarters from controlling and auditing their affairs. In 2008, Finnish Sampo Bank in Estonia turned into a branch of Danske Bank with the specially designed computer information systems. After the take-over, Danske Bank planned to convert the computer system at the Baltic subsidiary onto Danske Bank's IT platform, but someone quickly abandoned that plan. It is common to experience disagreement on IT platforms after mergers, where merging parties would like to keep computer systems that they know how to use. In this case, however, there was no merger, but a take-over, and normally the acquired organization has to implement systems from the acquiring organization, even when the acquired organization may claim they have a better computer system. Given the persistence of different systems, outside actors had no access to information of the business, and they could thus neither assess nor influence operation risks at the Estonian branch. The separate IT platform was an important part of the organizational opportunity structure for executive deviance in the Estonian branch as illustrated by decay in Fig. 5.2.

Officially, the abandonment of the migration plan occurred because it could be too expensive and take up too much capacity. The lack of migration would cause problems for the compliance function that they were unable to tackle. Disabled compliance function in the bank was thus another important part of the organizational opportunity structure for executive deviance in the Estonian branch. The same disability

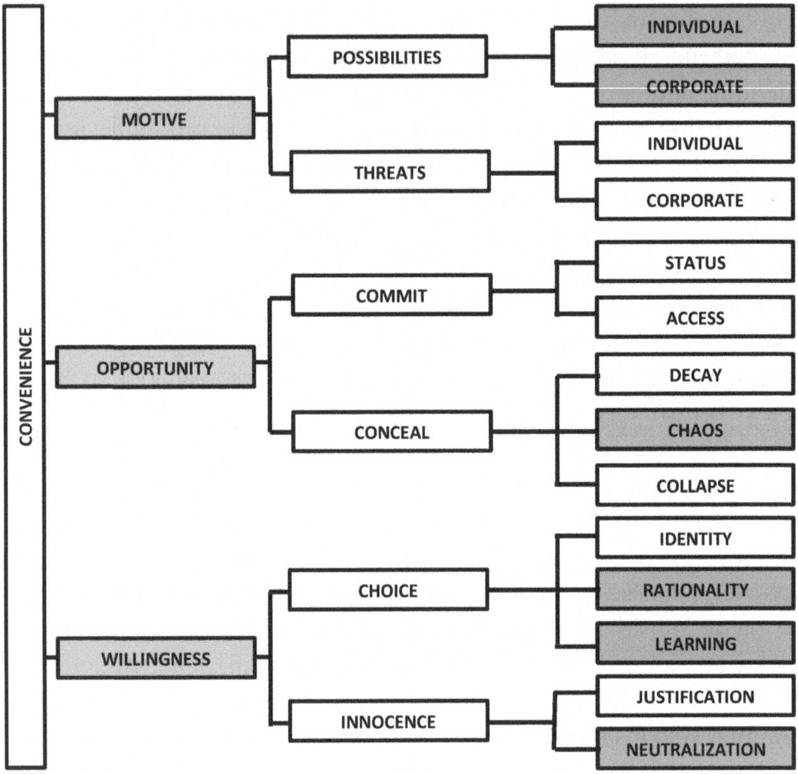

Fig. 5.2 Convenience themes in the case of Danske Bank

applied to internal auditors, external auditors, as well as other control functions in the bank. The inability for insight was even worse by the fact that "many documents at the Estonian branch, including information about customers, were written in Estonian or Russian" (Bruun Hjelje, 2018: 2).

When control functions knocked on the door to the branch, deviant executives reported that the non-resident customers department had improved considerably in applying know-your-customer principles. Since further control was difficult or impossible, Group Internal Audit at Danske Bank gave the branch a "satisfactory" rating for anti-money-laundering procedures, which was the second-best rating out of five

(Bruun Hjejle, 2018: 43). Again, as part of the opportunity structure, deviant executives had received seemingly confirmation that the group internal audit found no misconduct or crime. Local executives could continue conveniently their bank business with non-residents.

A similar outcome occurred when the Estonian financial supervisory authority performed an inspection regarding money-laundering control in the bank. This resulted in a final inspection report written in Estonian language. Local executives provided only an English summary to Danske Bank. According to the summary, the Estonian authority noted that the attitude of branch employees concerning the objectives of and compliance with statutory requirements had "improved considerably". The local authority also wrote that the branch office had "changed or updated its internal procedures in line with the legal amendments" (Bruun Hjejle, 2018: 42).

> "The lack of involvement from the Group meant that the Estonian branch was left on its own, and that the Group did not have sufficient oversight of the activities at the branch", says Bruun Hjejle (2018: 78), where Group means Danske Bank.

Bruun Hjejle (2018: 77) found that "a number of former and current employees in leading positions have not complied with their legal obligations under their employment terms and contracts with Danske Bank". Even worse, their report mentions collusion several times, for example: "cooperation between customers and employees with the Estonian branch (internal collusion)", and "it is also relevant to consider internal collusion due to the roles".

Examiners at Bruun Hjejle (2018: 8) summarize their views on collusion:

> Former and current employees and former agents (persons receiving commission for facilitating customers) of the Estonian branch have been examined for suspicious activity, ultimately with a view to determining whether they may have been colluding with customers in the Non-Resident Portfolio. 42 employees and agents have been deemed to have been involved in some suspicious activity. This is being reported to the Estonian FIU, again in an agreed format and in accordance with Estonian

> law. Further, eight former employees have been reported to the Estonian police by Danske Bank. Despite the SARs and police reports filed, it cannot be concluded with reasonable certainty to what extent criminal activity in the form of collusion has actually taken place.

The private investigators leave it to the police in Estonia to determine whether and to what extent criminal activity in the form of collusion had actually taken place. This is in accordance with guidelines for fraud examiners where it is the role of the criminal justice system eventually to prosecute and convict suspected individuals.

Explanations for behavioral willingness for executive deviance in the Estonian branch are difficult to derive explicitly from the Bruun Hjejle (2018) report. Therefore, we make assumptions based on behavioral perspectives in convenience theory. First, there seems to be support for the differential association perspective suggesting that offenders associate with those who agree with them, and distance themselves from those who disagree, which is illustrated by learning in Fig. 4.2.

A potential explanation of willingness is also the tradition of Russian influence in Estonia. Furthermore, there seems to be support for the rational choice perspective, where the benefits of misconduct related to non-residents exceed potential costs. Individual preferences determine whether crime is committed. Also, the obedience perspective can suggest that obedience by individuals in organizations is more strongly required in Eastern than in Western Europe.

Finally, and most importantly, neutralization techniques are attractive to offenders to minimize feelings of guilt. Deviant executives might claim appeal to higher loyalties and normality of action. They can claim entitlement, and they can argue the case of legal mistake. They find their own deviant behavior acceptable. They may argue that a dilemma arose, whereby they made a reasonable tradeoff before committing the act.

The separate computer system in Estonia made it convenient for local employees as bank agents to help non-residents with their money transfers without interference from bank principals. Lack of oversight and guardianship caused chaos. The agency perspective suggests that a principal is often unable to control an agent who does work for the principal. The agency perspective assumes narrow self-interest among both principals and agents. The interests of principal and agent tend to diverge, they may have different risk willingness or risk aversion, there is knowledge asymmetry between the two parties, and the principal has imperfect information about the agent's contribution (Bosse & Phillips, 2016; Chrisman et al., 2007; Pillay & Kluvers, 2014; Williams, 2008). According to principal–agent analysis, exchanges can encourage illegal gain for both principal and agent.

Picard (2009) found that IT systems in banks facilitate the commitment of fraud and, at the same time, complicates the investigation. Therefore, there is an attractive opportunity for fraud associated with low risk. What looks like an opportunity from the criminal standpoint represents an inherent risk from within organizations. One opportunity issue concerns the internal operations of a bank. Fraud aims at internal operations and exploits the many weaknesses or avoids the limited controls in place.

By applying neutralization techniques, white-collar offenders think they are doing nothing wrong. They deny responsibility, injury, and victim. They condemn the condemners. They claim appeal to higher loyalties and normality of action. They claim entitlement, and they argue the case of legal mistake. They find their own mistakes acceptable. They argue a dilemma arose, whereby they made a reasonable tradeoff before committing the act (Siponen & Vance, 2010). They claim rule complexity in handling anti-money laundering controls (Lehman et al., 2020). Such claims enable offenders to find crime convenient.

Benson and Simpson (2018: 145) found that white-collar criminals seldom think of injury or victims:

> Many white-collar offenses fail to match this common-sense stereotype because the offenders do not set out intentionally to harm any specific individual. Rather, the consequences of their illegal acts fall upon impersonal organizations or a diffuse and unseen mass of people.

The idea of neutralization techniques (Sykes & Matza, 1957) resulted from work on Sutherland's (1939, 1949) differential association theory. According to this theory, people are always aware of their moral obligation to abide by the law, and they are aware that they have the same moral obligation within themselves to avoid illegitimate acts. The theory postulates that criminal behavior learning occurs in association with those who find such criminal behavior favorable and in isolation from those who find it unfavorable (Benson & Simpson, 2018). Crime is relatively convenient when there is no guilt feeling for doing something learned from others.

Case Study of Internal Bank Fraud

Most studies regarding cybercrime and banks are concerned with external bank fraud. For example, Becker et al. (2017) studied fraudulent bank payments by abuse of payment cards by external offenders. This case study, however, has the neglected perspective of an internal trusted offender.

She was a trusted offender who was assigned a special task in the bank where she had access to and control over the computer system. Bente Selvaag was a bank executive in the Oslo branch of BNP Paribas. She embezzled 13 million Norwegian kroner (about 1.3 million US dollars) over a period of nine years by means of 260 transactions to her own and family member accounts. She received a prison sentence of three years (Kleppe, 2011: 6):

> After starting in an employment position as a "troubleshooting girl" during the financial crisis in the 1980ies, Selvaag gained, according to the fresh confession verdict, access to initiate transactions at the beginning of this century. Thereafter, the 59-year-old carried out 260 transactions for 'at least kr 13,670,000' of the bank's funds that she abused for her own and others' purposes. Bente Selvaag was an executive in the department for debt collection and follow-up on defaulting loans when she through transfers to an interim account diverted millions to herself and family member accounts.

It was her position as bank executive in the department for debt collection that Selvaag gained legitimate access to the bank's systems and accounts. She started on February 13, 2001 to move money out of the bank via transactions to a temporary account before moving the money on to her own and family member accounts. She teamed up with an acquaintance, and together they designed system functionality and data features, which made it difficult for the bank to detect deviant transactions.

It was not until February 25, 2010—nine years later—that regular control routines in the bank provided a signal. Selvaag had then been able to embezzle thirteen million during those nine years. After signal registration and detection in the audit function, the bank reported Bente Selvaag to the police where she faced the charge of fraud, while at the same time being immediately dismissed from her position at BNP Paribas. Almost two years later, on December 16, 2011, the district court in Oslo sentenced her to three years in prison. The judge emphasized that fraud harming the bank and its clients represents a serious breach of trust.

The bank immediately terminated the employment of Selvaag at the stage of crime detection, and she has later paid back the embezzled amount completely, which might have led to a somewhat milder conviction than the prosecution had suggested.

What in particular characterizes Bente Selvaag as an offender in the upper echelon in society was her position and access at BNP, which made it possible and convenient to commit substantial financial crime over a long period of many years. She enjoyed high social status. She lived in the best neighborhood in Oslo, close to the ski jumping arena Holmenkollen where many wealthy Norwegians have their homes. She lived in a house worth at that time more than one million US dollars, which today would be more than three million dollars. Crime occurred in her professional position at the bank, and she enjoyed complete confidence and trust from the top management at the bank. Therefore, she had convenient organizational opportunity to do what she did. The opportunity derived both from her high-level position and from her actual area of responsibility within bank operations. It was required for her to have access to systems and accounts to do her job as illustrated in Fig. 5.3.

Bente Selvaag also had a network that enabled her to establish contact with her conspirator. Her network, in addition to family members, did not react when they received money in their accounts from her. She belonged to the elite in society, and she spent the embezzled money to

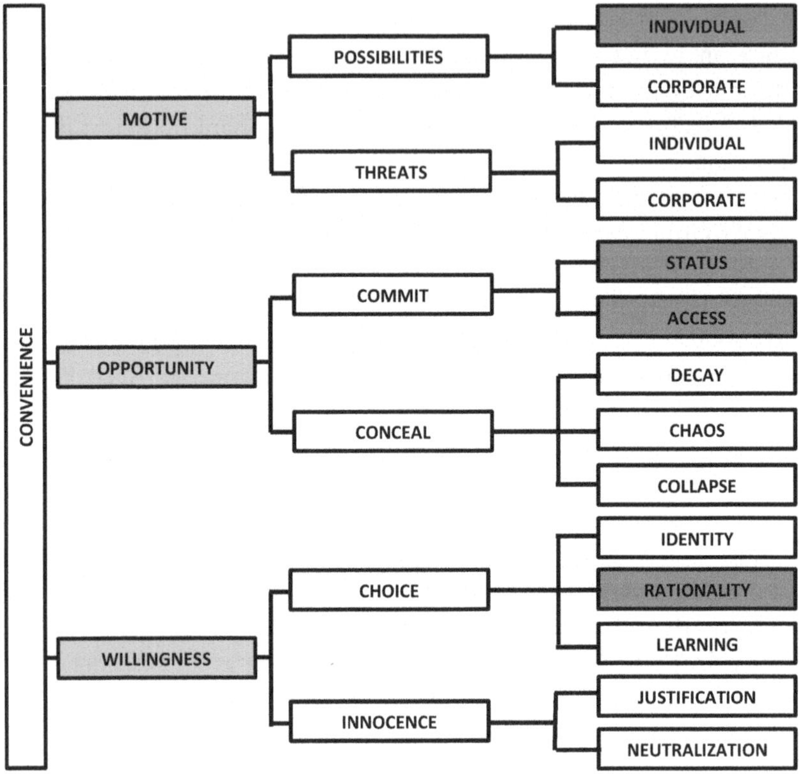

Fig. 5.3 Convenience themes in the case of BNP Paribas

finance the real estate at Holmenkollen. Her crime case popped up in the media, on TV, on the radio, on the internet and in the newspapers, which is one of the criteria in this book to define a person empirically as a woman in white-collar crime. Bente Selvaag and her husband Ivar Hagen purchased the house in Dagali road 19 at Holmenkollen in 2001 for six million Norwegian kroner and sold it in December 2010 for ten million kroner, some months after she realized she would face prosecution in court.

One interesting aspect of this crime case is the amount of money involved, which is above average for female white-collar offenders. Women are usually a little more careful and take a little here and a little there, rather than thirteen million in the same organization. In a Norwegian sample studied by Benson and Gottschalk (2015), the average economic gain from crime was far lower for female offenders than for male offenders.

Another interesting aspect is the duration of the wrongdoing by Selvaag, which must imply that there was no short-term motive to solve an acute financial problem, which typically characterizes much of what women do when they commit financial crime at work. A third interesting aspect is that Selvaag had a helper that seems uncommon among women where they are not followers of male leaders in crime. Convicted females typically worked alone when they committed embezzlement and fraud. In those cases where a man and a woman work together in crime, then the man is kind of a criminal leader and the main actor, while the woman is a follower and does what she is told (Gottschalk & Smith, 2011; Smith et al., 2020). This is evident in the Italian mafia, such as Cosa Nostra, where the role of women is to take care of communication between male offenders.

A fourth interesting aspect of this case is that detection occurred by regular control routines in the bank, despite the fact that deviance had taken place for nine years. Very few incidents of white-collar crime detection occur internally in organizations, especially not by regular control routines. Whistleblowers typically turn externally to the media when they do not trust the internal whistleblowing routine, or those persons assigned to follow up reports from whistleblowers.

A fifth interesting aspect is the quick refund of embezzled money. Selvaag sold her house for ten million and somehow added several million to pay back thirteen million in addition to interest rates. This is according to the court document (Kleppe, 2011).

Bente Selvaag had an external helper. He (61) died. People called him the shotgun man because he frequently went crazy. For example, a woman (59) and her daughter (41) should at one point only put their garden furniture out and fix the garden. Then the woman's ex-husband showed up with a shotgun. It happened outside the family house on Nesøya, a peninsula close to Oslo. The ex-husband killed them both, and then he took his own life (Hansen et al., 2009).

Figure 4.3 illustrates application of convenience theory to fraud by the bank executive. The motive was individual out of possibilities. The opportunity was based on status and access to resources. The willingness was based on rational choice. Status is an individual's social rank within a formal or informal hierarchy, or the person's relative standing along a valued social dimension. Status is the extent to which an individual is respected and admired by others, and status is the outcome of a subjective assessment process (McClean et al., 2018). High-status individuals enjoy greater respect and deference from, as well as power and influence over, those who are positioned lower in the social hierarchy (Kakkar et al., 2020: 532):

> Status is a property that rests in the eyes of others and is conferred to individuals who are deemed to have a higher rank or social standing in a pecking order based on a mutually valued set of social attributes. Higher social status or rank grants its holder a host of tangible benefits in both professional and personal domains. For instance, high-status actors are sought by groups for advice, are paid higher, receive unsolicited help, and are credited disproportionately in joint tasks. In innumerable ways, our social ecosystem consistently rewards those with high status.

Case Study of Manipulation

Accounting manipulation is a form of white-collar crime online where internal offenders change financial figures to benefit themselves. Misreporting in accounting is often a convenient way of concealing illegal transactions (Qiu & Slezak, 2019). Lack of transparency makes concealment in accounting convenient (Davidson et al., 2019; Goncharov & Peter, 2019). Managers can withhold bad news by accounting misrepresentation (Bao et al., 2019), since financial statements are a substantive component of a firm's communications with its stakeholders (Gupta et al., 2020). Balakrishnan et al. (2019) found that reduced corporate transparency in accounting is associated with increased corporate tax aggressiveness. Accounting fraud in terms of account manipulation is lacking transparency (Toolami et al., 2019).

Since accounting is no machine that can provide correct answers regarding the financial health of a company, since accounting information has limited representational properties, and since accounting cannot fully inform decision-makers (O'Leary & Smith, 2020), determination of final accounting figures is often left to the discretion of financial managers.

Concealing illegal transactions may result from the failure of auditors to do their job. Alon et al. (2019) argue that accounting and auditing functions have undergone a legitimacy crisis in recent years. Auditors are supposed to serve as gatekeepers to protect shareholders and other stakeholders, but deviant corporate managements tend to hire and control auditors instead of letting auditors report to the board of directors or the supervisory board (Hurley et al., 2019).

Nina Beate Tollefsen joined the cause, when the Norwegian government guaranteed all parents with small children that their youngsters could expect admission to nurseries and kindergartens at subsidized prices in the country. It was part of the government's struggle for gender equality. To succeed with full coverage of kindergartens and nurseries all over the country, the government relied on private entrepreneurs quickly to build and run such service premises for children (Grindaker, 2011).

Indeed, many more than Tollefsen joined the cause of full coverage of daycare for children in the nation. Soon, all kids could spend their days in a care facility close to their homes. Parents —sometimes the father, but more frequently the mother—deliver the child around 8 a.m., and pick up the child again around 4 p.m., although most premises are open from 7 a.m. to 5 p.m. Sometimes grandparents pick up grandchildren, and they typically do it already around 3 p.m. to spend some time playing before handing the children over to their parents. Independent of the length of daily stay, the state has limited the monthly fee to no more than 3135 Norwegian kroner (about 313 US dollars) per month. Most charge less, and the fee is lower for a number of groups, such as parents with several children in care premises, and parents with low income or disabilities.

It all works fine, except for one thing. The state does not allow childcare facility owners to make a profit. The owners should make sure to cover all their costs with the fee from parents, but they should not charge more than required to cover their costs. Therefore, what some of them do is to increase their costs artificially. They can increase their own salaries, if they at the same time as being owners also work in the childcare as managers or in other relevant positions. They can increase the rent if they own the building. They can make private expenses look like childcare expenses. There are thus various opportunities for fraud in the professional setting of being nursery and kindergarten owners (Grindaker, 2011).

The Norwegian national authority for investigation and prosecution of economic and environmental crime (Økokrim) charged Nina Beate Tollefsen and John Andrew McCracken with abuse of financial funds and fraud. The defendants were accused of overbilling own companies with skyrocketing rent for childcare premises and in addition charging private expenses to the companies. Økokrim claimed in court that the married couple had swindled their daycare organization for 9.5 million kroner (950,000 US dollars).

By means of overbilling of premises rent as well as cash withdrawals, the couple had depleted their four childcare facilities in Oslo named Tusseladden, Stomperud, Sohaugen, and Opplandsgate, which all eventually went bankrupt. While the fraud was going on, one of the defendants also received disability pension and thus additionally faced charges of fraud against the social security agency for 800,000 kroner (80,000 US dollars).

The married couple owned several companies that operated childcare facilities in Oslo. The indictment built on evidence that the couple through fake invoicing of rent, cash withdrawals, and refund of private expenses illegitimately charged the companies for 9.5 million kroner. The indictment regarded a period of about six years, and the depletion of funding in the companies led to bankruptcies (NTB, 2012).

The indictment also charged the couple with social security fraud and conspiracy to social security fraud by providing misleading information. The couple kept secret that the husband McCracken had income that exceeded the money level and thus excluded the justification for social benefits from the state.

State prosecutor Espen Haug at Økokrim made the following statement about the case (Grindaker, 2011: 13):

- This is a serious indictment in the sense that it has been committed financial infidelity against companies, which have received public funds to run kindergartens.
- We believe that the defendants have unlawfully taken away money so that it has harmed the operation of these kindergartens.

Offender Tollefsen had to go to prison for three years, while white-collar offender McCracken had to go to prison for two years and six months. It seems that Tollefsen was the leader in crime, while it is not obvious that McCracken was the follower in crime. In the perspective of leader and follower, a follower has a belief in the leader's pressure as morally right that can make the follower experience shame and guilt if failing to support the leader (Fehr et al., 2015). Glasø and Einarsen (2008) studied emotion regulation in leader–follower relationships (Gottfredson et al., 2020). They found that followers typically suppress negative emotions such as disappointment, uncertainty, and annoyance, while they typically express or fake positive emotions such as enthusiasm, interest, and calmness.

Asker and Bærum district court included in their verdict confiscation of 4.5 million kroner (450,000 US dollars). The court deprived both offenders of the right to conduct business for five years and three years, respectively. Again, there is a gender gap in seriousness where the court considered the female offense more serious than the male offense. Maybe the man with the English-sounding name was indeed a follower, and the woman with the Norwegian-sounding name was a leader. However, archival search has failed in exploring this possibility. The court sentenced them together to replace one million kroner to the bankrupt companies. Violations of the Norwegian penal law thus included bankruptcy crime, theft, and several types of accounting manipulation. Both were in the end convicted of social security fraud of 1.3 million kroner (130,000 US dollars) in Asker and Bærum district court (Asker Bærum, 2012).

The district court at Asker and Bærum wrote in their verdict about McCracken (Asker Bærum, 2012: 42):

> John A. McCracken has acknowledged criminal charges (negligence) for the matters. Based, among other things, on this acknowledgement, lack of accounting documentation, and the bankruptcy reports for the companies, the court finds it evidenced beyond any reasonable doubt that accounting in Stomperud Barnehage Ltd./NUF, Opplandsgt. Barnehage Ltd./NUF, Solhaugen Barnehage Ltd./NUF, and Tusseladden Barnehage Ltd./NUF in the period from January 2006 to the respective bankruptcy openings in 2007, were not updated in accordance with the rules in accounting legislation. Insufficient submission of supporting documents, inadequate accounting, and confusion in the companies' finances has made it difficult to process bankruptcy data and conduct auditing review. The circumstances, in isolation, constitute material breaches of the accounting act's rules. John A. McCracken as the formal and actual general manager of the companies intentionally committed the offenses.

This quote in a gender perspective is interesting. The man was general manager, while the woman was probably chairperson. Furthermore, the term Ltd. stands for Limited, which is a British abbreviation that is similar to Inc. in the United States, AG in Germany, and AS in Norway. Maybe the companies somehow had links to the UK where McCracken probably had a network of some sort.

Several years after his conviction in 2012 and following incarceration, McCracken emerged again in Norwegian media. Now he had taken the last name of Tollefsen as John Andrew Tollefsen. Although the court had deprived him of the right to conduct business for three years after release from prison, he had started a company offering summer camp to children. After a short while, his new company went bankrupt. He needed 750 registered children for financial break even, while only ten children signed up for his summer camp (Krokfjord, 2017) .

The married couple had astronomical private consumption compared to the average Norwegian. Their car fleet included Porsche 996 Carrera 4, Porsche 911 Turbo, BMW X3, BMW X5, Audi Q7, Mercedes ML63 AMG, and Mercedes S350. McCracken bought steadily new wristwatches of the type Rolex, Audemar Piquet, Omega, and Patek Philippe in the price range above ten thousand dollars. In 2005, the couple had a total debt of 31 million Norwegian kroner (Kleppe, 2012), which is the equivalent of three million US dollars.

Nina Tollefsen attempted in court to say that she did not understand what was going on, and that she had trusted her husband. The court did not believe her and said in the verdict that even if the husband was the potential brain behind all wrongdoing, they had nevertheless cooperated closely and conspired in crime. Formally, Nina Tollefsen had her name registered as owner and chief executive in most of the companies, nurseries, and kindergartens.

The two offenders lived in a nice neighborhood outside Oslo in a mansion of considerable size. In 2020, they had moved to an apartment in Oslo. Nina Tollefsen was then chairperson and chief executive at a company named Pearl, which reported financial loss according to public records for registered organizations.

Figure 5.4 illustrates application of convenience theory to kindergarten fraud by the company owner. The motive was individual greed. The opportunity was status and access to resources. The willingness was choice based on identity and rationality. Narcissistic identification is a special type of narcissism, where the offender sees little or no difference between self and the corporation. The company money is personal money that can be spent whatever way the narcissist prefers (Galvin et al., 2015). While grandiosity and admiration belong to the motivational dimension of convenience theory, empathy deficit belongs to the willingness dimension of convenience theory where the offender possesses a sense of entitlement (Nichol, 2019). The offender shows unreasonable expectations to receive and obtain preferential treatments (Zvi & Elaad, 2018).

Greed implies that the offender is never satisfied, as he, she, or the organization always wants more profit (Goldstraw-White, 2012). Greed represents socially constructed needs and desires that can never be completely covered or contended. There is a strong preference to maximize wealth for the corporation, possibly at the expense of violating the laws, rules, and guidelines. Economic greed is a strong motive for financial crime (Bucy et al., 2008; Hamilton & Micklethwait, 2006).

Nina Beate Tollefsen had also a convenient opportunity for concealment of her offenses. Decay occurred in the form of institutional deterioration (Barton, 2004; van Donk & Molloy, 2008). Institutions are the patterned, mutually shared ways that people develop for living

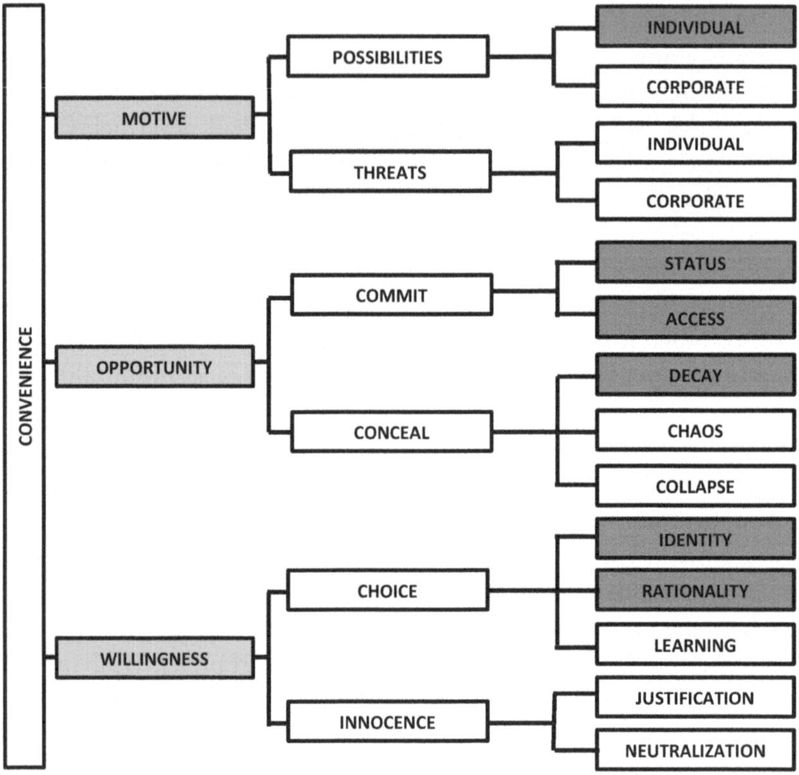

Fig. 5.4 Convenience themes for Tusseladden, etc.

together. Institutional deterioration improves conditions of convenience for corruption and other forms of financial crime (Kostova et al., 2008; Pinto et al., 2008; Rodriguez et al., 2005).

Institutional deterioration can occur conveniently, resulting from external legitimacy where deviance is the norm. An offender's actions have a superficial appearance of legitimacy also internally, since both legal and illegal actions in the company occur in a manner characterized by disorganization (Benson & Simpson, 2018). Conventional mechanisms of social control are weak and unable to regulate the behavior within the organization (Pratt & Cullen, 2005). Concealment of crime occurs conveniently by simply disappearing among other seemingly legitimate transactions.

Gendered White-Collar Crime

Three out of four case studies presented in this chapter are concerned with female white-collar offenders, which invite the introduction of the issue of gendered crime. Generally, there are two competing perspectives on gender and white-collar crime. The emancipation hypothesis suggests that incidents of women in white-collar crime will increase as access to opportunities increase as part of an emancipation process (Lutz, 2019; Steffensmeier et al., 2013). However, Benson and Gottschalk (2015) found very limited support for the emancipation hypothesis as they compared Norway with the United States, where the Norwegian gender gap is much smaller than the US gender gap. Even though gender inequality is much lower in Norway than the United States, the gender gap in Norwegian white-collar crime appears to be nearly identical to that observed in the United States.

The gendered focal concern hypothesis, on the other hand, contends that women socialize into accepting nurturing role obligations that emphasize the importance of social relationships and communalistic orientations toward others. Through the assimilation of these obligations, women develop identities as caregivers. Gendered focal concerns make illegitimate financial gain less attractive for women (Steffensmeier et al., 2013).

Historically, crime committed while using a computer has been stereotypically gendered, with young males being the perceived hacker (Alper, 2014; Thomas, 2002). Yet more recent evidence suggests that online crime is not only committed by males. However, the extent of female cybercrime is debated, with some studies finding males committing a higher proportion of cybercrime (e.g., Barlett & Coyne, 2014; Hinduja, 2007; Toupin, 2014), while other studies finding the opposite (e.g., Kowalski & Limber, 2007; Marcum et al., 2012).

One example of an offense that includes female cybercriminals is a romance or dating scam. These scams have emerged as the digital version of a paper-based scam, where criminals build an intimate relationship via the internet. They eventually request money claiming a dire situation such as unexpected hospital fees or travel expenses. In reality, the scammers simply abscond with the money and the relationship disappears.

While the victims are equally likely to be male and female (Whitty & Buchanan, 2012), in truth we do not know that offenders have a similar ratio. While the offender could have appeared as a female, their actual identity offline could have been male.

More relevant for our study of white-collar offenders online is gendered crime convenience. For example, female executives perceive greater termination vulnerability (Klein et al., 2021; Zhang & Qu, 2016). When women break through the "glass ceiling", Gupta et al. (2020) suggest that they end up on the "glass cliff" where they face more perils, risks, and difficulties compared to their male counterparts. The glass cliff metaphor captures the dangers of falling from the heights of elite positions. To avoid more scrutiny and criticism than men, financial crime might be a convenient avenue to survive on the glass cliff.

References

Agnew, R. (2014). Social concern and crime: Moving beyond the assumption of simple self-interest. *Criminology, 52*(1), 1–32.

Alon, A., Mennicken, A., & Samsonova-Taddei, A. (2019). Dynamics and limits of regulatory privatization: Reorganizing audit oversight in Russia. *Organization Studies, 40*(8), 1217–1240.

Alper, M. (2014). "Can our kids hack it with computers?" Constructing youth hackers in family computing magazines (1983–1987). *International Journal of Communication, 8*(1), 673–698.

Arjoon, S. (2008). Slippery when wet: The real risk in business. *Journal of Markets & Morality, 11*(1), 77–91.

Asker Bærum. (2012, February 28). Case 11–063509MED-AHER/1. *Asker and Bærum district court*.

Balakrishnan, K., Blouin, J. L., & Guay, W. R. (2019). Tax aggressiveness and corporate transparency. *The Accounting Review, 94*(1), 45–69.

Bao, D., Kim, Y., Mian, G. M., & Su, L. (2019). Do managers disclose or withhold bad news? *The Accounting Review, 94*(3), 1–26.

Barlett, C., & Coyne, S. M. (2014). A meta-analysis of sex differences in cyberbullying behavior: The moderating role of age. *Aggressive Behavior, 40*(5), 474–488.

Barton, H. (2004). Cultural reformation: A case for intervention within the police service. *International Journal of Human Resources Development and Management, 4*(2), 191–199.
BBC. (2020, February 18). Britta Nielsen: Danish social worker accused of stealing millions. *British Broadcasting Corporation.* www.bbc.com
Becker, I., Hutchings, A., Abu-Salma, R., Anderson, R., Bohm, N., Murdoch, S. J., Sasse, M. A., & Stringhini, G. (2017). International comparison of bank fraud reimbursement: Customer perceptions and contractual terms. *Journal of Cybersecurity, 3*(2), 109–125.
Benson, M. L., & Gottschalk, P. (2015). Gender and white-collar crime in Norway: An empirical study of media reports. *International Journal of Law, Crime and Justice, 43*(4), 535–552.
Benson, M. L., & Simpson, S. S. (2018). *Understanding white-collar crime—An opportunity perspective* (2nd ed.). Routledge.
Binham, C., & Milne, R. (2018, September 19). Danske bank fails to draw line under Euro 200billion scandal. *Financial Times.* https://www.ft.com/content/38306c04-bc1c-11e8-94b2-17176fbf93f5
Bosse, D. A., & Phillips, R. A. (2016). Agency theory and bounded self-interest. *Academy of Management Review, 41*(2), 276–297.
Bruun Hjejle. (2018). *Report on the non-resident portfolio at Danske bank's Estonian branch.* Report of investigation (p. 87). Law Firm Bruun Hjejle.
Bucy, P. H., Formby, E. P., Raspanti, M.S., & Rooney, K. E. (2008). Why do they do it? The motives, mores, and character of white collar criminals. *St. John's Law Review, 82*, 401–571.
Chrisman, J. J., Chua, J. H., Kellermanns, F. W., & Chang, E. P. C. (2007). Are family managers agents or stewards? An exploratory study in privately held family firms. *Journal of Business Research, 60*(10), 1030–1038.
Cohen, L. E., & Felson, M. (1979). Social change and crime rate trends: A routine activity approach. *American Sociological Review, 44*, 588–608.
Craig, J. M., & Piquero, N. L. (2017). Sensational offending: An application of sensation seeking to white-collar and conventional crimes. *Crime & Delinquency, 63*(11), 1363–1382.
Davidson, R. H., Dey, A., & Smith, A. J. (2019). CEO materialism and corporate social responsibility. *The Accounting Review, 94*(1), 101–126.
Donk, D.P., & Molloy, E. (2008). From organizing as projects, to projects as organizations. *International Journal of Project Management, 26*, 129–137.
Eberly, M. B., Holley, E. C., Johnson, M. D., & Mitchell, T. R. (2011). Beyond internal and external: A dyadic theory of relational attributions. *Academy of Management Review, 36*(4), 731–753.

Emmenegger, P. (2015). Swiss banking secrecy and the problem of international cooperation in tax matters: A nut too hard to crack? *Regulation & Governance, 11*(1), 24–40.

Engdahl, O. (2013). Ensuring regulatory compliance in banking and finance through effective controls: The principle of duality in the segregation of duties. *Regulation & Governance, 8*(3), 332–349.

Eren, C. P. (2021). Cops, firefighters, and scapegoats: Anti-money laundering (AML) professionals in an era of regulatory bulimia. *Journal of White Collar and Corporate Crime, 2*(1), 47–58.

Fehr, R., Yam, K. C., & Dang, C. (2015). Moralized leadership: The construction and consequences of ethical leader perceptions. *Academy of Management Review, 40*(2), 182–209.

Gago-Rodriguez, S., Marquez-Illescas, G., & Nunez-Nickel, M. (2020). Denial of corruption: Voluntary disclosure of bribery information. *Journal of Business Ethics, 162*, 609–626.

Galvin, B. M., Lange, D., & Ashforth, B. E. (2015). Narcissistic organizational identification: Seeing oneself as central to the organization's identity. *Academy of Management Review, 40*(2), 163–181.

Glasø, L., & Einarsen, S. (2008). Emotion regulation in leader-follower relationships. *European Journal of Work and Organizational Psychology, 17*(4), 482–500.

Goldstraw-White, J. (2012). *White-collar crime: Accounts of offending behavior*. Palgrave Macmillan.

Goncharov, I., & Peter, C. D. (2019). Does reporting transparency affect industry coordination? *The Accounting Review, 94*(3), 149–175.

Goodman-Delahunty, J., & Martschuk, N. (2020). Securing reliable information in investigative interviews: Coercive and noncoercive strategies preceding turning points. *Police Practice and Research, 21*(2), 152–171.

Gottfredson, M. R., & Hirschi, T. (1990). *A general theory of crime*. Stanford University Press, CA.

Gottfredson, R. K., Wright, S. L., & Heaphy, E. D. (2020). A critique of the leader-member exchange construct: Back to square one. *The Leadership Quarterly*. https://doi.org/10.1016/j.leaqua.2020.101385

Gottschalk, P., & Benson, M. L. (2020). The evolution of corporate accounts of scandals from exposure to investigation. *British Journal of Criminology, 60*, 949–969.

Gottschalk, P., & Smith, R. (2011). Criminal entrepreneurship, white-collar criminality, and neutralization theory. *Journal of Enterprising Communities: People and Places in the Global Economy, 5*(4), 300–308.

Gottschalk, P., & Tcherni-Buzzeo, M. (2017). Reasons for gaps in crime reporting: The case of white-collar criminals investigated by private fraud examiners in Norway. *Deviant Behavior, 38*(3), 267–281.
Grindaker, M. H. (2011, July 12). Tiltalt for barnehagebedrageri [Indicted for kindergarten fraud]. *Dagens Næringsliv*, p. 13.
Gupta, V. K., Mortal, S. C., Silveri, S., Sun, M., & Turban, D. B. (2020). You're fired! Gender disparities in CEO dismissal. *Journal of Management, 46*(4), 560–582.
Hamilton, S., & Micklethwait, A. (2006). *Greed and corporate failure: The lessons from recent disasters*. Palgrave Macmillan.
Hansen, F., Klungtveit, H. S., Fretland, R. A., Meldalen, S. G., Egeberg, K., Thoresen, K., Jappee, G., & Monsen, Ø. N. (2009, May 12). Drept etter bittert oppgjør [Killed after bitter settlement]. *Dagbladet*. www.dagbladet.no
Hinduja, S. (2007). Neutralization theory and online software piracy: An empirical analysis. *Ethics and Information Technology, 9*(3), 187–204.
Hurley, P. J., Mayhew, B. W., & Obermire, K. M. (2019). Realigning auditors' accountability: Experimental evidence. *The Accounting Review, 94*(3), 233–250.
Jaara, O. O., & Kadomi, A. M. (2017). Factors related to the Central Bank instructions on money laundering. *Journal of Money Laundering Control, 20*(3), 274–291.
Kakkar, H., Sivanathan, N., & Gobel, M. S. (2020). Fall from grace: The role of dominance and prestige in the punishment of high-status actors. *Academy of Management Journal, 63*(2), 530–553.
Kammeradvokaten. (2019). *Ansvarsvurdering vedrørende sagen om svindel med tilskudsmidler – Offentlig rapport* [Assessment of liability regarding the case of fraud with benefit funds—Public report], report of investigation (p. 163), law firm Kammeradvokaten Poul Schmith.
Keaveney, S. M. (2008). The blame game: An attribution theory approach to marketer-engineer conflict in high-technology companies. *Industrial Marketing Management, 37*, 653–663.
Klein, F. B., Chaigneau, P., & Devers, C. E. (2021). CEO gender-based termination concerns: Evidence from initial severance agreements. *Journal of Management, 47*(3), 567–596.
Kleppe, M. K. (2011, December 6). Banktopp dømt til tre års fengsel [Bank top convicted to three years prison]. *Finansavisen*, pp. 30–31.
Kleppe, M. K. (2012, March 3). Too easy to abuse public funds. *Finansavisen*, pp. 6–7.

Kostova, T., Roth, K., & Dacin, M. T. (2008). Institutional theory in the study of multinational corporations: A critique and new directions. *Academy of Management Review, 33*(4), 994–1006.

Kowalski, R. M., & Limber, S. P. (2007). Electronic bullying among middle school students. *Journal of Adolescent Health, 41*(6), S22–S30.

Krippendorff, K. (1980). *Content analysis: An introduction to its methodology*. Sage.

Krokfjord, T. P. (2017, April 19). Dømt for millionbedrageri, har brukt fire identiteter: Slik er John Andrew Tollefsens nye barnehageplan [Convicted of millions fraud, has used four identities: Such is John Andrew Tollefsen's new daycare plan]. *Dagbladet*. www.dagbladet.no

Lee, F., & Robinson, R. J. (2000). An attributional analysis of social accounts: Implications of playing the blame game. *Journal of Applied Social Psychology, 30*(9), 1853–1879.

Lehman, D. W., Cooil, B., & Ramanujam, R. (2020). The effects of rule complexity on organizational noncompliance and remediation: Evidence from restaurant health inspections. *Journal of Management, 46*(8), 1436–1468.

Lutz, J. R. (2019). Pink-collar crime. In F. P. Bernat & K. Frailing (Eds.), *The encyclopedia of women and crime* (pp. 791–796). Wiley.

Marcum, C. D., Higgins, G. E., Freiburger, T. L., & Ricketts, M. L. (2012). Battle of the sexes: An examination of male and female cyber bullying. *International Journal of Cyber Criminology, 6*(1), 904–911.

McClean, E. J., Martin, S. R., Emich, K. J., & Woodruff, T. (2018). The social consequences of voice: An examination of voice type and gender status and subsequent leader emergence. *Academy of Management Journal, 61*(5), 1869–1891.

McClelland, P. L., Liang, X., & Barker, V. L. (2010). CEO commitment to the status quo: Replication and extension using content analysis. *Journal of Management, 36*(5), 1251–1277.

Menon, S., & Siew, T. G. (2012). Key challenges in tackling economic and cybercrimes—Creating a multilateral platform for international co-operation. *Journal of Money Laundering Control, 15*(3), 243–256.

Mugarura, N. (2015). The jeopardy of the bank in enforcement of normative anti-money laundering and countering financing of terrorism regimes. *Journal of Money Laundering Control, 18*(3), 352–370.

Naheem, M. A. (2020). The agency dilemma in anti-money laundering regulation. *Journal of Money Laundering Control*. https://doi.org/10.1108/JMLC-01-2016-0007

Newth, M. (2018, November 5). Britta Nielsen (64) mistenkt for å ha stjålet 140 millioner (Britta Nielsen (64) suspected of having stolen 140 million). *VG*. www.vg.no
Nguyen, C. L. (2018). Preventing the use of financial institutions for money laundering and the implications for financial privacy. *Journal of Money Laundering Control, 21*(1), 47–58.
Nichol, J. E. (2019). The effects of contract framing on misconduct and entitlement. *The Accounting Review, 94*(3), 329–344.
Nielsen, M. K. (2019, March 1). New report concludes: How Britta Nielsen could swindle for DKK 120 million for 25 years. *Danmarks Radio*. www.dr.no
NTB. (2012, March 1). Ektepar dømt for grov utroskap [Married couple convicted of gross infidelity]. *Aftenposten*, p. 10.
NTB. (2019, October 24). Dansk kvinne for retten i storstilt svindelsak [Danish women prosecuted in court in a big fraud case]. ABC *nyheter*. www.abcnyheter.no
O'Leary, S., & Smith, D. (2020). Moments of resistance: An internally persuasive view of performance and impact reports in non-governmental organizations. *Accounting, Organization and Society, 85*, 1–21.
Obodaru, O. (2017). Forgone, but not forgotten: Toward a theory of forgone professional identities. *Academy of Management Journal, 60*(2), 523–553.
Ottermann, P. (2020, February 18). Danish social worker jailed for stealing £13m of government funds. *The Guardian*. www.theguardian.com
Patrucco, A. S., Luzzini, D., & Ronchi, S. (2017). Research perspectives on public procurement: Content analysis of 14 years of publications in the Journal of Public Procurement. *Journal of Public Procurement, 16*(2), 229–269.
Picard, M. (2009). Financial services in trouble: The electronic dimension. *Journal of Financial Crime, 16*(2), 180–192.
Pillay, S., & Kluvers, R. (2014). An institutional theory perspective on corruption: The case of a developing democracy. *Financial Accountability & Management, 30*(1), 95–119.
Pinto, J., Leana, C. R., & Pil, F. K. (2008). Corrupt organizations or organizations of corrupt individuals? *Academy of Management Review, 33*(3), 685–709.
Pontell, H. N., Black, W. K., & Geis, G. (2014). Too big to fail, too powerful to jail? On the absence of criminal prosecutions after the 2008 financial meltdown. *Crime, Law and Social Change, 61*(1), 1–13.

Pratt, T. C., & Cullen, F. T. (2005). Assessing macro-level predictors and theories of crime: A meta-analysis. *Crime and Justice, 32*, 373–450.

PwC. (2019). *Ekstern undersøgelse af tilskudsadministrationen 1977–2018: Udarbejdet for Socialstyrelsen* [External investigation of benefits administration 1977–2018: Provided to the social security administration]. Report of investigation, 80 pages, audit firm PricewaterhouseCoopers, Copenhagen, Denmark.

Qiu, B., & Slezak, S. L. (2019). The equilibrium relationships between performance-based pay, performance, and the commission and detection of fraudulent misreporting. *The Accounting Review, 94*(2), 325–356.

Rixen, T. (2013). Why reregulation after the crisis is feeble: Shadow banking, offshore financial centers, and jurisdictional competition. *Regulation & Governance, 7*(4), 435–459.

Rodriguez, P., Uhlenbruck, K., & Eden, L. (2005). Government corruption and the entry strategies of multinationals. *Academy of Management Review, 30*(2), 383–396.

Schoepfer, A., & Piquero, N. L. (2006). Exploring white-collar crime and the American dream: A partial test of institutional anomie theory. *Journal of Criminal Justice, 34*(3), 227–235.

Schoultz, I., & Flyghed, J. (2020a). From "we didn't do it" to "we've learned our lesson": Development of a typology of neutralizations of corporate crime. *Critical Criminology, 28*, 739–757.

Schoultz, I., & Flyghed, J. (2020b). Denials and confessions: An analysis of the temporalization of neutralizations of corporate crime. *International Journal of Law, Crime and Justice*. https://doi.org/10.1016/j.ijlcj.2020.100389

Schoultz, I., & Flyghed, J. (2021). "We have been thrown under the bus": Corporate versus individual defense mechanisms against transnational corporate bribery charges. *Journal of White Collar and Corporate Crime, 2*(1), 24–35.

Siponen, M., & Vance, A. (2010). Neutralization: New insights into the problem of employee information security policy violations. *MIS Quarterly, 34*(3), 487–502.

Slyke, S. V., & Bales, W. D. (2012). A contemporary study of the decision to incarcerate white-collar and street property offenders. *Punishment & Society, 14*(2), 217–246.

Smith, A. N., Watkins, M. B., Ladge, J. J., & Carlton, P. (2020). Making the invisible visible: Paradoxical effects of intersectional invisibility on the career experiences of executive black women. *Academy of Management Journal, 62*(6), 1705–1734.

Steffensmeier, D., Schwartz, J., & Roche, M. (2013). Gender and twenty-first-century corporate crime: Female involvement and the gender gap in Enron-era corporate frauds. *American Sociological Review, 78*(3), 448–476.

Sutherland, E. H. (1939). White-collar criminality. *American Sociological Review, 5*, 1–12.

Sutherland, E. H. (1949). *White collar crime*. Holt Rinehart and Winston.

Sykes, G., & Matza, D. (1957). Techniques of neutralization: A theory of delinquency. *American Sociological Review, 22*(6), 664–670.

Tejeiro, R., Alison, L., Hendricks, E., Giles, S., Long, M., & Shipley, D. (2020). Sexual behaviours in indecent images of children: A content analysis. *International Journal of Cyber Criminology, 14*(1), 121–138.

Thomas, D. (2002). *Hacker culture*. University of Minnesota Press.

Toolami, B. N., Roodposhti, F. R., Nikoomaram, H., Banimahd, B., & Vakilifard, H. (2019). The survey of whistleblowing intentions for accounting frauds based on demographic individual differences among accounting staff. *International Journal of Finance and Managerial Accounting, 4*(14), 1–13.

Toupin, S. (2014). Feminist hackerspaces: The synthesis of feminist and hacker cultures. *Journal of Peer Production, 5*(2014), 1–11.

Welsh, D. T., Ordonez, L. D., Snyder, D. G., & Christian, M. S. (2014). The slippery slope: How small ethical transgressions pave the way for larger future transgressions. *Journal of Applied Psychology, 100*(1), 114–127.

Whitty, M. T., & Buchanan, T. (2012). The online romance scam: A serious cybercrime. *Cyberpsychology, Behavior, and Social Networking, 15*(3), 181–183.

Williams, J. W. (2008). The lessons of 'Enron'—Media accounts, corporate crimes, and financial markets. *Theoretical Criminology, 12*(4), 471–499.

Zhang, Y., & Qu, H. (2016). The impact of CEO succession with gender change on firm performance and successor early departure: Evidence from China's publicly listed companies in 1997–2010. *Academy of Management Journal, 59*(5), 1845–1868.

Zvi, L., & Elaad, E. (2018). Correlates of narcissism, self-reported lies, and self-assessed abilities to tell and detect lies, tell truths, and believe others. *Journal of Investigative Psychology and Offender Profiling, 15*, 271–286.

6
Technology Issues

The risk of computer crime has become a global issue affecting almost all countries. Fundamentally, the proliferation of information and communication technology, virtual reality, artificial intelligence, and digitalization in general have directly challenged the traditional discourse of criminology and the police work informed by it, introducing new forms of deviance, crime, and social control. Cyberspace has significantly changed the nature and scope of offending and victimization.

Digitally Enabled Identity Gap

As illustrated and documented so far in this book, computer technology is not just another tool for committing and concealing white-collar crime. The technology does not only change the way privileged individuals in the elite use computers as enablers of crime. Rather, the technology causes changes to the identity of the offender as well. It is the digital version of the offender, and not the real version of the offender, that triggers reactions to the behaviors of the offender. The digital version, the double, will typically be different from the real version

P. Gottschalk and C. Hamerton, *White-Collar Crime Online*,
https://doi.org/10.1007/978-3-030-82132-6_6

of the person. The double version is not necessarily a result of manipulation; it can just as well be the result of mistakes. It is then typically called a data error or a system error. A data error is a piece of information that is wrong. A system error is a calculation that is wrong.

An example from the legal world can illustrate the identity gap for an individual. Assuming that the individual is entitled to social security benefits; then it is not a matter of facts about the individual and the rules applying to that individual, which will determine the extent of benefits. Rather, it is the data recorded about the individual and the programming of rules that determine the extent of benefits. If there are data errors regarding the person, and if there are calculation errors in the computer program, then the result will be wrong. The benefits to which the individual is entitled become ignored, while the benefits offered are a result of digital data about the recipient and the digital version of rules that apply to social benefits administration.

In addition to the identity gap by mistake, there is also ample opportunity for an identity gap by manipulation. For most external white-collar offenders online, hidden identities or fake identities are most relevant. As illustrated in the movie piracy case, the court had to pass a verdict on an "unknown perpetrator" (Borgarting, 2019; Høyesterett, 2019). In the case of foreign aid fraud, offenders applied the technique of business email compromise based on a stolen identity (Norfund, 2020; PwC, 2020). In the case of cryptocurrency crime, offenders were anonymous in handling cryptocurrency in the same way as traditional cash tells nothing about previous owners of the money (Braaten & Vaughn, 2019). In the case of industrial espionage, offenders at SAS could hide behind an identity of handling regular transactions on behalf of the airline (Borgarting, 2010; Grutle, 2010; Valvik & Strømsheim, 2010). In the case of Covid-19 fraud, the offender manipulated the identity to fit the requirements for receiving financial aid from the government during the pandemic (NTB, 2020; Ogre, 2020). In the case of CEO fraud, the offender changes identity to the executive to be able to communicate with organizational members pretending to be the chief executive officer (Keyworth & Wall, 2016).

For most internal white-collar offenders online, the identity cannot be manipulated digitally. Internal offenders abuse their access rights, but not by means of a manipulated identity, as exemplified by Britta Nielsen at the social security agency in Denmark (Kammeradvokaten, 2019; PwC, 2019), employees at the Estonian branch of Danske Bank (Bruun Hjejle, 2018), Bente Selvaag at BNP Paribas in Norway (Kleppe, 2011), and Nina Beate Tollefsen operating kindergartens in Norway (Asker Bærum, 2012; Grindaker, 2011; NTB, 2012). However, they may take on traditional deviant identities and adapt to potential labels assigned to them.

For example, internal offenders can accept deviant identities (Crank, 2018), and they can suffer from narcissistic identification with the organization by seeing themselves as central to the organization's identity (Galvin et al., 2015).

Some white-collar offenders take on a professional deviant identity (Obodaru, 2017). The identity perspective suggests that individuals develop professional identities where they commit to a chosen identity. It is a process of generating possible selves, selecting one, and discarding others. Professional identity is how an individual sees himself or herself in relation to work. The self-concept is a complex cognitive structure containing all of a person's self-representations. According to the identity perspective, roles and identities are interdependent concepts. Identity enactment refers to acting out an identity or claiming the identity by engaging in behaviors that conform to role expectations and that allow the identity to become manifest. Deviant behavior finds an anchor in a person's professional identity, where the deviant leader must claim and assume a leader identity by their followers.

Labeling can influence the deviant personality offender mind. The labeling perspective suggests that individuals adapt to the reputation created by others. The labeling perspective argues that the deviant reputation stigmatizes a person into a stereotype. Formal societal reaction to the individual can be a stepping-stone in the development of a criminal career. The deviant label is over time embedded in the individual (Mingus & Burchfield, 2012). The labeled person is increasingly likely to become involved in social groups that consist of social deviants and unconventional others without feeling any doubt or regret since the behavior is in accordance with the label glued to the person by others (Bernburg et al., 2006).

Eighteen Internet Characteristics

We are all familiar with online services on the internet. A typical example is online banking, where we complete our payments of bills at home. Most Norwegians have many years of personal experience using online services on the internet. According to the United Nations (2008), Norway is ranked third in the world in terms of online services provided by the government. Sweden and Denmark are on the top of the list, and Norway is followed by the United States and the Netherlands. The United Kingdom is ranked tenth on the list.

A number of characteristics of the internet for online services have been observed, which may shed light on methods white-collar offenders use online. The following list was generated based on a literature review:

1. *Disconnected personal communication.* While communication on the internet might be personal in content, it is not perceived as interpersonal in meaning. A typical example is email, where the sender might feel completely disconnected from the time and place the receiver reads the email message. Even when chatting in real time, sender and receiver may perceive both involvement and disconnectedness at the same time. Some may change their personality unconsciously when moving from face-to-face communication to email communication. For example, aggressive and threatening statements online might be unthinkable in a face-to-face situation. Internet victimization can be and often is different from "real world" victimization in that potential offenders spend little time chatting and will come straight to the point, sometimes instantly. This would suggest that the internet might act to remove inhibitions associated with face-to-face contact, which can be explained by the disconnected nature of personal communication on the internet, thereby avoiding unpleasant emotional states (Quayle et al., 2006). There are, however, some potential offenders who will still spend a considerable amount of time preparing a victim for harm, particularly in peer-to-peer networks, in order to prepare them for abuse (Davidson, 2008). Generally, there are a number of distinguishing

characteristics between the internet and the real world as the two principally different forms of victimization (Hutchings, 2018a, 2018b).

2. *Mediating technology.* According to Afuah and Tucci (2003), the internet is a mediating technology that interconnects parties that are independent. The interconnections can be business-to-business (B2B), business-to-consumer (B2C), government-to-business (G2B), person-to-person (P2P), person-to-system (P2S), or any other link between individuals and organizations. In the case of white-collar crime, internet serves as a mediating technology mainly for person-to-system (P2S) and person-to-person (P2P) communication, but person-to-group (P2G) and group-to-person (G2P) do also occur. In relation to victimization, changes in interconnections occur over time, where an initial contact may start as person-to-group, for example, group of executives, and then move into person-to-person, where the potential offender has singled out a potential victim in the form of the weakest link in a chain (Hutchings & Holt, 2018).
3. *Universality.* The universality of the internet refers to the internet's ability to both enlarge and shrink the world. It enlarges the world because anyone anywhere in the world can potentially make his or her services, messages, and requests available to anyone anywhere else in the world anytime. It shrinks the world in that distance is reduced on electronic highways (Afuah & Tucci, 2003). In the case of white-collar crime, the internet enables each offender potentially to contact anyone, anywhere, and anytime. Contact is established without the offender having to travel physically, all he or she needs to do is to travel electronically. The internet combines global communications with an incredible range of resources (Calder, 2004) . The global reach enabled by the internet permits victimization to cross cultural and national boundaries far more conveniently and cost effective than is true in traditional offending (Laudon & Laudon, 2010). However, cultural and communication issues exist between jurisdictions that can limit the extent of universality perceived by users in the upperworld, but not in the underworld (Becker et al., 2017).

4. *Network externalities*. A technology or product exhibits network externalities when it becomes more valuable to users as more people take advantage of it. A classic example is the first person in Norway who got himself a telephone. Until a second person got a telephone, there was nobody in Norway to talk to on the phone. The value of the telephone for each subscriber increases with the number of subscribers. Similarly, the value of the internet increases with the number of internet users. The more people and businesses that are connected to a network within the internet, the more valuable the network is to each user (Afuah & Tucci, 2003). The more computer systems that are connected to a network, the more valuable the network is to each offender since he or she is able to reach and get in contact with more potential victims. Since internet access is found in more and more organizations all over the world, and more and more internal computer systems are connected to the internet, the number of potential victims rises accordingly (Hutchings, 2016).
5. *Distribution channel*. The internet acts as a distribution channel for products that are information bits, such as software, music, video, news, tickets, and money. There is a replacement effect if the internet is used to serve the same deliveries, which were serviced by the old physical distribution channel. There is an extension effect if the internet is used by more people and for new services (Afuah & Tucci, 2003). When committing crime, the potential offender may use the internet not only for communications. He or she can also use it to send gifts and other digital items that the victim might be interested in. He or she can also send digital items that the victim is not always interested in, such as pornographic pictures and videos to test reactions. More importantly, however, the offender can complete the offense online as long as the gain is accessible in digital form, such as money, software, and music (Hutchings & Holt, 2016).
6. *Time moderator*. The internet has an ability to shrink and enlarge time. It shrinks time for people who want information when information sources are closed. It enlarges time when related work can be done at different points in time (Afuah & Tucci, 2003). Both dimensions of the internet as a time moderator can be important in online victimization of businesses. When victims are offline, offenders can

prepare for attacks and review system features without any interruptions. Furthermore, components of software and infrastructure as well as expert services on underground markets can be developed independent of time and space in parallel or sequentially (Caines et al., 2018).

7. *Low-cost standard*. White-collar offenders would not be able to exploit the properties of the internet if they could not adopt it. For two reasons, adoption has been easy. First and foremost, importantly, the internet and the web application are standards open to everyone and are very easy to use. Second, the cost of the internet is a lot lower than that of earlier means of electronic communication (Afuah & Tucci, 2003). Given the low-cost standard, access to the internet is not limited to affluent or well-educated people. Both adults and children have access independent of social class in most countries. For a white-collar offender, this enables access not only to a large number of enterprises but also to a large variety of enterprises. Universal technical standards of the internet enable any computer to link with any other computer regardless of the technology platform each is using (Laudon & Laudon, 2010; Vu et al., 2020).
8. *Electronic double*. It is not the real person who is present on the internet. It is a digital copy of the person who is present. The digital information about the person creates an image of the person, which we call the electronic double. The way in which an offender is perceived by a victim on the internet is thus dependent both on the information the person provides and the image this information creates in the victim's mind. Even if the offender is completely honest in all communication with the victim, the victim may perceive the offender as very different from reality and maybe similar to someone the victim already knows. Also, the offender may perceive the victim differently from reality and create an electronic double of the victim in his or her head, which can be far removed from reality, but which may serve his or her expectation (Keyworth & Wall, 2016).
9. *Electronic double manipulation*. The electronic double created on the internet represents an image of the real person. The real person can change his or her electronic double and make it more or less

similar to the real self. The most obvious change is role, where an offender may claim to be in a position more relevant, better, and different from the actual position. This requires consistency in all other information, so that the presented role matches other information about the person. Similarly, victims may come across with a distorted profile based on deviant terminology (Hughes et al., 2020).

10. *Information asymmetry*. Information asymmetry is often reduced on the internet. Information asymmetry exists when one party to a transaction has information that another party does not—information that is important to the transaction. The world wide web reduces such information asymmetries, as the other party can find the same information on the web (Afuah & Tucci, 2003). Neither the offender nor the victim has information monopoly in areas where information is available on the world wide web. However, the offender will typically be more knowledgeable than the victim, leading to an information asymmetry between potential offender and potential victim, which can be explored and exploited by the potential offender similar to principal–agent relationships (Bosse & Phillips, 2016; Chrisman et al., 2007; Pillay & Kluvers, 2014; Williams, 2008).
11. *Infinite virtual capacity*. Access to the internet is perceived as unlimited; you do not have to wait on hold or in a long line. For example, virtual communities like chatting houses have infinite capacity for members who can talk anytime of the day for as long as they want (Afuah & Tucci, 2003). However, in some parts of the world there are bandwidth and infrastructure limitations that reduce the virtual capacity. The amount of time online offenders spend in pursuit of victims will depend on a number of factors such as available virtual capacity. While there are underground markets for infrastructure services, there might be limitations in the supply since maintaining the infrastructure for cybercrime can be boring (Collier et al., 2020).
12. *Independence in time and space*. While a traditional meeting requires that participants are present at the same place at the same time, virtual meeting on the internet is possible even if different participants are present at different places at different times. Internet is a space unbounded in territory and time (Horgan et al., 2021) . The

online environment enables access to a wealth of information and communication across both distance and time (Kierkegaard, 2008). The independence in time and space is typically the case when using email. When participating in a chat room, participants are required to respond within a short time frame, eliminating independence in time, but still keeping independence in space. On the mobile phone, SMS messages have the same characteristic of independence in time and space. Calder (2004) has suggested that the internet promotes better social relationships as people will be freed from the constraints of time and place; however, it could also limit social relationships to the virtual world and reinforce isolation. The relevance to white-collar offenders online can be found in both relationships and isolation characteristics of the internet, such as anonymity on underground markets (Hutchings & Holt, 2016).

13. *Cyberspace*. Using the internet is not just a supplement to or add-on to real life. It is also an enabler of an alternative lifestyle in cyberspace with its own cyber culture. Cyberspace is an abstract space, rather than a physical space, where a culture has emerged from the use of computer networks for communication, entertainment, and business. Cyber culture can, for example, be found in virtual communities, which is a group of people that primarily interact via communication media such as newsletters, telephone, email, instant messages or as newsgroups, Facebook and Twitter, rather than face to face for social and other purposes (Whittaker, 2004). In terms of online victimization, both offenders and victims are sometimes members of virtual communities. Calder (2004) argues that there are many benefits that can be derived from the development of online relationships and online relationships that become trustworthy in cyberspace. Cyberspace can facilitate the formation of alternative business relationships, improve the chances of finding an optimal business partner, highlight that relationships can develop on attachments, and improve one's skills in interpersonal, yet virtual, communication. For example, social networks of malware writers and hackers develop in cyberspace (Holt et al., 2012) based on trust (Holt et al., 2016).

14. *Dynamic social network.* The emergence of social network services has radically challenged our understanding of traditional, territorial social networks. An average Westerner's social network comprises about 150 individuals. Once a physical social network is established, this number of members tends to change little over time, and the members themselves do not change very much. In contrast, the internet enables individuals to expand and reduce their social network and replace members in the network (CEOP, 2006). The internet provides a social context for more and more people to meet more and more people where people are replaced by other people over time. There is a dynamic social network rather than a stable social network on the internet when cartels move online (Goncharov & Peter, 2019). If both potential offenders and potential victims dynamically change their social networks, the likelihood of contact increases.
15. *Ubiquity.* In traditional white-collar crime, a place for crime is a physical place where the offender has legitimate access, such as an office and a computer terminal at home. Online victimization is ubiquitous, meaning that it is possible just about everywhere, at all times. It makes it possible to offend from a laptop, at home, at work, or even from a car, using mobile technology. The result is called an offense space—an offending place extended beyond traditional boundaries and removed from a temporal and geographic location (Hutchings, 2018a, 2018b). From an offender's point of view, ubiquity reduces transaction costs—the costs of victimizing externally as well as internally. To transact with systems and people online in the virtual world, it is no longer necessary that the potential offender spends time or money traveling to a place such as a bank or a customer, and much less mental effort is required to make an effort (Laudon & Laudon, 2010).
16. *Richness.* Information richness refers to the complexity and content of a message. Traditional communication channels have great richness. They are able to provide personal, face-to-face communication using aural and visual cues when making contact. The web makes it possible to deliver rich messages with text, audio, and video simultaneously to large numbers of people (Laudon & Laudon, 2010). The

variety of services available in the underground economy illustrates information richness for cybercriminals (Caines et al., 2018).

17. *Interactivity*. Systems used on the internet are interactive, meaning they allow for two-way communication between offender and victim. Interactivity allows an offender to engage a victim in ways similar to face-to-face experience but on a massive, global scale (Laudon & Laudon, 2010). Interactivity gives both potential victim and potential offender the possibility of communicating messages without interruption in distorted and anonymous ways (Steel, 2019).
18. *Digital knowledge transmission*. Knowledge cannot be stored in computers given the common definition of the term. Knowledge is defined as information combined with interpretation, context, and reflection. The only place those three activities can occur, particularly reflection, is in the heads of human beings. However, as emphasized by Hutchings (2014), knowledge transfer can indeed be supported and enabled online among cybercriminals. She emphasizes the role of co-offenders in knowledge transmission. Online portals and communication channels are used to learn and to teach others how to commit white-collar crime. Underground portals are useful for knowledge transfer, as portals also serve as marketplaces for code used to commit offences.

This list of 18 characteristics was derived from the research literature. The list might be refined in terms of exhaustiveness; overlap and hierarchy in future research.

Online Crime Terminology

Just like white-collar offenders offline use a language that potential whistleblowers may not understand (Ferraro et al., 2005; Holt & Cornelissen, 2014; Mawritz et al., 2017; Srivastava & Goldberg, 2017; Weick et al., 2005), white-collar crime online is associated with a terminology that potential victims and notifiers may not understand. It might not be the technology itself that is complicated, but rather the terminology that represents a barrier to insights into cybercrime.

Let us first review the issue of white-collar language offline. Executives and others in the elite may use language that followers do not necessarily understand. Followers nevertheless trust executive messages. Language shapes what people notice and ignore (Ferraro et al., 2005), and language is a window into organizational culture (Holt & Cornelissen, 2014; Srivastava & Goldberg, 2017; Weick et al., 2005). Offender language can cause obedience among followers (Mawritz et al., 2017).

Hughes et al. (2020: 1) studied the online crime terminology by reviewing underground hacking forums that contain a large collection of noisy text data around various topics, with misspellings, changing lexicons, and slang phrases:

> The evolving domain-specific lexicon includes homonyms, where "rat" may be identified as an animal by off-the-shelf tools but is typically defined as a "remote access trojan" in this context, a type of malware used to gain access to a victim's computer.

In this quote another term is used, which is malware. Malicious software or malware is any software intentionally designed to cause harm and damage. Computer viruses, worms, Trojan horses, ransomware, spyware, adware, rogue software, wiper, and scareware are some of the terms used for the variety of malware. Hughes et al. (2020) reviewed a large number of cyberterms by means of a statistical technique. For example, for online event terms, they identified terms like affiliate, betting, burst, fever, guide, iamb, laptop, mining, movie, movies, network, time, traffic, and videos. Some of these words in offline language do not have a meaning of an event, such as laptop, movie, or network.

Hughes et al. (2020) describe a terminology case of a known event. One of the largest organizations affected by the event was the National Health Service (NHS), which is the universal public healthcare system in the UK. The malware was WannaCry, which is a type of ransomware that encrypts data until the victim pays a ransom. Frequent terms used in the hacker terminology during the event include nuclear, nuke, border, amount, shopify, affiliate, laptop, and betting.

It is not just a matter of single words. It is a matter of understanding, where there are distinctions between data, information, knowledge, and wisdom. A term that does not make sense to an individual is called data. A data element that makes sense to an individual is called information. For example, the number 60 for a person can either be the weight in kilos or the age in years. When the number is clarified as weight or age, then the data element changes status into information. Information combined with interpretation, reflection, and context becomes knowledge. Knowledge accumulated over time as learning becomes wisdom.

From the perspective of the white-collar offender, online crime terminology can help both to commit and to conceal financial crime. Terminology is part of the opportunity structure in the theory of convenience where offenders online use digital techniques that people do not understand, similar to offline offenders (Ferraro et al., 2005; Holt & Cornelissen, 2014; Judge et al., 2009; Mawritz et al., 2017; Srivastava & Goldberg, 2017; Weick et al., 2005).

Executive language and online terminology are also complicated by data and information characteristics of statements. Data and information are the only kinds of messages that are communicated verbally, in writing, and in digital form. No knowledge can be stored in computer systems, and no knowledge can be communicated directly given the common definitions of data, information, knowledge, and wisdom in a hierarchical structure of understanding. Data are numbers, texts, and other materials without meaning. Data do not convey meaning in itself or meaning of facts, images, or sounds, since they lack relational elements indispensable to the establishment of a meaning, and they lack relational structure for a cognitive purpose. This structure is one of the attributes of information. When data are attached to certain and specific interpretations, then they become information. Data become information when their creators add meaning.

Information combined with interpretation, reflection, and context becomes knowledge. Information feeds knowledge. Knowledge has its origin and is applied in the minds of people. While data and information can be stored in computers, knowledge can only be present in the heads of individuals. Knowledge accumulated over time in the form of learning becomes wisdom. Knowledge is the most important issue in this hierarchy since it is knowledge that triggers what people do. Knowledge leads to action. While knowledge can only be stored between the ears in the heads of individuals, attempts are focused on codifying and packaging knowledge in the form of information in computer repositories to make it more accessible for reuse (Walsh, 2020).

In our perspective of understanding of crime terminology, what can be derived online is thus only data and information. The interpretation of data and information in an unfamiliar terminology contribute to the convenience structure for white-collar offenders online.

Underground Market Services

There are several different actors in a market for specialist cybercrime capabilities. First, there are competitors who offer the same kind of specialist services. Next, there are customers who are willing to pay for the services that they need to commit financial crime. Then there are providers of infrastructure on which specialists develop their capabilities. Fourth, new vendors attempt to enter the market with the same kind of services. Fifth and finally, there are vendors of substitute capabilities that can replace the services from the current specialists. Underground communities provide market access to the various actors (Caines et al., 2018).

The advertising and trading of airline tickets on online black markets is another example of underground market activities. Business organizations run by white-collar offenders are trading in airline tickets that have been obtained illicitly. Hutchings (2018a: 461) studied the trade in fraudulently obtained airline tickets:

> Every day, hundreds of people fly on airline tickets that have been obtained fraudulently. Tickets are purchased by complicit travelers or resellers from the online blackmarket. Victim travelers obtain tickets from fake travel agencies or malicious insiders. Compromised credit cards are used to be the main method to purchase tickets illegitimately.

Compromised credit cards were previously the main way in which offenders fraudulently obtained airline tickets. More common today are phishing techniques to obtain credentials for global distribution system companies, which provide booking services to travel agents. Other methods to obtain tickets illegally include the use of compromised loyalty point accounts, compromised business accounts, identity fraud, and voucher fraud (Hutchings, 2018b).

Similar to Vu et al. (2020), Holt et al. (2016) found that trust and reputation play a core role in underground cyber markets. They studied the signals of trust in advertisements for stolen data when analyzing the issues that influence the type of feedback received by sellers. In particular, they studied reactions from buyers of stolen credit card data. The study showed that signals of trust were dependent on payment mechanism, advertising language, and the type of market they operated within.

Trustworthiness in an otherwise untrusted environment is a particular challenge for white-collar offenders online when there is information asymmetry. In the perspective of principal–agent (Eisenhardt, 1989), information asymmetry suggests that the principal has imperfect information about the agent's contribution (Chrisman et al., 2007; Pillay & Kluvers, 2014; Williams, 2008). The principal–agent perspective assumes narrow self-interest among both principals and agents (Bosse & Phillips, 2016). Therefore, the principal is often unable to control an agent who does work for the principal (Jensen & Meckling, 1976; Naheem, 2020).

Trustworthiness in an otherwise untrusted environment can, for example, be the result of a satisfied buyer (Holt et al., 2016: 139):

> Once a buyer has made a successful payment and profited from the purchase, they will trust the same seller in the next transaction. This experiential learning process of product quality creates the trust between the parties.

The convenience for white-collar offenders is dependent on the trust in an otherwise untrusted environment. A white-collar offender online with a high user status can enjoy a high level of trust (Holt et al., 2016).

One kind of expert service available on underground markets is booter service. A booter service can enable distributed denial of service attacks that involves overloading a website or computer system with so much bogus traffic that legitimate access is unlikely to succeed (Sarre et al., 2018). For a white-collar offender online, overloading a website or a system can enable diverting attention and guardianship away from financial crime. An attack that prevents a business from operating can be followed by a demand for payment to make the attack cease. Hutchings and Clayton (2016) studied a booter service that offered customers a range of membership options, from basic to premium subscriptions with the higher levels allowing users to request longer attacks and attacks on more than just one target at a time. They found that attacks worked best during crucial times for business, such as before big sporting events for betting websites. Generally, an attacker will consider victim vulnerability in the light of crime profitability.

Underground markets offer a range of complementary products and services, from the supply of hardware and software to access valuable data, the sale of the stolen data itself, to the provision of services to turn information into money, and the procedure of money laundering (Hutchings & Holt, 2016). Online hidden markets link together various components of the underground economy, such as logistics, operational support, trading, and communications (Cai et al., 2018).

A software service offered on underground markets is SQL injection for website hacking (Leppänen et al., 2020: 64):

> SQL refers to Structured Query Language, which is used for controlling back-end SQL databases. In SQL injection, a perpetrator gets through malicious SQL queries and gains unauthorized access to a back-end database and is able to steal, alter or destroy information.

By SQL injection a program detects and exploits vulnerabilities in the target computer system to access valuable information. Database-driven interactive web sites typically consist of a back-end database, a computer program, and a web browser. The user can interact with the back-end database using the web browser that applies the computer program. The back-end database is a store of information. SQL injection enables the offender to send a query and receive a reply or update the back-end database in ways that it was not supposed to. A successful SQL injection may lead to manipulation of information, disclosure of information, or denial-of-service (Leppänen et al., 2020). In the latter case, the offender can request a fee for removing the cause of denial. Manipulation of information refers to altering or erasing the content of a back-end database to trigger, for example, transfer of funds out of the victim organization. Disclosure of information serves the purpose of collecting, trading, and abusing information such as credit card and bank account numbers and passwords.

Yip et al. (2013) suggest that there are two sources of uncertainty in underground markets. The first source of uncertainty is the quality of goods and services as merchandise bought on underground markets. There exists an incentive for the sellers to pass off a low-quality product as a higher quality one. The second source of uncertainty is the identity of the trader. Thus, aside from dishonest traders, cybercriminals also face the additional threat from fake traders pretending to be cybercriminals, or law enforcement associates such as undercover agents and informants pretending to be cybercriminals.

Yip et al. (2013) argue that by using carding forums, uncertainties surrounding the quality of traded commodities can be mitigated through two mechanisms: a sophisticated review system and an exchange service known as the escrow commonly used in legitimate forms of transaction. An escrow officer usually charges 5–10% commission for the service of controlling the quality of traded merchandise. Uncertainties around the identity of the traders can be mitigated by cybercriminals interacting socially in open discussions and knowledge exchange. These mechanisms tend to be enforced through a well-defined management hierarchy in the underworld. Cybercriminals can engage in reciprocal and mutually beneficial acts such as the exchange of valuable information. A picture of identities develops as cybercriminals interact with each other.

The most important mechanism for uncertainty reduction is reputation (Yip et al., 2013: 526):

> Reputation is the primary tool for trust preservation in the underground economy and reputation is attached to the nickname of a user. Therefore, nicknames are treated like brands. However, it is important to realize why reputation is needed in the first place. It is needed because many who want to collaborate have no prior knowledge or experience with each other. Accumulating a reputation by behaving well over time is difficult and requires too much time because many cybercriminals refuse to deal with those without a reputation in the first place. In other words, for cybercriminals to collaborate with one another, they must be able to trust each other without requiring previous experience. Therefore, there must be a mechanism capable of minimizing the risk of opportunistic intents and facilitates the development of initial trust.

The importance of reputation became evident in a court case in Norway, where the chief executive of a cannabis trading business was convicted to prison. He was a criminal entrepreneur labeled a hashish baron in the media. Entrepreneurs are often seen as important economic agents, driving forward employment, opportunities, and economic development. Entrepreneurship is associated with innovation, adaptation, change, and dynamism, hard work, willpower, and overcoming challenges and struggles. According to Welter et al. (2017), entrepreneurship is a broadly available social technology for creating organizations that may pursue a myriad of goals. Gjermund Cappelen, the Norwegian hashish baron, developed a terminology and a behavior that created trust among his business partners in the Netherlands who supplied cannabis to him. The quality of and the price for cannabis in the wholesale business in the Netherlands depends to a large extent on relationships. His patients on underground markets as well as his skills in communicating with the right people at the right time through the right channels enabled a continuous flow of high-quality cannabis at reasonable prices for more than a decade before his business enterprise with more than a dozen employees was detected (Gottschalk, 2019).

Gjermund Cappelen experienced trust with his business partners. As defined by Yip et al. (2013: 519), trust is a mechanism for people to cope with risk and uncertainty in interactions with others:

> Considering trust as a property of collective units such as ongoing relationships, groups and collectives, if person A trusts person B then person A relies on B's integrity in the absence of sufficient means to control this other person's behavior.

Yip et al. (2013) examined trust among cybercriminals on carding forums for underground market services. A carding forum is a place to share stolen credit card information and other kinds of valuable information. Participants discuss how to steal information. Carding forums serve to verify stolen credit card information. Carding forums are used for trading carding goods and services. Carding forums facilitate cybercrime because they offer a hybrid form of organizational structure that is able to address sources of uncertainty and minimize transaction costs to an extent that allows a competitive underground market to emerge. Characteristics of carding forums have implications for policing cybercrime as discussed later in this book.

Fake World Wide Web Sites

Fake websites have become increasingly pervasive and trustworthy in their appearance, generating billions of dollars in fraudulent revenue at the expense of unsuspecting Internet users. Abbasi et al. (2010) found that the growth in profitable fake websites is attributable to several factors, including their authentic appearance, a lack of user awareness regarding them, and the ability of fraudsters to undermine many existing mechanisms for protecting against them. The design and appearance of these websites makes it difficult for users to manually identify them as fake. Distinctions can be made between spoof sites and concocted sites. A spoof site is an imitation of an existing commercial website such as eBay or PayPal. A concocted site is a deceptive website attempting to create the impression of a legitimate, unique, and trustworthy entity.

Detecting fake websites is difficult. There is a need for both fraud cues as well as problem-specific knowledge. Fraud cues are important design elements of fake websites that may serve as indicators of their lack of authenticity. First, fake websites often use automatic content generation techniques to mass-produce fake web pages. Next, fraud cues include information, navigation, and visual design. Information in terms of web page text often contains fraud cues stemming from information design elements. Navigation in terms of linkage information and URL names for a website can provide relevant fraud cues relating to navigation design characteristics. For example, it is argued that 70% of ".biz" domain pages are fake sites. Fake websites frequently use images from existing legitimate or prior fake websites. For example, spoof sites copy company logos from the websites they are mimicking. The fact that it is copied can be detected in the system (Abbasi et al., 2010).

In addition to fraud cues, there is a need for problem-specific knowledge. Problem-specific knowledge regarding the unique properties of fake websites includes stylistic similarities and content duplication (Abbasi et al., 2010).

Abbasi et al. (2010) developed a prototype system for fake website detection. The system is based on statistical learning theory. Statistical learning theory is a computational learning theory that attempts to explain the learning process from a statistical point of view. The researchers conducted a series of experiments, comparing the prototype system against several existing fake website detection systems on a test sample encompassing 900 websites. The results indicate that systems grounded in statistical learning theory can more accurately detect various categories of fake websites by utilizing richer sets of fraud cues in combination with problem-specific knowledge.

A variation of fake websites is fraudulent email solicitation where the sender of an email claims an association with known and reputable corporations or organizational entities. For example, one email from the "Microsoft/AOL Award Team" notified its winners of a sweepstake by stating, "The prestigious Microsoft and AOL has set out and successfully organized a Sweepstakes marking the end of year anniversary we rolled out over 100,000.000.00 for our new year Anniversary Draw" (Nhan et al., 2009). The email proceeded to ask for the potential victim's personal information.

Nhan et al. (2009) examined 476 fraudulent email solicitations and found that the three most frequently alleged organizational associations were Microsoft, America Online, and PayPal. Fraudsters also attempt to establish trust through associating with credit-issuing financial corporations and authoritative organizations and groups.

References

Abbasi, A., Zhang, Z., Zimbra, D., & Chen, H. (2010). Detecting fake websites: The contribution of statistical learning theory. *MIS Quarterly, 34*(3), 435–461.

Afuah, A., & Tucci, C. L. (2003). *Internet business models and strategies* (2nd ed.). McGraw-Hill.

Asker Bærum. (2012, February 28). *Case 11–063509MED-AHER/1*. Asker and Bærum District Court.

Becker, I., Hutchings, A., Abu-Salma, R., Anderson, R., Bohm, N., Murdoch, S. J., Sasse, M. A., & Stringhini, G. (2017). International comparison of bank fraud reimbursement: Customer perceptions and contractual terms. *Journal of Cybersecurity, 3*(2), 109–125.

Bernburg, J. G., Krohn, M. D., & Rivera, C. (2006). Official labeling, criminal embeddedness, and subsequent delinquency. *Journal of Research in Crime and Delinquency, 43*(1), 67–88.

Borgarting. (2010, March 16). *Court case LB-2008–133972*. Borgarting lagmannsrett (Borgarting court of appleals), Oslo, Norway.

Borgarting. (2019, February 1). *Court case 17–170796AST-BORG/01*. Borgarting lagmannsrett (Borgarting court of appeals), judges Mats Wilhelm Ruland, Marit Bjørånesset Frogner and Bjørn E. Engstrøm. Prosecutor Esben Kyhring, defense attorney Christian Fredrik Bonnevie Hjort, Oslo, Norway.

Bosse, D. A., & Phillips, R. A. (2016). Agency theory and bounded self-interest. *Academy of Management Review, 41*(2), 276–297.

Braaten, C. N., & Vaughn, M.S. (2019). Convenience theory of cryptocurrency crime: A content analysis of U.S. federal court decisions. *Deviant Behavior*, published online. https://doi.org/10.1080/01639625.2019.1706706.

Bruun Hjejle (2018). *Report on the non-resident portfolio at Danske bank's Estonian branch* (Report of investigation, 87 pages). Law Firm Bruun Hjejle.

Cai, T., Du, L., Xin, Y., & Chang, L. Y. C. (2018). Characteristics of cybercrimes: Evidence from Chinese judgment documents. *Police Practice & Research, 19*(6), 582–595.

Caines, A., Pastrana, S., Hutchings, A., & Buttery, P. J. (2018). Automatically identifying the function and intent of posts in underground forums. *Crime Science, 7*(19), 1–14.

Calder, M. C. (2004). The internet: Potential, problems and pathways to hands-on sexual offending. In M. C. Calder (Ed.), *Child sexual abuse and the Internet: Tackling the new frontier* (pp. 1–23). Russell House Publishing.

CEOP. (2006). *Understanding online social network services and risks to youth.* Child Exploitation and Online Protection Centre. www.ceop.gov.uk.

Chrisman, J. J., Chua, J. H., Kellermanns, F. W., & Chang, E. P. C. (2007). Are family managers agents or stewards? An exploratory study in privately held family firms. *Journal of Business Research, 60*(10), 1030–1038.

Collier, B., Clayton, R., Hutchings, A., & Thomas, D. R. (2020). *Cybercrime is (often) boring: Maintaining the infrastructure of cybercrime economies.* Workshop on the Economics of Information Security, Brussels. www.weis2020.econinfosec.org.

Crank, B. R. (2018). Accepting deviant identities: The impact of self-labeling on intentions to desist from crime. *Journal of Crime and Justice, 41*(2), 155–172.

Davidson, J. (2008). *Child sexual abuse—Media representations and government reactions.* Routledge.

Eisenhardt, K. M. (1989). Agency theory: An assessment and review. *Academy of Management Review, 14*(1), 57–74.

Ferraro, F., Pfeffer, J., & Sutton, R. I. (2005). Economics language and assumptions: How theories can become self-fulfilling. *Academy of Management Review, 30*(1), 8–24.

Galvin, B. M., Lange, D., & Ashforth, B. E. (2015). Narcissistic organizational identification: Seeing oneself as central to the organization's identity. *Academy of Management Review, 40*(2), 163–181.

Goncharov, I., & Peter, C. D. (2019). Does reporting transparency affect industry coordination? Evidence from the duration of international cartels, *The Accounting Review, 94*(3), 149–175.

Gottschalk, P. (2019). Convenience in criminal entrepreneurship: The case of a Norwegian hashish baron. *Deviant Behavior, 40*(3), 326–333.

Grindaker, M. H. (2011, July 12). Tiltalt for barnehagebedrageri [Indicted for kindergarten fraud]. Norwegian daily business newspaper *Dagens Næringsliv,* p. 13.

Grutle, H. F. (2010, March 16). SAS dømt for industrispionasje mot Norwegian [SAS convicted of industrial espionage against Norwegian]. *TV2*. www.tv2nyhetene.no.

Holt, R., & Cornelissen, J. (2014). Sensemaking revisited. *Management Learning, 45*(5), 525–539.

Holt, T. J., Smirnova, O., & Hutchings, A. (2016). Examining signals of trust in criminal markets online. *Journal of Cybersecurity, 2*(2), 137–145.

Holt, T. J., Strumsky, D., Smirnova, O., & Kilger, M. (2012). Examining the social networks of malware writers and hackers. *International Journal of Cyber Criminology, 6*(1), 891–903.

Horgan, S., Collier, B., Jones, R., & Shepherd, L. (2021). Re-territorialising the policing of cybercrime in the post-Covid-19 era: Towards a new vision of local democratic cyber policing. *Journal of Criminal Psychology*, published online. https://doi.org/10.1108/JCP-08-2020-034.

Høyesterett. (2019). Dom avsagt 13. mai 2019 i anke over Borgarting lagmannsretts dom 23. oktober 2018 [Verdict announced May 13, 2019 regarding appeal for Borgarting court's verdict October 23, 2018]. Høyesterett (Norwegian Supreme Court).

Hughes, J., Aycock, S., Caines, A., Buttery, P., & Hutchings, A. (2020). *Detecting trending terms in cybersecurity forum discussions*. Workshop on Noisy User-generated Text (W-NUT), virtual event. www.noisy-text.github.io.

Hutchings, A. (2014). Crime from the keyboard: Organized crime, co-offending, initiation and knowledge transmission. *Crime, Law and Social Change, 62*(1), 1–20.

Hutchings, A. (2016). Cybercrime trajectories: An integrated theory of initiation, maintenance, and desistance. In T. J. Holt (Ed.), *Crime online: Correlates, causes, and context* (pp. 117–140). Carolina Academic Press.

Hutchings, A. (2018a). Leaving on a jet plane: The trade in fraudulently obtained airline tickets. *Crime, Law and Social Change, 70*, 461–487.

Hutchings, A. (2018b). Flying in cyberspace: Policing global travel fraud. *Policing: A Journal of Policy and Practice*, 1–16. https://doi.org/10.1093/police/pay063.

Hutchings, A., & Clayton, R. (2016). Exploring the provision of online booter services. *Deviant Behavior, 37*(10), 1163–1178.

Hutchings, A., & Holt, T. J. (2016). A crime script analysis of the online stolen data market. *British Journal of Criminology, 55*, 596–614.

Hutchings, A., & Holt, T. J. (2018). Interviewing cybercrime offenders. *Journal of Qualitative Criminal Justice & Criminology, 7*(1), 75–94.

Jensen, M. C., & Meckling, W. H. (1976). Theory of the firm: Managerial behavior, agency costs and ownership structures. *Journal of Financial Economics, 3*(4), 305–360.

Judge, T. A., Piccolo, R. F., & Kosalka, T. (2009). The bright and dark sides of leader traits: A review and theoretical extension of the leader trait paradigm. *The Leadership Quarterly, 20,* 855–875.

Kammeradvokaten. (2019). *Ansvarsvurdering vedrørende sagen om svindel med tilskudsmidler – Offentlig rapport* [Assessment of liability regarding the case of fraud with benefit funds—Public report], report of investigation (163 pages), law firm Kammeradvokaten Poul Schmith.

Keyworth, M., & Wall, M. (2016, January 8). The 'bogus boss' email scam costing firms millions. *BBC.* www.bbc.com.

Kierkegaard, S. (2008). Cybering, online grooming and ageplay. *Computer Law & Security Report, 24*, 41–55.

Kleppe, M. K. (2011, December 6). Banktopp dømt til tre års fengsel [Bank top convicted to three years prison]. Norwegian daily financial newspaper *Finansavisen,* pp. 30–31.

Laudon, K. C., & Laudon, J. P. (2010). *Management information systems: Managing the digital firm* (Eleventh). Pearson Education.

Leppänen, A., Toiviainen, T., & Kankaanranta, T. (2020). From vulnerability search to a criminal case: Script analysis of an SQL injection attack. *International Journal of Cyber Criminology, 14*(1), 63–80.

Mawritz, M. B., Greenbaum, R. L., Butts, M. M., & Graham, K. A. (2017). I just can't control myself: A self-regulation perspective on the abuse of deviant employees. *Academy of Management Journal, 60*(4), 1482–1503.

Mingus, W., & Burchfield, K. B. (2012). From prison to integration: Applying modified labeling theory to sex offenders. *Criminal Justice Studies, 25*(1), 97–109.

Naheem, M. A. (2020). The agency dilemma in anti-money laundering regulation. *Journal of Money Laundering Control*, published online. https://doi.org/10.1108/JMLC-01-2016-0007.

Nhan, J., Kinkade, P., & Burns, R. (2009). Finding a pot of gold at the end of an internet rainbow: Further examination of fraudulent email solicitation. *International Journal of Cyber Criminology, 3*(1), 452–475.

Norfund. (2020, May 15). *Norfund er utsatt for alvorlig svindel* [Norfund is exposed to serious fraud]. *Norfund*. www.norfund.no.

NTB. (2012, March 1). Ektepar dømt for grov utroskap [Married couple convicted of gross infidelity]. Norwegian daily business newspaper *Aftenposten,* p. 10.

NTB. (2020, December 17). Mann dømt til fengsel for koronasvindel [Man sentenced to prison for corona fraud]. Norwegian daily business newspaper *Sunnmørsposten.* www.smp.no.

Obodaru, O. (2017). Forgone, but not forgotten: Toward a theory of forgone professional identities. *Academy of Management Journal, 60*(2), 523–553.

Ogre, M. (2020, December 17). Mann dømt for massiv koronasvindel – Økokrim tror dette bare er begynnelsen [Man convicted of massive corona fraud – Økokrim thinks this is just the beginning]. *TV2.* www.tv2.no.

Pillay, S., & Kluvers, R. (2014). An institutional theory perspective on corruption: The case of a developing democracy. *Financial Accountability & Management, 30*(1), 95–119.

PwC. (2019). *Ekstern undersøgelse af tilskudsadministrationen 1977–2018: Udarbejdet for Socialstyrelsen* [External investigation of benefits administration 1977–2018: Provided to the social security administration]. Report of investigation, 80 pages, audit firm PricewaterhouseCoopers, Copenhagen, Denmark.

PwC. (2020, June 30). *Independent assessment of the LOLC incident: Report developed for Norfund, report of investigation* (p. 34). PricewaterhouseCoopers.

Quayle, E., Vaughan, M., & Taylor, M. (2006). Sex offenders, internet child abuse images and emotional avoidance: The importance of values. *Aggression and Violent Behavior, 11,* 1–11.

Sarre, R., Lau, L. Y. C., & Chang, L. Y. C. (2018). Responding to cybercrime: Current trends. *Police Practice & Research, 19*(6), 515–518.

Srivastava, S. B., & Goldberg, A. (2017). Language as a window into culture. *California Management Review, 60*(1), 56–69.

Steel, C. M. S. (2019). Stolen identity valuation and market evolution on the dark web. *International Journal of Cyber Criminology, 13*(1), 70–83.

United Nations. (2008). *United Nations e-government survey 2008.* Division for Public Administration and Development Management, United Nations.

Valvik, M. E., & Strømsheim, G. (2010, November 10). SAS dømt til å betale 570 millioner i bot [SAS convicted to pay 570 million kroner in fine]. Norwegian daily newspaper *Aftenposten.* www.aftenposten.no.

Vu, A. V., Hughes, J., Pete, I., Collier, B., Chua, Y. T., Shumailov, I., & Hutchings, A. (2020, October). Turning up the dial: The evolution of a cybercrime market through set-up, stable, and Covid-19 eras, IMC'20. In *Proceedings of the ACM Internet Measurement Conference* (pp. 551–566). https://doi.org/10.1145/3419394.3423636.

Walsh, J. N. (2020). Identifying and categorizing knowledge reuse activities in electronic repositories. *Journal of Information and Knowledge Management Systems*, published online. https://doi.org/10.1108/VJIKMS-04-2020-0066.

Weick, K. E., Sutcliffe, K. M., & Obstfeld, D. (2005). Organizing and the process of sensemaking. *Organization Science, 16*(4), 409–421.

Welter, F., Baker, T., Audretsch, D. B., & Gartner, W.B. (2017). Everyday entrepreneurship: A call for entrepreneurship research to embrace entrepreneurial diversity. *Entrepreneurship: Theory and Practice, 41*(3), 323–347.

Whittaker, J. (2004). *The cyberspace handbook.* Routledge, Taylor & Francis Group.

Williams, J. W. (2008). The lessons of 'Enron'—Media accounts, corporate crimes, and financial markets. *Theoretical Criminology, 12*(4), 471–499.

Yip, M., Webber, C., & Shadbolt, N. (2013). Trust among cybercriminals? Carding forums, uncertainty and implications for policing. *Policing & Society, 23*(4), 516–539.

7

Policing Cybercrime

Policing is an organized form of order maintenance, rule enforcement, crime investigation, and crime prevention (White, 2020). Policing has to be based on a police strategy concerned with choices to reach policing goals (Ortmeier & Davis, 2012: 29):

> A policing strategy is an approach to delivering police services based on specific assumptions about matters such as how police and community residents should interact, what causes crime to worsen, and how technology might be leveraged. Each strategy has unique advantages and disadvantages. Some strategies are mutually exclusive, while others complement or support one another.

The public expects law enforcement officers to be physically fit. It is a logical assumption that strength and stamina are necessary requirements for the job. Clearly, policing can be a physically demanding job. Officers encounter instances in which strength and endurance are an advantage. However, Bissett et al. (2012) raised the question, how important are physical strength and fitness to the job? Algarni (2013: 511)

P. Gottschalk and C. Hamerton, *White-Collar Crime Online*,
https://doi.org/10.1007/978-3-030-82132-6_7

redefined the same question as a contradictory characteristic of a late-modern crime control framework “in which expressive gestures, intended to demonstrate visibility that the sovereign state is addressing crime, sit alongside pragmatism and adaptation, with their emphasis on prevention and partnership”.

In policing white-collar crime, financial knowledge and business insights are more important than running or fighting skills. Relevant knowledge is based on criminology, psychology, sociology, and organizational behavior. Knowledge is applied in the value configuration of a value shop to solve crime cases. The value shop is an iterative rather than a sequential problem-solving technique. Knowledge sharing and knowledge development are of key importance in the value shop. Knowledge management is as important to investigating and preventing crime as it is to any other public or private sector organization in terms of improving performance (Collier, 2006).

In policing white-collar crime online, technology knowledge is certainly more important than running and fighting skills. As suggested in this book, the offender-based perspective is more important than the offense-based perspective on white-collar crime, as prosecuting offenders for offenses is the result of successful police investigations. Therefore, technology knowledge in policing white-collar offenders online should concentrate on offenders’ use of various tools and systems to commit and conceal financial crime.

Case Study of Global Travel Fraud

Hutchings (2018a) examined the trade of fraudulently obtained airline tickets. She followed up by examining how law enforcement could fight global travel fraud (Hutchings, 2018b). White-collar offenders online are in the business of obtaining airline tickets and selling them to travelers. The communication between those obtaining tickets fraudulently and those traveling on the tickets takes place not necessarily on black markets. The white-collar offenders may seemingly operate a travel agency where they advertise airline tickets around 20–75% of market price. The fake travel agency is an outside business that victimizes airlines by white-collar crime.

Previously, the tickets were typically obtained using stolen credit card information and online credentials. More common today are phishing techniques to obtain credentials for global distribution system companies, which provide booking services to travel agents. Other methods to obtain tickets illegally include the use of compromised loyalty point accounts, compromised business accounts, identity fraud, and voucher fraud (Hutchings, 2018b).

Hutchings (2018a: 462) found that some policing currently takes place in relation to travel fraud:

> Most notably, Europol runs 'Global Airline Action Days' on a regular basis, to identify and detain those travelling on tickets purchased using stolen credit card details. These operations, which are run in cooperation with the airline, travel, and payment card industries, have resulted in 2090 suspicious transactions being identified, and 1078 people being detained since 2013. Europol allege those arrested have been travelling in order to commit other offences, including trafficking of human beings, illegal immigration, smuggling of goods, drug trafficking, fraud, cybercrime, and terrorism.

However, most incidents left it unknown to Europol where the tickets were traded, although the police organization is aware of fake online travel agencies. Arrested travelers are rarely charged with crime. There are thus a number of challenges that the travel industry and law enforcement need to overcome in order better to police travel fraud (Hutchings, 2018b: 12):

- The low dollar amount for one-off purchases. This has been noted in the forums, where actors reassure each other that the risk is low for this reason. Some participants said that they could only get law enforcement involved when losses started to reach multiple hundreds of thousands of dollars.
- Fraud is not seen as a priority for law enforcement. Furthermore, adding complex international aspects can make investigations unattractive to pursue.

- A lack of international contacts. Like many interactions in life, having trusted relationships can take communications easier. However, due to the global nature of travel fraud, making connections with law enforcement all around the globe, with different time zones and languages, can prove difficult. While airlines advised that they often have good relationships with their local law enforcement agencies, this is more difficult in non-local jurisdictions.

In addition, Hutchings (2018b) mentions that some policing agencies are strictly local, local jurisdictions vary, awareness about travel fraud is low, and charging travelers can be problematic. There is also seldom any action taken after a flight has already occurred. In our convenience perspective of online offenders, many police agencies seem reluctant and incompetent to trace fake travel agencies and charge their owners and executives.

Some policing agencies are embedded in social, cultural, and institutional structures that favor traditional street crime to the detriment of white-collar crime generally and white-collar crime online particularly. Masculine power and physical action dominate many police agencies. Driving a police car is more exciting than sitting in front of a computer screen (Henry et al., 2018). It all starts with those applying to the police university colleges who typically are more interested than other people in guns and other arms.

Law Enforcement Approaches

As argued by Webster and Drew (2017), traditional, reactive law enforcement responses to crime typically involve obtaining details of the crime, usually provided by a complainant (victim), and preparation of a crime report. Instead, they suggest proactive law enforcement to identify and interrupt victimization. The term proactive is used to refer to the interruption of online victimization and thereby reducing potential harm. The term is not used to refer to prevention of initial online victimization. Proactive interventions are those designed to reduce the duration and severity of victimization, once identified.

Paek et al. (2020: 878) argue that policing cybercrime is a formidable task:

> Aside from a lack of a universal definition of cybercrime, the ambiguity of existing laws makes it difficult to punish illegal online activities. Furthermore, there is a dearth of police personnel who can conduct cybercrime investigation. Culturally, as a conservative organization with a hierarchical command structure and a strong emphasis on street crimes, the police tend to place a low priority on cybercrime cases, which explains the few resources being allotted for the online offenses as well as the low-level awareness and knowledge about cybercrime investigation.

The proactive approach suggested by Webster and Drew (2017) is followed up by Drew (2020), who argues that there is strong and urgent need to devise different ways to combat cybercrime and move much more toward a crime prevention focus that seeks to prevent victimization from occurring, constituting a primary crime prevention approach. Rather than waiting for an incident to occur, where the offender is usually impossible to bring to justice, the proactive approach suggests education for self-protection by potential victims. The law enforcement approach should thus be in the form of cybercrime prevention initiatives. Prevention themes include causing an increase in the required effort for crime to be committed and concealed, causing an increase in the risks surrounding the offense, causing a reduction in the rewards of committing the offence, causing a reduction in the provocations, and causing a removal of excuses. Prevention communication channels from the police to potential victims include social media (Procter et al., 2013; Williams et al., 2013).

While the proactive approach seems reasonable, white-collar offenses will still occur and will need reactive law enforcement response in terms of investigation, prosecution, and conviction. A possible interpretation of the emphasis on the proactive approach might be that if law enforcement agents are successful in preventing incidents of white-collar crime online, then they also have better and more relevant knowledge to investigate when actual white-collar offenses occur.

Koziarski and Lee (2020) suggest a law enforcement approach of linking the paradigm of evidence-based policing to cybercrime. They describe how the paradigm can assist, develop, and improve factors associated with policing cybercrime. Evidence-based policing is a paradigm where police detectives work together with academics to create and use the best available evidence to inform police practice. Evidence is anything that you see, experience, read, or are told that represent proof of something is true or has already happened. Evidence is something which shows that something else exists or is true. Proof is the evidence or argument of real existence or truth. The practice of hot spots policing is an example of evidence-based policing where experts concentrate their attention on digital locations that document high concentrations of cybercrime.

Koziarski and Lee (2020) argue that having a short, random, and intermittent police presence within crime hot spots can significantly lower crime and disorder both within and around the digital area. Evidence-based policing can be supplemented by problem-oriented policing where problems are diagnosed and solved in digital areas with comparatively high levels of crime. It is a matter of generating rigorous, clear, transparent, peer-reviewed, and replicable knowledge about white-collar crime hotspots. It is a matter of offending characteristics and behavioral traits by white-collar offenders online. In the end, it is a matter of effective criminalization and prosecution of cybercrime and its offenders.

Nowacki and Willits (2020) studied organizational success factors for dedication of specialist personnel to cybercrime response in police agencies. They found that larger agencies, agencies whose officers engage in more non-routine tasks, and agencies governed by an active collective bargaining agreement are more likely to dedicate specific resources to cybercrime. Furthermore, dedication of specific personnel to cybercrime was higher in agencies with more hierarchical layers, agencies that utilize more specialization, and agencies that make greater use of civilian employees as experts.

Burruss et al. (2020: 110) studied self-perceptions of English and Wales constables and sergeants' preparedness for online crime. Only 39% felt prepared, while 61% felt unprepared:

> The typical respondent was male (73 percent), a constable rather than sergeant (77.5 percent, and was between 35 and 44 years old (39 percent). A minority of respondents had received computer training regarding cybercrime (39 percent) or had responded frequently to cybercrime (47 percent). Interestingly, only a small percent had reported responding never or rarely to cybercrime (6.9 and 13 percent, respectively).

While cybercrime experienced an ascending position in national and international security agendas worldwide more than a decade ago (Wall & Williams, 2013), the associated strategies were not really implemented. Implementation is a procedure directed at installing planned change in an organization as well as the extent to which an innovation becomes ingrained within organizational behaviors. Barriers to implementation typically include resistance to change, lack of project champions, lack of people involvement and empowerment, and lack of leadership. While often emphasized, lack of resources is typically an excuse rather than a barrier.

This book frequently mentions the example of identity crime as an online white-collar offense. Identity crime is concerned with the theft of identities, fraud using stolen identities, as well as fraud using false identities. When policing identity crime, Wall (2013: 451) suggests a non-routine practice:

> Non-routine events include those created by the Internet, such as cross-border investigations, or types of deviant behavior not normally regarded as criminal by police officers.

This is in contrast to routine policing, where routine events are important in the development of police occupational culture, because they generate stories that are told to colleagues. Similarly, officers who are involved in non-routine practice need a terminology to generate stories that are told to colleagues. Just like data nerds are difficult to understand, so are cybercrime experts as long as they do not apply common language in their communication with colleagues. Non-routine practitioners in law enforcement need to translate the online crime terminology (Hughes et al., 2020) into police language to enable knowledge transfer and knowledge sharing.

Law enforcement approaches have not spread evenly across the wide spectrum of cybercrime categories. Rather, the dominant structure and pattern of policing has been concerned with Internet-based sex offences (Yar, 2013: 482):

> It is argued that the policing of Internet sex offences occupies an anomalous position, as compared to other forms of online offending.

White-collar crime online has certainly not been at the core of law enforcement attention. Rather, online victimization of minors both domestically and abroad still has very high priority in law enforcement against cybercrime. Yar (2013) finds that the reasons for this kind of police priority are the intense public concern, anxiety, and recurrent moral outrage. The policing approach toward sex offenses is typically to monitor social networking platforms and social media generally (Wall & Williams, 2013; Wilson-Kovacs, 2020; Yar, 2013), which seem irrelevant for the policing of white-collar offenders online.

Yip et al. (2013: 533) discuss implications for policing of carding forums for underground marked services:

> In essence, the market will fail in the absence of trust as transaction costs are too high. Therefore, it is vital for the law enforcement community to prevent cybercriminals from developing trust and particular attention should be placed on preventing cybercriminals from forming initial trust in the first instance.

Yip et al. (2013) suggest undercover agents, severe sentencing, and taking down carding forums. Since forums often are the primary facilitators for the development of trust among cybercriminals, it might be a feasible law enforcement approach to treat forum take-downs as priorities.

Digital Forensics Intelligence

The gathering of criminal intelligence is essential for all policing of cybercrime. It is central to national as well as transnational and international policing, where the latter is police cooperation and common action between officials and law enforcement agents who have their authority mainly in their own states. While transnational policing is law enforcement across borders where the focus is on cooperation, international policing involves the establishment and development of police organizations such as Europol and Interpol (Kowalick et al., 2018).

Criminal intelligence in cyberspace is dependent on digital forensics (Wilson-Kovacs, 2020: 77):

> It encompasses the extraction, examination, and interpretation of data from a range of personal and interconnected devices, including mobile phones, computers, navigation systems, gaming consoles, and increasingly, the Internet of Trings (IoT). It also extends to communication information and metadata from remove sources (e.g., websites, social media and IP logs) to obtain intelligence for ongoing investigations and provide evidence for criminal proceedings. Once confined to fraud inquiries and child sexual abuse cases, digital forensics has become key to the future of crime investigation. Critical to supplying evidence for most types of offences, it can help establish sequences of events, patterns of behavior and alibis. Consequently, law enforcement agencies have encountered an unprecedented pressure to deliver timely and effective digital examinations.

Holt et al. (2020) studied digital evidence recognition among officers and troopers in a sample of a state police force. Most respondents identified appropriate devices and locations where digital evidence may be stored on suspects and victims in a scenario call for service. The digital evidence awareness was high among respondents who recognized their own dependence on forensic evidence when investigating online incidents. The majority of respondents (88%) knew who to contact if they needed assistance with digital evidence in the field.

de Paoli et al. (2020) argue that part of the challenge of tackling cybercrime is that there are insufficient police officers with the appropriate investigative skills in digital forensics. They found that the forensic challenge thus related mainly to the capabilities of law enforcement to tackle cybercrime. As their recommendation, the need for increasing the numbers of personnel with a computer science and cybersecurity background may be most met by mixing civilian expertise with police officers. Similarly, Buil-Gil et al. (2021) recommend private businesses to invest in inhouse cybersecurity human resources and enhance employees' online self-protection by providing cybersecurity training, rather than just basic software protection and guidance about strong passwords.

Law Enforcement Knowledge Work

In a study of specialist police cybercrime units in Australia, Harkin et al. (2018) found that there was low institutional priority for policing cybercriminals. Many specialists suggested that the required skills in the units were not matched with the task of cyber policing. The staff of the cyber squads appeared rather pessimistic about the ability of the squads to respond to the challenges of cybercrime. 71% disagreed that they were adequately prepared. Only 10% agreed that they were adequately prepared. The problem was compounded by a feeling that training was inadequate for the nature of the work. There was a lack of education in computer science, internet, and criminality.

Some officers reported to Harkin et al. (2018) that various attempts to train staff in cybercrime units had taken place, but it was generally regarded as inadequate. Cyber squads faced the challenge of brain drain where skilled detectives left for the private sector. Cyber competence seemed harder to acquire when compared to drug squads, counterterrorism, or sexual assault units, for example. Furthermore, cyber expertise was found to have a shorter lifespan, where the nature of technological change creates pressures for renewal and updating of knowledge to reflect the rapidly evolving nature of cyber offending.

Similar to the findings in Australia are findings about police capability rather than police capacity in the United Kingdom (Loveday, 2017: 105):

> More worrying was the discovery that police forces almost universally were unable to provide an effective breakdown of their own workforce capability in understanding 'what their people can do and what skills they have and need to have. The evident failure by police to develop any appropriate capability and force-wide capability profile was highlighted in Her Majesty's Chief Inspector of Constabulary report. Forces were also unable to describe accurately the current strengths or weaknesses in their skills, either across the whole workforce or by rank or grade.

According to Popham et al. (2020), Canada's responses to cybercrime have contributed to insufficient guidelines for its policing, leaving many law enforcement agencies and their officers uncertain about strategy or responses. The challenge in Australia, Canada, the United Kingdom, and most other countries globally is the lack of cybercrime strategy, knowledge capability, and knowledge management as discussed in the next chapter.

Law enforcement knowledge work regarding white-collar offenders online is influenced by both organizational culture and organizational structure. The police culture can be traditional or innovative, cooperative or competitive, and transparent or closed. The police structure can be hierarchical or flat, divided into generalists or specialists, and according to geography or crime categories. Many countries have a combination of geography and national structure. For example, Norwegian police is organized in police districts along the geographical axis. To compensate for the lack of expertise and capability in the districts, there are some national agencies. In the area of cybercrime, the national criminal investigation service (Kripos) has established a national cybercrime center (NC3), which is presented on the internet (www.politiet.no):

> The NC3 will assist the Norwegian police in investigations and further develop police cybercrime expertise. By preventing, uncovering, and investigating threats and crime, the cybercrime center will help make digital space safer.

However, Kripos is not concerned with financial crime. They are only concerned with organized crime. A completely different national unit, the Norwegian national authority for investigation and prosecution of economic and environmental crime (Økokrim), is concerned with financial crime generally and white-collar crime particularly, but they have no cybercrime unit.

The office of the auditor general of Norway emphasizes in their report the lack of knowledge in Norwegian police when it comes to investigations of online financial crime (Riksrevisjonen, 2021: 5):

> The police's ability to detect and solve ICT crime has clear weaknesses that are serious overall. The police lack competence in the investigation of ICT crime. The measures to strengthen the police's capacity to investigate ICT crime are not keeping pace with the challenges. Weaknesses in support systems lead to inefficient use of resources and lack of clarification of ICT crime. Lack of coordination between police districts presents challenges for solving ICT crime. Challenges in international cooperation contribute to low resolution of ICT crime. The police lack an overview of ICT crime. The police give little priority to the detection and investigation of pure ICT crime. Tips and intelligence on internet-related sexual abuses increases and challenges the capacity of the police. The police lack the capacity to meet developments in economic ICT crime. ICT crime has to a small extent been a priority by the Norwegian police directorate and the ministry of justice and emergency preparedness.

In a study of technological innovation in the national police of the Netherlands, Ernst et al. (2021: 12) found that innovation processes within the police organization are often inhibited by organizational factors, whereas social factors can stimulate and promote these processes:

> New and innovative technology is often already developed and ready for use by the police organization but getting the police to actually start using the technology proves to be difficult and depends on many social and organizational factors that are of decisive importance, as shown in this (ongoing) study. Inhibiting factors are found predominantly in the organizational context and promoting factors in the social context.

All the above-mentioned shortcomings in policing cybercrime contribute to the convenience for white-collar offenders online. de Paoli et al.

(2020) summarize some of the shortcomings as the knowledge challenge, the legal challenge, the forensic challenge, the lack of definition and taxonomy for cybercrime, the lack of recording of cybercrime, the lack of international cooperation, the lack of police expertise, the lack of training, and the lack of equipment and funding.

References

Algarni, A. F. (2013). Policing internet fraud in Saudi Arabia: Expressive gestures or adaptive strategies? *Policing & Society, 23*(4), 498–515.

Bissett, D., Bissett, J., & Snell, C. (2012). Physical agility tests and fitness standards: Perceptions of law enforcement officers. *Police Practice and Research, 13*(3), 208–223.

Buil-Gil, D., Miro-Llinares, F., Moneva, A., Kemp, S., & Diaz-Castano, N. (2021). Cybercrime and shifts in opportunities during Covid-19: A preliminary analysis in the UK. *European Societies*, published online. https://doi.org/10.1080/14616696.2020.1804973.

Burruss, G., Howell, C. J., Bossler, A., & Holt, T. J. (2020). Self-perceptions of English and Welsh constables and sergeants preparedness for online crime: A latent analysis. *Policing: An International Journal, 43*(1), 105–119.

Collier, P. M. (2006, April). Policing and the intelligent application of knowledge. *Public Money & Management*, 109–116.

de Paoli, S., Johnstone, J., Coull, N., Ferguson, I., Sinclair, G., Tomkins, P., Brown, M., & Martin, R. (2020). A qualitative exploratory study of the knowledge, forensic, and legal challenges from the perspective of police cybercrime specialists. *Policing: A Journal of Policy and Practice*, published online. https://doi.org/10.1093/police/paaa027.

Drew, J. M. (2020). A study of cybercrime victimization and prevention: Exploring the use of online crime prevention behaviors and strategies. *Journal of Criminological Research, Policy and Practice, 6*(1), 17–33.

Ernst, S., Veen, H., & Kop, N. (2021). Technological innovation in a police organization: Lessons learned from the National Police of the Netherlands. *Policing: A Journal of Policy and Practice*, published online. https://doi.org/10.1093/police/paab003.

Harkin, D., Whelan, C., & Chang, L. (2018). The challenges facing specialist police cyber-crime units: An empirical analysis. *Police Practice & Research, 19*(6), 519–536.

Henry, N., Flynn, A., & Powell, A. (2018). Policing image-based sexual abuse: Stakeholder perspectives. *Police Practice & Research, 19*(6), 565–581.

Holt, T. J., Clevenger, S., & Navarro, J. (2020). Exploring digital evidence recognition among officers and troopers in a sample of a state police force. *Policing: An International Journal, 43*(1), 91–103.

Hughes, J., Aycock, S., Caines, A., Buttery, P., & Hutchings, A. (2020). *Detecting trending terms in cybersecurity forum discussions.* Workshop on Noisy User-generated Text (W-NUT), virtual event. www.noisy-text.github.io.

Hutchings, A. (2018a). Leaving on a jet plane: The trade in fraudulently obtained airline tickets. *Crime, Law and Social Change, 70*, 461–487.

Hutchings, A. (2018b). Flying in cyberspace: Policing global travel fraud. *Policing: A Journal of Policy and Practice*, 1–16. https://doi.org/10.1093/police/pay063.

Kowalick, P., Connery, D., & Sarre, R. (2018). Intelligence-sharing in the context of policing transnational serious and organized crime: A note on policy and practice in an Australian setting. *Police Practice & Research, 19*(6), 596–608.

Koziarski, J., & Lee, J. R. (2020). Connecting evidence-based policing and cybercrime. *Policing: An International Journal, 43*(1), 198–211.

Loveday, B. (2017). Still plodding along? The police response to the changing profile of crime in England and Wales. *International Journal of Police Science & Management, 19*(2), 101–109.

Nowacki, J., & Willits, D. (2020). An organizational approach to understanding police response to cybercrime. *Policing: An International Journal, 43*(1), 63–76.

Ortmeier, P. J., & Davis, J. J. (2012). *Police administration: A leadership approach.* McGraw Hill.

Paek, S. Y., Nalla, M. K., & Lee, J. (2020). Determinants of police officers' support for the public–private partnerships (PPPs) in policing cyberspace. *Policing: An International Journal, 43*(5), 877–892.

Popham, J., McCluskey, M., & Ouellet, M. (2020). Exploring police-reported cybercrime in Canada: Variation and correlates. *Policing: An International Journal, 43*(1), 35–48.

Procter, R., Crump, J., Karstedt, S., Voss, A., & Cantijoch, M. (2013). Reading the riots: What were the police doing in Twitter? *Policing & Society, 23*(4), 413–436.

Riksrevisjonen. (2021). *Riksrevisjonens undersøkelse av politiets innsats mot kriminalitet ved bruk av IKT* [The office of the Auditor General's investigation of police efforts against crime through the use of ICT] (147 Pages). The Office of the Auditor General of Norway, Oslo, Norway. www.riksrevisjonen.no.

Wall, D. S. (2013). Policing identity crimes. *Policing & Society, 23*(4), 437–460.

Wall, D. S., & Williams, M. L. (2013). Policing cybercrime: Networked and social media technologies and the challenges for policing. *Policing & Society, 23*(4), 409–412.

Webster, J., & Drew, J. M. (2017). Policing advance fee fraud (AFF): Experiences of fraud detectives using a victim-focused approach. *International Journal of Police Science & Management, 19*(1), 39–53.

White, A. (2020). What is the privatization of policing? *Policing: A Journal of Policy and Practice, 14*(3), 766–777.

Williams, M. L., Edwards, A., Housley, W., Burnap, P., Rana, O., Avis, N., Morgan, J., & Sloan, L. (2013). Policing cyber-neighbourhoods: Tension monitoring and social media networks. *Policing & Society, 23*(4), 461–481.

Wilson-Kovacs, D. (2020). Effective resource management in digital forensics: An exploratory analysis of triage practices in four English constabularies. *Policing: An International Journal, 43*(1), 77–90.

Yar, M. (2013). The policing of Internet sex offences: Pluralised governance versus hierarchies of standing. *Policing & Society, 23*(4), 482–497.

Yip, M., Webber, C., & Shadbolt, N. (2013). Trust among cybercriminals? Carding forums, uncertainty and implications for policing. *Policing & Society, 23*(4), 516–539.

8

Enforcement Knowledge

Law enforcement is not just a matter of policing as discussed in the previous chapter. Cybercrime is a concern of national states as well as international organizations. White-collar offenders online are business-people on the wrong side of the law. The case of fraudulent travel agencies who trade in airline tickets illustrates the helplessness of police agencies such as the European Europol in tracing offenders and not just victimized travelers (Hutchings, 2018a, 2018b). The knowledge asymmetry between online offenders and law enforcement agencies does not exist because online offenders are advanced in the way they commit and conceal crime. Rather, online offenders operate in an underworld that people do not understand. The lack of understanding is not mainly caused by complicated programming and infrastructure, smart attacks, and advanced money laundering, but rather caused by simple reasons such as terminology and lack of basic intelligence. Just like white-collar offenders offline use a language that potential whistleblowers may not understand (Ferraro et al., 2005; Holt & Cornelissen, 2014; Mawritz et al., 2017; Srivastava & Goldberg, 2017; Weick et al., 2005), white-collar crime online is associated with a terminology that potential victims and notifiers may not understand. It might not be the technology itself

P. Gottschalk and C. Hamerton, *White-Collar Crime Online*,
https://doi.org/10.1007/978-3-030-82132-6_8

that is complicated, but rather the terminology that represents a barrier to insights into cybercrime (Hughes et al., 2020).

The lack of understanding is also caused by the focus among researchers, politicians, and the media. The focus is on victims and crime. Almost every incident of cybercrime is reported as an action that has harmed somebody. Little or no attempt seems to be taken by researchers, law enforcement staff, and public administrators in tracing and understanding offenders. An admirable exception is the Computer Laboratory at the University of Cambridge. The laboratory updates its own Cambridge Computer Crime Database and publishes empirical work that contributes to our understanding of not just cybercrime but also cybercriminals (e.g., Collier et al., 2020; Hughes et al., 2020; Vu et al., 2020). This book contributes by emphasizing a number of case studies of external offenders as well as internal offenders online.

Theoretical Knowledge Requirements

Researchers need to frame their studies in terms of theoretical perspectives and crime hypotheses. As suggested by Barney (2018), a theoretical contribution is part of an ongoing conversation in the literature. The conversation in this book is concerned with white-collar offenders online as a phenomenon and its occurrences as incidents in different situations. One unresolved theoretical issue related to white-collar offenders online addressed in this book is crime convenience relative to legal means of reaching desired goals and ambitions for privileged individuals and organizations. This unresolved issue is important, as both prevention and detection of white-collar offenders rests on a relevant understanding of their motives, opportunities, and behaviors.

As argued by Haveman et al. (2019: 241), "it is theory that gives meaning to empirical results". Insights into white-collar crime occurrences are dependent on theory that guides experts and specialists to what questions to ask and tells why they are important. Theory provides a discipline of reasoning about occurrences that otherwise would end up as special cases of practice in the minds of observers. Rather than the case-by-case surprise of white-collar crime incidents often portrait in the media, the theoretical approach identifies patterns in the total set of incidents.

Researchers at the Computer Laboratory at the University of Cambridge apply a variety of theoretical and methodological approaches in their studies. Caines et al. (2018), Hughes et al. (2020) as well as Vu et al. (2020) applied statistical modeling approaches to classify forum posts, to identify trending terms, and to analyze the economic and social characteristics of the underground market, respectively. Hutchings and Holt (2016) and Leontiadis and Hutchings (2015) applied crime script analysis of the online stolen data market and the crime commission process in the illicit online prescription drug trade, respectively.

This book suggests the theory of convenience at a theoretical lens for studying white-collar offenders online. The theory is an umbrella for various perspectives on offender motive, offender opportunity, and offender willingness.

In the motive dimension, theoretical perspectives beyond greed (Bucy et al., 2008; Goldstraw-White, 2012; Hamilton & Micklethwait, 2006) should be understood. Important theoretical perspectives within individual possibilities themes for motive include the desire to satisfy the need for acclaim as a narcissist (Chatterjee & Pollock, 2017), restore the perception of equity and equality (Leigh et al., 2010), and satisfy the desire to help others as social concern (Agnew, 2014). Important theoretical perspectives within corporate possibilities themes for motive include the desire to reach business objectives that justify means (Jonnergård et al., 2010) and enjoy mutual benefits in exchange relationships (Huang & Knight, 2017).

Important theoretical perspectives within individual threat themes for motive include the desire to avoid loss of self-esteem after organizational failure (Crosina & Pratt, 2019), remove strain, pain, and uncertainty (Langton & Piquero, 2007), and avoid falling from position in the privileged elite (Piquero, 2012). Important theoretical perspectives within corporate threat themes for motive include the desire to avoid corporate collapse and bankruptcy (Kang & Thosuwanchot, 2017), adapt to profitable criminal market forces to stay in business (Leonard & Weber, 1970), and gain acceptance in profitable criminal networks and cartels to stay in business (Goncharov & Peter, 2019).

It is important to understand the motives of white-collar offenders online to apply relevant policing approaches. An example from street crime offline can illustrate the importance of contingent policing approaches. Rape was for a long time considered a sexual offense. However, Norwegian police discovered that it frequently was motivated by the desire for power and control rather than sexual satisfaction. In a country with a high degree of equality among genders (Benson & Gottschalk, 2015), there are some minority groups where gender equality is not the case. Therefore, prevention of rape focuses on gender equality issues rather than sexual issues. Similarly, for example, potential white-collar offenders online who have a motive of restoring the perception of equity and equality by financial crime (Leigh et al., 2010) might be prevented from offending by compensation efforts, especially in family-owned firms (Gottschalk & Asting, 2019, 2020). Furthermore, as mentioned in the previous chapter, prevention experience can help develop investigation skills. A possible interpretation of the emphasis on the proactive approach might thus be that if law enforcement agents are successful in preventing incidents of white-collar crime online, based on insights regarding motives, then they also have better and more relevant knowledge to investigate when actual white-collar offenses occur.

In the opportunity dimension, theoretical perspectives beyond opportunity creation by entrepreneurship (McElwee & Smith, 2015; Ramoglou & Tsang, 2016) should be understood. The lack of oversight and guardianship both at the victim site (Berghoff, 2018) and in law enforcement (de Paoli et al., 2020) contribute to convenience for white-collar offenders online. Other important theoretical perspectives within the opportunity structure to commit crime include language and terminology that people do not understand (Ferraro et al., 2005; Hughes et al., 2020), and the fact that some white-collar offenders can be elite members who are too big to fail and too powerful to jail (Pontell et al., 2014). Furthermore, the frequently missing evidence of the individual offender who operated an identified computer terminal enables the blame game by misleading attribution to others (Eberly et al., 2011).

Executive language and terminology, elite membership, and blame game are elements of convenience based on status of the offender. Status is an individual's social rank within a formal or informal hierarchy, or the person's relative standing along a valued social dimension. Status exists both in the real world and the virtual world. Status is the extent to which an individual is respected and admired by others, and status is the outcome of a subjective assessment process (McClean et al., 2018). High-status individuals enjoy greater respect and deference from, as well as power and influence over, those who are positioned lower in the social hierarchy (Kakkar et al., 2020).

Furthermore, in the opportunity dimension, white-collar offenders online have legitimate access to their own premises and systems from which they initiate an attack. If they attack from the inside, then they will typically have generalized access to premises and systems (Benson & Simpson, 2018) as well as specialized access in routine activities (Cohen & Felson, 1979). In addition, internal white-collar offenders online will have legitimate access to strategic resources (Adler & Kwon, 2002) that are valuable in wrongdoing activities.

Just like there are different approaches to policing high-ranking versus low-status offenders offline, there is a difference between people in the center of an online network versus people in the periphery of the network. White-collar offenders online may typically have a number of fences and gatekeepers depending on their status in the underworld. Identifying the network structure and the roles at different nodes in the network is a challenging task in cyber investigations.

In the willingness dimension, theoretical perspectives beyond lack of self-control (Gottfredson & Hirschi, 1990) or psychological deviance (Chatterjee & Pollock, 2017) should be understood. It is too simple to classify someone as a narcissist (Galvin et al., 2015; Zhu & Chen, 2015). Piquero et al. (2019) found no support for the suggestion of psychopathic traits among white-collar offenders, since individuals with adverse, anti-social behavior are unlikely to be able to climb to and stay in positions of power and trust. However, Pusch and Holtfreter (2020) found that negative personality traits, negative personal morality, lack of positive personality traits, and lack of self-control significantly and negatively predict white-collar offending. Dark personality traits may thus exist in many forms among elite members in society (Kholin et al., 2020).

Important willingness themes include rationality and learning. Rationality is based on the perception of benefits exceeding costs (Pratt &

Cullen, 2005), where there is little or no perceived deterrence effect (Comey, 2009). Learning can derive from differential association with others (Sutherland, 1983) and alignment to authority as obedience (Baird & Zelin, 2009). Other willingness themes include sensation seeking to experience adventure (Craig & Piquero, 2017) and deviant identity labeling (Mingus & Burchfield, 2012). The willingness themes mentioned so far indicate that the offender was aware of wrongdoing and committed crime as a choice.

Willingness can also stem from lack of awareness of wrongdoing or guilt. The perception of innocence might stem from moral justification of deviant acts (Schnatterly et al., 2018), upper echelon information selection (Gamache & McNamara, 2019), disappointing work context causes entitlement (Nichol, 2019), and blaming peer pressure (Gao & Zhang, 2019). The perception of innocence might also stem from application of neutralization techniques (Sykes & Matza, 1957) and sliding on the slippery slope (Welsh et al., 2014).

Theoretical knowledge about willingness of white-collar offenders can help law enforcement detect, investigate, and prosecute online crime. For example, the rational choice offender is influenced by perceived detection risk, while the innocent offender is influenced by perceived guilt.

Empirical Knowledge Requirements

Storytelling is a common mechanism for empirical knowledge transfer in policing. More experienced police officers tell less experienced colleagues about cases they have investigated in the past. However, empirical knowledge requirements in policing white-collar crime online are asking for more than just incidents experienced by officers in the past. There is a need for statistical analyses as well as intelligence studies. While statistical analysis is concerned with data from the past, intelligence studies are concerned with future incidents that might occur.

A statistical analysis of white-collar offenders online is to the best of the author's knowledge still not completed by any researcher so far. The author has only completed a statistical analysis of white-collar offenders that were offline, which might inspire future online studies. The offline study is a result of a statistical analysis of 405 convicted white-collar offenders in Norway from 2009 to 2015. There were 375 men and 30 women among the 405 white-collar criminals. The fraction of women was thus only 7.4%. The gender perspective is important, as women have slightly different motives, opportunities, and willingness compared to men (Benson & Gottschalk, 2015).

In the database with 405 offenders, the average age when crime was committed was 44 years old. The youngest was 21 years, while the oldest was 73 years. There was close to a normal distribution among offenders, which implies that there were many more criminals in their forties than criminals in other age groups. A total of five offenders committed crime after they had passed the age of 70 years. They were a fish exporter, a chief executive officer, a manager, a chairman of the board, and one retired person. The youngest offenders were a kebab shopper, an heir, a reality celebrity, a painter, and a self-employed person.

Average age at final conviction in court was 49 years. This implies that it took on average five years from criminal act to court ruling. The youngest convict was 25 years, while the oldest was 77 years. The oldest was Odd Arthur Olsen (born 1933) in the Swaco case. He was the father of Olav Olsen (born 1958). The father produced fictive invoices from his company for corruption payments and thereby contributed to money laundering of 7 million Norwegian kroner, which is the equivalent of eight hundred thousand US dollars (Gulating, 2009). The son was a warehouse manager at the oil service company Swaco. The father was sentenced to almost 3 years in prison, while the son was sentenced to almost 5 years. A reasonable hypothesis is that online offenders are younger than offline offenders.

Most of the criminals worked in privileged positions in the private business sector. Few criminals had positions in the public sector. There were 374 criminals from the private sector and 31 criminals from the public sector. Hence, public sector criminals represented only 7.7% of all criminals in the database.

Most offenders committed occupational crime rather than corporate crime. The organizational dimension of white-collar crime becomes particularly evident when financial crime is committed to benefit the organization rather than the individual. This is called corporate crime as opposed to occupational crime for personal benefit (Bittle & Hébert, 2020).

The most frequent victim was the offenders' own employers. Banks, tax authorities, and customers followed as victim categories. Fraud was the most frequent crime, followed by manipulation, corruption, and theft.

Much more statistical results could be presented here. However, it was the idea of statistical analysis to satisfy empirical knowledge requirements that is on the agenda here, rather than the specific database from Norway.

Intelligence studies are concerned with information about potential future incidents. Criminal intelligence is information compiled, analyzed, and disseminated in an effort to anticipate criminal activity. Information is collected from various sources on various topics. The reliability of the information sources has to be determined based on previous experiences with the sources. The information value in terms of its importance has to be assessed, in addition to information quality in terms of content, time, and form.

Traditionally, intelligence was understood to mean information from criminals about criminal activity by a covert source. Today, intelligence is a systematic approach to collecting information with the purpose of predicting crime to improve law enforcement. Intelligence analysists examining who is likely to commit crime, how, when, where, and why. They then provide recommendations on how to stop or curb the offences. As part of this, analysts produce profiles of crime problems and individual targets, and produce both strategic (overall, long-term) and tactical (specific, short-term) assessments within the confines set by the police force.

Hinduja (2007) suggests that leveraging knowledge from the past to address the future will improve computer crime investigations. Cybercrime is requiring law enforcement departments in general and criminal investigators in particular to tailor a significant amount of their efforts toward successfully identifying, apprehending, and assisting in the successful investigation and prosecution of perpetrators.

Ratcliffe (2005) argues that intelligence-led policing differs from other policing strategies in the focus on recidivist offenders, and the encouragement given to surveillance and the use of informants to gather intelligence that might not otherwise come to the attention of the police. Intelligence-led policing assumes that modern law enforcement needs more robust systems to interpret a complex criminal environment and to manage risk as effectively as possible. While the cybercrime environment is not necessarily complex, it represents a completely new landscape for many police agencies in need of interpretation.

Since storytelling is a common mechanism for empirical knowledge transfer in policing, we return to the case of business email compromise at Norfund in Norway (Norfund, 2020; PwC, 2020; Solgård, 2020; Speed, 2020; Stave, 2020). The auditor general in Norway tells the following story in their report (Riksrevisjonen, 2020).

In the spring of 2020, the Norwegian government investment fund for business in developing countries (Norfund) was defrauded of approximately NOK 100 million after a targeted computer attack. (At the time of writing, NOK 100 million is equivalent to USD 10 million.) Norfund is a key tool in Norwegian development aid policy. Through its mandate, the company shall combine the consideration of profitability with the overall goal of promoting sustainable development. Norfund is a wholly state-owned company that has received annual grants from the state budget since its establishment in 1997. In 2019, the number of employees was increased from 75 to 87, and in the budget proposal for 2020, an increase in the number of employees is planned, so that by the end of the year the company will have about 100 employees. Norfund's employees are distributed at the head office in Oslo and five regional offices in Ghana, Kenya, South Africa, Costa Rica, and Thailand. The company uses external suppliers of a number of services such as information and communication technology.

In 2019, the government allocation to Norfund amounted to NOK 1905 million. In addition, the company received NOK 105 million that was earmarked for a new scheme for project development and risk mitigation. Norfund's book equity was NOK 23 billion at the end of 2019. Norfund invested a total of NOK 4 billion in 2019. Over the ten-year period 2010–2020, Norfund received significant capital from the government. This means that Norfund could make several new investments. From 2018 to 2020, Norfund made around 2100 payments. On average, the company makes two payments and receives four payments per day (Riksrevisjonen, 2020).

Riksrevisjonen (2020: 4) found that many Norwegian companies are exposed to computer attacks every year, both with the goal of damaging the companies' activities and swindling money:

> Fraud through social manipulation, where the fraudster manipulates the payer to complete a transaction has increased in recent years. Statistics show that worldwide in the period 2016 to 2019 there have been about 166,000 cases of fraud with a cost of 26 billion dollars.
> In Norway, reported figures to the Financial Supervisory Authority indicate that in 2019 more than NOK 500 million was lost in such fraud. In about one-fifth of the cases, the recipient's account was changed. It is believed that the dark numbers are substantial, and that many companies do not report that they have been scammed. The risk posed by computer crime places increased demands on information security in companies that are exposed, both in terms of technical security solutions and internal routines.

The mandate for the investigation by the office of the auditor general in Norway was to assess Norfund's work on risk management in the area of information security based on the fraud that the company was exposed to in the spring of 2020 (Riksrevisjonen, 2020: 4): What happened when Norfund was scammed? How has Norfund worked with the management of information security? How has Norfund followed up the provider of ICT services? How has the ministry of foreign affairs followed up on risk management and information security at Norfund?

At the end of September 2019, an email account belonging to an employee at Norfund's regional office in Bangkok was compromised. This probably happened through phishing and without the use of malicious software. After the email account was compromised, it was monitored for several months by scammers who probably mapped Norfund's routines and communications. Through the monitoring, the fraudsters received information at the beginning of March 2020 about a transaction of NOK 100 million that was to take place in the same month between Norfund and the financial institution LOLC Plc. in Cambodia. The scammers then created fake email accounts and pretended to be Norfund and LOLC, respectively. In this way, they infiltrated the email communication, and had the payment details changed to that the money was transferred to the fraudsters' bank account in Mexico on March 16, 2020. After March 16, the fraudsters continued to send fake emails to both parties to postpone the discovery of the fraud. They wrote to LOLC that the payment was delayed due to Covid-19, while they wrote to Norfund that LOLC had received the payment. Following a request from LOLC that they had not received the payment, Norfund receives confirmation of the transfer from Norwegian bank DNB. In an email April 30, LOLC states that the account in Mexico does not belong to them. At about the same time, the payment details in a transaction that will go from Norfund to another recipient in Cambodia are attempted to be changed to the same bank in Mexico. However, an employee of Norfund questions this, and is confirmed by the rightful recipient that the bank account in Mexico does not belong to them. According to Norfund, it is not uncommon for payments to go to or via countries other than the country where the recipient is located. This is relevant for countries that lack professional and transparent financial institutions. Payments are routinely made from Norfund via corresponding banks in third countries. According to Norfund, it is not in itself unusual for payments to be made to banks in Mexico. However, according to Norfund, it is unusual for payments to Cambodia to be transferred via a bank in Mexico. Norfund claims that the company's payment routines were followed when the payment to the account in Mexico was made (Riksrevisjonen, 2020).

Knowledge Management Approaches

Knowledge can be defined within a hierarchy of data, information, knowledge, and wisdom. Data are numbers, texts, and other materials without meaning. Data do not convey meaning in itself or meaning of facts, images, or sounds, since they lack relational elements indispensable to the establishment of a meaning, and they lack relational structure for a cognitive purpose. This structure is one of the attributes of information. When data are attached to certain and specific interpretations, then they become information. Data become information when their creators add meaning.

As already emphasized in this book, information combined with interpretation, reflection, and context becomes knowledge. Information feeds knowledge. Knowledge has its origin and is applied in the minds of people. While data and information can be stored in computers, knowledge can only be present in the heads of individuals. Knowledge accumulated over time in the form of learning becomes wisdom. Knowledge is the most important issue in this hierarchy since it is knowledge that triggers what people do.

There are many definitions of knowledge. Nonaka et al. (2000) describe it as justified true belief. Definitions of organizational knowledge range from a complex, accumulated expertise that resides in individuals and is partly or largely inexpressible to a much more structured and explicit content. There are also several classifications of knowledge, e.g., far, explicit, embodied, encoded, embedded, event, procedural, and common. Knowledge has long been recognized as a valuable resource for the organizational growth and sustained competitive advantage, especially for organizations competing in uncertain environments. Recently, some researchers have argued that knowledge is an organization's most valuable resource because it represents intangible assets, operational routines, and creative processes that are hard to imitate (Wasko & Faraj, 2005). However, the effective management of knowledge is fundamental to the organization's ability to create and sustain competitive advantage.

Knowledge management as a practice involves the processes of knowledge creation and capture, storage and retrieval, transfer and sharing, application and integration into the operating philosophy and work practices of the police organization. Knowledge management is a systematic and integrative process of coordinating organization-wide knowledge sharing and knowledge development to achieve organizational goals and ambitions. Knowledge management encompasses the managerial efforts in facilitating activities of acquiring, creating, storing, sharing, diffusing, developing, and deploying knowledge by individuals and groups. Knowledge management practices need to fit with organizational context in order to make a difference. Practices of knowledge management are context-specific, and they influence organizational effectiveness (Zheng et al., 2010).

Three knowledge management approaches can be identified (Dean & Gottschalk, 2007):

1. *Stock strategy* is focused on collecting and storing all knowledge representations in information bases in the organization. Information is stored in databases and made available to knowledge workers in the organization and in knowledge networks. Knowledge workers use databases to keep updated on relevant problems, relevant methods, news, and opinions. Information on problems and methods accumulates over time in databases. This strategy can also be called officer-to-database strategy. Police officers have access to well-proven methods and previous cases, which enable them to handle the same policing situations in the same way as in the past.
2. *Flow strategy* is focused on collecting and storing knowledge representations in information bases in the organization as long as the information is used in knowledge work processes. If certain kinds of knowledge work disappear, then information for those work processes becomes obsolete and can be deleted from files and databases. This is a yellow-pages strategy where information on knowledge areas required in work processes in the organization is registered. The link to knowledge sources in the form of individuals performing tasks is made specific in the databases, so that the person source can be identified. When a knowledge worker starts on a new project, the person will search company databases to find colleagues who already have experience in solving these kinds of problem. This strategy can also be called officer-to-workflow strategy. Police officers have access to well proven methods that they apply to new policing situations.
3. *Growth strategy* is focused on developing new knowledge. New knowledge is developed in innovate work processes taking place when knowledge workers have to solve new problems with new methods. Often, several persons are involved in the innovation, and together

they have gone through a learning process. When a knowledge worker starts on a new project, the person will use the intra-organizational as well as the inter-organizational network to find information on work processes and learning environments, which colleagues have used successfully in previous innovation processes. This strategy can also be called officer-to-innovation strategy. Police officers have access to novel methods and novel cases that they apply to new policing situations in a creative manner.

The knowledge management approach most suited for a police organization depends on whether it is an efficiency-driven organization, an experience-driven organization, or an expertise-driven organization (Dean & Gottschalk, 2007):

1. *Efficiency-driven organization* solves known problems in known ways. The quality of the solution is found in fast and inexpensive application to meet needs. Law enforcement success is achieved in the ability to make small adjustments and improvements in existing procedures. An efficiency-driven organization is characterized by known problems and known methods for solution. An example might be a policing organization controlling car speeding on roads, where well-known approaches are applied to well-known situations.
2. *Experience-driven organization* solves large and complicated problems. The problems are new, but they can be solved with existing methods in a specific context every time. Law enforcement success is achieved through effective adaptation of existing problem-solving methodologies and techniques. Continuous improvement in effectiveness is important to be able to solve the next criminal problem more efficiently and more effectively than the previous one. An experience-based organization is characterized by new problems and existing methods for solution. An example might be a policing organization investigating homicides, where a well-known set of investigative procedures and thinking styles is applied to a variety of criminal situations.
3. *Expert-driven organization* solves large, complex, risky, new, and unusual problems. Law enforcement success is achieved through

continuous improvisation and innovation. Knowledge workers apply general high-level knowledge to understand, solve, and learn. Learning from problem solving is important to be able to solve the next new and unknown criminal problem. An expertise-driven organization is characterized by both new problems and new methods for solution. An example might be a policing organization fighting economic crime, where crime types are unfamiliar (such as money laundering), and procedures are not developed (such as working with banks and law firms when fighting money laundering).

Few knowledge-intensive organizations are only active in one of these businesses. Most policing organizations are active at several of these levels. For example, detectives in criminal investigations are mainly in the experience-driven business of solving new problems with known methods. Sometimes, they are in the expertise-driven business of solving new problems with new methods. Many police agencies are currently in the expertise-driven business of solving new problems in cybercrime with new methods.

As might have become evident, there is a strong link between the three types of organization and the three knowledge management strategies. Typically, efficiency-driven organizations will apply the stock strategy, while experience-driven organizations will apply the flow strategy, and expertise-driven organizations will apply the growth strategy.

As many police organizations struggle with their approach to law enforcement against cybercrime and white-collar offenders online, they need to define themselves as expertise-driven organizations and apply the growth strategy. However over time, as the expertise develops and expands to more staff, then in a dynamic perspective the characteristics of the police organization might change to experience-driven and also efficiency-driven, thereby changing strategy from growth via flow to stock.

Knowledge Organization Characteristics

Knowledge organization has emerged as the dominant structure of both public and private organizations in the transition from an industrial to a knowledge society (Lassen et al., 2006). Knowledge organization in the management sciences is concerned with structures within which knowledge workers solve knowledge problems (Bennet & Bennet, 2005a, 2005b; Bergström et al., 2009; Lassen et al., 2006; Smith, 2003; Uretsky, 2001).

Knowledge management research has described organizational knowledge flows in terms of the knowledge circulation process, consisting of five components: knowledge creation, accumulation, sharing, utilization, and internalization. Knowledge sharing within and between organizations is not a one-way activity, but a process of trial and error, feedback, and mutual adjustment of both the source and the recipient of knowledge. This mutuality in the knowledge sharing suggests that the process can be constructed as a sequence of collective actions in which the source and the recipient are involved. There are many different knowledge-sharing mechanisms: it can be informal and personal as well as formal and impersonal. Informal mechanisms include talk, unscheduled meetings, electronic bulletin boards, and discussion databases. More formal knowledge sharing channels include video conferencing, training sessions, organizational intranets, and databases.

Bennet and Bennet (2005a) define knowledge organizations as complex adaptive systems composed of a large number of self-organizing components that seek to maximize their own goals but operate according to rules in the context of relationships with other components. In an intelligent complex adaptive system, the agents are people. The systems (organizations) are frequently composed of hierarchical levels of self-organizing agents (or knowledge workers), which can take the forms of teams, divisions, or other structures that have common bonds. Thus, while the components (knowledge workers) are self-organizing, they are not independent from the system they comprise (the professional organization).

Knowledge in this book is referred to as information combined with interpretation, reflection, and context. In cybernetics, knowledge is defined as a reducer of uncertainty, a reducer of complexity, or as a relation to predict and to select those actions that are necessary in establishing a competitive advantage for organizational survival. That is, knowledge is the capability to draw distinctions, within a domain of actions. According to the knowledge-based view of the organization, the uniqueness of an organization's knowledge plays a fundamental role in its sustained ability to perform and succeed (Turner & Makhija, 2006).

According to the knowledge-based theory of the firm, knowledge is the main resource for a firm's competitive advantage. Knowledge is the primary driver of a firm's value. Performance differences across firms can be attributed to the variance in the firms' strategic knowledge. Strategic knowledge is characterized by being valuable, unique, rare, non-imitable, non-substitutable, non-transferable, combinable, and exploitable. Unlike other inert organizational resources, the application of existing knowledge has the potential to generate new knowledge (Garud & Kumaraswamy, 2005).

Inherently, however, knowledge resides within individuals and, more specifically in the employees who create, recognize, archive, access, and apply knowledge in carrying out their tasks (Liu & Chen, 2005). Consequently, the movement of knowledge across individual and organizational boundaries is dependent on employees' knowledge-sharing behaviors (Liebowitz, 2004). Bock et al. (2005) found that extensive knowledge sharing within organizations still appears to be the exception rather than the rule.

The knowledge organization is very different from the bureaucratic organization. For example, the knowledge organization's focus on flexibility and customer response is very different from the bureaucracy's focus on organizational stability and the accuracy and repetitiveness of internal processes. In the knowledge organization, current practices emphasize using the ideas and capabilities of employees to improve decision-making and organizational effectiveness. In contrast, bureaucracies utilize autocratic decision-making by senior leadership with unquestioned execution by the workforce (Bennet & Bennet, 2005b).

In knowledge organizations, transformational and charismatic leadership is an influential mode of leadership that is associated with high levels of individual and organizational performance. Leadership effectiveness is critically contingent on, and often defined in terms of, leaders' ability to motivate followers toward collective goals or a collective mission or vision (Kark & van Dijk, 2007).

In the knowledge society, knowledge organizations are expected to play a vital role in local economic development. For example, knowledge institutions such as universities are expected to stimulate regional and local economic development. Knowledge transfer units in universities such as Oxford in the UK and Grenoble in France are responsible for local and regional innovations (Smith, 2003).

Uretsky (2001) argues that the real knowledge organization is the learning organization. A learning organization is one that changes as a result of its experiences. Under the best of circumstances, these changes result in performance improvements. The phrases knowledge organization and learning organization are usually (but not necessarily) used to describe service organizations. This is because most, if not all, of the value of these organizations comes from how well their professionals learn from the environment, diagnose problems, and then work with clients or customers to improve their situations. The problems with which they work are frequently ambiguous and unstructured. The information, skills, and experience needed to address these problems vary with work cases. A typical example is detectives in police investigations of white-collar crime online.

Similarly, Bennet and Bennet (2005b) argue that learning and knowledge will have become two of the three most important emergent characteristics of the future world-class organization. Learning will be continuous and widespread, utilizing mentoring, classroom, and distance learning and will likely be self-managed with strong infrastructure support. The creation, storage, transfer, and application of knowledge will have been refined and developed such that it becomes a major resource of the organization as it satisfies customers and adapts to environmental competitive forces and opportunities.

The third characteristic of future knowledge organizations will be that of organizational intelligence. Organizational intelligence is the ability of an organization to perceive, interpret, and respond to its environment in a manner that meets its goals while satisfying multiple stakeholders. Intelligent behavior may be defined as being well prepared, providing excellent outcome-oriented thinking, choosing appropriate postures, and making outstanding decisions. Intelligent behavior includes acquiring knowledge continuously from all available resources and building it into an integrated picture, bringing together seemingly unrelated information to create new and unusual perspectives and to understand the surrounding world (Bennet & Bennet, 2005b).

In the context of policing and law enforcement, "intelligence" has another meaning as well, as discussed previously in this book. Brown (2007: 340) defines intelligence in this context as follows:

> Intelligence is information, which is significant or potentially significant for an enquiry or potential enquiry.

What establishes information as intelligence is that it is a subset of information defined by the special quality of being significant and relevant. If information is significant, it has value and it has relevance. Analysis does not create intelligence; it merely discovers, attributes, and refines it.

According to Bennet and Bennet (2005a), designing the knowledge organization of the future implies development of an intelligent complex adaptive system. In response to an environment of rapid change, increasing complexity and great uncertainty, the organization of the future must become an adaptive organic business. The intelligent complex adaptive system will enter into a symbiotic relationship with its cooperative enterprise, virtual alliances, and external environment, while simultaneously retaining unity of purpose and effective identification and selection of incoming threats and opportunities.

In the knowledge organization, innovation and creativity are of critical importance. The literature on creativity provides a view of organizing for innovation by focusing on how individuals and teams come to shape knowledge in unique ways. Innovation consists of the creative generation of a new idea and the implementation of the idea into a valuable product, and thus creativity feeds innovation and is particularly critical in complex and interdependent work. Taylor and Greve (2006) argue that creativity can be viewed as the first stage of the overall innovation process.

Innovative solutions in the knowledge organization arise from diverse knowledge, processes that allow for creativity, and tasks directed toward creative solutions. Creativity requires application of deep knowledge because knowledge workers must understand the knowledge domain to push its boundaries. Team creativity likewise relies on tapping into the diverse knowledge of a team's members (Taylor & Greve, 2006).

Within knowledge organizations, we often find communities of practice. Brown and Duguid (2001) argue that for a variety of reasons, communities of practice seem a useful organizational subset for examining organizational knowledge as well as identity. First, such communities are privileged sites for a tight, effective loop of insight, problem identification, learning, and knowledge production. Second, they are significant repositories for the development, maintenance, and reproduction of knowledge. Third, community knowledge is more than the sum of its parts. Fourth, organizational ability to adapt to environmental change is often determined by communities of practice.

References

Adler, P. S., & Kwon, S. W. (2002). Social capital: Prospects for a new concept. *Academy of Management Review, 27*(1), 17–40.

Agnew, R. (2014). Social concern and crime: Moving beyond the assumption of simple self-interest. *Criminology, 52*(1), 1–32.

Baird, J. E., & Zelin, R. C. (2009). An examination of the impact of obedience pressure on perceptions of fraudulent acts and the likelihood of committing occupational fraud. *Journal of Forensic Studies in Accounting and Business, 1*(1), 1–14.

Barney, J. (2018). Editor's comments: Positioning a theory paper for publication. *Academy of Management Review, 43*(3), 345–348.

Bennet, A., & Bennet, D. (2005a). Designing the knowledge organization of the future: The intelligent complex adaptive system. In C. W. Holsapple (Ed.), *Handbook of knowledge management* (Vol. 2, pp. 623–638). Springer Science & Business Media.

Bennet, D., & Bennet, A. (2005b). The rise of the knowledge organization. In C. W. Holsapple (Ed.), *Handbook of knowledge management* (Vol. 1, pp. 5–20). Springer Science & Business Media.

Benson, M. L., & Gottschalk, P. (2015). Gender and white-collar crime in Norway: An empirical study of media reports. *International Journal of Law, Crime and Justice, 43*(4), 535–552.

Benson, M. L., & Simpson, S. S. (2018). *Understanding white-collar crime—An opportunity perspective* (2nd ed.). Routledge.

Berghoff, H. (2018). "Organised irresponsibility?" The Siemens corruption scandal of the 1990s and 2000s. *Business History, 60*(3), 423–445.

Bergström, O., Hasselbladh, H., & Kärreman, D. (2009). Organizing disciplinary power in knowledge organization. *Scandinavian Journal of Management, 25*, 178–190.

Bittle, S., & Hébert, J. (2020). Controlling corporate crimes in times of deregulation and re-regulation. In M. L. Rorie (Ed.), *The handbook of white-collar crime* (Chapter 30, pp. 484–501). Wiley.

Bock, G. W., Zmud, R. W., & Kim, Y. G. (2005). Behavioral intention formation in knowledge sharing: Examining the roles of extrinsic motivators, social-psychological forces, and organizational climate. *MIS Quarterly, 29*(1), 87–111.

Brown, J. S., & Duguid, P. (2001). Knowledge and organization: A social-practice perspective. *Organization Science, 12*(2), 198–213.

Brown, S. D. (2007). The meaning of criminal intelligence. *International Journal of Police Science & Management, 9*(4), 336–340.

Bucy, P. H., Formby, E. P., Raspanti, M.S., & Rooney, K. E. (2008). Why do they do it? The motives, mores, and character of white collar criminals. *St. John's Law Review, 82*, 401–571.

Caines, A., Pastrana, S., Hutchings, A., & Buttery, P. J. (2018). Automatically identifying the function and intent of posts in underground forums. *Crime Science, 7*(19), 1–14.

Chatterjee, A., & Pollock, T. G. (2017). Master of puppets: How narcissistic CEOs construct their professional worlds. *Academy of Management Review, 42*(4), 703–725.

Cohen, L. E., & Felson, M. (1979). Social change and crime rate trends: A routine activity approach. *American Sociological Review, 44*, 588–608.

Collier, B., Clayton, R., Hutchings, A., & Thomas, D. R. (2020). *Cybercrime is (often) boring: Maintaining the infrastructure of cybercrime economies*. Workshop on the Economics of Information Security, Brussels. www.weis2020.econinfosec.org.

Comey, J. B. (2009). Go directly to prison: White collar sentencing after the Sarbanes-Oxley act. *Harvard Law Review, 122*, 1728–1749.

Craig, J. M., & Piquero, N. L. (2017). Sensational offending: An application of sensation seeking to white-collar and conventional crimes. *Crime & Delinquency, 63*(11), 1363–1382.

Crosina, E., & Pratt, M. G. (2019). Toward a model of organizational mourning: The case of former Lehman Brothers bankers. *Academy of Management Journal, 62*(1), 66–98.

de Paoli, S., Johnstone, J., Coull, N., Ferguson, I., Sinclair, G., Tomkins, P., Brown, M., & Martin, R. (2020). A qualitative exploratory study of the knowledge, forensic, and legal challenges from the perspective of police cybercrime specialists. *Policing: A Journal of Policy and Practice*, published online. https://doi.org/10.1093/police/paaa027.

Dean, G., & Gottschalk, P. (2007). *Knowledge management in policing and law enforcement—Foundations*. Oxford University Press.

Eberly, M. B., Holley, E. C., Johnson, M. D., & Mitchell, T. R. (2011). Beyond internal and external: A dyadic theory of relational attributions. *Academy of Management Review, 36*(4), 731–753.

Ferraro, F., Pfeffer, J., & Sutton, R. I. (2005). Economics language and assumptions: How theories can become self-fulfilling. *Academy of Management Review, 30*(1), 8–24.

Galvin, B. M., Lange, D., & Ashforth, B. E. (2015). Narcissistic organizational identification: Seeing oneself as central to the organization's identity. *Academy of Management Review, 40*(2), 163–181.

Gamache, D. L., & McNamara, G. (2019). Responding to bad press: How CEO temporal focus influences the sensitivity to negative media coverage of acquisitions. *Academy of Management Journal, 62*(3), 918–943.

Gao, P., & Zhang, G. (2019). Accounting manipulation, peer pressure, and internal control. *The Accounting Review, 94*(1), 127–151.

Garud, R., & Kumaraswamy, A. (2005). Vicious and virtuous circles in the management of knowledge: The case of Infosys Technologies. *MIS Quarterly, 29*(1), 9–33.

Goldstraw-White, J. (2012). *White-collar crime: Accounts of offending behavior*. Palgrave Macmillan.

Goncharov, I., & Peter, C. D. (2019). Does reporting transparency affect industry coordination? Evidence from the duration of international cartels, *The Accounting Review, 94*(3), 149–175.

Gottfredson, M. R., & Hirschi, T. (1990). *A general theory of crime*. Stanford University Press.

Gottschalk, P., & Asting, C. (2019). The family firm as an arena for white-collar crime. *International Journal of Business Continuity and Risk Management, 9*(4), 283–297.

Gottschalk, P., & Asting, C. (2020). Entitled to embezzlement? The case of successful executives working for rich heirs. *Deviant Behavior, 41*(3), 269–277.

Gulating. (2009, September 15). *Case number 08.196041AST-GULA/AVD2.* Gulating lagmannsrett [Gulating court of appeal].

Hamilton, S., & Micklethwait, A. (2006). *Greed and corporate failure: The lessons from recent disasters.* Palgrave Macmillan.

Haveman, H. A., Mahoney, J. T., & Mannix, E. (2019). Editors' comments: The role of theory in management research. *Academy of Management Review, 44*(2), 241–243.

Hinduja, S. (2007). Computer crime investigations in the United States: Leveraging knowledge from the past to address the future. *International Journal of Cyber Criminology, 1*(1), 1–26.

Holt, R., & Cornelissen, J. (2014). Sensemaking revisited. *Management Learning, 45*(5), 525–539.

Huang, L., & Knight, A. P. (2017). Resources and relationships in entrepreneurship: An exchange theory of the development and effects of the entrepreneur-investor relationship. *Academy of Management Review, 42*(1), 80–102.

Hughes, J., Aycock, S., Caines, A., Buttery, P., & Hutchings, A. (2020). *Detecting trending terms in cybersecurity forum discussions.* Workshop on Noisy User-generated Text (W-NUT), virtual event. www.noisy-text.github.io.

Hutchings, A. (2018a). Leaving on a jet plane: The trade in fraudulently obtained airline tickets. *Crime, Law and Social Change, 70*, 461–487.

Hutchings, A. (2018b). Flying in cyberspace: Policing global travel fraud. *Policing: A Journal of Policy and Practice*, 1–16. https://doi.org/10.1093/police/pay063.

Hutchings, A., & Holt, T. J. (2016). A crime script analysis of the online stolen data market. *British Journal of Criminology, 55*, 596–614.

Jonnergård, K., Stafsudd, A., & Elg, U. (2010). Performance evaluations as gender barriers in professional organizations: A study of auditing firms. *Gender, Work and Organization, 17*(6), 721–747.

Kakkar, H., Sivanathan, N., & Gobel, M. S. (2020). Fall from grace: The role of dominance and prestige in the punishment of high-status actors. *Academy of Management Journal, 63*(2), 530–553.

Kang, E., & Thosuwanchot, N. (2017). An application of Durkheim's four categories of suicide to organizational crimes. *Deviant Behavior, 38*(5), 493–513.

Kark, R., & van Dijk, D. (2007). Motivation to lead, motivation to follow: The role of the self-regulatory focus in leadership processes. *Academy of Management Review, 32*(2), 500–528.

Kholin, M., Kückelhaus, B., & Blickle, G. (2020). Why dark personalities can get ahead: Extending the toxic career model. *Personality and Individual Differences, 156*. https://doi.org/10.1016/j.paid2019.109792.

Langton, L., & Piquero, N. L. (2007). Can general strain theory explain white-collar crime? A preliminary investigation of the relationship between strain and select white-collar offenses. *Journal of Criminal Justice, 35,* 1–15.

Lassen, C., Laugen, B. T., & Næss, P. (2006). Virtual mobility and organizational reality—A note on the mobility needs in knowledge organizations. *Transportation Research, 11,* 459–463.

Leigh, A. C., Foote, D. A., Clark, W. R., & Lewis, J. L. (2010). Equity sensitivity: A triadic measure and outcome/input perspectives. *Journal of Managerial Issues, 22*(3), 286–305.

Leonard, W. N., & Weber, M. G. (1970). Automakers and dealers: A study of criminogenic market forces. *Law & Society Review, 4*(3), 407–424.

Leontiadis, N., & Hutchings, A. (2015). Scripting the crime commission process in the illicit online prescription drug trade. *Journal of Cybersecurity, 1*(1), 81–92.

Liebowitz, J. (2004). Will knowledge management work in the government? *Electronic Government: An International Journal, 1*(1), 1–7.

Liu, C. C., & Chen, S. Y. (2005). Determinants of knowledge sharing of e-learners. *International Journal of Innovation and Learning, 2*(4), 434–445.

Mawritz, M. B., Greenbaum, R. L., Butts, M. M., & Graham, K. A. (2017). I just can't control myself: A self-regulation perspective on the abuse of deviant employees. *Academy of Management Journal, 60*(4), 1482–1503.

McClean, E. J., Martin, S. R., Emich, K. J., & Woodruff, T. (2018). The social consequences of voice: An examination of voice type and gender status and subsequent leader emergence. *Academy of Management Journal, 61*(5), 1869–1891.

McElwee, G., & Smith, R. (2015). Towards a nuanced typology of illegal entrepreneurship: A theoretical and conceptual overview. In G. McElwee & R. Smith (Eds.), *Exploring criminal and illegal enterprise: New perspectives on research, policy & practice: Contemporary issues in entrepreneurship research* (Vol. 5). Emerald.

Mingus, W., & Burchfield, K. B. (2012). From prison to integration: Applying modified labeling theory to sex offenders. *Criminal Justice Studies, 25*(1), 97–109.

Nichol, J. E. (2019). The effects of contract framing on misconduct and entitlement. *The Accounting Review, 94*(3), 329–344.

Nonaka, I., Toyama, R., & Konno, N. (2000). Seci, ba and leadership: A Unified model of dynamic knowledge creation. *Long Range Planning, 33*(1), 5–34.

Norfund. (2020, May 15). *Norfund er utsatt for alvorlig svindel* [Norfund is exposed to serious fraud]. *Norfund*. www.norfund.no.

Piquero, N. L. (2012). The only thing we have to fear is fear itself: Investigating the relationship between fear of falling and white-collar crime. *Crime and Delinquency, 58*(3), 362–379.

Piquero, N. L., Piquero, A. R., Narvey, C., Boutwell, B., & Farrington, D. P. (2019). Are there psychopaths in white-collar jobs? *Deviant Behavior*, published online. https://doi.org/10.1080/01639625.2019.1708537.

Pontell, H. N., Black, W. K., & Geis, G. (2014). Too big to fail, too powerful to jail? On the absence of criminal prosecutions after the 2008 financial meltdown. *Crime, Law and Social Change, 61*(1), 1–13.

Pratt, T. C., & Cullen, F. T. (2005). Assessing macro-level predictors and theories of crime: A meta-analysis. *Crime and Justice, 32*, 373–450.

Pusch, N., & Holtfreter, K. (2020). Individual and organizational predictors of white-collar crime: A meta-analysis. *Journal of White-Collar and Corporate Crime*, 1–19. https://doi.org/10.1177/2631309X19901317.

PwC. (2020, June 30). *Independent assessment of the LOLC incident: Report developed for Norfund, report of investigation* (p. 34). PricewaterhouseCoopers.

Ramoglou, S., & Tsang, E. W. K. (2016). A realist perspective of entrepreneurship: Opportunities as propensities. *Academy of Management Review, 41*, 410–434.

Ratcliffe, J. (2005). The effectiveness of police intelligence management: A New Zealand case study. *Police Practice & Research, 6*(5), 435–451.

Riksrevisjonen. (2020). *Riksrevisjonens undersøkelse av informasjonssikkerhet i Norfund* [The office of the auditor general's investigation of information security at Norfund] (p. 25). The Office of the Auditor General of Norway. www.riksrevisjonen.no.

Schnatterly, K., Gangloff, K. A., & Tuschke, A. (2018). CEO wrongdoing: A review of pressure, opportunity, and rationalization. *Journal of Management, 44*(6), 2405–2432.

Smith, H. L. (2003). Knowledge organization and local economic development: The cases of Oxford and Grenoble. *Regional Studies, 37*(9), 899–909.
Solgård, J. (2020, July 9). Norfund ble svindlet for 100 millioner: -Vi har gjort mye, men ikke raskt nok for å styrke våre rutiner og systemer [Norfund was defrauded for 100 million: -We have done a lot, but not fast enough to strengthen our routines and systems]. *Dagens Næringsliv*. www.dn.no.
Speed, J. (2020, May 15). *Politiet: Lite trolig at Nordfun får igjen svindelpenger* [The police: It is unlikely that Norfund will get back fraud money]. *BistandsAktuelt*. www.bistandsaktuelt.no.
Srivastava, S. B., & Goldberg, A. (2017). Language as a window into culture. *California Management Review, 60*(1), 56–69.
Stave, T. K. (2020, July 9). Norfund tar selvkritikk etter gigantsvindel [Norfund takes self-criticism after giant fraud]. *Aftenposten*. www.e24.no.
Sutherland, E. H. (1983). *White collar crime—The uncut version*. Yale University Press.
Sykes, G., & Matza, D. (1957). Techniques of neutralization: A theory of delinquency. *American Sociological Review, 22*(6), 664–670.
Taylor, A., & Greve, H. R. (2006). Superman or the fantastic four? Knowledge combination and experience in innovative teams. *Academy of Management Journal, 49*(4), 723–740.
Turner, K. L., & Makhija, M. V. (2006). The role of organizational controls in managing knowledge. *Academy of Management Review, 31*(1), 197–217.
Uretsky, M. (2001). Preparing for the real knowledge organization. *Journal of Organizational Excellence, 21*(1), 87–93.
Vu, A. V., Hughes, J., Pete, I., Collier, B., Chua, Y. T., Shumailov, I., & Hutchings, A. (2020, October). Turning up the dial: The evolution of a cybercrime market through set-up, stable, and Covid-19 eras, IMC'20. In *Proceedings of the ACM Internet Measurement Conference* (pp. 551–566). https://doi.org/10.1145/3419394.3423636.
Wasko, M. M., & Faraj, S. (2005). Why should I share? Examining social capital and knowledge contribution in electronic networks of practice. *MIS Quarterly, 29*(1), 35–57.
Weick, K. E., Sutcliffe, K. M., & Obstfeld, D. (2005). Organizing and the process of sensemaking. *Organization Science, 16*(4), 409–421.
Welsh, D. T., Ordonez, L. D., Snyder, D. G., & Christian, M. S. (2014). The slippery slope: How small ethical transgressions pave the way for larger future transgressions. *Journal of Applied Psychology, 100*(1), 114–127.

Zheng, W., Yang, B., & McLean, G. N. (2010). Linking organizational culture, structure, strategy, and organizational effectiveness: Mediating role of knowledge management. *Journal of Business Research, 63*, 763–771.

Zhu, D. H., & Chen, G. (2015). CEO narcissism and the impact of prior board experience on corporate strategy. *Administrative Science Quarterly, 60*(1), 31–65.

9

Online Grooming

This book is concerned with white-collar offenders online who victimize individuals and organizations by financial crime. A very different offender category online is sex groomers who attract victims for sexual abuse (Aljuboori et al., 2021). While very different, this offender group is of interest because we know much more about them than we know about white-collar offenders online (Hamerton, 2020: 73):

> Considering the typology and character of contemporary white-collar cybercrime in particular, it can be argued that the genre incorporates analogous processes common to a number of other types of crime that appear as emblematic for cybercrime generally. Typical examples that employ comparable and often complex techniques are hacking and cracking, online grooming of specific targets, and sharp practice in accessing illicit or restricted information.

We might learn from offender characteristics, for example, why they choose online rather than offline when they want to attract the attention of their victims for sexual abuse. Therefore, this chapter presents research regarding online grooming to identify characteristics of cyberspace that

P. Gottschalk and C. Hamerton, *White-Collar Crime Online*,
https://doi.org/10.1007/978-3-030-82132-6_9

make online offending so different from offline offending (Davidson & Gottschalk, 2008, 2010, 2011a, 2011b, 2015; Gottschalk, 2011a, 2011b; Webster et al., 2015).

While we focus on white-collar financial crime in this book on computer crime, we must thus not forget that there are a number of other types of crime that are typical for cybercrime and internet crime as well, from which we can learn. Typical examples are hacking, child pornography, and online child grooming. In this chapter, we present the case of child grooming as computer crime.

An interesting aspect of child grooming is the stepwise approach often used by offenders. They start out widely to meet potential victims in various chat rooms at different locations. It is a random search before they start to narrow it down. After a while, they decide to target some children. If they do not succeed, they move down on their list of potential targets. A similar multi-stage approach might be applied by white-collar offenders online who initially do not know what organizations are vulnerable and which employees within targeted organizations that will cooperate voluntarily or involuntarily with the offenders. The operational mode of white-collar offenders is little explored, while we know much more about the mode of operation among grooming offenders. However, we know that both groups search for opportunities.

Ramoglou and Tsang (2016: 738) argue that opportunities are not the result of innovation, discovery or creation: "They are objectively existing propensities to be creatively actualized". Criminal entrepreneurs thus actualize illegal opportunities in the shadow economy (McElwee & Smith, 2015). Criminal entrepreneurship represents the dark side of entrepreneurialism. To understand entrepreneurial behavior by white-collar criminals, important behavioral areas include "modus essendi", "modus operandi", and "modus vivendi". Modus essendi is a philosophical term relating to modes of being. Modus operandi is method of operating, which is an accepted criminological concept for classifying generic human actions from their visible and consequential manifestations. Modus vivendi represents the shared symbiotic relationship between different entrepreneurial directions (Smith, 2009).

Internet use has grown considerably in the last decade. Information technology now forms a core part of the formal education system in many countries, ensuring that each new generation of internet users is more adept than the last. Research studies in the UK suggest that the majority of young people aged 9–19 accessed the internet at least once a day. The internet provides the opportunity to interact with friends on social networking sites such as Myspace and Bebo and enables young people to access information in a way that previous generations would not have thought possible. The medium also allows users to post detailed personal information, which may be accessed by any site visitor and provides a platform for peer communication hitherto unknown (Davidson & Martellozzo, 2008). There is, however, increasing evidence that the internet is used by some adults to access children and young people in order to groom them for the purposes of sexual abuse (Winters et al., 2017). Myspace have expelled 29,000 suspected sex offenders and is being sued in the United States by parents who claim that their children were contacted by sex offenders on the site and consequently abused (BBC, 2007). The internet also plays a role in facilitating the production and distribution of indecent illegal images of children, which may encourage and complement online grooming.

Online Sexual Offenders

Recent advances in computer technology have been aiding sexual sex offenders, stalkers, child pornographers, child traffickers, and others with the intent of exploiting children (Kierkegaard, 2008: 41):

> Internet bulletin boards, chat rooms, private websites, and peer-to-peer networks are being used daily by pedophiles to meet unsuspecting children. Compounding the problem is the lack of direct governance by an international body, which will curb the illegal content and activity. Most countries already have laws protecting children, but what is needed is a concerted law enforcement and international legislation to combat child sex abuse.

Men who target young people online for sex are pedophiles (Kierkegaard, 2008; Wolak et al., 2009). According to Dunaigre (2001), the pedophile is an emblematic figure, made into a caricature and imbued with all the fears, anxieties, and apprehensions rocking our society today. Pedophile acts are—according to the World Health Organization (WHO)—sexual behavior that an adult major (16 years or over), overwhelmingly of the male sex, acts out toward prepubescent children (13 years or under). According to the WHO, there must normally be a five-year age difference between the two, except in the case of pedophilic practices at the end of adolescence where what counts is more the difference in sexual maturity. However, the definition of criminal behavior varies among countries. Pedophile acts in Norway are sexual behavior that a person carries out toward children of 16 years or under. There is no minimum age definition for the grooming person in Norwegian criminal law, but age difference and difference in sexual maturity are included as criteria for criminal liability.

Online groomers are people who engage in a communications process by which a perpetrator applies affinity-seeking strategies, while simultaneously engaging in sexual desensitization and information acquisition about targeted victims in order to develop relationships that result in need fulfilment. Wolak et al. (2009: 4) present two case examples of crimes by online sex offenders in the United States:

- Police in West Coast state found child pornography in the possession of the 22-year-old offender. The offender, who was from a Northeastern state, confessed to befriending a 13-year-old local boy online, traveling to the West Coast, and meeting him for sex. Prior to the meeting, the offender and victim had corresponded online for about six months. The offender had sent the victim nude images via web cam and email, and they had called and texted each other hundreds of times. When they met for sex, the offender took graphic pictures of the encounter. The victim believed he was in love with the offender. He lived alone with his father and was struggling to fit in and come to terms with being gay. The offender possessed large quantities of child pornography that he had downloaded from the Internet. He was sentenced to 10 years in prison.
- A 24-year-old man met a 14-year-old girl at a social networking site. He claimed to be 19. Their online conversation became romantic and

sexual, and the victim believed she was in love. They met several times for sex over a period of weeks. The offender took nude pictures of the victim and gave her alcohol and drugs. Her mother and stepfather found out and reported the crime to the police. The victim was lonely, had issues with drugs and alcohol, and problems at school and with her parents. She had posted provocative pictures of herself on her social networking site. She had met other men online and had sex with them. The offender was a suspect in another online enticement case. He was found guilty but had not been sentenced at time of the interview.

According to Davidson and Martellozzo (2008: 277), internet sex offender behavior can include: "the construction of sites to be used for the exchange of information, experiences, and indecent images of children; the organization of criminal activities that seek to use children for prostitution purposes and that produce indecent images of children at a professional level; the organization of criminal activities that promote sexual tourism".

Child grooming is a process that commences with sex offenders choosing a target area that is likely to attract children. In the physical world, this could be venues visited by children such as schools, shopping malls, or playgrounds (Wild et al., 2020). A process of grooming then commences when offenders take a particular interest in targeted child and make them feel special with the intention of forming a bond. The internet has greatly facilitated this process in the virtual world. Offenders now seek out their victims by visiting internet relay chat rooms from their home or internet cafés at any time. Once a child victim is identified, the offender can invite it into a private area of the chat room to engage in private conversations on intimate personal details including the predator's sex life (Australian, 2008).

Internet Characteristics

The internet is an international network of networks that connects people all over the world. Any computer can communicate with almost any other computer linked to the internet. The internet has created a universal technology platform on which to build all sorts of new products, services, communities, and solutions. It is reshaping the way information technology is used by individuals and organizations. The internet has provided an expedient mode of communication and access to a wealth of information (Dombrowski et al., 2007).

In less than three decades, the internet has moved from a strange communications medium to an obvious tool in our homes, schools, workplaces, and travels. It enables us to search information, perform routine tasks, and communicate with others. The technological aspects of the internet are developing at the same high speed as the number of users globally. The internet provides a social context for us to meet with others and to exchange information (Quayle et al., 2006). During the Covid-19 pandemic in 2020 and 2021, the internet represented the main and sometimes the only communication platform to meet with others.

The World Wide Web is a system with universally accepted standards for storing, retrieving, formatting, changing, and displaying information in a networked environment. Information is stored and displayed as electronic pages that can contain numbers, text, pictures, graphics, sound, and video. These web pages can be linked electronically to other web pages, independent of where they are located. Web pages can be viewed by any type of computer.

In a survey of young people in Norway between the ages 8 and 18 years old, 78% of the respondents said that they are involved in chatting. The use of chatting for communication is more common than the use of email in this age group. In the age group 17–18 years old, all respondents said they do chat. The percentage reporting that they have been plagued while chatting was 9%. Among chatters about one third had met persons in reality that they first met while chatting. The survey was conducted more than a decade ago, so it can be assumed that the internet use and the internet dependence have further increased.

The internet is a valuable tool; however, it can also be detrimental to the wellbeing of children due to numerous online hazards (Dombrowski et al., 2007: 153):

> There is the potential for children to be abused via cyberspace through online sexual solicitation and access to pornography. Indeed, the Internet is replete with inappropriate material, including pornography, chat rooms with adult themes and access to instant messaging wherein others could misrepresent themselves. Because children are actively utilizing the Internet where unknown others can have access to them or where they can be exposed to inappropriate sexual materials, they require safeguarding and education in safe Internet use.

Online grooming might be compared to online learning and other forms of online activity. The purpose of such analogies is to identify both similarities and differences. Learning on the internet, for example, is structured as a formal and non-anonymous activity. To some it is scary rather than safe because students can be asked to expose their (lack of) knowledge on the internet and share it with others. Active and extrovert students enjoy this, while other students choose to be passive on-lookers.

Generally, going online enables individuals to play a personality role, which might be more or less different from their real personality. There will always be a difference between your role in virtual reality and in real world. We play roles as adults and parents, or children and students, both in the real world and in virtual realities. However, in the virtual world we may find it easier to live our dreams and fantasies. In the type "second life" environments on the internet, people tend to be unfaithful and to build their dream existence alone or with others.

What is then so special about being online? One answer to this question is that you can be in a different, informal, and anonymous setting to live out dreams and fantasies.

Internet Relationships

Just like the stage approach seems common among child grooming offenders and possibly also among white-collar offenders as the modus operandi, relationships established on the internet might be different from offline social contacts for both groups of offenders. Relationships online are built using social software. The internet is a special artifact system that has enormous technical and social positive impacts on modern society (Kierkegaard, 2008: 41):

> The online environment enables access to a wealth of information and communication across both distance and time. There is a vast amount of data available on virtually every subject, making it an effective learning tool.

However, the internet is also a double-edged sword with negative and positive consequences (Kierkegaard, 2008: 41):

> It has a potential for misuse and has generated societal concerns. Today, the danger for children is even greater because the Internet provides anonymity to predators.

Recent advances in computer technology have been aiding sexual predators, stalkers, child pornographers, child traffickers, and others with the intent of exploiting children. While they have existed prior to the internet, the advent of the new technology three decades ago has allowed for easier and faster distribution of pornographic materials and communication across national and international boundaries (Kierkegaard, 2008).

On the other hand, the Internet is not all negative concerning sexual communication (Calder, 2004: 3):

> It can be used for healthy sexual expression. For example, the Internet offers the opportunity for the formulation of online or virtual communities where isolated or disenfranchised individuals e.g., gay males and lesbians can communicate with each other around sexual topics of shared

> interest; it offers educational potential; and it may allow for sexual experimentation in a safer forum, thus facilitating identity exploration and development.

The internet allows sex offenders instant access to other sex offenders worldwide, forums facilitate open discussion of their sexual desires, shared ideas about ways to lure victims, mutual support of their adult–child sex philosophies, instant access to potential child victims worldwide, disguised identities for approaching children, even to the point of presenting as a member of teen groups. Furthermore, the internet allows potential offenders ready access to chat areas and social networking sites reserved for teenagers and children, to discover how to approach and who to target as potential victims. The internet provides a means to identify and track down home contact information, and the internet enables adults to build long-term virtual relationships with potential victims, prior to attempting to engage the child in physical contact (Davidson & Gottschalk, 2008, 2010, 2011a, 2011b, 2015; Gottschalk, 2011a, 2011b; Webster et al., 2015).

Relationships are built using social software. Through the internet, people are discovering and inventing new ways to share knowledge and interests. People communicate on the Internet with each other in a human voice. These conversations using social software are collectively referred to as social media, a wide-ranging term than encompasses the practice and resulting output of all kinds of information created online by those who were previously consumers of that media (Cook, 2008: 7):

> Philosophically, social media describes the way in which content (particularly news and opinion) has become democratized by the Internet and the role people now play not only in consuming information and conveying it to others, but also in creating and sharing content with them, be it textual, aural or visual.

For this reason, social media is interchangeably referred to as consumer- or user-generated content. Social media is often defined by the categories of software tools that people use to undertake this consuming, conveying, creating, and sharing content with each other, including blogs, pod casts, wikis, and social networking that have found their place on the Internet (Cook, 2008).

Blogs in terms of online personal journals are one of the examples mentioned by Cook (2008), and Mitchell et al. (2008) phrased the following question: Are blogs putting youth at risk of online sexual solicitation or harassment? They conducted a telephone survey of 1500 youth internet users, ages 10–17, in the USA. They found that 16% of youth internet users reported blogging in the past year. Teenagers and girls were the most common bloggers, and bloggers were more likely than other youth to post personal information online.

However, Mitchell et al. (2008) found that bloggers were not more likely to interact with people they met online and did not know in person. Youth who interacted with people they met online, regardless of whether or not they blogged, had higher odds of receiving online sexual solicitations. Bloggers who did not interact with people they met online were at no increased risk for sexual solicitation. Moreover, posting personal information did not add to risk. The only difference found was related to harassment, since youthful bloggers were found to be at increased risk for online harassment, regardless of whether they also interacted with others online.

Online Grooming Legislation

The concept of sexual grooming is well documented in the sex offender literature (Finkelhor, 1984; Mitchell et al., 2008; Wolak et al., 2009), and is now filtering into legislation policy, crime detection, and prevention initiatives. A newspaper report more than a decade ago suggested that the Child Exploitation and Online Protection Centre in the UK received an average of 4 phone calls per day from young people planning to meet people with whom they have developed an online, sexual relationship.

Potential offenders using the internet to perpetrate sexual offences against children fall into two principal categories: Those who use the Internet to target and "groom" children for the purposes of sexual abuse, and those who produce and/or download indecent illegal images of children from the Internet and distribute them (Finkelhor, 1984; Mitchell et al., 2008; Wolak et al., 2009). Recent legislation has sought to protect young people from internet abuse through the introduction of a grooming clause. This new offence category was introduced in the Sexual Offences Act (2003) in England and Wales (this section of the Act also applies to Northern Ireland). Section 15 makes meeting a child following sexual grooming an offence; this applies to the internet, to other technologies such as mobile phones and to the real world.

Grooming involves a process of socialization through which a potential offender seeks to interact with a child under the age of 16, possibly sharing their hobbies and interests in an attempt to gain trust in order to prepare them for sexual abuse. The concept of grooming is now also recognized in legislation in the UK. The Sexual Offences Act (2003) in England and Wales, and Northern Ireland and the Protection of Children and Prevention of Sexual Offences Act (2005) in Scotland include the offence of "meeting a child following certain preliminary contact" (section 1). "Preliminary contact" refers to occasions where a person arranges to meet a child who is under 16, having communicated with them on at least one previous occasion (in person, via the internet or via other technologies), with the intention of performing sexual activity on the child.

Several countries are beginning to follow the UK in legislating against grooming behavior. Sexual grooming has been added to the Crimes Amendment Act in New Zealand. In the United States, it is an offence to transmit information electronically about a child aged 16 or under, for the purpose of committing a sexual offence. The Australian Criminal Code makes similar restrictions, as does the Canadian Criminal Code. The legislation in the UK differs in that the sexual grooming offence applies both to the new technologies including the internet and mobile phones, and also to the real world, while legislation in other countries addresses only electronic grooming via the internet and mobile phones.

Norway was among the first European countries to adopt the grooming legislation. The relevant sections in the General Civil Penal Code ("straffeloven") concerned with sexual offenders in Norway include Section 195: Any person who engages in sexual activity with a child who is under 14 years of age shall be liable to imprisonment for a term not exceeding 10 years. If the said activity was sexual intercourse the penalty shall be imprisonment for not less than 2 years. Furthermore, Section 196 says: Any person who engages in sexual activity with a child who is under 16 years of age shall be liable to imprisonment for a term not exceeding 5 years. Section 201a is the new grooming section in Norwegian criminal law. This section was included in The General Civil Penal Code in April 2007: "With fines or imprisonment of not more than 1 year is any person liable, who has agreed a meeting with a child who is under 16 years of age, and who with intention of committing an act as mentioned in sections 195, 196 or 200 second part has arrived at the meeting place or a place where the meeting place can be observed".

In Norwegian law, the grooming section refers to the intention of committing an act. However, the perpetrator must actually appear for a meeting (sometimes a police trap). An intention to meet is not enough, it is possible that it should be, but it is difficult to prove beyond doubt. Therefore, the legislation is phrased as follows: "…has arrived at the meeting place or a place where the meeting place can be observed". It is the potential scene of the crime, which is the meeting place where the offence is intended to take place, that the offender has arrived at, or the offender can observe the potential crime scene from where he is located. We refer to the potential offender and offender as "he", although little is known in the literature about the gender of all online groomers.

Virtual Offender Communities

Kierkegaard (2008) argues that the anonymity, availability of extremely sensitive personal information, and ease of contacting people make social networking sites a useful tool for online child predators. The sites enable both potential offenders and potential victims to explore and exploit all eighteen characteristics of the internet listed earlier in this book. While many of the sites have age restrictions, it is possible for potential offenders to misrepresent their age. How far the MySpace threat to remove those believed to be over 18, but posing as less than 18 years, is carried out in practice, for example, is questionable. To hide their

IP addresses and locations, they piggyback on WiFi connections or use proxy servers. Decentralized peer-to-peer networks prevent material from being tracked to a specific server, and encryption lets them keep online chats private from those policing the web.

Social networking sites have been studied in different contexts. For example, Tufekci (2008) explored the rapid adoption of online social network sites by students on a US college campus. Using quantitative and qualitative data based on a diverse sample of college students, demographic and other characteristics of social networking site, users and non-users were compared. A distinction was made between social grooming and presentation of self. In the study, non-users displayed an attitude toward social grooming (gossip, small-talk and generalized, non-functional people-curiosity) that ranged from incredulous to hostile. Contrary to expectations in the study, non-users did not report a smaller number of close friends compared with users, but they did keep in touch with fewer people. Users were also heavier users of the expressive Internet, which is the practice and performance of technologically mediated sociality.

Thus, while social grooming through language may well be an important human activity, there seems to be no reason to presuppose that everyone will be equally disposed to such activity. Interest in exchange and browsing social information about friends and acquaintances, and curiosity about people, is likely to be related to interest in how an application specifically facilitates such activity (Tufekci, 2008).

When we apply Tufekci's (2008) terminology to online grooming, online groomers are likely to be heavier users of the expressive Internet than pedophilic non-users of social networking sites. As users of the expressive Internet, online groomers use the internet as an instrument to express opinions and communicate information. Expressive Internet is the practice and performance of technologically mediated sociality. It is the use of the internet to perform and realize interactions, self-presentations, public performance, social capital management, social monitoring, and the production, maintenance, and furthering of social ties. The expressive Internet might be recognized as a social ecology involving other people, values, norms, and social contexts.

Instrumental internet, on the other hand, refers to information seeking, knowledge gathering, and commercial transactions on the internet, and non-social communication involved in such transactions. This is typically the internet of online banking, shopping, and checking the weather. Tufekci (2008) found no difference in the use of instrumental Internet for users versus non-users of social networking sites.

The expressive Internet has been expanding rapidly, a process often described in the popular press as the rise of social computing. These tools have been assimilated as a means of social interaction and social integration for increasing numbers of people and communities. People are increasingly using the expressive Internet in ways that complement or further their offline sociality (Tufekci, 2008).

The distinction between the two groups of users is a point also raised by some of the probation officers interviewed by Davidson (2008) in the UK. The probation officers were working with groomers in treatment programs. They spoke about offenders for whom the internet played a significant role in their lives and who had many online relationships. Using the Internet to offend was almost a natural progression for these offenders as it played such a big part in other areas of their lives.

The internet has afforded potential sex offenders the opportunity to create their own virtual communities, by allowing instant access to other offenders by worldwide reach, open discussion of their sexual desires, shared ideas about ways to lure victims, and mutual support of their adult–child sex philosophies. Computer technology and the internet enable potential sex offenders to locate and interact with other offenders more readily than before. The organizational aspects of a common gathering place and the resultant support child predators are providing each other is probably their most significant advantage—and the most troublesome for a concerned public.

Child predators are forming online communities and bonds using the internet. They are openly uniting against legal authorities and discussing ways to influence public thinking and legislation on child exploitation. While sex offender web sites are being tracked down and removed from internet servers in countries all over the world, they are popping up again at a higher pace in most parts of the world, and many sites are hosted in the United States and Russia.

The forming of communities for white-collar offenders online and cybercriminals is similar to virtual communities for sex offenders. Underground communities provide market access to the various actors (Caines et al., 2018). Trustworthiness in an otherwise untrusted environment is a particular challenge for financial offenders as well as sex offender. Trustworthiness can, for example, be the result of a satisfied buyer (Holt et al., 2016).

An example of a web site representing a virtual community for sex offenders is "Boylove". It is one of the largest sex offender networks on the internet. On the web site, The Boylove Manifesto could be found, which argued the case for intergenerational relationships (www.prevent-abuse-now.com):

> As boy lovers we distance ourselves from the current discussion about "child sexual abuse". Human sexuality plays the same part in a boy love relationship as it undoubtedly does in any relationship between human beings. A boy lover desires a friendly and close relationship with a boy.

Similar text can be found on BoyLover.net:

> Over the years, pedophilia, or boy love as it is sometimes known, has come under heavy criticism from those who are opposed to it in the media, government and general society. Often, this can be very one-sided and extremely vitriolic in nature.
> Here at BoyLover.net, we believe that people deserve the chance to hear both sides of the argument. Doubtless, by now you will have read or heard many opinions against pedophilia. With this in mind, we have taken the opportunity to present different views so that people can make an informed decision regarding the subject.

BoyLover.net seems important to mention here, as sex offender research in countries such as Norway, Sweden, and the UK tends to focus on girls more than boys. Lillywhite and Skidmore (2006) argue that the view that boys are not sexually exploited is very common among many professionals working with vulnerable young men. Do potential sex offenders interested in boys perform online grooming different from potential sex offenders that are interested in girls? Different grooming behaviors may be employed with different genders.

D'Ovidio et al. (2009) conducted a content analysis of 64 websites that promote, advocate, and convey information in support of sexual relationships between adults and children to determine whether these sites were structured as learning environments for crime involving the sexual exploitation of children. Their findings indicate that the adult–child advocacy websites analyzed were criminal in that they contained a variety of communication tools (e.g., chat rooms, instant messengers, and message boards) to foster interaction among site users and expose users to rationalizations for offending and, in turn, definitions favorable to sexual violations against minors.

Given these research findings, D'Ovidio et al. (2009) recommend law enforcement to consider expanding restrictions for companies offering website hosting services to modify their terms of service agreements to ban content advocating sexual relationships between adults and children. Out of 64 websites studied, 40 websites were registered in the United States, 9 in the Netherlands, 5 in Canada, 4 in the United Kingdom, and 1 in each of the countries Brazil, Czech Republic, Finland, France, Liechtenstein, and Slovakia.

While little is known about white-collar communities compared to pedophile communities on the internet, it is quite likely that cybercrime communities exist for several of the case studies presented earlier in this book. Movie piracy and music piracy are typical examples (Hinduja, 2012; Popham & Volpe, 2018; Smallridge & Roberts, 2013; Stone, 2015), where businesspeople exchange ideas, services, and software in social communities on the internet. The case study of foreign aid fraud is another example, where white-collar offenders online exchange ideas and solutions for business email compromise (Bakarich & Baranek, 2020). Also, the case study of cryptocurrency crime by Braaten and Vaughn (2019) reflects the likely existence of communities dealing in Bitcoin and other cryptocurrencies. During the Covid-19 pandemic, communities of practice probably developed for knowledge sharing in defrauding digital government (Horgan et al., 2021; Niesche, 2020; Vu et al., 2020).

European Grooming Project

The sexual abuse of young people via the internet is an international problem, a crime without geographical boundaries. A report from the Center for Missing and Exploited Children described 2660 incidents of adults using the internet to befriend and establish an emotional connection with a child, in order to entice them into meeting. As more young people use the internet to socially network with friends, the potential for contact with sexual offenders will increase. There is, however, limited information available about the behaviors of internet sexual offenders to inform effective risk management strategies for policy-makers, law enforcement agencies, parents, and young people. In response to this, the European Commission Safer Internet Plus Program commissioned a consortium of leading experts from the UK and across Europe to develop an understanding of the different ways in which sexual offenders approach, communicate, and groom young people online.

The consortium comprised Stephen Webster (National Centre for Social Research, UK); Julia Davidson and Antonia Bifulco (Kingston University, UK), Thierry Pham (UMons university, Belgium), Vincenzo Caretti (University of Rome and Palermo, Italy), and Petter Gottschalk (BI Norwegian Business School, Norway).

The overarching set of objectives of the research was to:

- Describe the behavior of offenders who groom and their account of young people who are groomed and explore differences (e.g., in demographics, behavior or profiles) within offender and victim group and how these differences may have a bearing on offence outcome.
- Describe how information and communication technology (ICT) is used to facilitate the process of online grooming.
- Further the current low knowledge base about the way in which young people are selected and prepared for abuse online.
- Make a significant contribution to the further development of educational awareness and preventative initiatives aimed at parents and young people.
- Contribute to the development of online sex offender risk assessment and management knowledge.

To meet this set of objectives, the project involved three separate but inter-linked phases. First, a scoping phase that encompassed a review of recent police case files, interviews with key stakeholders working to prevent online grooming, and a literature review. The fieldwork and analysis of phase two of the research consisted of in-depth interviews with men who have been convicted of online grooming in each consortium country. These research interviews investigated in detail the behavior of Internet sexual offenders and described the variation in their actions according to the characteristics and response of different young people (Davidson & Gottschalk, 2008, 2010, 2011a, 2011b, 2015; Gottschalk, 2011a, 2011b; Webster et al., 2015).

The first step in developing a robust understanding of online grooming was to assess the hypothetical model developed in the scoping phase. Thematic analysis of offender interviews indicated that some refinement was necessary to reflect the complexity of online grooming. The first high-level refinement was to rename the model as "features of online grooming". There were two reasons for this: first, "model" assumes a linear pathway through phases—our interviews with online groomers showed this is not the case. Online groomers enter and exit particular phases according to their objectives and the perceived "needs" of the young people targeted. Second, the word model assumes that all aspects of the described process are relevant to the population of groomers. Again, our research indicates this not to be the case. That is, although some groomers described taking a measured and lengthy approach through a sequence of pre-determined steps, there was also evidence of fast and almost random approaches to young people. Below we briefly describe our typology of online grooming that explains these diverse offending behaviors.

As noted above, the key features of grooming behavior the study identified do not apply to all groomers in all contacts they have with young people. These features of online grooming include factors that help maintain the behavior such as the online environment, dissonance, and offenders' perceptions of young people and their behavior. The research also identified salient behaviors in the grooming process such as: scanning the online environment for potential people to contact, the identity adopted by the groomer (be it their own or another); the nature of contact with the young person; the different ways in which the online groomer can intensify the process of grooming and the diverse range of outcomes toward the end of the process. In particular, it is clear from the research that not all episodes of online grooming result in a physical meeting.

Development of the thematic framework was followed by detailed within and between case analysis to identify and understand associations between broad grooming features and individual offender characteristics. These analyses led to the development of a classification that encompassed three types of online groomer across nine behavioral dimensions. These analytical dimensions included whether the offender: had any previous convictions for sexual offending; used their own or another identity; the nature and extent of indecent image use; contacted other offenders online; the type of offence-supportive beliefs described; the speed of contact made with young people; how contact was made and sustained; and finally, the outcome of the offence (online offending and/or offline meeting).

The first "type" of groomer identified is the **distorted attachment** offender. Men in this group had offence supportive beliefs that involved seeing contact with the young person as a "*relationship*". As such, they did not get involved in other online behaviors that indicated to them, and others, that they were sexually offending. Men within this group did not have any indecent images of children and they did not have any contact with any other sexual offenders online. This group also seemed to spend a significant amount of time online talking to the young person before they met the victim. All men in this group went on to meet the victim to develop or further the "*relationship*".

The second type is the **adaptable online groomer**. This group of men had offence supportive beliefs that involved their own needs and seeing the victim as mature and capable. Unlike the group above, they did not seem to have discussed the encounter in terms of a relationship. Some men in this group had collections of indecent images of children but they were not significant collections in terms of size. They also tended not to have significant contact with other sexual offenders online. Men in this group were adept at adopting their identity and grooming style according to how the young person presented online. Similarly, the speed at which contact developed could be fast and/or slow according to how the victim responded to contact.

Finally, the **hyper-sexualized** group of men was characterized by extensive indecent image collections of children and significant online contact with other sexual offenders or offender groups. Some men in this group also had significant collections of extreme adult pornography. They adopted different identities altogether or had an identity picture that was not of their face but of their genitals. Their contacts with young people were highly sexualized and escalated very quickly. Their offence supportive beliefs involved "dehumanizing" young people. They tended not to personalize contact and so did not seem to be using the phone or other personal media like the other groups of offenders.

The final aspect of the analysis at phase two of the research encompassed understanding the behavior of young people online via the interviews with online groomers. Despite the research not directly interviewing young people that have been harmed online, the offender interviews provided an insight to the diverse behavior of young people. It was clear from the accounts of offenders that safety messages are getting through to a resilient group of young people. However, those young people who seemed to be susceptible to the approaches of online groomers displayed a range of vulnerability features that could include loneliness, low self-esteem, self-harming behavior, family break-up, and incidence of ongoing sexual abuse by other offenders.

Analysis of the offender accounts of their contact with young people made it clear that online grooming cannot be comprehensively understood and managed without understanding the interaction between the offender, online environment, and young person. Reflecting on the research project, the development of the typology represents an important contribution of this research to the literature, as it *challenges* some of the common grooming myths such as:

- "All online groomers want to meet young people…"
- "Pornography and indecent images cause online offending…"
- "Young people are passive when communicating with adults…"
- "All online offending involves socialization…"

In testing and challenging these assumptions, the research empowers policy-makers to understand the complexity of offenders and young people's online behavior and may assist in the development of effective intervention programs (Davidson & Gottschalk, 2008, 2010, 2011a, 2011b, 2015; Gottschalk, 2011a, 2011b; Webster et al., 2015).

Furthermore, in our main perspective of online white-collar offenders as trusted cybercriminals who find it convenient to commit and conceal financial crime, it might be a relevant path for future research to explore different types of offenders. While the labels for groomer types certainly will not fit, building on offline categories might be a start. For example, as suggested by the theory of convenience, some offenders commit occupational crime to benefit themselves, while others commit corporate crime to benefit the organization. Hopefully, future research will challenge some of the common myths about cybercriminals.

The idea of profiling offenders in different groups can help introduce a contingent approach to law enforcement in cyberspace, where policing is dependent on the assumed profile of offenders. In the case of groomers, distorted attachment offenders, adaptable online groomers, and hyper-sexualized group require different approaches in policing. Since there is so much to learn from the sexual offender literature, one more classification is worthwhile to include. van Gijn-Grosvenor and Lamb (2021) suggest the following online groomer typology scheme:

- Intimacy-seeking groomers: These offenders engage in addressing topics such as hobbies, school, occupation, friends, and family rather than sexual activities or concealment. They show great interest in the children's lives, they complement the children on their physical appearance, and they promise children presents and fun activities.
- Dedicated, hyper-sexual groomers: They are highly cautious, but talk a lot about sexual matters. They are very keen to meet the children offline for sexual purposes, and they use every possible strategy to avoid getting caught. They work hard to foster children's trust and to force children into complying with their sexual desires.
- Social groomers: Compared to the first two groups, these offenders communicate more about non-sexual matters than about sexual matters and ways to prevent disclosure. They build a relation over time

where they are less concerned about disclosure of the contact. The relational orientation through interaction is important to offenders.

- Opportunistic-asocial groomers. The offenders in this fourth cluster make very little effort to build relationships. They are somewhat comparable to the social groomers because they mention sexual matters the same number of times, but they are concerned about detection and therefore spend little time talking online.

For white-collar offender, there is a possibility to find clusters based on theories. For example, some are greedy, while others are adventurous. However, the interesting thing about works by Webster et al. (2015) and van Gijn-Grosvenor and Lamb (2021) is their empirical basis of interviewed offenders.

References

Aljuboori, D., Seneviratne-Eglin, E., Swiergala, E., & Guerra, C. (2021). Association between family support and online sexual abuse in Chilean adolescents: The mediational role of online risk behaviors. *Journal of Child Sexual Abuse*. https://doi.org/10.1080/10538712.2021.1875280

Australian. (2008). *Online child grooming laws*. Australian Institute of Criminology, Project 0074a, Australian Government. www.aic.gov.au

Bakarich, K. M., & Baranek, D. (2020). Something phish-y is going on here: A teaching case on business email compromise. *Current Issues in Auditing, 14*(1), A1–A9.

BBC. (2007, July 25). MySpace bars 29,000 sex offenders. *BBC*. http://news.bbc.co.uk/2/hi/technology/6914870.stm

Braaten, C. N., & Vaughn, M.S. (2019). Convenience theory of cryptocurrency crime: A content analysis of U.S. federal court decisions. *Deviant Behavior*, published online. https://doi.org/10.1080/01639625.2019.1706706

Caines, A., Pastrana, S., Hutchings, A., & Buttery, P. J. (2018). Automatically identifying the function and intent of posts in underground forums. *Crime Science, 7*(19), 1–14.

Calder, M. C. (2004). The internet: Potential, problems and pathways to hands-on sexual offending. In M. C. Calder (Ed.), *Child sexual abuse and the Internet: Tackling the new frontier* (pp. 1–23). Russell House Publishing.

Cook, N. (2008). *Enterprise 2.0: How social software will change the future of work*. Gower Publishing Limited.

Davidson, J. (2008). *Child sexual abuse—Media representations and government reactions*. Routledge.

Davidson, J., & Gottschalk, P. (2008). Digital forensics in law enforcement: The case of online victimization of children. *Electronic Government—An International Journal, 5*(4), 445–451.

Davidson, J., & Gottschalk, P. (2010). *Online groomers: Profiling*. Russell House Publishing.

Davidson, J., & Gottschalk, P. (2011a). Characteristics of the internet for criminal child sexual abuse by online groomers. *Criminal Justice Studies, 24*(1), 23–36.

Davidson, J., & Gottschalk, P. (2011b). *Child internet abuse: Current research and policy*. Routledge, Taylor & Francis Group.

Davidson, J., & Gottschalk, P. (2015). The context of online abuse: Policy and legislation. In S. Webster, J. Davidson, & A. Bifulco (Eds.), *Online offending behaviour and child victimisation* (pp. 1–20). Palgrave Macmillan.

Davidson, J., & Martellozzo, E. (2008). Protecting vulnerable young people in cyberspace from sexual abuse: Raising awareness and responding globally. *Police Practice & Research, 9*(4), 277–289.

Dombrowski, S. C., Gischlar, K. L., & Durst, T. (2007). Safeguarding young people from cyber pornography and cyber sexual predation: A major dilemma of the internet. *Child Abuse Review, 16*, 153–170.

D'Ovidio, R., Mitman, T., El-Burki, I. J., & Shumar, W. (2009). Adult-child sex advocacy websites as social learning environments: A content analysis. *International Journal of Cyber Criminology, 3*(1), 421–440.

Dunaigre, P. (2001). Paedophilia: A psychiatric and psychoanalytical point of view. In C. A. Arnaldo (Ed.), *Child abuse on the internet—Ending the silence* (pp. 43–49). UNESCO and Beghahn Books.

Finkelhor, D. (1984). *Child sexual abuse: New theory and research*. The Free Press.

van Gijn-Grosvenor, E. L., Lamb, M. E. (2021). Online groomer typology scheme. *Psychology, Crime & Law*, published online. https://doi.org/10.1080/1068316X.2021.1876048

Gottschalk, P. (2011a). Characteristics of the internet and child abuse. In J. Davidson & P. Gottschalk (Ed.), *Internet child abuse—Current research and policy* (pp. 27–51). Routledge, Taylor & Francis Group.

Gottschalk, P. (2011b). Stage model for online grooming offenders. In J. Davidson & P. Gottschalk (Eds.), *Internet child abuse—Current research and policy* (pp. 79–103). Routledge, Taylor & Francis Group.

Hamerton, C. (2020). White-collar cybercrime: Evaluating the redefinition of a criminological artifact. *Journal of Law and Criminal Justice, 8*(2), 67–79.

Hinduja, S. (2012). General strain, self-control, and music piracy. *International Journal of Cyber Criminology, 6*(1), 951–967.

Holt, T. J., Smirnova, O., & Hutchings, A. (2016). Examining signals of trust in criminal markets online. *Journal of Cybersecurity, 2*(2), 137–145.

Horgan, S., Collier, B., Jones, R., & Shepherd, L. (2021). Re-territorialising the policing of cybercrime in the post-Covid-19 era: Towards a new vision of local democratic cyber policing. *Journal of Criminal Psychology*, published online. https://doi.org/10.1108/JCP-08-2020-034

Kierkegaard, S. (2008). Cybering, online grooming and ageplay. *Computer Law & Security Report, 24*, 41–55.

Lillywhite, R., & Skidmore, P. (2006). Boys are not sexually exploited? A challenge to practitioners. *Child Abuse Review, 15*, 351–361.

McElwee, G., & Smith, R. (2015). Towards a nuanced typology of illegal entrepreneurship: A theoretical and conceptual overview. In G. McElwee & R. Smith (Eds.), *Exploring criminal and illegal enterprise: New perspectives on research, policy & practice: Contemporary issues in entrepreneurship research* (Vol. 5). Emerald.

Mitchell, K. J., Wolak, J., & Finkelhor, D. (2008). Are blogs putting youth at risk for online sexual solicitation or harassment? *Child Abuse & Neglect, 32*, 277–294.

Niesche, C. (2020, October–November). Thei heightened risk of fraud in the Covid era. *Acuitymag*. www.acuitymag.com

Popham, J. F., & Volpe, C. (2018). Predicting moral disengagement from the harms associated with digital music piracy: An exploratory, integrative test of digital drift and the criminal interaction order. *International Journal of Cyber Criminology, 12*(1), 133–150.

Quayle, E., Vaughan, M., & Taylor, M. (2006). Sex offenders, internet child abuse images and emotional avoidance: The importance of values. *Aggression and Violent Behavior, 11*, 1–11.

Ramoglou, S., & Tsang, E. W. K. (2016). A realist perspective of entrepreneurship: Opportunities as propensities. *Academy of Management Review, 41*, 410–434.

Smallridge, J. L., & Roberts, J. R. (2013). Crime specific neutralizations: An empirical examination of four types of digital piracy. *International Journal of Cyber Criminology, 7*(2), 125–140.

Smith, R. (2009). Understanding entrepreneurial behavior in organized criminals. *Journal of Enterprising Communities: People and Places in the Global Economy, 3*(3), 256–268.

Stone, B. (2015, March 2–March 8). Too good to be legal. *Bloomberg Businessweek*, pp. 31–33.

Tufekci, Z. (2008). Grooming, gossip, Facebook and MySpace: What can we learn about these sites from those who won't assimilate? *Information, Communication & Society, 11*(4), 544–564.

Vu, A. V., Hughes, J., Pete, I., Collier, B., Chua, Y. T., Shumailov, I., & Hutchings, A. (2020, October). Turning up the dial: The evolution of a cybercrime market through set-up, stable, and Covid-19 eras, IMC'20. In *Proceedings of the ACM Internet Measurement Conference* (pp. 551–566). https://doi.org/10.1145/3419394.3423636

Webster, S., Davidson, J., & Gottschalk, P. (2015). Understanding online grooming—Findings from the EOGP study. In S. Webster, J. Davidson, & A. Bifulco (Eds.), *Online offending behaviour and child victimisation* (pp. 55–90). Palgrave Macmillan.

Wild, T. S. N., Müller, I., Fromberger, P., Jordan, K., Klein, L., & Müller, J. L. (2020). Prevention of sexual child abuse: Preliminary results from an outpatient therapy program. *Frontiers in Psychiatry, 11*(88), 96–110.

Winters, G. M., Kaylor, L. E., & Jeglic, E. L. (2017). Sexual offenders contacting children online: An examination of transcripts of sexual grooming. *Journal of Sexual Aggression, 23*(1), 62–76.

Wolak, J., Finkelhor, D., & Mitchell, K. (2009). *Trends in arrests of "online sex offenders"*. Crimes Against Children Research Center. www.unh.edu/ccrc

10

Offline Case Studies

A number of online case studies have been presented so far in this book. The case studies presented convenience themes for external offenders (movie pirates, cryptocurrency abusers, espionage, corona fraud) and internal offenders (embezzlement, money laundering, bank fraud, manipulation). This chapter presents three offline case studies for comparison. The case studies are based on investigation reports made public in 2020 and 2021. The case studies include assessments of the investigations. It is important to emphasize that these case studies are concerned with suspected individuals and not convicted white-collar offenders.

Austria: Biathlon Union

The International Biathlon Union is headquartered in Salzburg in Austria. Biathlon is a winter sport that combines cross-country skiing and rifle shooting. It is treated as a race, with contestants skiing through a cross-country trail whose distance is divided into shooting rounds. Major biathlon nations include France, Russia, Sweden, and Norway. Biathlon

P. Gottschalk and C. Hamerton, *White-Collar Crime Online*, https://doi.org/10.1007/978-3-030-82132-6_10

is a very popular sport among spectators, both present at shooting stadiums and in front of television screens all over the world. The business of biathlon events has grown significantly in recent decades, and rumors of both corruption and doping have flourished for several years in the media.

Russian doping whistleblower Grigory Rodchenkov told the media about organized doping of Russian athletes at the Sochi Winter Olympics. He had been the head of Russia's national anti-doping laboratory. Rodchenkov's allegations were confirmed by the independent McLaren report, leading to Russia's partial bans from the 2016 Summer Olympics and 2018 Winter Olympics. Rodchenkov's allegations and the McLaren findings led to an investigation particularly targeted at the management at the International Biathlon Union (IBU). When the IBU report was released (IBU Commission, 2021), the *New York Times* wrote about it under the heading "Hunting trips, sex, and cash: How grooming biathlon's leader paid off for Russia: An investigation accuses biathlon's longtime president of accepting gifts from Russians and then doing the country's bidding as a doping scandal swirled" (Panja, 2021):

> The president of the International Biathlon Union told the police that the young woman who had come to his hotel in Moscow was a prostitute, but he was hazy on the details. He did not remember the date or even who had paid for her services, he said, but it had assuredly not been him. The president, Anders Besseberg, had led biathlon's governing body for more than two decades by then, and he was accustomed to receiving gifts from his Russian hosts. Like a chocolate on his pillow or a gift bag placed on a chair in his hotel room, the company of a young woman during a trip to a World Cup biathlon event was not uncommon.
>
> And for decades, according to a report commissioned by biathlon's new leadership, Besseberg repaid the Russian favors by doing the country's bidding – defending its athletes, assailing its critics and even blocking efforts to root out doping by its teams. The yearlong effort to groom Besseberg, and later his top deputy, was so effective that at the height of Russia's state-run doping scandal one Russian official boasted to a colleague that the country had little to fear in biathlon – a grueling endurance sport that combines precision shooting with cross-country ski racing – because he had Besseberg "under his control".

The potential offender in this case study is Anders Besseberg who appears in the view of the commission to have had no regard for ethical values and no real interest in protecting the sport from cheating. IBU Commission (2021) claims that Besseberg was enabled by a complete lack of basic governance safeguards that left integrity decisions in the sole hands of himself and his allies on the IBU executive board, with no checks and balances, no transparency, and no accountability. Integrity is the quality of acting in accordance with the moral values, norms, and rules that are considered valid and relevant within the context in which the actor operates (Loyens et al., 2021). The external review commission found that Besseberg had been bribed by Russian officials by more than three hundred thousand Euros.

In the financial motive dimension of convenience theory, he was interested in hunting trips and sex paid for by others, in addition to cash (IBU Commission, 2021: 63):

> The police also seized thirteen watches at Mr Besseberg's home. Four of them were from specific sporting events, the other nine watches being luxury brands like RAM (2), Omega Broad Arrow, Ulysee Nardin (2), Huboldt Geneve, Poljot, and two unknown brands (both probably Russian) . Mr Besseberg confirmed that he had received the Omega watch (worth about Euro 20,000) as a personal present in March 2011 in Khanty-Mansysk, to mark the occasion of the 100th IBU Executive Board meeting and his 65th birthday. He said a blue watch (brand unknown, probably *Naprer') was given to him by Alexander Tikhonov, but he could not provide the occasion or the date of the gift, just that it was at an IBU World Cup event at Holmenkollen. That leaves seven watches of unclear provenance. Mr Besseberg himself did not state that he had bought them or indicate how he had obtained them.

Besseberg climbed the hierarchy of needs for status and success (Maslow, 1943). He had contributed to the success of biathlon sport and probably wanted to satisfy the need for acclaim as a narcissist (Chatterjee & Pollock, 2017). He was greedy as well (Goldstraw-White, 2012). The motive was individual possibilities as indicated in Fig. 10.1.

In the opportunity dimension of convenience theory, IBU Commission (2021: 1) argue that Besseberg's corrupt behavior was "enabled

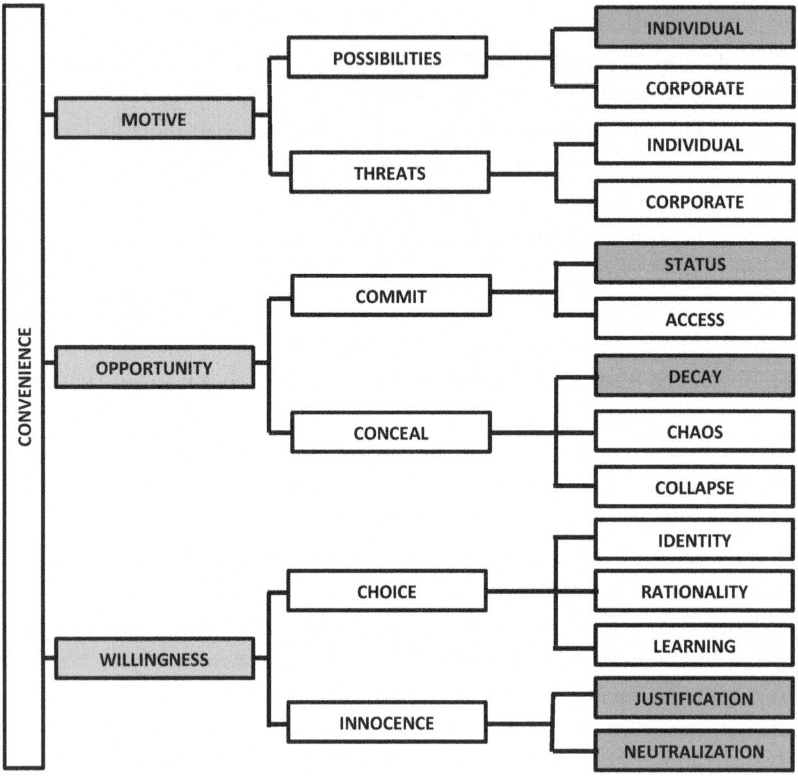

Fig. 10.1 Convenience themes for the IBU president

by a complete lack of basic governance safeguards that left integrity decisions in the sole hands of the President and his allies on the IBU Executive Board, with no checks and balances, no transparency, and no accountability whatsoever to keep them honest", which made that "Mr. Besseberg's proclaimed commitment to clean sport was, in the Commission's view, a charade". As indicated in Fig. 10.1, there was a combination of status and decay that made wrongdoing convenient. While status enabled commitment of wrongdoing (Patel & Cooper, 2014; Pontell et al., 2014), decay enabled concealment of wrongdoing (Crosina & Pratt, 2019; Eberl et al., 2015; Rooij & Fine, 2020).

In the willingness dimension of convenience theory, IBU Commission (2021: 1) claims that Besseberg could justify and neutralize his deviant behavior:

> This final report of the independent IBU External Review Commission (the Commission) identifies what the Commission considers to be evidence of systematic corrupt and unethical conduct at the very top of the IBU for a decade (2008 to 2018) and more, by a president (Anders Besseberg, IBU President 1993 to 2018) who appears, in the view of the Commission, to have had no regard for ethical values and no real interest in protecting the sport from cheating.

His behavior seems to be in accordance with the differential association perspective, where an offender associates with those who agree with him, and distances himself from those who are critical to his activities (Sutherland, 1983). It is a matter of learning from others, who in this case are Russian officials. It was a rational choice, where perception of benefits exceeded perceptions of costs (Pratt & Cullen, 2005). Probably did behavioral reinforcement of deviance occur over time (Benartzi et al., 2017). Besseberg may have slided on the slippery slope (Welsh et al., 2014) with a lack of self-control (Gottfredson & Hirschi, 1990) .

In view of the commission, the evidentiary record that the commission has gathered established that both Besseberg and Resch have a case to answer for breach of their duties under the IBU constitution, IBU disciplinary rules, and/or the IBU code of ethics. These regulations require people at IBU to act at all times with the utmost integrity, to protect the rights of clean athletes, and not to undertake any actions that are contrary to the interests of the biathlon sport. In the commission's view, the evidence uncovered suggests that IBU president Anders Besseberg consistently preferred and protected Russian interests in virtually everything that he did. The commission claims that they have identified provision of bribes and extensive favors by the Russians to Besseberg, particularly in the form of free hunting trips and the services of prostitutes (IBU Commission, 2021: 64):

> Another way of gaining improper influence over someone is by obtaining compromising material that can be used to blackmail them. In this regard, the Commission notes that there is evidence of Mr Besseberg's use of prostitutes in Russia, some or all of them arranged for him by his hosts. It was notorious within IBU circles that Mr Besseberg's hosts would often provide him with the services of a young, female 'interpreter' when he visited Russia. An IBU Board Member stated to the Commission: 'in this regard Anders was a special man. It was well known that when he was in Russia, he had an interpreter on his side'. The interpreter indeed translated speeches and other conversation, but 'what kind of the role of the interpreters of Mr Besseberg are doing later after official events, I don't know, if it was a double role'. He understood that 'the RBU hired these interpreters'. Nicole Resch said to the police: 'Because of the way Anders Besseberg treated these women, I got the impression of an intimate relationship'. But she could not say definitively if these women were paid or who paid them.

Examiners exemplify how Besseberg protected Russian interests in the case of the 2018 IBU World Cup event in Tuymen in Russia. In advance it had been agreed to move the event away from Russia if further Russian doping cases were detected (IBU Commission, 2021: 160):

> When interviewed by the Commission, Max Cobb and Ivor Lehotan were both very clear in their recollection that the agreement of the IBU Executive Board was that if the new LIMS evidence that WADA had obtained led to any further cases against Russian biathletes (beyond the four already pending: Glazyrina, Romanova, Vilukhina, and Zaitseva), the 2018 IBU World Cup Final event would be moved from Tyumen. In contrast, Dr Leistner said he could not really remember any such discussion. However, a press release issued by the IBU stated that 'all members of the Association of the International Olympic Winter Sports Federations (AIOWF) agreed at a conference call on 9 December 2017 that all competitions in Russia will be conducted as planned for the ongoing season 2017/2018, unless new important and legally backed evidence is brought up'.
>
> The Commission also has evidence that Mr Besseberg was well aware of the situation and was also apparently himself of the view that there had been a conspiracy between the Moscow laboratory and the Ministry of Sports. On 9 January 2018, Mr Besseberg met with athletes and coaches

> at the IBU World Cup event in Ruhpolding, and they expressed significant concern about competing in Russia. In addition, the IBU Athletes' Committee passed on to the IBU Executive Board a letter setting out their position that it was simply wrong to have the final 2018 IBU World Cup event and two IBU Cups in Russia, noting that there had even been threats of physical harm made to athletes who travelled to Russia, and that they were also worried about dope tests being tampered with (...) According to Max Cobb; 'During the discussion Mr Besseberg threatened that if the World Cup in Tyumen would not take place, we all could be held liable with our private assets'. Mr Besseberg told the criminal prosecutors that it was not him who said that. Rather, as far as he could recall, 'noted that there is a risk that in the event of a withdrawal the board members could be liable with their private assets'.

The IBU Commission (2021) concluded that both Anders Besseberg and Nicole Resch improperly favored Russian interests, in breach of their duties to the IBU and to the sport.

The IBU external review commission was chaired by Jonathan Taylor. He was a lawyer and a partner at law firm Bird & Bird in the UK. He was head of the sports group in London, where he advised governing bodies, event organizers, and others active in the sector. He appeared regularly before the Court of Arbitration for Sport in Lausanne on doping and other matters. The review committee included Vincent Defrasne (former French biathlete), Christian Dorda (Austrian lawyer), Tanja Haug (German lawyer), Anja Martin (German lawyer), and Lauren Pagé (legal secretary). The mandate for the work by commission had three items:

1. Assist Wada and the criminal authorities with their investigations. Allegations that triggered the investigations: Anders Besseberg covered up anti-doping rule violations by Russian biathletes, with the assistance of Nicole Resch; vote in favor of 2021 IBU world cup in Tyumen in Russia was corrupted. Wada handed over its investigation to the external review commission, with close cooperation ever since. The external review commission has provided support to Austrian criminal authorities and offered its support to Norwegian criminal authorities regarding biathlon investigations. The commission

has also been in contact with the German and Austrian authorities involved in Operation Aderlass (blood doping in different sports).

2. Support the updating and strengthening of the IBU governance system in accordance with best practice. Next steps are criminal investigations in Austria and Norway that are ongoing. Austrian and Norwegian authorities have set up a joint investigation team that Europol has joined. At IBU, the Biathlon Integrity Unit will take over responsibility to support the criminal authorities as necessary from the IBU's side.
3. Determine whether anyone has a case to answer for breach of the IBU rules. Both substantive rules as well as procedural rules apply. Is there admissible and credible evidence that would be sufficient, if accepted by the hearing panel, to prove each element of the rule breach charged to the requisite standard (comfortable satisfaction/balance of probabilities)? In corruption cases, unlikely to be much direct evidence, but use indirect/circumstantial evidence and inferences that strand together to create a strong enough cable to sustain charges. The Biathlon Integrity Unit may bring charges before the CAS.

The commission compiled more than 70,000 documents and electronic files. They interviewed 60 people, and they accessed anti-doping evidence from criminal proceedings in Austria. The commission failed in interviewing Anders Besseberg as well as Nicole Resch. This is an obvious shortcoming in the investigation that reduces investigation report maturity since Besseberg and Resch are important information sources as well as persons entitled to contradict allegations against them as well as contradict conclusions drawn by examiners. While Besseberg denied cooperation with the examiners with an excuse that criminal investigations against him were pending in both Norway and Austria, Resch denied cooperation for health-related reasons. An important skill for examiners is to approach suspects as information sources in a manner that makes potential interviewees motivated for questioning. Obviously, Taylor and his colleagues on the commission failed in their approach.

As argued by King (2020), an important element in determining investigation maturity is the applied maturity level of financial fraud investigative interviewing since interviewing is at the heart of the investigation process. The aim of an investigative interview is to elicit an accurate and detailed account of an incident for the purpose of reconstructing past events and sequences of events. An investigative interview should be carried out in a manner that does not place significant stress or strain on the interviewee.

Both Besseberg and Resch declined the opportunity to comment substantially on the allegations and evidence set out in the commission report. However, in accordance with Austrian law, the commission was granted access to the Austrian criminal investigation file and therefore had copies of the statements that Besseberg and Resch, respectively, made to the police, and which they both referred the commission to as explanation of their respective positions. Such files represent secondary information compared to primary information in an interview, which reduces their value. The files are of less value also because the purpose of crime interviews is different from the purpose of rule-breaking interviews.

The investigation report seems biased toward wrongdoing. For example, examiners claim that all interpreters for Besseberg were prostitutes. While Besseberg had admitted to the police that he received the service of a prostitute on one single occasion between 2010 and 2014 in Moscow, he denied that interpreters were prostitutes.

Similarly, examiners jump to the conclusion of corruption (IBU Commission, 2021: 68):

> Although the Commission has not found direct evidence that Mr Besseberg received cash bribes from Russian parties, there are significant apparent gaps in his explanation of his personal finances, as well as direct evidence that he received expensive hunting trips paid for by his Russian hosts.

In most civilized and democratic countries, this kind of evidence would not be sufficient to cause conviction in criminal court. Any doubt must always benefit defendants, and here there is doubt left for insights into the context. In civil court, where some apply the rule of more-likely than less-likely incident, with a probability of 50% and above being sufficient, then the outcome might be different. Maybe the threshold of 50% is sufficient for IBU constitution, rules, and ethics. However, in fair proceedings, and especially in criminal courts, an incident should be documented beyond any reasonable doubt before conviction.

Based on these shortcomings, the IBU investigation is allocated at level 2 as a problem-oriented investigation in Fig. 10.2. At this level, the investigation focused on issues that needed clarification. Examiners were looking for answers. Once examiners believed they had found answers, the investigation was terminated. The client had an unresolved problem, and the client regulated premises for the investigation. There was probably no room for investigators to pursue other paths than those that addressed the predefined problem. Lawyers are typically in charge of investigations at this level, where they map the facts. They find out what happened and how it happened, but they are reluctant to find out why it happened.

The low level of investigative maturity contrasts reactions in the media and elsewhere. After release of the report, it seems that nobody read the

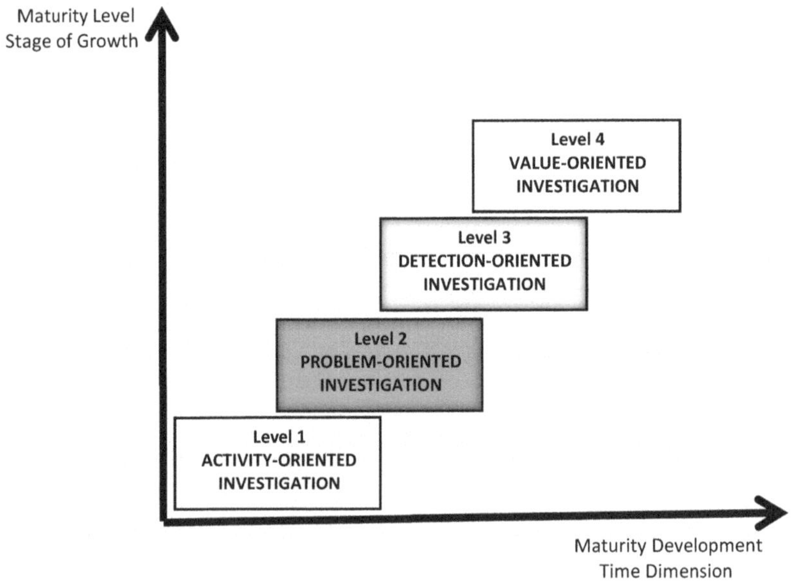

Fig. 10.2 Maturity assessments for the IBU Commission (2021) report

two-hundred-and-twenty pages, but rather relied on the press conference presentation by commission leader Jonathan Taylor. Nobody questioned, for example, the commission's suggestion and indication that because the interpreters helping Besseberg understand Russian in talks in Russia were young Russian females, they were probably all prostitutes.

After the report, Besseberg was facing punishment from four different actors (Christiansen, 2021): (i) Austrian police where doping in legal terms is considered fraud; (ii) Norwegian police where improper favors, gifts, and services are considered corruption; (iii) IBU Integrity Group where violations of rules and regulations can cause dismissal, and (iv) Norwegian Sports Association where violations of rules and regulations can cause dismissal as well as revocation of honorary award.

Congo: Mercy Corps Aid

Mercy Corps is a charity. The international non-government organization (NGO) experienced a scam in the Democratic Republic of Congo (DRC). The scam involved corrupt aid workers, business owners, and community leaders (Kleinfeld, 2020):

> Together they zeroed in on the humanitarian sector's flagship rapid response programmes – the main mechanism for helping displaced people in Congo, where hundreds of millions of dollars of foreign aid are spent every year.

Some $636,000 was lost by Mercy Corps and partners in just a few months. It was estimated that the charity had last $6 million in about two years. Kleinfeld (2020) describes the modus operandi in some of the wrongdoing:

> When a conflict or natural disaster occurred, aid groups would receive reports from local community leaders that exaggerated the number of people who had fled their homes. Businesspeople would then pay kickbacks to corrupt aid workers to register hundreds of additional people for cash support who were not actually displaced. The merchants would then receive the aid payments and share with the local leaders. Of the

> nineteen Mercy Corps aid workers alleged to be involved in the scam, some were using the extra cash to buy new cars, Armani glasses, and iPhones, according to several of their colleagues who spoke to The New Humanitarian (TNH). One even started building a hotel, colleagues said.

UN agencies and aid groups in Congo created an anti-fraud task to conduct an operational review after the NGO Mercy Corps discovered the fraud scheme. The investigating team consisted of three international consultants and two Congolese researchers contracted by Adam Smith International, an aid consultancy. The anti-fraud task was funded with a grant from the UK government (Henze et al., 2020).

Assuming that the allegations against local charity aid workers regarding corruption are correct, convenience themes can be identified for this group of offenders in the Mercy Corps case as illustrated in Fig. 10.3. A potential motive is the need to restore the perception of equity and equality (Leigh et al., 2010). Being an aid worker is a job, but aid organizations tend to believe that their employees are idealists who do not necessarily need a decent salary.

The equity perspective suggests that an individual compares his or her work efforts to another person or group of persons chosen as reference. A situation evaluated being without equity will initiate behavior to remove the feeling of discomfort (Huseman et al., 1987; Kamerdze et al., 2014; Martin & Peterson, 1987; Roehling et al., 2010).

The equity perspective is linked to the social exchange perspective, where there is a norm of reciprocity. Social exchange considers trusted employees as partners with the employer, who exchange valued contributions. The organization provides trusted employees material and socio-emotional rewards in exchange for their work effort and loyalty (Cropanzano & Mitchell, 2005). If a trusted employee perceives that the norm of reciprocity is violated, then the retaliation principle implies that the emphasis is placed both on the return of benefits and on the return of injuries (Caesens et al., 2019). Disloyalty is to defect from supporting someone. A trusted individual who feels mistreated might reciprocate by behaving in a manner that harms the source of this mistreatment (Gibney et al., 2009). Restoring the perception of equity and equality might also be a matter of responding to dehumanization, which is a

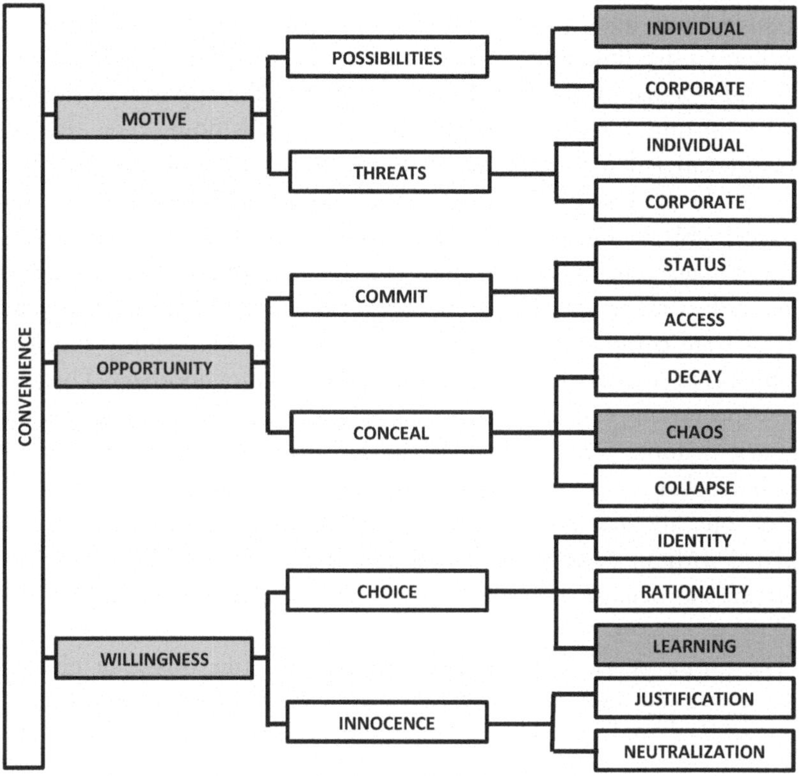

Fig. 10.3 Convenience themes for aid workers at Mercy Corps

feeling of being a tool or an instrument based on a perception of a treatment as lesser than or different from others (Bell & Khoury, 2016; Väyrynen & Laari-Salmela, 2015).

The organizational opportunity structure is mainly a result of trust-based management typically found in charities. Uygur (2020) studied fraud in the charity sector in England and Wales. He analyzed 42 fraud and 42 no-fraud charities. His findings suggest that excessive trust toward the charities creates the opportunity for fraud to take place.

Trust is an important contribution to the convenience of white-collar crime. Dearden (2016) argues that violation of trust is at the core of white-collar crime opportunity. Trust implies that vulnerability is accepted based upon positive expectations of the motives and actions of another. Controlling a trusted person is often considered both unnecessary and a signal of mistrust. In many cultures, the opposite of showing trust is to monitor and question what a person is doing. For example, a board can tell management what to do, but they do not tell them how to do it. The board shows trust that management will do it in an acceptable manner. If the board would move from only controlling what management has done to how management did it, then it might be perceived as mistrust. Kim et al. (2009: 401) define trust as "a psychological state comprising the intention to accept vulnerability based on positive expectations of the intentions or behavior of another". The positive expectations can relate to what another does, how it is done, and when it is done. The positive expectations can relate to the reaction of another, where it is expected that the reaction will be understandable, acceptable, and favorable. Vulnerability means that trust can easily be violated without detection or correction of deviant behavior.

Trust is associated with dependence and risk (Chan et al., 2020: 3):

> The trustor depends on something or someone (the trustee or object of trust), and there is a possibility that expectations or hopes will not be satisfied, and that things will go wrong. Trust is not absolute, but conditional and contextual.

Just like the concept of trust is relational, such that trust inherently requires a target, so too is the concept of felt trust relational. It is the felt trust that can influence an individual's tendency to crime, while it is the actual trust that is part of the opportunity structure for crime.

The gap between the two represents how accurately people understand others' perceptions of them (Campagna et al., 2020: 994):

> The concept of felt trust reflects what the more general interpersonal perception literature refers to as a dyadic meta-perception – one person's belief about the thought, attitude, or perception held by another person.

Control is replaced by trust in principal–agent relationships creating chaos in terms of guardianship as illustrated in Fig. 10.3. Chaos in humanitarian assistance is often resulting from the pressure to act quickly in emergencies primarily because human life may be at risk, but also because fundraising and media pressure demand fast action (Maxwell et al., 2008: 8):

> Operations are sometimes conducted in completely unfamiliar environments or may involve massive scale-up (and speed-up) to existing programs. And the normal physical, administrative, legal, and financial infrastructure and services have often been substantially or entirely damaged or destroyed.

The final dimension in convenience theory is individual willingness for deviant behavior. Learning from others by differential association is a possible explanation as indicated in Fig. 10.2. The differential association perspective suggests that offenders associate with those who agree with them, and distance themselves from those who disagree. The choice of crime is thus caused by social learning from others with whom offenders associate (Akers, 1985; Sutherland, 1983).

The report by Henze et al. (2020) is not examining the Mercy Corps scam. However, the investigation was triggered by the scam that raised the alarm about widespread corruption and problems with the systems designed to root it out. The two main objectives of the operational review were to:

- Produce an analysis of the risks related to corruption and fraud along all stages of the project cycle as well as supply chains common to the humanitarian sector in DRC that is also gender-sensitive and protection oriented.
- Examine which existing prevention and mitigation measures are effective and indispensable to curb the risks of corruption. Further identify potential solutions to decrease corruption risks within specific program modalities and emergency response systems. These would be actionable and affordable operational and strategic recommendations for the humanitarian community in DRC.

Reviewers found that corruption in DRC is endemic, and no sector in the country is immune from the diversity of modes with which corruption is practiced, including humanitarian aid. As well as routine bribery, corruption practices in the country extend to nepotism, abuses of budgets, embezzlement, and other forms of misappropriation. Nepotism is a form of favoritism that is granted to relatives.

Reviewers found that corruption starts early in the project cycle. When an aid project is designed, both people with good intentions and people with bad intentions present their views on the scope of the emerging project. At the next stage of resource mobilization, corruption is frequent when selecting partner organizations. Kickback payments, diversion, favoritism, and nepotism appear common (Henze et al., 2020: 22):

> Many interviewees cited recruitment of national staff as an entry point for corruption, though a few reported not having issues of this nature. Similar to kickbacks in procurement, there is a strong perception amongst interviewees that corruption in recruitment in the aid sector is the norm or at the very least expected. Corruption practices may be initiated from within the organization or by the jobseeker. Corruption practices described by interviewees included: actors internal to the organization will coach external candidates on how to orient their CVs in accordance with the terms of reference; insiders provide questions and answers prepared for job tests to their preferred candidates. This facilitation is rewarded with kickbacks by successful candidates. The practice of procuring sex in recruitment was acknowledged as widely practiced in the DRC.

At the next stage of project implementation, examiners found that the main risk in this area of the project cycle is the inclusion of persons who are not eligible to receive aid according to set criteria. This might be in addition to eligible recipients or instead of them.

The main risks identified during the monitoring stage are the manipulation of monitoring reports and the failure to detect wrongdoing through traditional complaint mechanisms. Potential whistleblowers can be bribed together with monitoring officers as part of efforts to hide poor project performance and corruption.

The methodological approach applied by Henze et al. (2020) combined the collection of primary data with a review of secondary data. Primary data was collected almost exclusively during field research through semi-structured interviews, focus group discussions, a problem-description and solution-identification workshop and observation. A shortcoming in their approach was the selection of experts and victims, but no offenders. Statements from experts, stakeholders and especially victims can become biased in the direction of overstating problems to make their statements more interesting. Offenders are an important source of information as they know more about motive, opportunity, and willingness.

A total of 402 interviewees were consulted during the review. However, their responses are in no way systematized and presented in the report. Rather, the information sources seem more or less ignored by reviewers.

Furthermore, the report itself is problematic, as it confuses findings with recommendations. Sometimes findings are presented, while suddenly normative statements about how it should be are in the text.

The most important criticism is that there is nothing previously unknown presented in the report. There is no reconstruction of past events and sequences of events. Therefore, there are no insights to be gained from the report by Henze et al. (2020). Accordingly, the investigation is at the lowest level of maturity as indicated in Fig. 10.4. It was an activity-oriented investigation, where the reviewers interviewed a substantial number of people about well-known corrupt activities. The examiners made up their minds that the activities were reprehensible. They describe what is going on, but they do not reveal key enablers and barriers of corruption. They do not analyze causal relationships in terms of causes and effects of corruption.

Mercy Corps presents itself as a global team of humanitarians working together on the front lines of today's biggest crises to create a future of possibilities, where everyone can prosper. The mission of the organization is to alleviate suffering, poverty, and oppression by helping people build secure, productive, and just communities. In more than forty countries, over five thousand team members work side by side with people living through poverty, disaster, and violent conflicts, according to the website www.mercycorps.org.

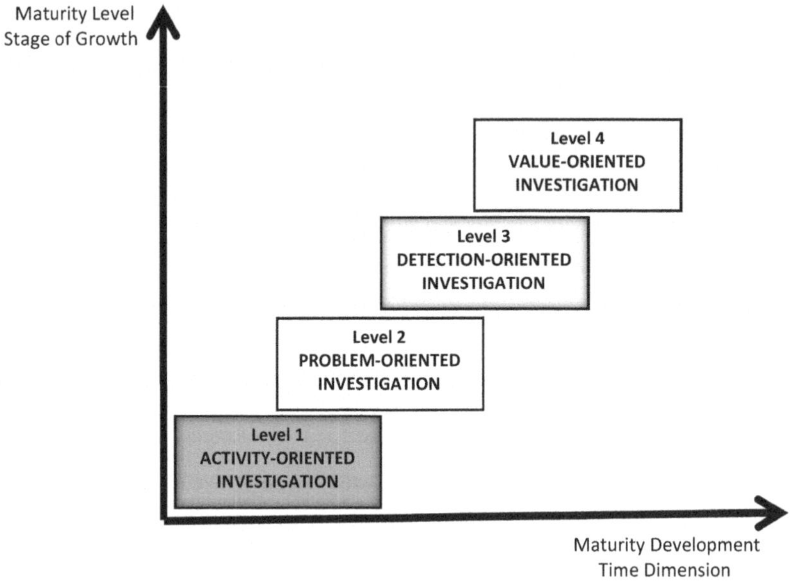

Fig. 10.4 Maturity assessments for the Henze et al. (2020) report

Fleckenstein and Bowes (2000) phrased the question: Do members often betray trust in terms of white-collar crime in religious institutions? Similarly, it is relevant to ask the question: Do humanitarians in global teams of humanitarians often betray trust in terms of financial crime in foreign aid organizations? According to Owens and Shores (2010), most white-collar crime incidents are exploitations of trust, where trust may originate from a shared religious identity between the victim and the perpetrator. Similarly, trust among aid workers may originate from a shared aid identity between the victim and the perpetrator. Shores (2010) phrased the questions: Are social religious networks an attractive arena for white-collar criminals? Is the morale of not acting illegally blinded from a chance when an attractive opportunity arises? While shared religious beliefs may lead to less acceptability of white-collar crime (Corcoran et al., 2012), the extent of opportunity for white-collar offenders may be greater in religious settings, mainly because of the trust-based culture found in religious institutions (Fleckenstein & Bowes, 2000; Owens & Shores, 2010; Shores, 2010).

Maxwell et al. (2008: 7) found that the majority of humanitarian aid workers interviewed across several aid agencies did not rate prevention of corruption particularly high on the priorities of the agency:

> Corruption was generally perceived as an unavoidable part of the emergency environment, and the prevention of corruption was often considered as just another routine part of doing business. Whether this reflects justified confidence or complacency remains to be seen, but what is clear is that there are few incentives within the systems of reporting and accountability that currently exist for corruption to be uncovered or reported.

While the general perception of foreign aid workers might be individuals with high moral and ethical standards, the opposite can be the case. Both in recruiting aid workers and in learning from other aid workers, the tendency to accept law violations such as corruption benefitting oneself might be stronger than commonly known. While most studies focus on situational factors such as corrupt countries with no public authorities in place, the Mercy Corps scam documents that local executives from the aid organization can be involved in corruption as well, for example, in the form of kickbacks.

Denmark: Public Railroad

Investigative journalist at a Danish newspaper learned about potential fraud at Banedanmark, a governmental body under the ministry of transportation and housing in Denmark. The state-owned company is responsible for tracks, signals, and safety systems for the railroad traffic. They renovate the rail network and build new lines. They monitor rail traffic and steer trains in and out of stations and across the entire rail network. The Danish newspaper Berlingske reported in 2020 that they had started their inquiries in 2018 and that Banedanmark had reported suspects to the police two years later (Jessen & Jung, 2020):

> Banedanmark suspects employees of bribery and illegal circumstances. Banedanmark has reported an employee and a contractor to the police for potential bribery. This is happening on the basis of a request for access to documents by Berlingske in 2018. The minister takes the matter "very seriously".

Banedanmark hired Danish law firm Kammeradvokaten (2020) to investigate allegations against 23 named individuals who were former and current employees at the state-owned company. The individuals were suspected of bribery, abuse of office, and theft.

When assuming that the allegations against 23 named individuals at Banedanmark are correct, then it is possible to analyze their wrongdoings by application of convenience theory to identify convenience themes in the case. Focus here is on corruption, where external vendors have bribed internal employees. Employees have received various gifts such as season tickets to football matches. Both briber and bribed are of interest here, where briber themes are marked in light grey while bribed themes are marked in dark grey in Fig. 10.5.

For bribing vendors, the possibilities of achieving more corporate business with Banedanmark are the financial motive. It can be a matter of reaching business objectives that justify means (Jonnergård et al., 2010; Welsh et al., 2019), and of enjoying benefits in exchange relationships (Huang & Knight, 2017). For individual employees, the possibilities of achieving more personal benefits are the financial motive. It can be a matter of climbing the hierarchy of needs for status and success (Maslow, 1943), realize the American dream of prosperity (Schoepfer & Piquero, 2006), and satisfy the desire to help others as social concern (Agnew, 2014).

For bribing vendors, the organizational opportunity to commit corruption is the access to relevant resources that enable bribing. It can be a matter of legitimate access to premises and systems (Benson & Simpson, 2018), opportunity creation by entrepreneurship (Ramoglou & Tsang, 2016), and legitimate access to strategic resources (Adler & Kwon, 2002). The opportunity to conceal corruption can be found in the criminal market structure where corruption is a marketing tool. It can be a matter of the usual way of business in markets with

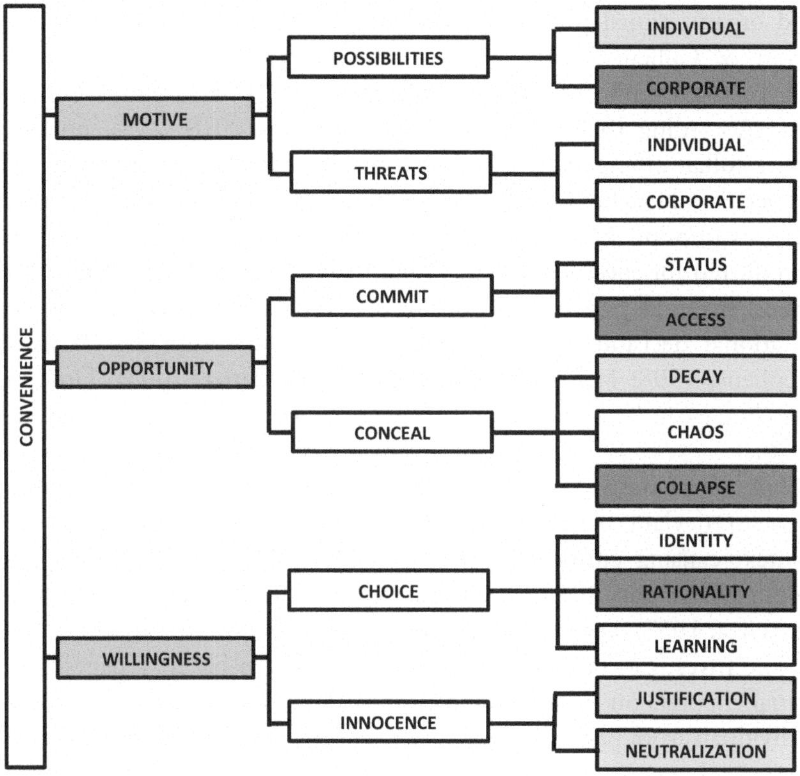

Fig. 10.5 Convenience themes for Banedanmark employees and vendors

crime forces (Chang et al., 2005), and participation in crime networks of vendors such as cartels (Nielsen, 2003). For bribed individuals, the organizational opportunity structure is mainly the lack of guardianship and controls representing decay. It can be a matter of institutional deterioration based on legitimacy (Rodriguez et al., 2005), inability to control because of social disorganization, and interference and noise in crime signals (Karim & Siegel, 1998).

For bribing vendors, corruption is a rational choice where expected benefits exceed expected costs. The rational choice assumption about offending is based on a normative foundation where advantages and disadvantages are subjectively compared (Müller, 2018). Individual and organizational preferences determine whether crime is committed (Pratt & Cullen, 2005). The greater benefits of crime are, and the less costs of crime are, the more attractive it is to commit criminal acts. According to Berghoff and Spiekermann (2018: 293), potential white-collar offenders "act on cost–benefit calculations involving the expected utility, the likelihood of being caught, and punishment costs". The assumption of rational choice is that every crime is chosen and committed for specific reasons. Individuals consciously and deliberately choose criminal behavior of their own free will. Financial crime is thus a rational decision where advantages exceed disadvantages (Barry & Stephens, 1998; Hefendehl, 2010; Lyman & Potter, 2007). However, the choice can be bounded and constrained by personal and situational factors.

For bribed individuals, justification and neutralization create willingness for deviant behavior. It can be a matter of disappointing work context causing entitlement (Engdahl, 2013), sliding on the slippery slope (Welsh et al., 2014), application of neutralization techniques (Sykes & Matza, 1957), and lack of self-control (Gottfredson & Hirschi, 1990).

The investigation report by Kammeradvokaten has 191 pages. After initial chapters on rules and regulations, the report reviews all of the 23 individuals from page 79 to page 185. For each individual, various email messages between employees and vendors are reviewed. The payments and benefits are modest, but seem to fit into the picture of a corrupt culture that existed for many years (Kammeradvokaten, 2020: 187):

> On the basis of the above review of the material concerning the 23 persons who were selected for the present investigation, Kammeradvokaten has made a number of general observations, which are described in more detail below.
> Based on the overall review of the material included in this study, it is Kammeradvokaten's assessment that in a number of areas there has been criticisable behavior among a number of Banedanmark employees. At the same time, the documentation shows that a number of suppliers have also shown reprehensible behavior. As can be seen from the report, the overall picture is that the problems have clearly diminished over the entire period examined from 2011 to March 2020. Thus, the vast majority of the criticisable circumstances that appear in the reviewed material took place in

> the period from 2011 to 2015. During that period, the circumstances concern gift receipts, including invitations to events paid for by partners, a possible violation of the rules regarding secondary employment, as well as excessive help and guidance for partners, including help at offer writing. Only two cases of reprehensible behavior have been found in the period after 2015. This is about an external consultant in 2016 sending a confidential interview report to his own e-mail account. In addition, it is a matter of an employee in 2018 in connection with the revocation of a security permit (which, however, was later handed out again) did not comply with the administrative rules.

The potential wrongdoing in the period before 2016 consists partly of rule violations in the public sector, and partly of violations of criminal law regarding bribery and abuse of office. Examiners found examples of contractors inviting a number of current and former Banedanmark employees to participate in Christmas lunches, circus performances, and go-kart events, and to provide Christmas presents to current and former employees (Kammeradvokaten, 2020: 187):

> In relation to the invitations, it is worth noting that these have to a large extent either been rejected, or that it cannot be documented whether the Banedanmark employees in question participated. In relation to invitations from partners, it is also important to emphasize that the very fact of receiving an invitation does not in itself trigger criticism of the individual employees, as it is not possible for them to control which e-mails they receive.

The examiners concluded that the frequency of offers from vendors has exceeded the extent of requests for bribes from employees, and that employees frequently have not responded to offers of benefits from vendors to Banedanmark. Furthermore, examiners found that the close friendship that existed between some employees and vendor representatives was harming the business of both parties, as contract negotiations and other formal situations were handled too informally (Kammeradvokaten, 2020).

On their website, Danish law firm Kammeradvokaten claims that the firm has grown to become one of Denmark's largest and leading full-service law firms. Fraud examiners at the law firm have previously completed several internal investigations. An example is their investigation into embezzlement by a trusted employee at the government social security agency (Kammeradvokaten, 2019; Newth, 2018; Nielsen, 2019; NTB, 2019; PwC, 2019), where Britta Nielsen later was sentenced to six and half years in prison for embezzlement (BBC, 2020; Ottermann, 2020).

At the time of examining the Banedanmark case, investigators knew that the company had submitted two reports to the police (Kammeradvokaten, 2020: 8):

- Police report of a former employee and contractor regarding a sponsorship of DKK 4000 to a football club in 2014. The police report was later supplemented as a result of the contractor in 2012 had invited a number of employees from Banedanmark to a Christmas lunch.
- Police report of a former employee and the same contractor that was covered by the previous police report, regarding a sponsorship of DKK 5000 in 2014 in connection with a swimming competition, a sponsorship of DKK 7500 in 2012 for a Christmas lunch, and an invitation in 2013 to go-karting and dining.

The police and subsequently the public prosecutor in Copenhagen refused to initiate an investigation as a result of the first-mentioned police report, while the police had not yet returned to Banedanmark regarding the case of the swimming competition. Kammeradvokaten then assessed in their report that there was no basis for further police involvement based on the public prosecutor's first decision. Given the status of knowledge and assessment of wrongdoing at the time of Kammeradvokaten's investigation, it was not obvious what kind of contribution, if any, could be expected from their investigation. The mandate for the investigation was vaguely formulated with a focus on the relationship between employees and vendors. The only specific issue in the mandate was the task of considering whether Banedanmark should formulate claims for damages against involved vendors. However, the report fails to present a conclusion for this issue.

There seems to be little value from the report. Nothing seems to be detected by examiners. No problems were solved. Therefore, the examination belongs at the lowest level of activity-oriented investigation in Fig. 10.6.

The investigation focused on activities that may have been carried out in a reprehensible manner. The report presents detailed accounts of minor incidents for a number of employees at Banedanmark. Then examiners made up their minds whether the activities were reprehensible or not. Given the outcome of the first police report, examiners seemed reluctant to emphasize any particular incident as relevant for criminal prosecution. Instead, the report says that most wrongdoing was a while back, and that improvements in the organization can be noticed since then. Investigations at maturity level 1 are typically passive, fruitless, and characterized by unnecessary use of resources.

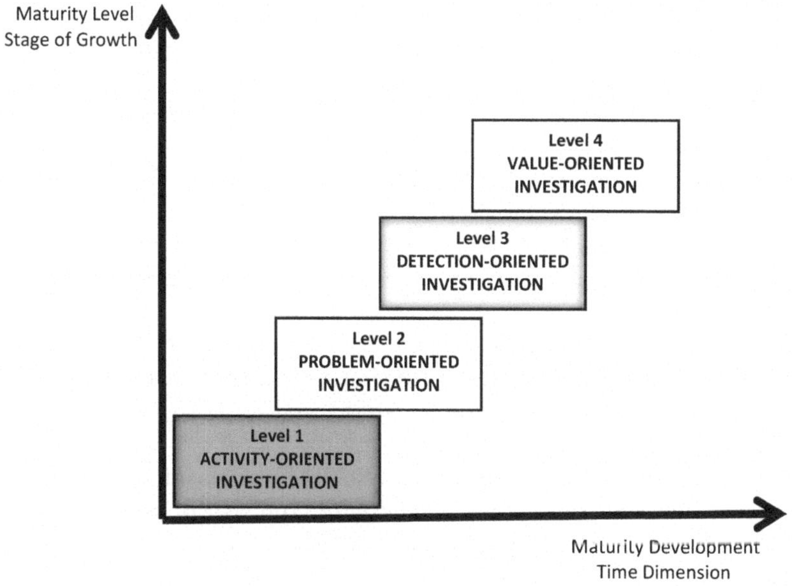

Fig. 10.6 Maturity assessments for the Kammeradvokaten (2020) report

References

Adler, P. S., & Kwon, S. W. (2002). Social capital: Prospects for a new concept. *Academy of Management Review, 27*(1), 17–40.

Agnew, R. (2014). Social concern and crime: Moving beyond the assumption of simple self-interest. *Criminology, 52*(1), 1–32.

Akers, R. L. (1985). *Deviant behavior: A social learning approach* (3rd ed.). Wadsworth.

Barry, B., & Stephens, C. U. (1998). Objections to an objectivist approach to integrity. *Academy of Management Review, 23*(1), 162–169.

BBC. (2020, February 18). Britta Nielsen: Danish social worker accused of stealing millions. *British Broadcasting Corporation.* www.bbc.com.

Bell, C. M., & Khoury, C. (2016). Organizational powerlessness, dehumanization, and gendered effects of procedural justice. *Journal of Managerial Psychology, 31,* 570–585.

Benartzi, S., Beshears, J., Milkman, K. L., Sunstein, C. R., Thaler, R. H., Shankar, M., Tucker-Ray, W., Congdon, W. J., & Galing, S. (2017). Should governments invest more in nudging? *Psychological Science, 28*(8), 1041–1055.

Benson, M. L., & Simpson, S. S. (2018). *Understanding white-collar crime—An opportunity perspective* (2nd ed.). Routledge.

Berghoff, H., & Spiekermann, U. (2018). Shady business: On the history of white-collar crime. *Business History, 60*(3), 289–304.

Caesens, G., Nguyen, N., & Stinglhamber, F. (2019). Abusive supervision and organizational dehumanization. *Journal of Business and Psychology, 34*, 709–728.

Campagna, R. L., Dirks, K. T., Knight, A. P., Crossley, C., & Robinson, S. L. (2020). On the relation between felt trust and actual trust: Examining pathways to and implications of leader trust meta-accuracy. *Journal of Applied Psychology, 105*(9), 994–1012.

Chan, J., Logan, S., & Moses, L. B. (2020). Rules in information sharing for security. *Criminology & Criminal Justice* (pp. 1–19), published online. https://doi.org/10.1177/1748895820960199.

Chang, J. J., Lu, H. C., & Chen, M. (2005). Organized crime or individual crime? Endogeneous size of a criminal organization and the optimal law enforcement. *Economic Inquiry, 43*(3), 661–675.

Chatterjee, A., & Pollock, T. G. (2017). Master of puppets: How narcissistic CEOs construct their professional worlds. *Academy of Management Review, 42*(4), 703–725.

Christiansen, A. K. (2021, February 3). Skiskyttertoppen risikerer straff fra 4 kanter [The Biathlon President risks punishment from 4 sides]. Norwegian daily newspaper *Aftenposten*, Wednesday, p. 39.

Corcoran, K. E., Pettinicchio, D., & Robins, B. (2012). Religion and the acceptability of white-colar crime: A crossnational analysis. *Journal of the Scientific Study of Religion, 51*(3), 542–567.

Cropanzano, R., & Mitchell, M. S. (2005). Social exchange theory: An interdisciplinary review. *Journal of Management, 31*(6), 874–900.

Crosina, E., & Pratt, M. G. (2019). Toward a model of organizational mourning: The case of former Lehman Brothers bankers. *Academy of Management Journal, 62*(1), 66–98.

Dearden, T. E. (2016). Trust: The unwritten cost of white-collar crime. *Journal of Financial Crime, 23*(1), 87–101.

Eberl, P., Geiger, D., & Assländer, M. S. (2015). Repairing trust in an organization after integrity violations: The ambivalence of organizational rule adjustments. *Organization Studies, 36*(9), 1205–1235.

Engdahl, O. (2013). Ensuring regulatory compliance in banking and finance through effective controls: The principle of duality in the segregation of duties. *Regulation & Governance, 8*(3), 332–349.

Fleckenstein, M. P., & Bowes, J. C. (2000). When trust is betrayed: Religious institutions and white collar crime. *Journal of Business Ethics, 23*(1), 111–115.

Gibney, R., Zagenczyk, T. J., & Masters, M. F. (2009). The negative aspects of social exchange: An introduction to perceived organizational obstruction. *Group and Organization Management, 34*, 665–697.

Goldstraw-White, J. (2012). *White-collar crime: Accounts of offending behavior*. Palgrave Macmillan.

Gottfredson, M. R., & Hirschi, T. (1990). *A general theory of crime*. Stanford University Press.

Hefendehl, R. (2010). Addressing white collar crime on a domestic level. *Journal of International Criminal Justice, 8*, 769–782.

Henze, N., Grünewald, F., & Parmar, S. (2020, July). *Operational review of exposure to corrupt practices in humanitarian aid implementation mechanisms in the DRC*. Adam Smith International. www.reliefweb.int.

Huang, L., & Knight, A. P. (2017). Resources and relationships in entrepreneurship: An exchange theory of the development and effects of the entrepreneur-investor relationship. *Academy of Management Review, 42*(1), 80–102.

Huseman, R. C., Hatfield, J. D., & Miles, E. W. (1987). A new perspective on equity theory: The equity sensitivity construct. *Academy of Management Review, 12*(2), 222–234.

IBU Commission. (2021, January 28). *Final report of the IBU External Review Commission* (220 pages). IBU External Review Commission: Jonathan Taylor, Vincent Defrasne, Christian Dorda, Tanja Haug, Anja Martin, and Lauren Pagé.

Jessen, C. K., & Jung, E. (2020, March 7). Banedanmark mistænker medarbeidere for bestikkelse og ulovlige forhold [Banedenmark suspects employees for bribe and illegal circumstances]. Danish daily newspaper *Berlingske*. www.berlingske.dk.

Jonnergård, K., Stafsudd, A., & Elg, U. (2010). Performance evaluations as gender barriers in professional organizations: A study of auditing firms, *Gender, Work and Organization, 17*(6), 721–747.

Kamerdze, S., Loughran, T., Paternoster, R., & Sohoni, T. (2014). The role of affect in intended rule breaking: Extending the rational choice perspective. *Journal of Research in Crime and Delinquency, 51*(5), 620–654.

Kammeradvokaten. (2019). *Ansvarsvurdering vedrørende sagen om svindel med tilskudsmidler – Offentlig rapport* [Assessment of liability regarding the case of fraud with benefit funds—Public report]. Report of investigation, 163 pages, law firm Kammeradvokaten Poul Schmith, Copenhagen, Denmark.

Kammeradvokaten. (2020, October 5). *Undersøgelse af forholdet mellem visse ansatte hos Banedanmark og private virksomheder* [Investigation of the relationship between certain employees at Banedanmark and private companies] (191 pages), law firm Poul Schmith Kammeradvokaten, Copenhagen, Denmark.

Karim, K. E., & Siegel, P. H. (1998). A signal detection theory approach to analyzing the efficiency and effectiveness of auditing to detect management fraud. *Managerial Auditing Journal, 13*(6), 367–375.

Kim, P. H., Dirks, K. T., & Cooper, C. D. (2009). The repair of trust: A dynamic bilateral perspective and multilevel conceptualization. *Academy of Management Review, 34*(3), 401–422.

King, M. (2020). Financial fraud investigative interviewing—Corporate investigators' beliefs and practices: A qualitative inquiry. *Journal of Financial Crime*. https://doi.org/10.1108/JFC-08-2020-0158.

Kleinfeld, P. (2020, June 11). Congo aid scam triggers sector-wide alarm. *The New Humanitarian*. www.thenewhumanitarian.org.

Leigh, A. C., Foote, D. A., Clark, W. R., & Lewis, J. L. (2010). Equity sensitivity: A triadic measure and outcome/input perspectives. *Journal of Managerial Issues, 22*(3), 286–305.

Loyens, K., Claringbould, I., Heres-van Rossem, L., & van Eekeren, Frank. (2021). The social construction of integrity: A qualitative case study in Dutch football. *Sports in Society*, published online. https://doi.org/10.1080/17430437.2021.1877661.

Lyman, M. D., & Potter, G. W. (2007). *Organized crime* (4th ed.). Pearson Prentice Hall.

Martin, J., & Peterson, M. M. (1987). Two-tier wage structures: Implications for equity theory. *Academy of Management Journal, 30*(2), 297–315.

Maslow, A. H. (1943). A theory of human motivation. *Psychological Review, 50*(4), 370–396.

Maxwell, D., Walker, P., Church, C., Harvey, P., Savage, K., & Bailey, S. (2008). *Preventing corruption in humanitarian assistance*. Transparency International, Berlin, Germany. www.transparency.org.

Müller, S. M. (2018). Corporate behavior and ecological disaster: Dow Chemical and the Great Lakes mercury crisis, 1970–1972. *Business History, 60*(3), 399–422.

Newth, M. (2018, November 5). Britta Nielsen (64) mistenkt for å ha stjålet 140 millioner [Britta Nielsen (64) suspected of having stolen 140 million], daily Norwegian newspaper *VG*. www.vg.no.

Nielsen, M. K. (2019, March 1). New report concludes: How Britta Nielsen could swindle for DKK 120 million for 25 years, Danish public broadcasting. *Danmarks Radio*. www.dr.no.

Nielsen, R. P. (2003). Corruption networks and implications for ethical corruption reform. *Journal of Business Ethics, 42*(2), 125–149.

NTB. (2019, October 24). Dansk kvinne for retten i storstilt svindelsak [Danish women prosecuted in court in a big fraud case]. ABC *nyheter*. www.abcnyheter.no.

Ottermann, P. (2020, February 18). Danish social worker jailed for stealing £13m of government funds. *The Guardian*. www.theguardian.com.

Owens, E. G., & Shores, M. (2010). *Informal networks and white collar crime: Evidence from the Madoff scandal* (54 pages). Social Science Research Network. www.pars.ssm.com.

Panja, T. (2021, January 28). Hunting trips, sex and cash: How grooming biathlon's leader paid off for Russia—An investigation accuses biathlon's longtime president of accepting gifts from Russians and then doing the

country's bidding as a doping scandal swirled. *The New York Times*. www.nytimes.com.
Patel, P. C., & Cooper, D. (2014). Structural power equality between family and nonfamily TMT members and the performance of family firms. *Academy of Management Journal, 57*(6), 1624–1649.
Pontell, H. N., Black, W. K., & Geis, G. (2014). Too big to fail, too powerful to jail? On the absence of criminal prosecutions after the 2008 financial meltdown. *Crime, Law and Social Change, 61*(1), 1–13.
Pratt, T. C., & Cullen, F. T. (2005). Assessing macro-level predictors and theories of crime: A meta-analysis. *Crime and Justice, 32*, 373–450.
PwC. (2019). *Ekstern undersøgelse af tilskudsadministrationen 1977–2018: Udarbejdet for Socialstyrelsen* [External investigation of benefits administration 1977–2018: Provided to the Social security administration]. Report of investigation, 80 pages, audit firm PricewaterhouseCoopers, Copenhagen, Denmark.
Ramoglou, S., & Tsang, E. W. K. (2016). A realist perspective of entrepreneurship: Opportunities as propensities. *Academy of Management Review, 41*, 410–434.
Rodriguez, P., Uhlenbruck, K., & Eden, L. (2005). Government corruption and the entry strategies of multinationals. *Academy of Management Review, 30*(2), 383–396.
Roehling, M. V., Roehling, P., & Boswell, W. R. (2010). The potential role of organizational setting in creating 'entitled' employees: An investigation of the antecedents of equity sensitivity. *Employee Responsibilities & Rights Journal, 22*, 133–145.
Rooij, B., & Fine, A. (2020). Preventing corporate crime from within: Compliance management, whistleblowing, and internal monitoring. In M. L. Rorie (Ed.),*The handbook of white-collar crime* (Chapter 15, pp. 229–245). Hoboken, NJ: Wiley.
Schoepfer, A., & Piquero, N. L. (2006). Exploring white-collar crime and the American dream: A partial test of institutional anomie theory. *Journal of Criminal Justice, 34*(3), 227–235.
Shores, M. (2010). *Informal networks and white collar crime: An extended analysis of the Madoff scandal*. www.dspace.library.cornell.edu.
Sutherland, E. H. (1983). *White collar crime—The uncut version*. Yale University Press.
Sykes, G., & Matza, D. (1957). Techniques of neutralization: A theory of delinquency. *American Sociological Review, 22*(6), 664–670.

Uygur, S. A. (2020). *Fraud in the charity sector in England and Wales: Accountability and stakeholder oversight*. A thesis submitted in fulfillment of the requirement for the degree of Doctor of Philosophy of Royal Holloway, University of London, United Kingdom.

Väyrynen, T., & Laari-Salmela, S. (2015). Men, mammals, or machines? Dehumanization embedded in organizational practices. *Journal of Business Ethics, 147*, 1–19.

Welsh, D. T., Bush, J., Thiel, C., & Bonner, J. (2019). Reconceptualizing goal setting's dark side: The ethical consequences of learning versus outcome goals. *Organizational Behavior and Human Decision Processes, 150*, 14–27.

Welsh, D. T., Ordonez, L. D., Snyder, D. G., & Christian, M. S. (2014). The slippery slope: How small ethical transgressions pave the way for larger future transgressions. *Journal of Applied Psychology, 100*(1), 114–127.

11

Conclusion

As argued in this book, white-collar offenders who are familiar with computer terminology can conveniently acquire malware and services to commit and conceal financial crime. They can hide behind the perceived complexity of new computer science that most people do not understand. The perception of complexity is caused by the lack of knowledge of simple elements in information technology. Software and hardware, networks and servers are all elements in a technological infrastructure that is not too difficult to understand. However, those who join law enforcement agencies such as police units seem more interested in cars and action rather than the specific traces that can be found in cyberspace. There is a knowledge gap between offenders and inspectors mainly caused by low knowledge levels among inspectors and not by high knowledge levels among offenders.

The risk of computer crime has become a global issue affecting all countries and regions. Salifu (2008) argued that the Internet is a double-edged sword providing many opportunities for individuals and organizations to develop and prosper, but at the same time has brought with it new opportunities to commit crime. Amateur offenders online include those who send Nigeria letters about a heritage or suggesting love. Also

P. Gottschalk and C. Hamerton, *White-Collar Crime Online*,
https://doi.org/10.1007/978-3-030-82132-6_11

attempts of CEO fraud seem mostly amateurish, where offenders only succeed if the victim is extremely vulnerable. More advanced offenders online include those who commit business email compromise, where there are several stages over time to commit and to conceal financial crime.

Fundamentally, the proliferation of information and communication technology (ICT), virtual reality, computer-mediated communications and the growing establishment of artificial intelligence (AI) has directly challenged the traditional discourse of criminology and the police work informed by it, introducing new forms of deviance, crime, and social control. Since the 1990s, a growing group of academics and practitioners has observed how cyberspace has emerged as a new field of criminal activity. Cyberspace has fundamentally changed the nature and scope of offending and victimization. Scholars such as Hutchings (2014, 2016, 2018a, 2018b)and Holt (2013, 2015, 2017a, 2017b) have contributed significantly to increased insights into online offending, sometimes together with other scholars (Holt et al., 2016, 2020; Hutchings & Clayton, 2016; Hutchings & Holt, 2016, 2018; Hutchings & Jorna, 2015).

References

Holt, T. J. (2013). Exploring the social organization and structure of stolen data markets. *Global Crime, 14*(2–3), 155–174.

Holt, T. J. (2015). Qualitative criminology in online spaces. In H. Copes & J. M. Miller (Eds.), *The Routledge handbook of qualitative criminology* (pp. 189–204). Routledge.

Holt, T. J. (2017a). Situating the problem of cybercrime in a multidisciplinary context. In T. J. Holt (Ed.), *Cybercrime through an interdisciplinary lens* (pp. 1–16). Routledge.

Holt, T. J. (2017b). On the value of honeypots to produce policy recommendations. *Criminology & Public Policy, 16*(3), 739–747.

Holt, T. J., Smirnova, O., & Hutchings, A. (2016). Examining signals of trust in criminal markets online. *Journal of Cybersecurity, 2*(2), 137–145.

Holt, T.J., Clevenger, S., & Navarro, J. (2020). Exploring digital evidence recognition among officers and troopers in a sample of a state police force, *Policing: An International Journal, 43* (1), 91–103.

Hutchings, A. (2014). Crime from the keyboard: Organized crime, co-offending, initiation and knowledge transmission. *Crime, Law and Social Change, 62*(1), 1–20.

Hutchings, A. (2016). Cybercrime trajectories: An integrated theory of initiation, maintenance, and desistance. In T. J. Holt (Ed.), *Crime online: Correlates, causes, and context* (pp. 117–140). Carolina Academic Press.

Hutchings, A. (2018a). Leaving on a jet plane: The trade in fraudulently obtained airline tickets. *Crime, Law and Social Change, 70*, 461–487.

Hutchings, A. (2018b). Flying in cyberspace: Policing global travel fraud, *Policing: A Journal of Policy and Practice, 15*, 1–16. https://doi.org/10.1093/police/pay063

Hutchings, A., & Clayton, R. (2016). Exploring the provision of online booter services. *Deviant Behavior, 37*(10), 1163–1178.

Hutchings, A., & Holt, T. J. (2016). A crime script analysis of the online stolen data market. *British Journal of Criminology, 55*, 596–614.

Hutchings, A., & Holt, T. J. (2018). Interviewing cybercrime offenders. *Journal of Qualitative Criminal Justice & Criminology, 7*(1), 75–94.

Hutchings, A., & Jorna, P. (2015). Misuse of information and communications technology within the public sector, *Trends & Issues in Crime & Criminal Justice Series*, No. 470. Australian Institute of Criminology.

Salifu, A. (2008). The impact of internet crime on development. *Journal of Financial Crime, 15*(4), 432–443.

References

Abbasi, A., Zhang, Z., Zimbra, D., & Chen, H. (2010). Detecting fake websites: The contribution of statistical learning theory. *MIS Quarterly, 34*(3), 435–461.

ACFE. (2008). *2008 Report to the nations on occupational fraud and abuse*. Association of Certified Fraud Examiners.

ACFE. (2014). *2014 Report to the nations on occupational fraud and abuse, 2014 Global Fraud Study*. Association of Certified Fraud Examiners.

ACFE. (2016). *CFE code of professional standard*. Association of Certified Fraud Examiners. www.acfe.com/standards/

Adler, P. S., & Kwon, S. W. (2002). Social capital: Prospects for a new concept. *Academy of Management Review, 27*(1), 17–40.

Afuah, A., & Tucci, C. L. (2003). *Internet business models and strategies* (2nd ed.). McGraw-Hill.

Agnew, R. (2014). Social concern and crime: Moving beyond the assumption of simple self-interest. *Criminology, 52*(1), 1–32.

Akdemir, N., & Lawless, C. J. (2020). Exploring the human factor in cyber-enabled and cyber-dependent crime victimization: A lifestyle routine activities approach. *Internet Research, 30*(6), 1665–1687.

Akers, R. L. (1985). *Deviant behavior: A social learning approach* (3rd ed.). Wadsworth.

P. Gottschalk and C. Hamerton, *White-Collar Crime Online*,
https://doi.org/10.1007/978-3-030-82132-6

Akinbowale, O. E., Klingelhöfer, H. E., & Zerihun, M. F. (2020). Analysis of cyber-crime effects on the banking sector using the balanced score card: A survey of literature. *Journal of Financial Crime*, 945–958.

Al-Suwaidi, N., Nobanee, H., & Jabeen, F. (2018). Estimating causes of cyber crime: Evidence from panel data FGLS estimator. *International Journal of Cyber Criminology, 12*(2), 392–407.

Albanese, J. S. (2012). Deciphering the linkages between organized crime and transnational crime. *Journal of International Affairs, 66*(1), 1–16.

Algarni, A. F. (2013). Policing internet fraud in Saudi Arabia: Expressive gestures or adaptive strategies? *Policing & Society, 23*(4), 498–515.

Aljuboori, D., Seneviratne-Eglin, E., Swiergala, E., & Guerra, C. (2021). Association between family support and online sexual abuse in Chilean adolescents: The mediational role of online risk behaviors. *Journal of Child Sexual Abuse*. https://doi.org/10.1080/10538712.2021.1875280

Alon, A., Mennicken, A., & Samsonova-Taddei, A. (2019). Dynamics and limits of regulatory privatization: Reorganizing audit oversight in Russia. *Organization Studies, 40*(8), 1217–1240.

Alper, M. (2014). "Can our kids hack it with computers?" Constructing youth hackers in family computing magazines (1983–1987). *International Journal of Communication, 8*(1), 673–698.

Ampratwum, E. F. (2009). Advance fee fraud "419" and investor confidence in the economies of sub-Saharan African (SSA). *Journal of Financial Crime, 16*(1), 67–79.

Andresen, M. S., & Button, M. (2019). The profile and detection of bribery in Norway and England & Wales: A comparative study. *European Journal of Criminology, 16*(1), 18–40.

Arjoon, S. (2008). Slippery when wet: The real risk in busines. *Journal of Markets & Morality, 11*(1), 77–91.

Artello, K., & Albanese, J. S. (2021). Culture of corruption: Prosecutions, persistence, and desistence. *Public Integrity*, 1–21, published online. https://doi.org/10.1080/10999922.2021.1881300

Ashforth, B. E., Gioia, D. A., Robinson, S. L., & Trevino, L. K. (2008). Re-reviewing organizational corruption. *Academy of Management Review, 33*(3), 670–684.

Asker Bærum. (2012, February 28). *Case 11–063509MED-AHER/1*. Asker and Bærum District Court.

Australian. (2008). *Online child grooming laws*. Australian Institute of Criminology, Project 0074a, Australian Government. www.aic.gov.au

Baird, J. E., & Zelin, R. C. (2009). An examination of the impact of obedience pressure on perceptions of fraudulent acts and the likelihood of committing occupational fraud. *Journal of Forensic Studies in Accounting and Business, 1*(1), 1–14.

Bakarich, K. M., & Baranek, D. (2020). Something phish-y is going on here: A teaching case on business email compromise. *Current Issues in Auditing, 14*(1), A1–A9.

Balakrishnan, K., Blouin, J. L., & Guay, W. R. (2019). Tax aggressiveness and corporate transparency. *The Accounting Review, 94*(1), 45–69.

Bao, D., Kim, Y., Mian, G. M., & Su, L. (2019). Do managers disclose or withhold bad news? Evidence from short interest. *The Accounting Review, 94*(3), 1–26.

Barlett, C., & Coyne, S. M. (2014). A meta-analysis of sex differences in cyber-bullying behavior: The moderating role of age. *Aggressive Behavior, 40*(5), 474–488.

Barney, J. (2018). Editor's comments: Positioning a theory paper for publication. *Academy of Management Review, 43*(3), 345–348.

Barry, B., & Stephens, C. U. (1998). Objections to an objectivist approach to integrity. *Academy of Management Review, 23*(1), 162–169.

Barton, H. (2004). Cultural reformation: A case for intervention within the police service. *International Journal of Human Resources Development and Management, 4*(2), 191–199.

BBC. (2007, July 25). MySpace bars 29,000 sex offenders. *BBC*. http://news.bbc.co.uk/2/hi/technology/6914870.stm

BBC. (2020, February 18). Britta Nielsen: Danish social worker accused of stealing millions. *British Broadcasting Corporation*. www.bbc.com.

Becker, I., Hutchings, A., Abu-Salma, R., Anderson, R., Bohm, N., Murdoch, S. J., Sasse, M. A., & Stringhini, G. (2017). International comparison of bank fraud reimbursement: Customer perceptions and contractual terms. *Journal of Cybersecurity, 3*(2), 109–125.

Bell, C. M., & Khoury, C. (2016). Organizational powerlessness, dehumanization, and gendered effects of procedural justice. *Journal of Managerial Psychology, 31*, 570–585.

Benartzi, S., Beshears, J., Milkman, K. L., Sunstein, C. R., Thaler, R. H., Shankar, M., Tucker-Ray, W., Congdon, W. J., & Galing, S. (2017). Should governments invest more in nudging? *Psychological Science, 28*(8), 1041–1055.

Bennet, A., & Bennet, D. (2005a). Designing the knowledge organization of the future: The intelligent complex adaptive system. In C. W. Holsapple

(Ed.), *Handbook of knowledge management* (Vol. 2, pp. 623–638). Springer Science & Business Media.

Bennet, D., & Bennet, A. (2005b). The rise of the knowledge organization. In C. W. Holsapple (Ed.), *Handbook of knowledge management* (Vol. 1, pp. 5–20). Springer Science & Business Media.

Benson, M. L. (1985). Denying the guilty mind: Accounting for involvement in a white-collar crime. *Criminology, 23*(4), 583–607.

Benson, M. L. (2020). Theoretical and empirical advances in the study and control of white-collar offenders. *Justice Evaluation Journal*, published online. https://doi.org/10.1080/24751979.2020.1808855

Benson, M. L., & Gottschalk, P. (2015). Gender and white-collar crime in Norway: An empirical study of media reports. *International Journal of Law, Crime and Justice, 43*(4), 535–552.

Benson, M. L., & Simpson, S. S. (2018). *Understanding white-collar crime—An opportunity perspective* (2nd ed.). Routledge.

Berghoff, H. (2018). "Organised irresponsibility?" The Siemens corruption scandal of the 1990s and 2000s. *Business History, 60*(3), 423–445.

Berghoff, H., & Spiekermann, U. (2018). Shady business: On the history of white-collar crime. *Business History, 60*(3), 289–304.

Bergström, O., Hasselbladh, H., & Kärreman, D. (2009). Organizing disciplinary power in knowledge organization. *Scandinavian Journal of Management, 25*, 178–190.

Bernburg, J. G., Krohn, M. D., & Rivera, C. (2006). Official labeling, criminal embeddedness, and subsequent delinquency. *Journal of Research in Crime and Delinquency, 43*(1), 67–88.

Bigley, G. A., & Wiersma, M. F. (2002). New CEOs and corporate strategic refocusing: How experience as heir apparent influences the use of power. *Administrative Science Quarterly, 47*, 707–727.

Binham, C., & Milne, R. (2018, September 19). Danske bank fails to draw line under Euro 200billion scandal. *Financial Times*. https://www.ft.com/content/38306c04-bc1c-11e8-94b2-17176fbf93f5

Bissett, D., Bissett, J., & Snell, C. (2012). Physical agility tests and fitness standards: Perceptions of law enforcement officers. *Police Practice and Research, 13*(3), 208–223.

Bittle, S., & Hébert, J. (2020). Controlling corporate crimes in times of de-regulation and re-regulation. In M. L. Rorie (Ed.), *The handbook of white-collar crime* (Chapter 30, pp. 484–501). Wiley.

Bjørkelo, B., Einarsen, S., Nielsen, M. B., & Matthiesen, S. B. (2011). Silence is golden? Characteristics and experiences of self-reported whistleblowers. *European Journal of Work and Organizational Psychology, 20*(2), 206–238.

Blickle, G., Schlegel, A., Fassbender, P., Klein, U. (2006). Some personality correlates of business white-collar crime. *Applied Psychology: An International Review, 55*(2), 220–233.

Bock, G. W., Zmud, R. W., & Kim, Y. G. (2005). Behavioral intention formation in knowledge sharing: Examining the roles of extrinsic motivators, social-psychological forces, and organizational climate. *MIS Quarterly, 29*(1), 87–111.

Bookman, Z. (2008). Convergences and omissions in reporting corporate and white collar crime. *DePaul Business & Commercial Law Journal, 6*, 347–392.

Borgarting. (2010a, September 8). *Court case LB-2010–18170.* Borgarting lagmannsrett (Borgarting court of appeals), Oslo, Norway.

Borgarting. (2010b, March 16). *Court case LB-2008–133972.* Borgarting lagmannsrett (Borgarting court of appleals), Oslo, Norway.

Borgarting. (2019, February 1). *Court case 17–170796AST-BORG/01.* Borgarting lagmannsrett (Borgarting court of appeals), judges Mats Wilhelm Ruland, Marit Bjørånesset Frogner and Bjørn E. Engstrøm. Prosecutor Esben Kyhring, defense attorney Christian Fredrik Bonnevie Hjort, Oslo, Norway.

Bosse, D. A., & Phillips, R. A. (2016). Agency theory and bounded self-interest. *Academy of Management Review, 41*(2), 276–297.

Bowman, D., & Gilligan, G. (2008). Public awareness of corruption in Australia. *Journal of Financial Crime, 14*(4), 438–452.

Braaten, C. N., & Vaughn, M. S. (2019). Convenience theory of cryptocurrency crime: A content analysis of U.S. federal court decisions. *Deviant Behavior*, published online. https://doi.org/10.1080/01639625.2019.1706706

Broadhurst, R., Grabosky, P., Alazab, M., & Chon, S. (2014). Organizations and cyber crime: An analysis of the nature of groups engaged in cyber crime. *International Journal of Cyber Criminology, 8*(1), 1–20.

Brown, J. O., Hays, J., & Stuebs, M. T. (2016). Modeling accountant whistleblowing intentions: Applying the theory of planned behavior and the fraud triangle. *Accounting and the Public Interest, 16*(1), 28–56.

Brown, J. S., & Duguid, P. (2001). Knowledge and organization: A social-practice perspective. *Organization Science, 12*(2), 198–213.

Brown, S. D. (2007). The meaning of criminal intelligence. *International Journal of Police Science & Management, 9*(4), 336–340.

Bruggen, M., & Blokland, A. (2021). Profiling darkweb child sexual exploitation material forum members using longitudinal posting history data. *Social Science Computer Review*, published online. https://doi.org/10.1177/0894439321994894

Bruun Hjejle (2018). *Report on the non-resident portfolio at Danske bank's Estonian branch* (Report of investigation, 87 pages). Law Firm Bruun Hjejle.

Bucy, P. H., Formby, E. P., Raspanti, M. S., & Rooney, K. E. (2008). Why do they do it? The motives, mores, and character of white collar criminals. *St. John's Law Review, 82*, 401–571.

Buil-Gil, D., Lord, N., & Barrett, E. (2020). The dynamics of business, cybersecurity and cyber-victimization: Foregrounding the internal guardian in prevention. *Victims & Offenders, 16*(3), 286–315.

Buil-Gil, D., Miro-Llinares, F., Moneva, A., Kemp, S., & Diaz-Castano, N. (2021). Cybercrime and shifts in opportunities during Covid-19: A preliminary analysis in the UK. *European Societies*, published online. https://doi.org/10.1080/14616696.2020.1804973

Burruss, G., Howell, C. J., Bossler, A., & Holt, T. J. (2020). Self-perceptions of English and Welsh constables and sergeants preparedness for online crime: A latent analysis. *Policing: An International Journal, 43*(1), 105–119.

Bussmann, K. D., Niemeczek, A., & Vockrodt, M. (2018). Company culture and prevention of corruption in Germany, China and Russia. *European Journal of Criminology, 15*(3), 255–277.

Button, M., Nicholls, C. M., Kerr, J., & Owen, R. (2015). Online fraud victims in England and Wales: Victims' views on sentencing and the opportunity for restorative justice. *The Howard Journal of Criminal Justice, 54*(2), 193–211.

Caesens, G., Nguyen, N., & Stinglhamber, F. (2019). Abusive supervision and organizational dehumanization. *Journal of Business and Psychology, 34*, 709–728.

Cai, T., Du, L., Xin, Y., & Chang, L. Y. C. (2018). Characteristics of cybercrimes: Evidence from Chinese judgment documents. *Police Practice & Research, 19*(6), 582–595.

Caines, A., Pastrana, S., Hutchings, A., & Buttery, P. J. (2018). Automatically identifying the function and intent of posts in underground forums. *Crime Science, 7*(19), 1–14.

Calder, M. C. (2004). The internet: Potential, problems and pathways to hands-on sexual offending. In M. C. Calder (Ed.), *Child sexual abuse and the Internet: Tackling the new frontier* (pp. 1–23). Russell House Publishing.

Campagna, R. L., Dirks, K. T., Knight, A. P., Crossley, C., & Robinson, S. L. (2020). On the relation between felt trust and actual trust: Examining pathways to and implications of leader trust meta-accuracy. *Journal of Applied Psychology, 105*(9), 994–1012.

Campbell, J. L., & Göritz, A. S. (2014). Culture corrupts! A qualitative study of organizational culture in corrupt organizations. *Journal of Business Ethics, 120*(3): 291–311.

CEOP. (2006). *Understanding online social network services and risks to youth.* Child Exploitation and Online Protection Centre. www.ceop.gov.uk

Chan, F., & Gibbs, C. (2020). Integrated theories of white-collar and corporate crime. In M. L. Rorie (Ed.), *The handbook of white-collar crime* (Chapter 13, pp. 191–208). Wiley.

Chan, J., Logan, S., & Moses, L. B. (2020). Rules in information sharing for security. *Criminology & Criminal Justice*, 1–19, published online. https://doi.org/10.1177/1748895820960199

Chang, L. Y. C. (2013). Formal and informal modalities for policing cybercrime across Taiwan Strait. *Policing & Society, 23*(4), 540–555.

Chang, J. J., Lu, H. C., & M. Chen. (2005). Organized crime or individual crime? Endogeneous size of a criminal organization and the optimal law enforcement. *Economic Inquiry, 43*(3), 661–675.

Chatterjee, A., & Pollock, T. G. (2017). Master of puppets: How narcissistic CEOs construct their professional worlds. *Academy of Management Review, 42*(4), 703–725.

Chen, Y., & Moosmayer, D. C. (2020). When guilt is not enough: Interdependent self-construal as moderator of the relationship between guilt and ethical consumption in a Confucian context. *Journal of Business Ethics, 161*, 551–572.

Chrisman, J. J., Chua, J. H., Kellermanns, F. W., & Chang, E. P. C. (2007). Are family managers agents or stewards? An exploratory study in privately held family firms. *Journal of Business Research, 60*(10), 1030–1038.

Christiansen, A. K. (2021, February 3). Skiskyttertoppen risikerer straff fra 4 kanter [The Biathlon President risks Punishment from 4 sides]. Norwegian daily newspaper *Aftenposten*, Wednesday, p. 39.

Clifford Chance. (2020). *Report of investigation on Swedbank* (Report of investigation, 218 pages, law firm Clifford Chance). Washington, DC.

Cloutier, C., & Ravasi, D. (2020). Identity trajectories: Explaining long-term patterns of continuity and change in organizational identities. *Academy of Management Journal, 63*(4), 1196–1235.

Cohen, L. E., & Felson, M. (1979). Social change and crime rate trends: A routine activity approach. *American Sociological Review, 44*, 588–608.

Collier, B., Clayton, R., Hutchings, A., & Thomas, D. R. (2020). *Cybercrime is (often) boring: Maintaining the infrastructure of cybercrime economies*. Workshop on the Economics of Information Security, Brussels. www.weis2020.econinfosec.org

Collier, P. M. (2006, April). Policing and the intelligent application of knowledge. *Public Money & Management*, 109–116.

Collins, M., Theis, M., Trzeciak, R., Strozer, J., Clark, J., Costa, D., Cassidy, T., Albrethsen, M., & Moore, A. (2016). *Common sense guide to mitigating insider threats* (5th ed.). Software Engineering Institute.

Corcoran, K. E., Pettinicchio, D., & Robins, B. (2012). Religion and the acceptability of white-colar crime: A crossnational analysis. *Journal of the Scientific Study of Religion, 51*(3), 542–567.

Comey, J. B. (2009). Go directly to prison: White collar sentencing after the Sarbanes-Oxley act. *Harvard Law Review, 122*, 1728–1749.

Cook, N. (2008). *Enterprise 2.0: How social software will change the future of work*. Gower Publishing Limited.

Craig, J. M., & Piquero, N. L. (2016). The effects of low self-control and desire-for-control on white-collar offending: A replication. *Deviant Behavior, 37*(11), 1308–1324.

Craig, J. M., & Piquero, N. L. (2017). Sensational offending: An application of sensation seeking to white-collar and conventional crimes. *Crime & Delinquency, 63*(11), 1363–1382.

Crank, B. R. (2018). Accepting deviant identities: The impact of self-labeling on intentions to desist from crime. *Journal of Crime and Justice, 41*(2), 155–172.

Cressey, D. (1972). *Criminal organization: Its elementary forms*. Harper and Row.

Cropanzano, R., & Mitchell, M. S. (2005). Social exchange theory: An interdisciplinary review. *Journal of Management, 31*(6), 874–900.

Crosina, E., & Pratt, M. G. (2019). Toward a model of organizational mourning: The case of former Lehman Brothers bankers. *Academy of Management Journal, 62*(1), 66–98.

Cross, C. (2018). Victims' motivations for reporting to the 'fraud justice network.' *Police Practice & Research, 19*(6), 550–564.

Cullen, F. T. (2010). Cloward, Richard A., and Lloyd E. Ohlin: Delinquency and opportunity. In F. T. Cullen & P. Wilcox (Eds.), *Encyclopedia of criminological theory* (Vol. 1, pp. 170–174). Sage .

D'Ovidio, R., Mitman, T., El-Burki, I. J., & Shumar, W. (2009). Adult-child sex advocacy websites as social learning environments: A content analysis. *International Journal of Cyber Criminology, 3*(1), 421–440.

Davidson, J. (2008). *Child sexual abuse—Media representations and government reactions*. Routledge.

Davidson, J., & Gottschalk, P. (2008). Digital forensics in law enforcement: The case of online victimization of children. *Electronic Government—An International Journal, 5*(4), 445–451.

Davidson, J., & Gottschalk, P. (2010). *Online groomers: Profiling*. Russell House Publishing.

Davidson, J., & Gottschalk, P. (2011a). Characteristics of the internet for criminal child sexual abuse by online groomers. *Criminal Justice Studies, 24*(1), 23–36.

Davidson, J., & Gottschalk, P. (2011b). *Child internet abuse: Current research and policy*. Routledge, Taylor & Francis Group.

Davidson, J., & Gottschalk, P. (2015). The context of online abuse: Policy and legislation. In S. Webster, J. Davidson, & A. Bifulco (Eds.), *Online offending behaviour and child victimisation* (pp. 1–20). Palgrave Macmillan.

Davidson, J., & Martellozzo, E. (2008). Protecting vulnerable young people in cyberspace from sexual abuse: Raising awareness and responding globally. *Police Practice & Research, 9*(4), 277–289.

Davidson, R. H., Dey, A., & Smith, A. J. (2019). CEO materialism and corporate social responsibility. *The Accounting Review, 94*(1), 101–126.

de Paoli, S., Johnstone, J., Coull, N., Ferguson, I., Sinclair, G., Tomkins, P., Brown, M., & Martin, R. (2020). A qualitative exploratory study of the knowledge, forensic, and legal challenges from the perspective of police cybercrime specialists. *Policing: A Journal of Policy and Practice*, published online. https://doi.org/10.1093/police/paaa027

Dean, G., & Gottschalk, P. (2007). *Knowledge management in policing and law enforcement—Foundations*. Oxford University Press.

Dean, G., Fahsing, I., & Gottschalk, P. (2010). *Organized crime—Policing illegal business entrepreneurialism*. Oxford University Press.

Dearden, T. E. (2016). Trust: The unwritten cost of white-collar crime. *Journal of Financial Crime, 23*(1), 87–101.

Dion, M. (2010). Advance fee fraud letters as Machiavellian/narcissistic narratives. *International Journal of Cyber Criminology, 4*(1–2), 630–642.

Dodge, M. (2009). *Women and white-collar crime*. Prentice Hall.

Dombrowski, S. C., Gischlar, K. L., & Durst, T. (2007). Safeguarding young people from cyber pornography and cyber sexual predation: A major dilemma of the internet. *Child Abuse Review, 16*, 153–170.

Dotinga, W. (2017, April 26). EU court finds copyright issues with streaming player. *Courthouse News Service*. www.courthousenews.com

Drew, J. M. (2020). A study of cybercrime victimization and prevention: Exploring the use of online crime prevention behaviors and strategies. *Journal of Criminological Research, Policy and Practice, 6*(1), 17–33.

Drew, J. M., & Farrell, L. (2018). Online victimization risk and self-protective strategies: Developing police-led cyber fraud prevention programs. *Police Practice & Research, 19*(6), 537–549.

Dunaigre, P. (2001). Paedophilia: A psychiatric and psychoanalytical point of view. In C. A. Arnaldo (Ed.), *Child abuse on the internet —Ending the silence* (pp. 43–49). UNESCO and Beghahn Books.

Eberl, P., Geiger, D., & Assländer, M. S. (2015). Repairing trust in an organization after integrity violations. The ambivalence of organizational rule adjustments. *Organization Studies, 36*(9), 1205–35.

Eberly, M. B., Holley, E. C., Johnson, M. D., & Mitchell, T. R. (2011). Beyond internal and external: A dyadic theory of relational attributions. *Academy of Management Review, 36*(4), 731–753.

Eisenhardt, K. M. (1989). Agency theory: An assessment and review. *Academy of Management Review, 14*(1), 57–74.

Elisha, O. S., Johnson, U. J., Olugbemi, K. O., Olugbemi, M. D., & Emefiele, C. C. (2020). Forensic accounting and fraud detection in Nigerian universities. *Journal of Accounting and Financial Management, 6*(4), 1–12.

Emmenegger, P. (2015). Swiss banking secrecy and the problem of international cooperation in tax matters: A nut too hard to crack? *Regulation & Governance, 11*(1), 24–40.

Engdahl, O. (2013). Ensuring regulatory compliance in banking and finance through effective controls: The principle of duality in the segregation of duties. *Regulation & Governance, 8*(3), 332–349.

Eren, C. P. (2021). Cops, firefighters, and scapegoats: Anti-money laundering (AML) professionals in an era of regulatory bulimia. *Journal of White Collar and Corporate Crime, 2*(1), 47–58.

Ernst, S., Veen, H., & Kop, N. (2021). Technological innovation in a police organization: Lessons learned from the National Police of the Netherlands. *Policing: A Journal of Policy and Practice*, published online. https://doi.org/10.1093/police/paab003

Farquhar, J. D., & Rowley, J. (2009). Convenience: A services perspective. *Marketing Theory, 9*(4), 425–438.

Fehr, R., Yam, K. C., & Dang, C. (2015). Moralized leadership: The construction and consequences of ethical leader perceptions. *Academy of Management Review, 40*(2), 182–209.

Ferraro, F., Pfeffer, J., & Sutton, R. I. (2005). Economics language and assumptions: How theories can become self-fulfilling. *Academy of Management Review, 30*(1), 8–24.

Finkelhor, D. (1984). *Child sexual abuse: New theory and research.* The Free Press.

Fleckenstein, M. P., & Bowes, J. C. (2000). When trust is betrayed: Religious institutions and white collar crime. *Journal of Business Ethics, 23*(1), 111–115.

Fletcher, N. (2007). Challenges for regulating financial fraud in cyberspace. *Journal of Financial Crime, 14*(2), 190–207.

Fried, Y., & Slowik, L. H. (2004). Enriching goal-setting theory with time: An integrated approach. *Academy of Management Review, 29*(3), 404–422.

Friedrichs, D. O. (2010). Integrated theories of white-collar crime. In F. T. Cullen & P. Wilcox (Eds.), *Encyclopedia of criminological theory* (Vol. 1, pp. 479–486). Sage.

Friedrichs, D. O., Schoultz, I., & Jordanoska, A. (2018). *Edwin H. Sutherland, Routledge key thinkers in criminology.* Routledge.

Gago-Rodriguez, S., Marquez-Illescas, G., & Nunez-Nickel, M. (2020). Denial of corruption: Voluntary disclosure of bribery information. *Journal of Business Ethics, 162,* 609–626.

Gallaher, M. P., Link, A. N., & Rowe, B. R. (2008). *Cyber security—Economic strategies and public policy alternatives.* Edward Elgar.

Galvin, B. M., Lange, D., & Ashforth, B. E. (2015). Narcissistic organizational identification: Seeing oneself as central to the organization's identity. *Academy of Management Review, 40*(2), 163–181.

Gamache, D. L., & McNamara, G. (2019). Responding to bad press: How CEO temporal focus influences the sensitivity to negative media coverage of acquisitions. *Academy of Management Journal, 62*(3), 918–943.

Gao, P., & Zhang, G. (2019). Accounting manipulation, peer pressure, and internal control. *The Accounting Review, 94*(1), 127–151.

Garud, R., & Kumaraswamy, A. (2005). Vicious and virtuous circles in the management of knowledge: The case of Infosys Technologies. *MIS Quarterly, 29*(1), 9–33.

Ghazi-Tehrani, A. K., & Pontell, H. N. (2021). Phishing evolves: Analyzing the enduring cybercrime. *Victims & Offenders, 16*(3), 316–342.

Gibney, R., Zagenczyk, T. J., & Masters, M. F. (2009). The negative aspects of social exchange: An introduction to perceived organizational obstruction. *Group and Organization Management, 34*, 665–697.

Glasø, L., & Einarsen, S. (2008). Emotion regulation in leader-follower relationships. *European Journal of Work and Organizational Psychology, 17*(4), 482–500.

Goldstraw-White, J. (2012). *White-collar crime: Accounts of offending behavior*. Palgrave Macmillan.

Goncharov, I., & Peter, C. D. (2019). Does reporting transparency affect industry coordination? Evidence from the duration of international cartels, *The Accounting Review, 94*(3), 149–175.

Goodman-Delahunty, J., & Martschuk, N. (2020). Securing reliable information in investigative interviews: Coercive and noncoercive strategies preceding turning points. *Police Practice and Research, 21*(2), 152–171.

Gottfredson, M. R., & Hirschi, T. (1990). *A general theory of crime*. Stanford University Press.

Gottfredson, R. K., Wright, S. L., & Heaphy, E. D. (2020). A critique of the leader-member exchange construct: Back to square one. *The Leadership Quarterly*. https://doi.org/10.1016/j.leaqua.2020.101385

Gottschalk, P. (2011a). Characteristics of the internet and child abuse. In J. Davidson & P. Gottschalk (Ed.), *Internet child abuse—Current research and policy* (pp. 27–51). Routledge, Taylor & Francis Group.

Gottschalk, P. (2011b). Stage model for online grooming offenders. In J. Davidson & P. Gottschalk (Eds.), *Internet child abuse—Current research and policy* (pp. 79–103). Routledge, Taylor & Francis Group.

Gottschalk, P. (2017). White-collar crime: Detection and neutralization in religious organizations. *International Journal of Police Science & Management, 19*(2), 120–126.

Gottschalk, P. (2019). Convenience in criminal entrepreneurship: The case of a Norwegian hashish baron. *Deviant Behavior, 40*(3), 326–333.

Gottschalk, P. (2020). *Convenience dynamics and white-collar crime*. Routledge Publishing.

Gottschalk, P., & Asting, C. (2019). The family firm as an arena for white-collar crime. *International Journal of Business Continuity and Risk Management, 9*(4), 283–297.

Gottschalk, P., & Asting, C. (2020). Entitled to embezzlement? The case of successful executives working for rich heirs. *Deviant Behavior*, *41*(3), 269–277.

Gottschalk, P., & Benson, M. L. (2020). The evolution of corporate accounts of scandals from exposure to investigation. *British Journal of Criminology, 60*, 949–969.

Gottschalk, P., & Gunnesdal, L. (2018). *White-collar crime in the shadow economy: Lack of detection, investigation, and conviction compared to social security fraud*. Springer.

Gottschalk, P., & Markovic, V. (2016, June–December). Transnational criminal organizations (TCOs): The case of combating criminal biker gangs. *International Journal of Criminal Justice Sciences*, 30–44.

Gottschalk, P., & Smith, R. (2011). Criminal entrepreneurship, white-collar criminality, and neutralization theory. *Journal of Enterprising Communities: People and Places in the Global Economy, 5*(4), 300–308.

Gottschalk, P., & Tcherni-Buzzeo, M. (2017). Reasons for gaps in crime reporting: The case of white-collar criminals investigated by private fraud examiners in Norway. *Deviant Behavior, 38*(3), 267–281.

Graham, K. A., Resick, C. J., Margolis, J. A., Shao, P., Hargis, M. B., & Kiker, J. (2020). Egoistic norms, organizational identification, and the perceived ethicality of unethical pro-organizational behavior: A moral maturation perspective. *Human Relations, 73*(9), 1249–1277.

Graham, A., Kulig, T. C., & Cullen, F. T. (2020). Willingness to report crime to the police. *Policing: An International Journal, 43*(1), 1–16.

Grindaker, M. H. (2011, July 12). Tiltalt for barnehagebedrageri [Indicted for kindergarten fraud]. Norwegian daily business newspaper *Dagens Næringsliv*, p. 13.

Grutle, H. F. (2010, March 16). SAS dømt for industrispionasje mot Norwegian [SAS convicted of industrial espionage against Norwegian]. *TV2*. www.tv2nyhetene.no

Guccione, D. (2019, November 18). What is the dark web? How to access it and what you'll find, The state of cybersecurity. *CSO Online*. www.csoonline.com

Gulating. (2009, September 15). *Case number 08.196041AST-GULA/AVD2*. Gulating lagmannsrett [Gulating court of appeal].

Gupta, V. K., Mortal, S. C., Silveri, S., Sun, M., & Turban, D. B. (2020). You're fired! Gender disparities in CEO dismissal. *Journal of Management, 46*(4), 560–582.

Hagen, J. M., Sivertsen, T. K., & Rong, C. (2008). Protection against unauthorized access and computer crime in Norwegian enterprises. *Journal of Computer Security, 16*, 341–366.

Hambrick, D. C., & Lovelace, J. B. (2018). The role of executive symbolism in advancing new strategic themes in organization: A social influence perspective. *Academy of Management Review, 43*(1), 110–131.

Hamerton, C. (2020). White-collar cybercrime: Evaluating the redefinition of a criminological artifact. *Journal of Law and Criminal Justice, 8*(2), 67–79.

Hamilton, S., & Micklethwait, A. (2006). *Greed and corporate failure: The lessons from recent disasters*. Palgrave Macmillan.

Hansen, L. L. (2009). Corporate financial crime: Social diagnosis and treatment. *Journal of Financial Crime, 16*(1), 28–40.

Hansen, L. L. (2020). Review of the book "convenience triangle in white-collar crime: Case studies of fraud examinations". *ChoiceConnect, 57*(5). Association of College and Research Libraries.

Hansen, F., Klungtveit, H. S., Fretland, R. A., Meldalen, S. G., Egeberg, K., Thoresen, K., Jappee, G., & Monsen, Ø. N. (2009, May 12). Drept etter bittert oppgjør [Killed after bitter settlement]. Norwegian daily newspaper *Dagbladet*. www.dagbladet.no

Harkin, D., Whelan, C., & Chang, L. (2018). The challenges facing specialist police cyber-crime units: An empirical analysis. *Police Practice & Research, 19*(6), 519–536.

Harrison, A. J., Dilla, W. N., & Mennecke, B. E. (2020). Relationships within the fraud diamond: The decision processes that influence fraudulent intentions in online consumer fraud. *Journal of Information Systems, 34*(1), 61–80.

Hausman, W. J. (2018). Howard Hopson's billion dollar fraud: The rise and fall of associated gas & electric company. *Business History, 60*(3), 381–398.

Haveman, H. A., Mahoney, J. T., & Mannix, E. (2019). Editors' comments: The role of theory in management research. *Academy of Management Review, 44*(2), 241–243.

Haynes, K. T., Josefy, M., & Hitt, M. A. (2015). Tipping point: Managers' self-interest, greed, and altruism. *Journal of Leadership & Organizational Studies, 22*, 265–279.

Heath, J. (2008). Business ethics and moral motivation: A criminological perspective. *Journal of Business Ethics, 83*, 595–614.

Hefendehl, R. (2010). Addressing white collar crime on a domestic level. *Journal of International Criminal Justice, 8*, 769–782.

Henning, J. (2009). Perspectives on financial crimes in Roman-Dutch law: Bribery, fraud and the general crime of falsity. *Journal of Financial Crime, 16*(4), 295–304.

Henry, N., Flynn, A., & Powell, A. (2018). Policing image-based sexual abuse: Stakeholder perspectives. *Police Practice & Research, 19*(6), 565–581.

Henze, N., Grünewald, F., & Parmar, S. (2020, July). *Operational review of exposure to corrupt practices in humanitarian aid implementation mechanisms in the DRC*. Adam Smith International. www.reliefweb.int

Hern, A. (2017, June 15). European court of justice rules Pirate Bay is infringing copyright. *The Guardian*. www.theguardian.com

Hinduja, S. (2007a). Neutralization theory and online software piracy: An empirical analysis. *Ethics and Information Technology, 9*(3), 187–204.

Hinduja, S. (2007b). Computer crime investigations in the United States: Leveraging knowledge from the past to address the future. *International Journal of Cyber Criminology, 1*(1), 1–26.

Hinduja, S. (2012). General strain, self-control, and music piracy. *International Journal of Cyber Criminology, 6*(1), 951–967.

Hoffmann, J. P. (2002). A contextual analysis of differential association, social control, and strain theories of delinquency. *Social Forces, 81*(3), 753–785.

Holt, T. J. (2013). Exploring the social organization and structure of stolen data markets. *Global Crime, 14*(2–3), 155–174.

Holt, T. J. (2015). Qualitative criminology in online spaces. In H. Copes & J. M. Miller (Eds.), *The Routledge handbook of qualitative criminology* (pp. 189–204). Routledge.

Holt, T. J. (2017a). Situating the problem of cybercrime in a multidisciplinary context. In T. J. Holt (Ed.), *Cybercrime through an interdisciplinary lens* (pp. 1–16). Routledge.

Holt, T. J. (2017b). On the value of honeypots to produce policy recommendations. *Criminology & Public Policy, 16*(3), 739–747.

Holt, R., & Cornelissen, J. (2014). Sensemaking revisited. *Management Learning, 45*(5), 525–539.

Holt, T. J., & Graves, D. C. (2007). A qualitative analysis of advance fee fraud e-mail schemes. *International Journal of Cyber Criminology, 1*(1), 137–154.

Holt, T. J., Smirnova, O., & Hutchings, A. (2016). Examining signals of trust in criminal markets online. *Journal of Cybersecurity, 2*(2), 137–145.

Holt, T. J., Strumsky, D., Smirnova, O., & Kilger, M. (2012). Examining the social networks of malware writers and hackers. *International Journal of Cyber Criminology, 6*(1), 891–903.

Holt, T. J., Clevenger, S., & Navarro, J. (2020). Exploring digital evidence recognition among officers and troopers in a sample of a state police force. *Policing: An International Journal, 43*(1), 91–103.

Holtfreter, K. (2015). General theory, gender-specific theory, and white-collar crime. *Journal of Financial Crime, 22*(4), 422–431.

Holtfreter, K., Beaver, K. M., Reisig, M. D., & Pratt, T. C. (2010). Low self-control and fraud offending. *Journal of Financial Crime, 17*(3), 295–307.

Horgan, S., Collier, B., Jones, R., & Shepherd, L. (2021). Re-territorialising the policing of cybercrime in the post-Covid-19 era: Towards a new vision of local democratic cyber policing. *Journal of Criminal Psychology*, published online. https://doi.org/10.1108/JCP-08-2020-034

Huang, L., & Knight, A. P. (2017). Resources and relationships in entrepreneurship: An exchange theory of the development and effects of the entrepreneur-investor relationship. *Academy of Management Review, 42*(1), 80–102.

Huang, J., Diehl, M. R., & Paterlini, S. (2020). The influence of corporate elites on women on supervisory boards: Female directors' inclusion in Germany. *Journal of Business Ethics, 165*, 347–364.

Huff, R., Desilets, K., & Kane, J. (2010). *The national public survey on white collar crime*. National White Collar Crime Center, Fairmont. www.nw3c.org

Hughes, J., Aycock, S., Caines, A., Buttery, P., & Hutchings, A. (2020). *Detecting trending terms in cybersecurity forum discussions*. Workshop on Noisy User-generated Text (W-NUT), virtual event. www.noisy-text.github.io

Huisman, W., & Erp, J. (2013). Opportunities for environmental crime. *British Journal of Criminology, 53*, 1178–1200.

Hurley, P. J., Mayhew, B. W., & Obermire, K. M. (2019). Realigning auditors' accountability: Experimental evidence. *The Accounting Review, 94*(3), 233–250.

Huseman, R. C., Hatfield, J. D., & Miles, E. W. (1987). A new perspective on equity theory: The equity sensitivity construct. *Academy of Management Review, 12*(2), 222–234.

Hutchings, A. (2014). Crime from the keyboard: Organized crime, co-offending, initiation and knowledge transmission. *Crime, Law and Social Change, 62*(1), 1–20.

Hutchings, A. (2016). Cybercrime trajectories: An integrated theory of initiation, maintenance, and desistance. In T. J. Holt (Ed.), *Crime online: Correlates, causes, and context* (pp. 117–140). Carolina Academic Press.

Hutchings, A. (2018a). Leaving on a jet plane: The trade in fraudulently obtained airline tickets. *Crime, Law and Social Change, 70*, 461–487.

Hutchings, A. (2018b). Flying in cyberspace: Policing global travel fraud. *Policing: A Journal of Policy and Practice*, 1–16. https://doi.org/10.1093/police/pay063

Hutchings, A., & Clayton, R. (2016). Exploring the provision of online booter services. *Deviant Behavior, 37*(10), 1163–1178.

Hutchings, A., & Holt, T. J. (2016). A crime script analysis of the online stolen data market. *British Journal of Criminology, 55*, 596–614.

Hutchings, A., & Holt, T. J. (2018). Interviewing cybercrime offenders. *Journal of Qualitative Criminal Justice & Criminology, 7*(1), 75–94.

Hutchings, A., & Jorna, P. (2015). *Misuse of information and communications technology within the public sector*. Trends & Issues in Crime & Criminal Justice Series, No. 470. Australian Institute of Criminology.

Hällgren, M., Lindberg, O., & Rantatalo, O. (2020). Sensemaking in detective work: The social nature of crime investigation. *International Journal of Police Science and Management*, published online. https://doi.org/10.1177/1461355720980759

Høyesterett. (2019). Dom avsagt 13. mai 2019 i anke over Borgarting lagmannsretts dom 23. oktober 2018 [Verdict announced May 13, 2019 regarding appeal for Borgarting court's verdict October 23, 2018]. Høyesterett (Norwegian Supreme Court).

IBU Commission. (2021, January 28). *Final report of the IBU external review commission* (220 pages). IBU External Review Commission: Jonathan Taylor, Vincent Defrasne, Christian Dorda, Tanja Haug, Anja Martin, and Lauren Pagé.

Interpol. (2009). *Financial and high-tech crimes*. International Criminal Police Organizaton (Interpol). http://www.interpol.int/Public/FinancialCrime/

Jaara, O. O., & Kadomi, A. M. (2017). Factors related to the Central Bank instructions on money laundering. *Journal of Money Laundering Control, 20*(3), 274–291.

Jaishankar, K. (2007). Cyber criminology: Evolving a novel discipline with a new journal. *International Journal of Cyber Criminology, 1*(1), 1–6.

Jaishankar, K. (2010). The future of cyber criminology: Challenges and opportunities. *International Journal of Cyber Criminology, 4*(1 & 2), 26–31.

Jaishankar, K. (2018). Cyber criminology as an academic discipline: History, contribution, and impact. *International Journal of Cyber Criminology, 12*(1), 1–8.

Jansen, J., & Leukfeldt, R. (2016). Phishing and malware attacks on online banking customers in the Netherlands: A qualitative analysis of factors leading to victimization. *International Journal of Cyber Criminology, 10*(1), 79–91.

Jensen, M. C., & Meckling, W. H. (1976). Theory of the firm: Managerial behavior, agency costs and ownership structures. *Journal of Financial Economics, 3*(4), 305–360.

Jessen, C. K., & Jung, E. (2020, March 7). Banedanmark mistænker medarbeidere for bestikkelse og ulovlige forhold [Banedenmark suspects Employees for Bribe and illegal circumstances]. Danish daily newspaper *Berlingske*. www.berlingske.dk

Jones, S., Lyman, D. R., & Piquero, A. R. (2015). Substance use, personality, and inhibitors: Testing Hirschi's predictions about the reconceptualization of self-control. *Crime & Delinquency, 61*(4), 538–558.

Jonnergård, K., Stafsudd, A., & Elg, U. (2010). Performance evaluations as gender barriers in professional organizations: A study of auditing firms. *Gender, Work and Organization, 17*(6), 721–747.

Jordanoska, A. (2018). The social ecology of white-collar crime: Applying situational action theory to white-collar offending. *Deviant Behavior, 39*(11), 1427–1449.

Jordanoska, A., & Schoultz, I. (2020). The discovery of white-collar crime: The legacy of Edwin Sutherland. In M. Rorie (Ed.), *The handbook of white-collar crime* (Chapter 1, pp. 3–15). Wiley.

Joyce, E. (2005). Expanding the international regime on money laundering in response to transnational organized crime, terrorism, and corruption. In P. Reichel (Ed.), *Handbook of transnational crime and justice* (pp. 79–97). Sage.

Judge, T. A., Piccolo, R. F., & Kosalka, T. (2009). The bright and dark sides of leader traits: A review and theoretical extension of the leader trait paradigm. *The Leadership Quarterly, 20*, 855–875.

Kakkar, H., Sivanathan, N., & Gobel, M. S. (2020). Fall from grace: The role of dominance and prestige in the punishment of high-status actors. *Academy of Management Journal, 63*(2), 530–553.

Kamerdze, S., Loughran, T., Paternoster, R., & Sohoni, T. (2014). The role of affect in intended rule breaking: Extending the rational choice perspective. *Journal of Research in Crime and Delinquency, 51*(5), 620–654.

Kammeradvokaten. (2019). *Ansvarsvurdering vedrørende sagen om svindel med tilskudsmidler – Offentlig rapport* [Assessment of liability regarding the case of fraud with benefit funds—Public report], report of investigation (163 pages), law firm Kammeradvokaten Poul Schmith.

Kammeradvokaten. (2020, October 5). *Undersøgelse af forholdet mellem visse ansatte hos Banedanmark og private virksomheder* [Investigation of the relationship between certain employees at Banedanmark and private companies], law firm Poul Schmith Kammeradvokaten (191 pages).

Kang, E., & Thosuwanchot, N. (2017). An application of Durkheim's four categories of suicide to organizational crimes. *Deviant Behavior, 38*(5), 493–513.

Kaptein, M., & Helvoort, M. (2019). A model of neutralization techniques. *Deviant Behavior, 40*(10), 1260–1285.

Karim, K. E., & Siegel, P. H. (1998). A signal detection theory approach to analyzing the efficiency and effectiveness of auditing to detect management fraud. *Managerial Auditing Journal, 13*(6), 367–375.

Kark, R., & van Dijk, D. (2007). Motivation to lead, motivation to follow: The role of the self-regulatory focus in leadership processes. *Academy of Management Review, 32*(2), 500–528.

Kawasaki, T. (2020). Review of comparative studies on white-collar and corporate crime. In M. L. Rorie (Ed.), *The handbook of white-collar crime* (Chapter 27, pp. 437–447). Wiley.

Keaveney, S. M. (2008). The blame game: An attribution theory approach to marketer-engineer conflict in high-technology companies. *Industrial Marketing Management, 37*, 653–663.

Keil, M., Tiwana, A., Sainsbury, R., & Sneha, S. (2010). Toward a theory of whistleblowing intentions: A benefit-cost differential perspective. *Decision Sciences, 41*(4), 787–812.

Kempa, M. (2010). Combating white-collar crime in Canada: Serving victim needs and market integrity. *Journal of Financial Crime, 17*(2), 251–264.

Kennedy, J. P. (2020). Organizational and macro-level corporate crime theories. In M. L. Rorie (Ed.), *The handbook of white-collar crime* (Chapter 12, pp 175–190). Wiley.

Keyworth, M., & Wall, M. (2016, January 8). The 'bogus boss' email scam costing firms millions. *BBC*. www.bbc.com

Kholin, M., Kückelhaus, B., & Blickle, G. (2020). Why dark personalities can get ahead: Extending the toxic career model. *Personality and Individual Differences, 156*. https://doi.org/10.1016/j.paid2019.109792

Kierkegaard, S. (2008). Cybering, online grooming and ageplay. *Computer Law & Security Report, 24*, 41–55.

Kim, P. H., Dirks, K. T., & Cooper, C. D. (2009). The repair of trust: A dynamic bilateral perspective and multilevel conceptualization. *Academy of Management Review, 34*(3), 401–422.

King, M. (2020). Financial fraud investigative interviewing—Corporate investigators' beliefs and practices: A qualitative inquiry. *Journal of Financial Crime*. https://doi.org/10.1108/JFC-08-2020-0158.

Kireenko, A. P., Nevzorova, E. N., & Fedotov, D. Y. (2019). Sector-specific characteristics of tax crime in Russia. *Journal of Tax Reform, 5*(3), 249–264.

Kleijn, M., & Bogaerts, S. (2020). Sexual offending pathways and chat conversations in an online environment. *Sexual Abuse*, 1–20, published online. https://doi.org/10.1177/1079063220981061

Klein, F. B., Chaigneau, P., & Devers, C. E. (2021). CEO gender-based termination concerns: Evidence from initial severance agreements. *Journal of Management, 47*(3), 567–596.

Kleinfeld, P. (2020, June 11). Congo aid scam triggers sector-wide alarm. *The New Humanitarian*. www.thenewhumanitarian.org

Kleppe, M. K. (2011, December 6). Banktopp dømt til tre års fengsel [Bank top convicted to three years prison]. Norwegian daily financial newspaper *Finansavisen*, pp. 30–31.

Kleppe, M. K. (2012, March 3). Too easy to abuse public funds. Norwegian daily financial newspaper *Finansavisen*, pp. 6–7.

Klimek, L. (2020). European responses criminalizing online solicitation of children for sexual purposes. *Balkan Social Science Review, 16*, 7–21.

Kolthoff, E. (2020). Criminological responses to corruption. In A. Graycar (Ed.), *Handbook on corruption, ethics and integrity in public administration* (Chapter 30, pp. 434–448). Edward Elgar.

Kostova, T., Roth, K., & Dacin, M. T. (2008). Institutional theory in the study of multinational corporations: A critique and new directions. *Academy of Management Review, 33*(4), 994–1006.

Kowalick, P., Connery, D., & Sarre, R. (2018). Intelligence-sharing in the context of policing transnational serious and organized crime: A note on policy and practice in an Australian setting. *Police Practice & Research, 19*(6), 596–608.

Kowalski, R. M., & Limber, S. P. (2007). Electronic bullying among middle school students. *Journal of Adolescent Health, 41*(6), S22–S30.

Koziarski, J., & Lee, J. R. (2020). Connecting evidence-based policing and cybercrime. *Policing: An International Journal, 43*(1), 198–211.

Krippendorff, K. (1980). *Content analysis: An introduction to its methodology*. Sage.

Krokfjord, T. P. (2017, April 19). Dømt for millionbedrageri, har brukt fire identiteter: Slik er John Andrew Tollefsens nye barnehageplan [Convicted of millions fraud, has used four identities: Such is John Andrew Tollefsen's new daycare plan]. Norwegian daily newspaper *Dagbladet*. www.dagbladet.no

Kroneberg, C., & Schulz, S. (2018). Revisiting the role of self-control in situational action theory. *European Journal of Criminology, 15*(1), 56–76.

Kshetri, N. (2005). Pattern of global cyber war and crime: A conceptual framework. *Journal of International Management, 11*(4), 541–562.

Langton, L., & Piquero, N. L. (2007). Can general strain theory explain white-collar crime? A preliminary investigation of the relationship between strain and select white-collar offenses. *Journal of Criminal Justice, 35,* 1–15.

Larsson, P. (2006). Developments in the regulation of economic crime in Norway. *Journal of Financial Crime, 13*(1), 65–76.

Lassen, C., Laugen, B. T., & Næss, P. (2006). Virtual mobility and organizational reality—A note on the mobility needs in knowledge organizations. *Transportation Research, 11,* 459–463.

Laudon, K. C., & Laudon, J. P. (2010). *Management information systems: Managing the digital firm* (Eleventh). Pearson Education.

Leasure, P., & Zhang, G. (2018). "That's how they taught us to do it": Learned deviance and inadequate deterrents in retail banking. *Deviant Behavior, 39*(5), 603–616.

Lee, F., & Robinson, R. J. (2000). An attributional analysis of social accounts: Implications of playing the blame game. *Journal of Applied Social Psychology, 30*(9), 1853–1879.

Lehman, D. W., Cooil, B., & Ramanujam, R. (2020). The effects of rule complexity on organizational noncompliance and remediation: Evidence from restaurant health inspections. *Journal of Management, 46*(8), 1436–1468.

Leigh, A. C., Foote, D. A., Clark, W. R., & Lewis, J. L. (2010). Equity sensitivity: A triadic measure and outcome/input perspectives. *Journal of Managerial Issues, 22*(3), 286–305.

Leonard, W. N., & Weber, M. G. (1970). Automakers and dealers: A study of criminogenic market forces. *Law & Society Review, 4*(3), 407–424.

Leontiadis, N., & Hutchings, A. (2015). Scripting the crime commission process in the illicit online prescription drug trade. *Journal of Cybersecurity, 1*(1), 81–92.

Leppänen, A., Toiviainen, T., & Kankaanranta, T. (2020). From vulnerability search to a criminal case: Script analysis of an SQL injection attack. *International Journal of Cyber Criminology, 14*(1), 63–80.

Leukfeldt, R., & Jansen, J. (2015). Cyber criminal networks and money mules: An analysis of low-tech and high-tech fraud attacks in the Netherlands. *International Journal of Cyber Criminology, 9*(2), 173–184.

Lie, T. (2020, December 26). UiT gir opp forsøk på å få tilbake svindel-millioner [UiT gives up attempt to get scam millions back]. Norwegian web-based newspaper *Khrono*.

Liebowitz, J. (2004). Will knowledge management work in the government? *Electronic Government: An International Journal, 1*(1), 1–7.

Lillywhite, R., & Skidmore, P. (2006). Boys are not sexually exploited? A challenge to practitioners. *Child Abuse Review, 15*, 351–361.

Liu, C. C., & Chen, S. Y. (2005). Determinants of knowledge sharing of e-learners. *International Journal of Innovation and Learning, 2*(4), 434–445.

Locke, S. L., & Blomquist, G. C. (2016). The cost of convenience: Estimating the impact of communication antennas on residential property values. *Land Economics, 92*(1), 131–147.

Lokanan, M., & Liu, S. (2021). Predicting fraud victimization using classical machine learning. *Entropy, 23*, 1–19.

Loveday, B. (2017). Still plodding along? The police response to the changing profile of crime in England and Wales. *International Journal of Police Science & Management, 19*(2), 101–109.

Loyens, K., Claringbould, I., Heres-van Rossem, L., & van Eekeren, Frank. (2021). The social construction of integrity: A qualitative case study in Dutch football. *Sports in Society*, published online. https://doi.org/10.1080/17430437.2021.1877661

Lutz, J. R. (2019). Pink-collar crime. In F. P. Bernat & K. Frailing (Eds.), *The encyclopedia of women and crime* (pp. 791–796). Wiley.

Lyman, M. D., & Potter, G. W. (2007). *Organized crime* (4th ed.). Pearson Prentice Hall.

Malladi, R. K., & Dheeriya, P. L. (2021). Time series analysis of cryptocurrency returns and volatilities. *Journal of Economics and Finance, 45*, 75–94.

Marcum, C. D., Higgins, G. E., Freiburger, T. L., & Ricketts, M. L. (2012). Battle of the sexes: An examination of male and female cyber bullying. *International Journal of Cyber Criminology, 6*(1), 904–911.

Martin, J., & Peterson, M. M. (1987). Two-tier wage structures: Implications for equity theory. *Academy of Management Journal, 30*(2), 297–315.

Maslow, A. H. (1943). A theory of human motivation. *Psychological Review, 50*(4), 370–396.

Mawritz, M. B., Greenbaum, R. L., Butts, M. M., & Graham, K. A. (2017). I just can't control myself: A self-regulation perspective on the abuse of deviant employees. *Academy of Management Journal, 60*(4), 1482–1503.

Maxwell, D., Walker, P., Church, C., Harvey, P., Savage, K., & Bailey, S. (2008). *Preventing corruption in humanitarian assistance*. Transparency International. www.transparency.org

McClean, E. J., Martin, S. R., Emich, K. J., & Woodruff, T. (2018). The social consequences of voice: An examination of voice type and gender status and subsequent leader emergence. *Academy of Management Journal, 61*(5), 1869–1891.

McClelland, P. L., Liang, X., & Barker, V. L. (2010). CEO commitment to the status quo: Replication and extension using content analysis. *Journal of Management, 36*(5), 1251–1277.

McDonald, M. L., & Westphal, J. D. (2003). Getting by with the advice of their friends: CEOs' advice networks using content analysis. *Administrative Science Quarterly, 48*(1), 1–32.

McElwee, G., & Smith, R. (2015). Towards a nuanced typology of illegal entrepreneurship: A theoretical and conceptual overview. In G. McElwee & R. Smith (Eds.), *Exploring criminal and illegal enterprise: New perspectives on research, policy & practice: Contemporary issues in entrepreneurship research* (Vol. 5). Emerald.

Menon, S., & Siew, T. G. (2012). Key challenges in tackling economic and cybercrimes—Creating a multilateral platform for international co-operation. *Journal of Money Laundering Control, 15*(3), 243–256.

Mesmer-Magnus, J. R., & Viswesvaran, C. (2005). Whistleblowing in an organization: An examination of correlates of whistleblowing intentions, actions, and retaliation. *Journal of Business Ethics, 62*(3), 266–297.

Mingus, W., & Burchfield, K. B. (2012). From prison to integration: Applying modified labeling theory to sex offenders. *Criminal Justice Studies, 25*(1), 97–109.

Miro-Llinares, F., Drew, J., & Townsley, M. (2020). Understanding target suitability in cyberspace: An international comparison of cyber victimization processes. *International Journal of Cyber Criminology, 14*(1), 139–155.

Mitchell, K. J., Wolak, J., & Finkelhor, D. (2008). Are blogs putting youth at risk for online sexual solicitation or harassment? *Child Abuse & Neglect, 32*, 277–294.

Mpho, B. (2017). Whistleblowing: What do contemporary ethical theories say? *Studies in Business and Economics, 12*(1), 19–28.

Mugarura, N. (2015). The jeopardy of the bank in enforcement of normative anti-money laundering and countering financing of terrorism regimes. *Journal of Money Laundering Control, 18*(3), 352–370.

Murphy, P. R., & Dacin, M. T. (2011). Psychological pathways to fraud: Understanding and preventing fraud in organizations. *Journal of Business Ethics, 101*, 601–618.

Müller, S. M. (2018). Corporate behavior and ecological disaster: Dow chemical and the Great Lakes mercury crisis, 1970–1972. *Business History, 60*(3), 399–422.

Naheem, M. A. (2020). The agency dilemma in anti-money laundering regulation. *Journal of Money Laundering Control*, published online. https://doi.org/10.1108/JMLC-01-2016-0007

Naumovska, I., Wernicke, G., & Zajac, E. J. (2020). Last to come and last to go? The complex role of gender and ethnicity in the reputational penalties for directors linked to corporate fraud. *Academy of Management Journal, 63*(3), 881–902.

Newth, M. (2018, November 5). Britta Nielsen (64) mistenkt for å ha stjålet 140 millioner [Britta Nielsen (64) suspected of having stolen 140 million]. Norwegian daily newspaper *VG*. www.vg.no

Nguyen, C. L. (2018). Preventing the use of financial institutions for money laundering and the implications for financial privacy. *Journal of Money Laundering Control, 21*(1), 47–58.

Nhan, J., Kinkade, P., & Burns, R. (2009). Finding a pot of gold at the end of an internet rainbow: Further examination of fraudulent email solicitation. *International Journal of Cyber Criminology, 3*(1), 452–475.

Nichol, J. E. (2019). The effects of contract framing on misconduct and entitlement. *The Accounting Review, 94*(3), 329–344.

Nielsen, M. K. (2019, March 1). New report concludes: How Britta Nielsen could swindle for DKK 120 million for 25 years. *Danmarks Radio*. www.dr.no

Nielsen, R. P. (2003). Corruption networks and implications for ethical corruption reform. *Journal of Business Ethics, 42*(2), 125–149.

Niesche, C. (2020, October–November). Thei heightened risk of fraud in the Covid era. *Acuitymag*. www.acuitymag.com

Nodeland, B., & Morris, R. (2020). The impact of low self-control on past and future cyber offending. *International Journal of Cyber Criminology, 14*(1), 106–120.

Nonaka, I., Toyama, R., & Konno, N. (2000). Seci, ba and leadership: A Unified model of dynamic knowledge creation. *Long Range Planning, 33*(1), 5–34.

Norfund. (2020, May 15). *Norfund er utsatt for alvorlig svindel* [Norfund is exposed to serious fraud]. *Norfund*. www.norfund.no

Nowacki, J., & Willits, D. (2020). An organizational approach to understanding police response to cybercrime. *Policing: An International Journal, 43*(1), 63–76.

NTB. (2011, July 1). Fem tiltalt for Nordea-bedrageri [Five charged with Nordea fraud]. Norwegian daily business newspaper *Dagens Næringsliv*. www.dn.no

NTB. (2012, March 1). Ektepar dømt for grov utroskap [Married couple convicted of gross infidelity]. Norwegian daily business newspaper *Aftenposten*, p. 10.

NTB. (2018, January 19). Nordmenn brøt loven ved å se filmer gjennom popcorn time [Norwegians violated the law by watching movies through Popcorn Time]. Norwegian daily business newspaper *Aftenposten*. www.aftenposten.no

NTB. (2019, October 24). Dansk kvinne for retten i storstilt svindelsak [Danish women prosecuted in court in a big fraud case]. ABC *nyheter*. www.abcnyheter.no

NTB. (2020, December 17). Mann dømt til fengsel for koronasvindel [Man sentenced to prison for corona fraud]. Norwegian daily business newspaper *Sunnmørsposten*. www.smp.no

Nykodym, N., Taylor, R., & Vilela, J. (2005). Criminal profiling and insider cyber crime. *Computer Law & Security Report, 21*, 408–414.

O'Leary, S., & Smith, D. (2020). Moments of resistance: An internally persuasive view of performance and impact reports in non-governmental organizations. *Accounting, Organization and Society, 85*, 1–21.

Obodaru, O. (2017). Forgone, but not forgotten: Toward a theory of forgone professional identities. *Academy of Management Journal, 60*(2), 523–553.

Ogre, M. (2020, December 17). Mann dømt for massiv koronasvindel – Økokrim tror dette bare er begynnelsen [Man convicted of massive corona fraud – Økokrim thinks this is just the beginning]. *TV2*. www.tv2.no

Ortmeier, P. J., & Davis, J. J. (2012). *Police administration: A leadership approach*. McGraw Hill.

Ottermann, P. (2020, February 18). Danish social worker jailed for stealing £13m of government funds. *The Guardian*. www.theguardian.com

Owens, E. G., & Shores, M. (2010). *Informal networks and white collar crime: Evidence from the Madoff scandal* (54 pages). Social Science Research Network. www.pars.ssm.com

Paek, S. Y., Nalla, M. K., & Lee, J. (2020). Determinants of police officers' support for the public-private partnerships (PPPs) in policing cyberspace. *Policing: An International Journal, 43*(5), 877–892.

Panja, T. (2021, January 28). Hunting trips, sex and cash: How grooming biathlon's leader paid off for Russia—An investigation accuses biathlon's longtime president of accepting gifts from Russians and then doing the country's bidding as a doping scandal swirled. *The New York Times*. www.nytimes.com

Paraschiv, G. (2013). Conceptualizing transnational organized crime. *Economics, Management, and Financial Markets, 8*(2), 173–178.

Park, H., Bjørkelo, B., & Blenkinsopp, J. (2020). External whistleblowers' experiences of workplace bullying by superiors and colleagues. *Journal of Business Ethics, 161*, 591–601.

Patel, P. C., & Cooper, D. (2014). Structural power equality between family and nonfamily TMT members and the performance of family firms. *Academy of Management Journal, 57*(6), 1624–1649.

Patrucco, A. S., Luzzini, D., & Ronchi, S. (2017). Research perspectives on public procurement: Content analysis of 14 years of publications. *Journal of Public Procurement, 16*(2), 229–269.

Payne, B. K., & Hadzhidimova, L. (2020). Disciplinary and interdisciplinary trends in cybercrime research: An examination. *International Journal of Cyber Criminology, 14*(1), 1–25.

Picard, M. (2009). Financial services in trouble: The electronic dimension. *Journal of Financial Crime, 16*(2), 180–192.

Pickett, K. H. S., & Pickett, J. M. (2002). *Financial crime investigation and control*. Wiley.

Pillay, S., & Kluvers, R. (2014). An institutional theory perspective on corruption: The case of a developing democracy. *Financial Accountability & Management, 30*(1), 95–119.

Pinto, J., Leana, C. R., & Pil, F. K. (2008). Corrupt organizations or organizations of corrupt individuals? Two types of organization-level corruption. *Academy of Management Review, 33*(3), 685–709.

Piquero, N. L. (2012). The only thing we have to fear is fear itself: Investigating the relationship between fear of falling and white-collar crime. *Crime and Delinquency, 58*(3), 362–379.

Piquero N. L., & Schoepfer A. (2010). Theories of white-collar crime and public policy. In H. D. Barlow & S. H. Decker (Eds.), *Criminology and public policy: Putting theory to work*. Temple University Press.

Piquero, N. L., Piquero, A. R., Narvey, C., Boutwell, B., & Farrington, D. P. (2019). Are there psychopaths in white-collar jobs? *Deviant Behavior*, published online. https://doi.org/10.1080/01639625.2019.1708537

Podgor, E. S. (2007). The challenge of white collar sentencing. *Journal of Criminal Law and Criminology, 97*(3), 1–10.

Pontell, H. N., Black, W. K., & Geis, G. (2014). Too big to fail, too powerful to jail? On the absence of criminal prosecutions after the 2008 financial meltdown. *Crime, Law and Social Change, 61*(1), 1–13.

Pontell, H. N., Tillman, R., & Ghazi-Tehrani, A. K. (2021). In-your-face Watergate: Neutralizing government lawbreaking and the war against white-collar crime. *Crime, Law and Social Change*, 19, published online. https://doi.org/10.1007/s10611-021-09954-1

Popham, J., McCluskey, M., & Ouellet, M. (2020). Exploring police-reported cybercrime in Canada: Variation and correlates. *Policing: An International Journal, 43*(1), 35–48.

Popham, J. F., & Volpe, C. (2018). Predicting moral disengagement from the harms associated with digital music piracy: An exploratory, integrative test of digital drift and the criminal interaction order. *International Journal of Cyber Criminology, 12*(1), 133–150.

Porter, M. E., Lorsch, J. W., & Nohria, N. (2004, October). Seven surprises for new CEOs. *Harvard Business Review*, p. 62.

Pratt, T. C., & Cullen, F. T. (2005). Assessing macro-level predictors and theories of crime: A meta-analysis. *Crime and Justice, 32*, 373–450.

Procter, R., Crump, J., Karstedt, S., Voss, A., & Cantijoch, M. (2013). Reading the riots: What were the police doing in Twitter? *Policing & Society, 23*(4), 413–436.

Pusch, N., & Holtfreter, K. (2020). Individual and organizational predictors of white-collar crime: A meta-analysis. *Journal of White-Collar and Corporate Crime*, 1–19. https://doi.org/10.1177/2631309X19901317

PwC. (2019). *Ekstern undersøgelse af tilskudsadministrationen 1977–2018: Udarbejdet for Socialstyrelsen* [External investigation of benefits administration 1977–2018: Provided to the social security administration]. Report of investigation, 80 pages, audit firm PricewaterhouseCoopers, Copenhagen, Denmark.

PwC. (2020, June 30). *Independent assessment of the LOLC incident: Report developed for Norfund, report of investigation* (p. 34). PricewaterhouseCoopers.

Qiu, B., & Slezak, S. L. (2019). The equilibrium relationships between performance-based pay, performance, and the commission and detection of fraudulent misreporting. *The Accounting Review, 94*(2), 325–356.

Quayle, E., Vaughan, M., & Taylor, M. (2006). Sex offenders, internet child abuse images and emotional avoidance: The importance of values. *Aggression and Violent Behavior, 11*, 1–11.

Ramoglou, S., & Tsang, E. W. K. (2016). A realist perspective of entrepreneurship: Opportunities as propensities. *Academy of Management Review, 41*, 410–434.

Ratcliffe, J. (2005). The effectiveness of police intelligence management: A New Zealand case study. *Police Practice & Research, 6*(5), 435–451.

Rawat, P. (2020). A systematic review of multiple terminologies for ICT in government: A mesh of concentric and overlapping circles. *Bulletin of Science, Technology & Society*, published online. https://doi.org/10.1177/0270467620980996

Rehg, M. T., Miceli, M. P., Near, J. P., & Scotter, J. R. V. (2009). Antecedents and outcomes of retaliation against whistleblowers: Gender differences and power relationships. *Organization Science, 19*(2), 221–240.

Resodihardjo, S. L., Carroll, B. J., Eijk, C. J. A., & Maris, S. (2015). Why traditional responses to blame games fail: The importance of context, rituals, and sub-blame games in the face of raves gone wrong. *Public Administration, 94*(2), 350–363.

Reyns, B. W. (2013). Online routines and identity theft victimization: Further expanding routine activity theory beyond direct-contact offenses. *Journal of Research in Crime and Delinquency, 50*, 216–238.

Reyns, B. W. (2018). Routine activity theory and cybercrime. In K. Steinmetz & M. Nobles (Eds.), *Technocrime and criminological theory*. Routledge.

Riksrevisjonen. (2020). *Riksrevisjonens undersøkelse av informasjonssikkerhet i Norfund* [The office of the auditor general's investigation of information security at Norfund] (25 pages). The Office of the Auditor General of Norway. www.riksrevisjonen.no

Riksrevisjonen. (2021). *Riksrevisjonens undersøkelse av politiets innsats mot kriminalitet ved bruk av IKT* [The office of the auditor general's investigation of police efforts against crime through the use of ICT] (147 pages). The Office of the Auditor General of Norway. www.riksrevisjonen.no

Rixen, T. (2013). Why reregulation after the crisis is feeble: Shadow banking, offshore financial centers, and jurisdictional competition. *Regulation & Governance, 7*(4), 435–459.

Rodriguez, P., Uhlenbruck, K., & Eden, L. (2005). Government corruption and the entry strategies of multinationals. *Academy of Management Review, 30*(2), 383–396.

Roehling, M. V., Roehling, P., & Boswell, W. R. (2010). The potential role of organizational setting in creating 'entitled' employees: An investigation of the antecedents of equity sensitivity. *Employee Responsibilities & Rights Journal, 22*, 133–145.

Rooij, B., & Fine, A. (2020). Preventing corporate crime from within: Compliance management, whistleblowing, and internal monitoring. In Rorie, M. L. (Eds.), *The handbook of white-collar crime* (Chapter 15, pp. 229–245). Wiley.

Salifu, A. (2008). The impact of internet crime on development. *Journal of Financial Crime, 15*(4), 432–443.

Sarre, R., Lau, L. Y. C., & Chang, L. Y. C. (2018). Responding to cybercrime: Current trends. *Police Practice & Research, 19*(6), 515–518.

Scheaf, D. J., & Wood, M. S. (2021). Entrepreneurial fraud: A multidisciplinary review and synthesized framework. *Theory and Practice*, published online. https://doi.org/10.1177/04225872110018l8,pages1-36

Schnatterly, K., Gangloff, K. A., & Tuschke, A. (2018). CEO wrongdoing: A review of pressure, opportunity, and rationalization. *Journal of Management, 44*(6), 2405–2432.

Schneider, S. (2006). Privatizing economic crime enforcement: Exploring the role of private sector investigative agencies in combating money laundering. *Policing & Society, 16*(3), 285–312.

Schoenmueller, V., Netzer, O., & Stahl, F. (2020). The polarity of online reviews: Prevalence, drivers and implications. *Journal of Marketing Research, 57*(5), 853–877.

Schoepfer, A., & Piquero, N. L. (2006). Exploring white-collar crime and the American dream: A partial test of institutional anomie theory. *Journal of Criminal Justice, 34*(3), 227–235.

Schoultz, I., & Flyghed, J. (2020a). From "we didn't do it" to "we've learned our lesson": Development of a typology of neutralizations of corporate crime. *Critical Criminology, 28*, 739–757.

Schoultz, I., & Flyghed, J. (2020b). Denials and confessions: An analysis of the temporalization of neutralizations of corporate crime. *International Journal*

of Law, Crime and Justice, published online. https://doi.org/10.1016/j.ijlcj.2020.100389
Schoultz, I., & Flyghed, J. (2021). "We have been thrown under the bus": Corporate versus individual defense mechanisms against transnational corporate bribery charges. *Journal of White Collar and Corporate Crime, 2*(1), 24–35.
Shawver, T., & Clements, L. H. (2019). The impact of value preferences on whistleblowing intentions of accounting professionals. *Journal of Forensic and Investigative Accounting, 11*(2), 232–247.
Shores, M. (2010). *Informal networks and white collar crime: An extended analysis of the Madoff Scandal*. www.dspace.library.cornell.edu
Siponen, M., & Vance, A. (2010). Neutralization: New insights into the problem of employee information security policy violations. *MIS Quarterly, 34*(3), 487–502.
Slyke, S. V., & Bales, W. D. (2012). A contemporary study of the decision to incarcerate white-collar and street property offenders. *Punishment & Society, 14*(2), 217–246.
Smallridge, J. L., & Roberts, J. R. (2013). Crime specific neutralizations: An empirical examination of four types of digital piracy. *International Journal of Cyber Criminology, 7*(2), 125–140.
Smith, H. L. (2003). Knowledge organization and local economic development: The cases of Oxford and Grenoble. *Regional Studies, 37*(9), 899–909.
Smith, R. (2009). Understanding entrepreneurial behavior in organized criminals. *Journal of Enterprising Communities: People and Places in the Global Economy, 3*(3), 256–268.
Smith, A. N., Watkins, M. B., Ladge, J. J., & Carlton, P. (2020). Making the invisible visible: Paradoxical effects of intersectional invisibility on the career experiences of executive black women. *Academy of Management Journal, 62*(6), 1705–1734.
Solem, L. K., & Kleppe, M. K. (2014, December 3). Seks dømt for korrupsjon i Unibuss-saken [Six convicted in the Unibuss case]. Norwegian daily business newspaper *Dagens Næringsliv*. https://www.dn.no/korrupsjon/unibuss/kriminalitet/seks-domt-for-korrupsjon-i-unibuss-saken/1-1-5245586
Solgård, J. (2020, July 9). Norfund ble svindlet for 100 millioner: -Vi har gjort mye, men ikke raskt nok for å styrke våre rutiner og systemer [Norfund was defrauded for 100 million: -We have done a lot, but not fast enough to strengthen our routines and systems]. Norwegian daily business newspaper *Dagens Næringsliv*. www.dn.no

Speed, J. (2020, May 15). *Politiet: Lite trolig at Nordfun får igjen svindelpenger* [The police: It is unlikely that Norfund will get back fraud money]. Foreign aid magazine *BistandsAktuelt*. www.bistandsaktuelt.no

Srivastava, S. B., & Goldberg, A. (2017). Language as a window into culture. *California Management Review, 60*(1), 56–69.

Stadler, W. A., Benson, M. L., & Cullen, F. T. (2013). Revisiting the special sensitivity hypothesis: The prison experience of white-collar inmates. *Justice Quarterly, 30*(6), 1090–1114.

Stamatel, J. P. (2018). The international trafficking of human organs. *Police Practice & Research, 19*(6), 618–620.

Stave, T. K. (2020, July 9). Norfund tar selvkritikk etter gigantsvindel [Norfund takes self-criticism after giant fraud]. Norwegian daily newspaper *Aftenposten*. www.e24.no

Steel, C. M. S. (2019). Stolen identity valuation and market evolution on the dark web. *International Journal of Cyber Criminology, 13*(1), 70–83.

Steffensmeier, D., Schwartz, J., & Roche, M. (2013). Gender and twenty-first-century corporate crime: Female involvement and the gender gap in Enron-era corporate frauds. *American Sociological Review, 78*(3), 448–476.

Stone, B. (2015, March 2–March 8). Too good to be legal. *Bloomberg Businessweek*, pp. 31–33.

Sundström, M., & Radon, A. (2015). Utilizing the concept of convenience as a business opportunity in emerging markets. *Organizations and Markets in Emerging Economies, 6*(2), 7–21.

Sutherland, E. H. (1939). White-collar criminality. *American Sociological Review, 5*, 1–12.

Sutherland, E. H. (1949). *White collar crime*. Holt Rinehart and Winston.

Sutherland, E. H. (1983). *White collar crime—The uncut version*. Yale University Press.

Sykes, G., & Matza, D. (1957). Techniques of neutralization: A theory of delinquency. *American Sociological Review, 22*(6), 664–670.

Szalma, J. L., & Hancock, P. A. (2013). A signal improvement to signal detection analysis: Fuzzy SDT on the ROCs. *Journal of Experimental Psychology: Human Perception and Performance, 39*(6), 1741–1762.

Tankebe, J. (2019). Cooperation with the police against corruption: Exploring the roles of legitimacy, deterrence and collective action theories. *British Journal of Criminology, 59*, 1390–1410.

Taylor, A., & Greve, H. R. (2006). Superman or the fantastic four? Knowledge combination and experience in innovative teams. *Academy of Management Journal, 49*(4), 723–740.

Tejeiro, R., Alison, L., Hendricks, E., Giles, S., Long, M., & Shipley, D. (2020). Sexual behaviours in indecent images of children: A content analysis. *International Journal of Cyber Criminology, 14*(1), 121–138.

Teubner, R. A., & Stockhinger, J. (2020). Literature review: Understanding information systems strategy in the digital age. *Journal of Strategic Information Systems*, published online. https://doi.org/10.1016/j.jsis.2020.101642

Thaxton, S., & Agnew, R. (2018). When criminal coping is likely: An examination of conditioning effects in general strain theory. *Journal of Quantitative Criminology, 34*, 887–920.

Thomas, D. (2002). *Hacker culture*. University of Minnesota Press.

Toner, G. A. (2009). New ways of thinking about old crimes: Prosecuting corruption and organized criminal groups engaged in labor-management racketeering. *Journal of Financial Crime, 16*(1), 41–59.

Tonoyan, V., Strohmeyer, R., Habib, M., & Perlitz, M. (2010). Corruption and entrepreneurship: How formal and informal institutions shape small firm behavior in transition and mature market economies. *Entrepreneurship: Theory & Practice, 34*(5), 803–831.

Toolami, B. N., Roodposhti, F. R., Nikoomaram, H., Banimahd, B., & Vakilifard, H. (2019). The survey of whistleblowing intentions for accounting frauds based on demographic individual differences among accounting staff. *International Journal of Finance and Managerial Accounting, 4*(14), 1–13.

Toupin, S. (2014). Feminist hackerspaces: The synthesis of feminist and hacker cultures. *Journal of Peer Production, 5*(2014), 1–11.

Tufekci, Z. (2008). Grooming, gossip, Facebook and MySpace: What can we learn about these sites from those who won't assimilate? *Information, Communication & Society, 11*(4), 544–564.

Turner, K. L., & Makhija, M. V. (2006). The role of organizational controls in managing knowledge. *Academy of Management Review, 31*(1), 197–217.

United Nations. (2008). *United Nations e-government survey 2008*. Division for Public Administration and Development Management, United Nations.

Uretsky, M. (2001). Preparing for the real knowledge organization. *Journal of Organizational Excellence, 21*(1), 87–93.

Uygur, S. A. (2020). *Fraud in the charity sector in England and Wales: Accountability and stakeholder oversight*. A thesis submitted in fulfillment of the requirement for the degree of Doctor of Philosophy of Royal Holloway, University of London, United Kingdom.

van Donk, D. P., & Molloy, E. (2008). From organizing as projects, to projects as organizations. *International Journal of Project Management, 26*, 129–137.

van Gijn-Grosvenor, E. L., Lamb, M. E. (2021). Online groomer typology scheme. *Psychology, Crime & Law*, published online. https://doi.org/10.1080/1068316X.2021.1876048

Valvik, M. E., & Strømsheim, G. (2010, November 10). SAS dømt til å betale 570 millioner i bot [SAS convicted to pay 570 million kroner in fine]. Norwegian daily newspaper *Aftenposten*. www.aftenposten.no

Vasiu, V. I., & Podgor, E. S. (2019, July). Organizational opportunity and deviant behavior: Convenience in white-collar crime. In *Criminal Law and Criminal Justice Books*. Rutgers, The State University of New Jersey. www.clcjbooks.rutgers.edu

Väyrynen, T., & Laari-Salmela, S. (2015). Men, mammals, or machines? Dehumanization embedded in organizational practices. *Journal of Business Ethics, 147*, 1–19.

Victor, B., & Cullen, J. B. (1988). The organizational bases of ethical work climates. *Administrative Science Quarterly, 33*, 101–125.

Vu, A. V., Hughes, J., Pete, I., Collier, B., Chua, Y. T., Shumailov, I., & Hutchings, A. (2020, October). Turning up the dial: The evolution of a cybercrime market through set-up, stable, and Covid-19 eras, IMC'20. In *Proceedings of the ACM Internet Measurement Conference* (pp. 551–566). https://doi.org/10.1145/3419394.3423636

Walburg, C. (2020). White-collar and corporate crime: European perspectives. In M. L. Rorie (Ed.), *The handbook of white-collar crime* (Chapter 21, pp. 337–346). Wiley.

Wall, D. S. (2013). Policing identity crimes. *Policing & Society, 23*(4), 437–460.

Wall, D. S., & Williams, M. L. (2013). Policing cybercrime: Networked and social media technologies and the challenges for policing. *Policing & Society, 23*(4), 409–412.

Wall-Parker, A. (2020). Measuring white collar crime. In M. L. Rorie (Ed.), *The handbook of white-collar crime* (Chapter 3, pp. 32–44). Wiley.

Walsh, J. N. (2020). Identifying and categorizing knowledge reuse activities in electronic repositories. *Journal of Information and Knowledge Management Systems*, published online. https://doi.org/10.1108/VJIKMS-04-2020-0066

Wang, P. (2020). How to engage in illegal transactions: Resolving risk and uncertainty in corrupt dealings. *British Journal of Criminology, 60*, 1282–1301.

Wasko, M. M., & Faraj, S. (2005). Why should I share? Examining social capital and knowledge contribution in electronic networks of practice. *MIS Quarterly, 29*(1), 35–57.

Webster, J., & Drew, J. M. (2017). Policing advance fee fraud (AFF): Experiences of fraud detectives using a victim-focused approach. *International Journal of Police Science & Management, 19*(1), 39–53.

Webster, S., Davidson, J., & Gottschalk, P. (2015). Understanding online grooming—Findings from the EOGP study. In S. Webster, J. Davidson, & A. Bifulco (Eds.), *Online offending behaviour and child victimisation* (pp. 55–90). Palgrave Macmillan.

Weick, K. E., Sutcliffe, K. M., & Obstfeld, D. (2005). Organizing and the process of sensemaking. *Organization Science, 16*(4), 409–421.

van de Weijer, S., Leukfeldt, R., & van der Zee, S. (2020). Reporting cybercrime victimization: Determinants, motives, and previous experiences. *Policing: An International Journal, 43*(1), 17–34.

Welsh, D. T., & Ordonez, L. D. (2014). The dark side of consecutive high performance goals: Linking goal setting, depletion, and unethical behavior. *Organizational Behavior and Human Decision Processes, 123*, 79–89.

Welsh, D. T., Ordonez, L. D., Snyder, D. G., & Christian, M. S. (2014). The slippery slope: How small ethical transgressions pave the way for larger future transgressions. *Journal of Applied Psychology, 100*(1), 114–127.

Welsh, D. T., Bush, J., Thiel, C., & Bonner, J. (2019). Reconceptualizing goal setting's dark side: The ethical consequences of learning versus outcome goals. *Organizational Behavior and Human Decision Processes, 150*, 14–27.

Welter, F., Baker, T., Audretsch, D. B., & Gartner, W.B. (2017). Everyday entrepreneurship: A call for entrepreneurship research to embrace entrepreneurial diversity. *Entrepreneurship: Theory and Practice, 41*(3), 323–347.

White, A. (2020). What is the privatization of policing? *Policing: A Journal of Policy and Practice, 14*(3), 766–777.

Whittaker, J. (2004). *The cyberspace handbook*. Routledge, Taylor & Francis Group.

Whitty, M. T., & Buchanan, T. (2012). The online romance scam: A serious cybercrime. *Cyberpsychology, Behavior, and Social Networking, 15*(3), 181–183.

Whyte, D. (2016). It's common sense, stupid! Corporate crime and techniques of neutralization in the automobile industry. *Crime, Law and Social Change, 66*(2), 165–181.

Wild, T. S. N., Müller, I., Fromberger, P., Jordan, K., Klein, L., & Müller, J. L. (2020). Prevention of sexual child abuse: Preliminary results from an outpatient therapy program. *Frontiers in Psychiatry, 11*(88), 96–110.

Wikstrom, P. O. H., Mann, R. P., & Hardie, B. (2018). Young people's differential vulnerability to criminogenic exposure: Bridging the gap between people- and place-oriented approaches in the study of crime causation. *European Journal of Criminology, 15*(1), 10–31.

Williams, J. W. (2008). The lessons of 'Enron'—Media accounts, corporate crimes, and financial markets. *Theoretical Criminology, 12*(4), 471–499.

Williams, M. L., Edwards, A., Housley, W., Burnap, P., Rana, O., Avis, N., Morgan, J., & Sloan, L. (2013). Policing cyber-neighbourhoods: Tension monitoring and social media networks. *Policing & Society, 23*(4), 461–481.

Williams, M. L., Levi, M., Burnap, P., & Gundur, R. V. (2019). Under the corporate radar: Examining insider business cybercrime victimization through an application of routine activities theory. *Deviant Behavior, 40*(9), 1119–1131.

Wilson-Kovacs, D. (2020). Effective resource management in digital forensics: An exploratory analysis of triage practices in four English constabularies. *Policing: An International Journal, 43*(1), 77–90.

Winters, G. M., Kaylor, L. E., & Jeglic, E. L. (2017). Sexual offenders contacting children online: An examination of transcripts of sexual grooming. *Journal of Sexual Aggression, 23*(1), 62–76.

Wolak, J., Finkelhor, D., & Mitchell, K. (2009). *Trends in arrests of "online sex offenders"*. Crimes Against Children Research Center. www.unh.edu/ccrc

Yam, K. C., Christian, M. S., Wei, W., Liao, Z., & Nai, J. (2018). The mixed blessing of leader sense of humor: Examining costs and benefits. *Academy of Management Journal, 61*(1), 348–369.

Yar, M. (2013). The policing of Internet sex offences: Pluralised governance versus hierarchies of standing. *Policing & Society, 23*(4), 482–497.

Yip, M., Webber, C., & Shadbolt, N. (2013). Trust among cybercriminals? Carding forums, uncertainty and implications for policing. *Policing & Society, 23*(4), 516–539.

Zhang, Y., & Qu, H. (2016). The impact of CEO succession with gender change on firm performance and successor early departure: Evidence from China's publicly listed companies in 1997–2010. *Academy of Management Journal, 59*(5), 1845–1868.

Zheng, W., Yang, B., & McLean, G. N. (2010). Linking organizational culture, structure, strategy, and organizational effectiveness: Mediating role of knowledge management. *Journal of Business Research, 63*, 763–771.

Zhu, D. H., & Chen, G. (2015). CEO narcissism and the impact of prior board experience on corporate strategy. *Administrative Science Quarterly, 60*(1), 31–65.

Zvi, L., & Elaad, E. (2018). Correlates of narcissism, self-reported lies, and self-assessed abilities to tell and detect lies, tell truths, and believe others. *Journal of Investigative Psychology and Offender Profiling, 15*, 271–286.

Index

P. Gottschalk and C. Hamerton, *White-Collar Crime Online*,
https://doi.org/10.1007/978-3-030-82132-6